Charles Lindsey

Rome in Canada

The Ultramontane Struggle for Supremacy over the Civil Authority

Charles Lindsey

Rome in Canada
The Ultramontane Struggle for Supremacy over the Civil Authority

ISBN/EAN: 9783744782180

Printed in Europe, USA, Canada, Australia, Japan

Cover: Foto ©Suzi / pixelio.de

More available books at **www.hansebooks.com**

ROME IN CANADA.

ROME

IN

CANADA.

THE ULTRAMONTANE STRUGGLE

FOR

SUPREMACY OVER THE CIVIL AUTHORITY.

BY

CHARLES LINDSEY.

––––––––

TORONTO:
LOVELL BROTHERS.
1877.

LOVELL BROS., BOOK AND JOB PRINTERS, 39 & 41 MELINDA ST., TORONTO.

ROME IN CANADA.

THE term 'Church Militant,' is, in Canada, more than a figure of speech. When the temporal power of the Papacy was in the agony of dissolution, between five and six hundred French Canadian youths took up arms, with a feeling akin to rapture, and flew across the sea to the succour of the Pope. This expedition, set on foot in defiance of the law of nations, took part in a quarrel in which neither Canada nor England had any share. These Papal Zouaves of Canada, who were at war while their Sovereign was at peace, bore a flag the device on which, as seen on the cover of this book, was intended to typify their errand. This flag, the gift of the Abbé Rousselot, Curé of Montreal, was designed by M. Napoleon Bourassa, embroidered by the Nuns of the Hôpital-Général of that city, blessed by Bishop Bourget, and borne to Rome in an expedition which the Canadian Zouaves regarded as a modern Crusade Among the organizers, officers and leaders of these Zouaves, the fiercest of Ultramontanes, were men who, when they laid down the sword, took up the pen to assail the representatives of what remained of Gallican principles, in their native land, and to demand absolute and unconditional submission to Rome. They are now panting for an opportunity to fight for the restoration of the temporal power. The device on the flag of these ardent and enthusiastic fillibusters, in which the battle-axe figures conspicuously, fitly typifies the movement which it is the object of this work to describe.

TABLE OF CONTENTS.

I.

PREMONITIONS OF THE STRUGGLE.

The Vatican Council is sometimes assumed to be the starting point of a retrograde movement in the Roman Catholic Church which has for its object the revival of the medieval spirit in the nineteenth century. But the origin of the movement is a little more remote in point of time. The Vatican Council was rather its official consummation than the initial point. Pius IX. had previously renewed several bulls framed with the view of enabling the Church of Rome to encroach on the domain of the civil power: bulls which had fallen into disuse for a long period of time, and some of which had from the first been rejected by nearly every government in Christendom.

The tone of the Papal Court, gradually increasing in arrogance, carried its fatal contagion slowly but surely to the remotest nations in which a considerable portion of the population was Roman Catholic. In some countries, the change had not been so great as to attract general attention before the Vatican Council was held. But the decrees of that Council did not spring out of the earth ; the way had been prepared for them, and it was perfectly understood at Rome before the Council met what was required of it and what it could be relied upon to do. The formal adoption of the dogma of the Immaculate Conception led up to the declaration of Papal Infallibility.

Except in the diocese of Montreal, there was no part of Canada in which the Ultramontane contagion had produced much, if any, visible effect before the promulga-

I

tion of the Vatican decrees. The episcopal assault on the *Institut Canadien* had commenced several years before. Liberal journals had been denounced by the Bishop of Montreal, and he had refused to admit that laymen had any right to liberty of opinion.

But at this time Bishop Bourget, the leader of the Ultramontane movement in Lower Canada, had neither the sympathy nor the concurrence of his episcopal colleagues. The palace of the Archbishop of Quebec was still the lingering refuge of Gallicanism, and the other bishops were far more in sympathy with the Archbishop than with the Bishop of Montreal.

It is undeniable that the Roman Catholic Bishops of Quebec had, at different times, raised their voices on questions of political or national interest ; but in doing so they acted in perfect accord with the national instincts, and aided the Government in periods of national crisis. Such action on their part is clearly distinguishable from the modern assertions of the right of the Church of Rome to control political elections in her own interest. On the breaking out of the war of 1812, Bishop Plessis encouraged the spirit of volunteering ; when the rebellion reared its head in Lower Canada, Bishop Lartigne, of Montreal, condemned the revolt in a pastoral which he ordered to be read in all the parish churches. In 1868 Bishop Bourget denounced the Fenians as a secret society, and instructed the priests to refuse them the sacraments unless they renounced their connection with the order. This, of course, was not done from any national or political motive, but in deference to a rule of the Church under which all secret societies come under condemnation.

It is quite true that the Government welcomed the aid of the Bishops on these several occasions ; but only moral blindness could lead any one to confound these acts of the Bishops with the attempts which they now make to obtain absolute control of political elections, by directing electors how to vote, and holding over their heads the menace of the refusal of the sacraments as the penalty of disobedience.

While Canada was under the French dominion, the principles of the Gallican Church, though not always free from assault, were practically predominant in the colony.

When Canada fell under the dominion of a Protestant crown, it was inevitable that the new subjects of England should draw nearer to Rome. Out of a religion which was proscribed in the mother country, nothing bearing the semblance of a national Church could be formed, in . the newly acquired colony. While the free exercise of the Roman Catholic religion was accorded in the very terms of the capitulation, attempts continued to be made, for many years, to prevent the exercise within the colony of any authority centred in Rome. But, one by one, the restraints which had been imposed, for what were considered prudential reasons, were removed, and the authority of Rome came in time to be far greater in the British than it had ever been in the French colony.

But the time came, after the publication of the Syllabus, and especially after the promulgation of the Vatican decrees, when the fullest liberty and the most perfect equality no longer sufficed for the Church of Rome. She now claims religious dominance and political control. These pretensions will certainly be met, as they deserve to be, with determined resistance.

In this contest, it will be desirable as much as possible to distinguish the dogmatic from the civil aspect of the question. But this is not always possible. There are many cases in which the two are inextricably blended. Intolerance, or a denial of the right of any other form of religion than that of Rome to public celebration, is a dogma which strikes at the root of civil liberty. When a person who has received Christian baptism outside of the Church of Rome is told that he is bound by the decrees of the Congregation of the *Index* and of the Inquisition, and that he is not at liberty to read a book treating of law or philosophy without special permission of the Pope, he feels that this is a theory which, if it could be enforced, would deprive him of one of his most cherished rights. When a person who has been married according to the laws of the land is told that, according to the dogma of the Church of Rome, he is living in a state of concubinage, and is bound to separate from his wife, he sees that those who hold this doctrine only want the power, not the will, to do him a grievous injury.

If those who make loud profession of these dogmas could grasp in their hands the whole political power of the country, what guarantee would remain for the maintenance of the rights and liberties of the rest of the population?

In this refusal of Rome to reconcile herself to civilization and modern progress, there are those who see grave dangers : the elements of a contest between medieval ecclesiasticism and the civilization of the nineteenth century. Others admit themselves to be so morally purblind as not to be able to recognize the danger. A man would be accounted wilfully imprudent who, if threatened every day with the deprivation of his liberty or his life on the first favourable opportunity, failed to take reasonable precautions against the threat being carried into effect.

The Ultramontanes of Quebec, by a systematic plan of attack upon the old moderate, reasonable, tolerant, and respectable Gallicans, have already obtained the advantages of having had the last word, and are joyously hugging the conviction that there is not moral courage

enough left in that section of the ecclesiastics and their adherents, whom they have treated as enemies, to renew
the defence.

To trace the difference between the New School—as the
late Bishop of Montreal calls it—and the old will be
equally interesting and instructive.

The resignation of Bishop Bourget is an event to which
too much significance might easily be attached. Scarcely
voluntary, it was eagerly accepted at Rome. The
Bishop's imprudence could not be denied, and the necessity of allowing him to give place to another was clear.
Complaint had been made at Rome that the policy of the
episcopate, led by Bishop Bourget, would, if continued,
prove disastrous to the Church. There is no reason to
suppose that Bishop Bourget had done anything that
was distasteful to Rome. But his manner of doing many
things was unfortunate. Prudence counselled the acceptance of his resignation. But it was desirable to let him
fall as easily as possible. In ceasing to be Bishop of
Montreal, he acquired the title of Archbishop of Martin-
opolis (Mesia). The empty title was a poor exchange
for the real power ; and his admirers will sympathize
with the late Bishop under the effect of a blow which
seemed to have a stunning and might have a fatal effect.
His whole life had been given to the service of Rome ; it
had been one of almost heroic devotion and constant sac-
rifice ; and his friends evidently think it was a poor
return that he got for all that mortal man can give.

In vain did Bourget's friends in the priesthood try to recover the lost ground : to induce the Papal Court to recall
the acceptance of the resignation. The Court of Rome
found it necessary to dissemble for a moment. The Archbishop of Quebec about this time issued a mandement, in
which he, in effect, condemned everything the united
episcopate of the Province had done for the past three

years. The priests of his diocese he forbade voluntarily to interfere in elections. His pastoral read like an arraignment of the fifth Council of Quebec, and a condemnation of the joint action of the episcopate dating back no further than the previous September.

Has Rome, people asked, really commanded a halt in the Province of Quebec? Has the Archbishop power to tear up the joint letter of the episcopate, at the head of the signatures to which stood his own name? Fear not, the re-assurance of the clerical organs ran: the joint letter, which obliges the priests to interfere in elections, and to enforce their interference with the terrible sanctions of their holy office, remains in full force and vigour.

At this juncture the Archbishop of Quebec re-appeared upon the scene, to volunteer an explanation. His mandement of May 5, 1876, did not supersede the collective letter of September 22, 1875. To the truth of the principles of the letter he was a witness; and these principles, which were but a development of the decrees of the fourth and the fifth Councils of Quebec, his mandement left intact. Between the two mandements he found no contradiction. All he intended was to put his clergy on their guard against overstepping certain boundaries in the exercise of rights long since prescribed by competent authority. The collective pastoral was addressed to all Catholics in the Province; his mandement was intended to enlighten the electors on certain duties which it fell to them to perform on occasion of political elections.

It remains true, nevertheless, that the instructions of the two documents are as wide as the poles asunder. The truth seems to be that the Archbishop felt called upon to say something to satisfy the exigency of the moment, though there was no real intention greatly to alter the policy previously pursued; and when he found he was taken at his word, he had to explain that that word was without meaning. We need, not therefore expect any real change of conduct on the part of the Roman Catholic clergy of Quebec as a consequence of the resignation of Bishop Bourget, or any hint from Rome on which the Archbishop may have acted when he penned his pastoral letter of May 5. Pius IX. has, in fact, since upheld the bishops in the ground they took in their joint letter of September, 1875.

There is probably no country in the world, unless it be Belgium, in which the Ultramontanes raise their demands so high as in the Province of Quebec. The City of Quebec, the mother of sixty dioceses, enjoys at Rome the distinction of being considered the metropolis of the Roman Catholic religion in North America.* The New France of other days occupies, in that part of the world, a position not dissimilar to that of the eldest son of the Church in Europe. Quebec is proud of the pre-eminence, and seems resolved that no rival shall supplant her in the affections of the Holy See, if blind obedience to papal authority bring its due reward. In Quebec, the Ultramontanes are attempting to occupy all the avenues that lead to power, secular as well as ecclesiastical. One portion of the press they aim to control, the other to silence. They claim the direction of political elections, and they demand immunity for their political acts, because these acts are performed under the shadow of the sanctuary. Such a career of aggression, pursued with unflagging persistency, was sure to provoke opposition. No one therefore was surprised when, some months ago, a public man, reading the signs of the times, declared that a great battle between Ultramontanism and the defenders of the citadel of civil liberty was about to be fought in Canada.

* Bull of Pius IX., May 15, 1876, canonically erecting the University of Laval, Quebec.

The battle has already opened. The right of the clergy to exercise undue influence over elections has been contested in the civil tribunals, and the attacks which are made upon other forms of immunity—especially the immunity from municipal taxation which Church property enjoys—show on what line the next battle will be fought.

The Church of Rome is all but omnipotent in Quebec, and to obtain over her, when she confronts the civil power in a hundred ways, more than partial victories, varied by defeats, will probably long be impossible. A repressive policy, in the shape of a revival of old, restrictive laws, is neither possible nor desirable. But it would be rash to say that there is no conceivable case in which it might not be the duty of the State to protect itself by a rigid enactment against the assaults of Rome on its authority. Protestant leagues, or Protestant and Liberal alliances, would, if resorted to as remedies, probably do more harm than good. There seems to be but one hope; and that is, that the people on whom the weight of clerical domination falls with greatest force, finding the burden intolerable, will make a supreme effort to cast it off. But the time when that effort can be made has not yet come.

Among Roman Catholics in Ontario there is, so far as I have been able to learn, no sympathy with the arrogant pretensions of the Quebec Ultramontanes; and not one educated Roman Catholic out of a hundred in the former Province is even aware of the extremes to which the episcopate of the latter has gone.

II.

THE RISE OF THE NEW SCHOOL.

While the din of the battle between the old Gallicans and the New school of Ultramontanes in Quebec is ringing in our ears, the successful party is revelling in the arrogance of victory, and claiming for Rome the right to set its foot on the neck of the State. It is my purpose to trace the origin and progress of this contest; to examine the weapons which the aggressors have brought into play ; to show how the Jesuits and priests who formed the *entourage* of the late Bishop of Montreal have trailed in the dust the reputations of dignitaries of their own Church whom two generations of French Canadian Catholics had learned to revere, and whose sin was that they were suspected of desiring to retain some share of those ancient liberties which the teachings of the Syllabus and the decrees of the Vatican Council threatened with annihilation.

I shall show that this internecine war, which was intended to silence all opposition to Romish assumption in the bosom of the Canadian Church, was only a preliminary step to the general assault upon the liberties of the nation. The Gallican element is reduced to silence ; but the Jesuits still perform the part of jailors over the prostrate forms of the liberal members of their own Church whom they have overcome. The ready jibe, the ungenerous taunt, of these jailors smite our ears with their harsh accents. But while these aggressive Ultramontanes hold their prisoners with one hand, they assail liberty, in all its forms, so hateful to them, with the other.

Bishop Bourget boasts the formation of a 'New School' in Quebec, who find their duty and their plea-

sure in unlimited devotion to the Pope ; who accept without question all his teachings ; who approve of everything
he approves, and condemn everything he condems ; who
reject liberalism, philosophy, Cæsarism, rationalism, and
other errors which are described as gliding like venomous
serpents in all ranks of society. This school, he adds,
comprises a good number of Catholics of mark in the various degrees of the social hierarchy, especially young men.
Among the latter are distinguished the Pontifical Zouaves,
whom no ties of international obligation prevented being
organized in Canada. The devotees of the new school are
described as belonging to good families, and being fitted
by their talents and their knowledge to appear to advantage in the *salon*, to shine in the literary circle, and to
make their way to important positions in the State. In
a few years, it is predicted, their number will increase,
and they will be strong enough, by the aid of the Church,
to force open the doors of the legislature and to take possession of the judicial bench.

When that day of triumph arrives, the obnoxious *Code
des Curés*, written by the Judge Baudry, will cease to be
recognized as an authority in the courts ; and another
wish of Bishop Bourget, and one which is dear to his
heart, will have been gratified. The voice of Rome will
find an echo within the walls of the Canadian Parliament,
in the judicial tribunals, in the legal opinions of the bar, at
the hustings and in the lecture room, in school and college,
everywhere.

The Bishop has not explained how it will be possible to
educate lawyers when Pothier shall have been banished
from the University of Laval, and all the other text-books
of Gallican authors which have been honored with a
place in the *Index* shall have been burnt. The Bishop
of Birtha, the right hand of the late Bishop of Montreal,
who acted as administrator of the diocese in the absence

of Mgr. Bourget, laments that it is a very rare thing to find an advocate *qui écrit à la lumière de la foi.* The light of dogma would prove a will-o'-the-wisp to one destined to pursue the career of civil law.

This school, though still young, is old enough to have made its mark ;* and it has undeniably made great progress during the last four years. By means of an implacable war, through journals founded at the instance of Bishop Bourget, against the liberal element in the Catholic Church, it has obtained its first victory ; it boasts of successes secured through its influence on the court's of justice, and of having successfully combated the rights of the State by the learning and eloquence of the forum.

Bishop Bourget encouraged the study of the writers of this school, and the sound of his applause formerly mingled with the anathema which struck the directors of journals which propagated—we cannot write the word in the present tense—*mauvais principes;* that is, journals which defended the assailed rights of the civil authority.

Much is expected from M. Pagnuelo's attack upon Cæsarism ; in other words, upon the rights of the State, the head of which monstrous serpent the good virgin is expected to crush with her immaculate heel.†

The writers on whom Bishop Bourget showers his applause form a motley crowd of journalists, pamphleteers, and authors of more pretensions ; priests, Jesuits, bishops, *attachés* of the *Nouveau Monde* and the *Franc-Parleur.*

* For the programme of the Ultramontane party, see a Circulaire au clergé, by Bishop Bourget, concernant un ouvrage intitulé études historiques et légales sur la liberté religieuse en Canada, par M. l'Avocat S. Pagnuelo, March 19, 1872.

† Ces *Etudes* combattent directment le *Cæsarisme* ; que est se second monstre venimeux que le St. Siége signala, le 9 Déc., 1854, à l'attention et au zèle d'environ deux cents Cardinaux, Patriarches, Archevêques et Evêques, réuni à Rome pour la mémorable solemnité de la definition dogmatique de l'Immaculée Conception de la glorieuse Vierge Marie Mère de Dieu. Espérons, que cette Vierge, bonne et puissante, écrasera de son pied immaculé la tête de ce monstreux serpent, qui se glisse dans toutes les sociétés, pour la boulverser de fond en comble.—Bishop Bourget, *Circulaire*, March, 9 1872.

Within the last four years they have produced a pyramid of worthless but not innocuous literature, which probably contains not less than a hundred separate publications, all in the French language, and varying in size from the small pamphlet to the heavy octavo. Sometimes the authors write anonymously, and sometimes under their own signatures; some hide themselves under the anonymous veil for a while, and when they throw aside the screen to accept, in their own persons, the applause of the New School, it not unfrequently happens that a priest or a bishop stands revealed. Through this process Alp. Villeneuve, one of the most furious assailants of the liberal section of the Catholic clergy that has ever appeared in the bosom of the Church, and the Bishop of Birtha, who undertook to instruct members of Parliament in their duty, both went.

It is my intention to bring under the eyes of the reader several of the works which have been ushered into the world with the direct approbation or the tacit consent of the late Bishop of Montreal. Their authors proclaim the sacred duty of intolerance ; and the mildest of them insist that the dogma of intolerance must never be surrendered.* Some of them admit exceptions founded on necessity, such as the inability of the Church of Rome to compel the civil power to suppress all other forms of religion ; † but their liberality and moderation are treated by the aggressive party as a scandal and an error which place them in rebellion to the See of Rome. ‡

The writers who take part in this ' implacable war ' boldly assert that Protestantism has no rights ; that it is

---

* L'Abbé Paquet, docteur en théologie et professeur a la faculté de théologie, à Université Laval. *La Libéralisme.*

† In this category are Vicar-General Raymond (L'Eglise et l'Etat) of St. Hyacinthe, and Abbé Paquet.

‡ Binan. Broc. Anon. The style of this writer, and his mode of attack, have a striking resemblance to those of the Jesuit priest Braün.

not even a religion ; that it is the embodiment of ͵error and rebellion, neither of which can have any rights ; rebellion which owes the duty of repentance and submission to the Church.

The doctors of the New School teach that the laws of the Church are universal, and are binding on heretics ; § and that no one, Catholic or Protestant, has a right to read any book, of any kind, without the special permission of the Bishop ; and that leave to peruse a prohibited book can only be given when the object of perusal is a preparation for refuting the author.

They teach that the Church has a divine power over Christian marriage ; ‖ that every lay judge who pretends that he has a right to decide matrimonial causes incurs anathema ; that a marriage which the Canadian Parliament assumes to annul for adultery, remains after the sentence of divorce has been pronounced in full force ; and that the children of either the man or the woman born of a second marriage contracted according to the laws of the land are illegitimate.

It was an article of the Gallican liberties that no ecclesiastic should presume to censure or anathematize a lay judge for any decision he had given ; but Father Braün tells us that the Council of Trent had saved him the trouble. He forgets to add that France never accepted the decrees of the Council of Trent in matters of ecclesiastical policy or discipline.

The crusade of the late Bishop of Montreal was directed against every branch of the civil power, legislative, executive, and judicial ; and included the intimidation of the judiciary. In one of his pastorals he attacked the *Côde des Curés*, and called upon the clergy to assist him in pre-

§ Braün. Institutes Dogmatiques.

‖ Braün, pp. 33, 59, and 55.

venting its being accepted as authority in the civil tribunals.

For a hundred years and more after the conquest it was usual to defend the rights of the Roman Catholic Church by appeals to the capitulation of Montreal, to the treaty of cession, to the Quebec Act, to the Edicts and Ordinances, the Arrêts of the Superior Council of Quebec, during the French Dominion. They were held to contain the charter of the liberties of the Catholic Church in French Canada. They are still sometimes appealed to, but with an infrequency which is constantly becoming greater. The professors of that New School, whose rise and growth have been so rapid and so great, would joyfully burn half of them to-morrow. Some the New School would find it convenient to retain, and they have many ingenious contrivances for getting rid of such as stand in the way of their plans of aggression.

The Edicts and Ordinances have been codified, and the Code is acknowledged at Rome to be the most Romish Code of which any country can boast the possession ; * at least, any country in which the Church of Rome is not strong enough to exclude the open profession of any other form of religion. If, in any case, the Code seems to be less favourable to any pretension the New School may make, it rejects the code and falls back on the original instruments ; if it seems to give more, the New School accepts the Code as having superseded the Edicts and Ordinances. If neither will suit, the New School discovers that a new custom has superseded both.

But this stage of the controversy may almost be said to have been passed. The New School finds in the Syllabus and the Vatican decrees the infallible rule of truth. Against infallibility nothing can stand ; it cuts short all argument ; there is nothing left but the duty of obe-

* Vicar-General Raymond.

dience. Any one, we read in the modern gospel of the New School, who does not obey all commands of the Pope without question, is no longer a Catholic.†

Fortunately, as it may yet prove, there are some things to which the Roman Catholic subjects of Her Majesty cannot legally consent. If they could, there is every reason to believe the authority of the Inquisition would now be recognized in Quebec. It was partly because the decrees of the Congregation of the Index had not been in force, and the authority of the Inquisition had never been recognized, in Canada, that the New School lost its suit in the Guibord case. The Lords of the Privy Council tell us, in their decree, that " since the passing of the 13 Geo. III., c. 83, which (s. 5.) incorporates the 1st of Elizabeth, the Roman Catholic subjects of the Queen could not legally consent to be bound by such a rule " as the Church was seeking to enforce.

But it is far from being certain that the same object cannot be attained by a side-wind. The Bishops have obtained a reinforcement of power since the decree of the Privy Council was rendered : a dozen lines put into the shape of an Act of the Quebec Legislature, and giving them the power to say in which part of the cemetery any one shall be buried—the consecrated or the unconsecrated part—a power which, if it had existed before, would have given the Church of Rome the victory in the Guibord trial. The Bishops have now all the power which the adoption of the decrees of the Congregation of the Index and the recognition of the authority of the Inquisition by the civil power could give them. They can excommunicate a person for the crime of possessing a prohibited book ; they can, for the same crime, refuse absolution and the right of burial in the consecrated part of the cemetery. In any case they could do no more.

† Binan.

Several of the Canadian bishops seconded the aggressive policy of the Court of Rome with reluctance; some of them even showed signs of resistance at first. The late Archbishop of Quebec republished the celebrated letter of Mgr. Dupanloup, Bishop of Orleans, on the Vatican Council and distributed it among his clergy. Vicar-General Cazeau shared the liberal sentiments of the Archbishop, and resisted, as far as it was prudent—farther, as the event proved—the policy of aggression. Vicar-General Raymond, one of the great lights of the Catholic Church in Quebec, and whose literary labours in its behalf are not equalled by any other ecclesiastic, pleaded for moderation, as the safest policy for the Church. The clergy, as a body, would have preferred to continue to live in peace with the rest of the population.

But the New School of ecclesiastics, who had adopted opinions of the latest pattern from Rome, would not stand quietly by in presence of what they deemed a scandal so great as this indifference, this semi-opposition, this pestilent moderation. Its band of journalists, pamphleteers, playwrights, orators, and the allied Jesuits, made a concerted attack upon the offenders. They showed their respect for episcopal authority—a virtue on which they never ceased to insist—when Bishop Bourget resolved on dividing the parish of Montreal and virtually confiscating the property of the Sulpicians, by violent assaults on the Archbishop of Quebec, the Primate of Lower Canada. To his Vicar-General they meted out similar treatment; and for the Vicar-General of St. Hyacinthe their deadliest hostility was reserved.

One of the priests who formed the *entourage* of the late Bishop of Montreal, Alp. Villeneuve, wrote a comedy of between five and six hundred pages, and laid the scene in the palace of Pandemonium in hell. Thither he dragged bishops, priests, statesmen—all who opposed the dismemberment of the parish of Montreal, or questioned the right of the Church of Rome to usurp the functions of the State in the formation of parishes.

A layman, Hon. M. Dessaulles, answered *La Comédie Infernale*, with considerable effect, though perhaps not altogether in the most judicious way; when Bishop Bourget, who had enjoyed in silence the acting of Villeneuve's infernal play, at once swooped down upon his critic, and, usurping the functions of the Congregation of the Index, forbade anyone to read the reply, or to possess a copy of it, without leave from him, or to possess it at all for any other purpose than to refute it.

The battle now raged along the whole line; but the defenders of the ancient citadel fought with their hands tied. Jesuit spies stood ready to report any utterance on their part which would be unwelcome at the Vatican; and free speech was branded as a crime.

The fierce onslaught of the Ultramontanes on whatever was respected and respectable among the old Canadian ecclesiastics bears a sinister resemblance to that made upon Port Royal by the Jesuits two centuries ago. The victory remained with the Jesuits; and from Port Royal were driven its old inmates, by whom, whatever their faults, it had been made famous. But in those days the Jesuits, instead of writing comedies in which ecclesiastics are made to play a discreditable part in Pandemonium, made it the great sin of Racine's life that he had given to the world his immortal plays. To the remains of Molière, the great French comedian, a grave was refused in consecrated ground, until the King softened the bishop into allowing a private burial to take place under cover of darkness. But then Molière did not show the world Archbishops and Vicars-General inspired by the breath of demons.

The gradual renewal of the episcopate will do much
2

temporarily to realize the aims of the New School. Only Ultramontanes will be selected when a bishopric becomes vacant. A bishop who shows any lingering signs of a recalcitrant spirit, and neglects to die, may be made as unhappy as his enemies could well wish to see him. He may have at his side a coadjutor, with the right of future succession, waiting for his vacant shoes, and daily doing things, which may put into his superior's head the thought of resignation as a means of escape from an intolerable tor- ˙ ment; for for bishops there is a kind of ecclesiastical Chiltern Hundreds. By this ingenious process, Bishop Pinsonneault, of London, became Bishop of Birtha, and removed to Montreal, where he fell into all the plans of Bishop Bourget.

It is doubtful whether the late Archbishop of Quebec ever gave a hearty assent to the Vatican decrees. As late as May, 1872, when asked for a puff episcopal of Pagnuelo's *Liberté Religieuse en Canada*, of which the Bishop of Montreal could not find words strong enough adequately to describe the merits, the Archbishop, frankly expressing his opinion of works of this kind, wrote: 'There is danger of taking for absolute truth what is matter of opinion : what the Church has not thought proper to condemn, is sometimes ill-spoken of ; the ideal of what ought to be tends to cause the reality to be forgotten ; a future looked forward to with impatience, the real past and the difficulties of the present not being sufficiently taken into account.'

The Archbishop evidently had misgivings about the discretion of M. Pagnuelo's zeal which he tried to conceal; and yet this writer is one of the most respectable and the least aggressive of the New School.

The New School teaches that the Church of Rome alone has the right to say whether the decrees of the Council of Trent are in force in any particular country ;*

though these decrees, so far as they related to discipline, were rejected by the Government of France and never allowed to take effect in Canada.

The New School teaches what is not new, and what only slaves can accept as true : that the Church has the power to depose sovereigns and to release subjects from their oath of allegiance.† *

The New School teaches that the Roman Catholic episcopate of Canada is as much above the civil power as the supernatural is superior to the natural ; that the Pope is the Church ; and that the Church contains the State ; that every human being is subject to the Pope ; that the Pope has the right to command the obedience of the king, and to control his armies ; that the civil authority can place no limit to the ecclesiastical power ; and that it is a ' pernicious doctrine ' to allege that it has the right to do so ;‡ that to deny the priests the right to use their spiritual authority to control the elections is to exclude God from the regulation of human affairs ;§ that civil laws which are contrary to the pretensions of Rome are null and void ; and that the judiciary has no power to interpret the true sense of laws so passed, which are, in fact, not laws at all ;‖ that civil society is inferior to the Church ; and that it is contrary to the natural order of

---

* Bishop Bourget. Lettre Pastorale concerning la Sepulchre de Joseph Guibord, Oct. 3, 1875.

† A Ouimet, in a note to the *pièces justificatives* of *La Comedie Infernale*, says of a Sulpician priest who had expressed a different opinion : ' It may be seen by this phrase that M. Bedard, in spite of his clear mind, had not entirely free himself of the ideas current at St. Sulpice, Montreal. If he had had the happiness to live in a more Catholic society, he would not have doubted the right of the Pope to depose sovereigns, as the Church teaches.'

‡ Mgr. de Rimouski. Lettre au clergé seculier et régulier et aux fidèles du diocèse, issued on the occasion of the late Provincial elections in Quebec.

§ Sermon de La Grandeur Monseigneur A. Pinsonneault, Evêque de Birtha, prononcé dans l'Eglise de St. Henri des Tanneries, Dimanche, le 4 Juillet, 1875.

‖ M. R. Lefranc. Les influences indues dans le Comté de Montmagny, 15th Sept., 1875.

things to pretend that, the Church, can be cited before the
·civil tribunals ; as if Pope Pius IX., in the concordat with
Austria, had not agreed that the secular judges should
have cognizance of the civil causes of clerks, such as
contracts, debts, and the right of succession to private ·
property.

The New School is too avaricious of power to be satisfied with the tremendous influence which the pulpit and
the confessional place at its disposal.   It turns the altar
into a tribune, and seeks to wield the power of the period-
ical press.

The late Bishop of Montreal knew how to use, as well
as to curb, the press.   In 1854, he recommended the setting up of a journal to propagate ' sound principles ' *(les
bons principes)*, and he foresaw that it would be more
·effective and would excite less prejudice if conducted by
laymen, than if known to be exclusively in the hands of
priests.   But both priests and bishops figure among the
contributors of the journals whose mission it is to dis-
seminate *les bons principes.*   Even when these journals are
written by laymen, the effective control is admitted to be
in the hands of priests.*   And the whole clerical army is
under the supreme control of Rome.

Bishop Bourget has given a vivid picture of the liberal
press. †   The ' liberal journal,' he says, ' is that which
pretends to be liberal in its religious and political opinions.'   ' No one,' he adds, 'is allowed to exercise freedom
in his religious or political opinions ; it is for the Church
to teach its children to be good citizens, as well as good
Christians.   In teaching them the true principle of faith
and morals, of which she alone is the depository . . . her
mission is to teach sovereigns to govern with wisdom, and
subjects to obey with joy.'

* Bishop Bourget. Circulaire 11 Mai, 1850.
† Fioretti Vescovili.

The Bishop arrives at the conclusion 'that every journal which pretends to be free in its religious and political opinions is in error;' and that 'liberty of opinion is nothing else than the liberty of error, which causes the death of the soul, which can only live by truth;' 'thus,' he adds, 'every journal which professes liberty of opinions causes its readers to walk in the ways of error, which conducts society, as well as individuals, to ruin and to death.'   %

Sometimes Bishop Bourget directs his maledictions against a particular journal which has presumed to use the liberty he condemns. Twice he denounced *Le Pays*.* Its offence was, that it had applauded Victor Emanuel; had expressed opinions similar to those found in the Paris *Siècle*, liberal opinions in fact; that its Paris correspondent desired to see the whole of Italy put under Victor Emanuel; that it had published the proclamations of that chief of rebels, Garibaldi, and done a great many other forbidden things. In *Le Pays* the right of theatrical criticism, if not condemnatory, was denied, though that privilege can be indulged with immunity by journals which defend *les bons principes* and are recognized as arms of the Church militant; and the Jesuit priests give additional proofs of piety by opening a theatre, provided with stage and scenery, in the basement of their church, in Rue Beaudry, Montreal. The professed object is the cultivation of music; but as a matter of fact tragedies and even comedies are there put on the stage. The clergy were told that it was their duty to use every means to prevent *Le Pays* seducing the faithful committed to their care. The hint was acted upon, and their persistent opposition finally made it necessary to bring the career of the liberal journal to a close.

The *National*, a journal of pale and almost neutral tint,.

---

* Supplément au mandement du 31 Mai, 1860. Circulaire 31 Mai, 1860.

has survived a denunciation publicly made in the Cathedral of St. Hyacinthe, for having presumed to question the wisdom of observing so many days' fast in Lent. It is not probable that this journal will ever again be honoured in the same way. It now disclaims all sympathy with the Liberals and Radicals of Europe; avers that it is in sympathy only with those who are occupied with the administration of the affairs of the country in an economical point of view; and that it is above all things practical. L'Evénement, a journal conducted by a Senator of Canada, found it necessary formally to retract the statement that it is 'always dangerous to introduce religious principles into political contests;' and more recently it received a warning from the Archbishop for publishing an analysis of a sermon in which the tribunals have since found evidence of undue clerical influence. A parish priest has recently denounced from the altar the Gazette de Sorel, and forbidden his parishioners to receive or read it. All this shows the keen and all-pervading surveillance exercised by the Church of Rome over the expressions of opinion daily made in the press, and the power of the clergy in repressing free discussion. The condemned expression of the Quebec journalist was intended to be nothing more than a mild protest against the interference of the clergy in political elections; it was tortured and twisted by a host of antagonistic writers, who had no difficulty in finding in it the essence of impiety.

The Fifth Council of Quebec took upon itself the regulation of the press, and it claimed immunity from criticism for all establishments to which the bishops extend their protection.*

Some of the advice given, such as that adversaries

* Il ne faut pas traduire devant le tribunal incompétent de l'opinion publique des établissements dont les évêques sont les protecteurs et les juges naturels. Arch Taschereau, Mand. Juin 16, 1875.

should be treated with charity, moderation, and respect, besides being good, was much needed. The writers of the New School have, in this respect, been great offenders.

But this Council made it the duty of the clergy to wage perpetual war upon the independent, non-clerical press. The instructions are to make the faithful avoid the danger of reading ' bad journals ; ' all journals being bad which do not unhesitatingly accept the *Syllabus* and the Encyclical for their guide. To journalists who surrender themselves to this guidance every encouragement is to be given. In judging a public journal, the priests are to be guided by the dogmas of the Church, the teaching found in the decrees of general councils, in the constitutions of the Popes, and in orthodox fathers and doctors. The whole debatable ground on which Roman Catholics take different sides is to remain free ; and opinions not yet condemned by the Church are to enjoy exemption from censure.

Armed with this authority, and burthened with this duty, the priests take care that no newspaper, printed in the French language, which does not come up to the required standard shall find among their flocks countenance enough to ensure its continued existence. For the conduct of the clerical organs, even those which are in closest connection with the episcopate, the Church disclaims all responsibility.

The worst offenders against the rules laid down by the Council may safely reckon on immunity, provided they take up the cudgels in favour of the Church. The University of Laval may be spitefully assailed by an unworthy son whom she had cast from her bosom without forfeiting his position as an approved Catholic journalist. And this may take place, though there is a corps of ten priests at Montreal whose duty it is to exercise a constant surveillance over every form of publication issued, with a view of directing replies to be made to what is distaste-fnl, procuring episcopal prohibition of obnoxious works, or denouncing them to the Congregation of the Index.

A journalist whose profession of faith is put in these words may, for the rest, do what he likes : 'I believe in the *Syallabus* and in ecclesiastical immunities, in the rights of the Church and its supremacy over the State.' * Such an one is an acceptable apostle of the doctrines of the New School ; and one in this position may safely curse even those whom the Pope blesses, provided it is done in the interest of the 'good cause.' Proof: On the 11th April, 1876, the Pope gave the apostolic benediction to each of the directors, professors, and pupils of the University of Laval ; and M. Langlier, one of the professors, was, from about that date for some months afterwards, almost daily described as little short of a monster, by the clerical press of the city of Quebec, because, in his capacity of advocate, he held a brief in the Charlevoix election case, and would be obliged to press charges of undue in-fluence against certain of the parish priests in that county.

It has become the habit of the curés, in the country parishes, to denounce in the church every journal which is displeasing to them on political grounds ; to proscribe and anathematize it as pernicious ; to threaten to refuse the sacraments to all who still persist in continuing to receive it. The confessional is used as a means of discovering the dis-obedient ; and even the wives of the subscribers to the obnoxious journals are refused absolution, if they fail to influence their husbands to obey the priest's command.†

When the authority of the bishops is insufficient to constrain the journals, and obtain perfect obedience to

* Canadien, July 3, 1876
† Le Réveil, Dec. 23, 1876

their mandates, recourse is had to the Congregation of
the Propaganda at Rome, from which an injunction
comes, forbidding the faithful to read the recalcitrant
prints. Three years ago a rescript came from Rome forbidding the faithful to read certain journals in whose col-
umns the conduct of the ecclesiastical authorities had
been criticised.* This direction of the Holy See every
one to whom it comes is obliged to obey; no one is at
liberty to reply, or to oppose (il n'est permis à personne
de rèpliquer et de s'insurger).

The Congregation of the Propaganda, Bishop Bourget
is frank enough to tell us, is charged with the apostolic
surveillance of Canada, and he seems to infer that its
watchful eye is kept upon the Canadian press, with which
it may at any time interfere, without special direction.†
Armed with this authority from Rome, the Bishop instructed the priests of his dioceses to refuse the sacraments to all who read, or give effectual encouragement to,
journals in which criticism of the conduct of the clergy is
to be found; and the editors are to be subjected to the
same treatment. Such are the means to which, in these
days, Rome resorts in the Province of Quebec to stifle the
voice of free discussion.

Ten years ago, the *Nouveau Monde* was brought into
existence, as the organ of Bishop Bourget; the priests of
the diocese became canvassing agents to extend its circulation, and in some cases they sounded its praises from
the altar. The writers were the intimate friends of the
Bishop, and most of them were ecclesiastics under his
control. So strictly has this journal spoken for Bishop

---

* 'Curent (Episcopi) ne hujusmodi contentiones per ephemerides et libellos a
catholicis exerceantur, utque eos qui in hoc deliquerint coercere, et si opus fuerit ear-
umdem ephemeridum lectionem fidelibus prohibere non omittant:' (Rescrit du 23.
Mars, 1873.)

† *Lettre Pastorale* concernant le libéralisme catholique,les journaux, etc. Fevrier 1,.
1876.

Bourget, that, far from respecting the authority of his ecclesiastical superior, it attacked with fierceness and ran-
cour, which are more completely developed under the
soutane than elsewhere, the late Archbishop of Quebec.

To this order of writers comfort and encouragement
came from Rome ; and Bishop Bourget hastened to make
known the glad tidings.* The priests are called upon to
load with eulogy the young men who, as journalists and
authors, place their pens at the service of the Church.
What line they are to take is distinctly marked out.
They are to propagate ' Conservative principles, which
can alone make the people good, moral, peaceable, in-
dustrious, and above all sincerely religious.' ' It is,' the
Bishop adds, ' to accomplish the noble task that the Immortal Pontiff invites us, in his admirable encyclical *Inter
Multiplices.'*

Pius IX. instructs the Bishops to excite the ardour of
Roman Catholic writers to defend the cause of Catholic
society, and to admonish with fatherly prudence remiss-
ness of duty. Bishop Bourget interprets this encyclical
to mean that these writers are to be encouraged in ' the
defence of the rights of the Holy See and the execution
of its decrees in all their force ; in the discussions and
contests against the authority of the Holy See, and the
pursuit of errors even in the most obscure retreats.' It
cannot be complained that the writers of the New School
have not carried out these instructions to the letter. .

The Holy Office condemned the *Courrier de St. Hyacinthe* in 1860; and in 1876, the Pope gave his benediction
to that ' good Catholic journalist' of the *Courrier du Canada,* with right of his children, to the third generation, to
a reversion in the benediction. As the *Courrier* has several times changed its editor, it is to be presumed that
the dew of the Papal blessing fell upon the more stable

* Circulaire 6 Mai., 1871.

element of the *Courrier* represented by the proprietor.
A blessing descending to the third generation, it is conceivable, may fall upon the head of something far less
worthy than that of an approved Catholic journalist.

The *Courrier de St. Hyacinthe* now ranks among
the obedient echoes of the Church. To a journal in the
position which it occupied in 1860, forcible conversion or
death was the only alternative. On the condition of submission it is enabled to illustrate the theory of the survival of the fittest.

The Bishops are willing to concede freedom of discussion to one side; they are willing to concede the greatest
license to one side; but they will allow no liberty to the
other. Vicar-General Langevin, of Rimouski, in the
summer of 1875, identified the preachers of liberalism
with the Rouges;* and in a private letter to a curé, which
got into print, he stigmatized as an offence against God
the voting for such a candidate. The *Journal de Quebec*
had been guilty of the offence of contending, in opposition to the Ultramontanes, that 'the citizens have the right
and are at liberty to express their opinions, on political
subjects, by tongue or pen, or in any other way, without
having their rights interfered with by the ecclesiastica
authorities.'

The Vicar-General confounded the audacious journalist, pointing triumphantly to the Encyclical of December
8th, 1864. That free discussion is a natural and imprescriptible right, this ecclesiastic brands as a false assumption ; and he asks, with the air of a man who feels that he is
crushing his adversary, 'If you ask so much liberty for
yourself, why refuse to the priest the rights of the citizen ?'
But this was precisely what the *Journal* had not done.
It had denied the right of priest to interfere with the

---

* Lettre de M. le Grand Vicar Langevin aux M. le Rédacteur du *Journal de Québec*, 23 Août, 1876.

free choice of the electors, by exerting the influence of his sacred office and the bringing to bear terrors of spiritual censure ; but it distinctly admitted his right, as a citizen, to express his opinion. The separation of the two characters is all but impossible, and the priest is at present not in mood to make the attempt. How a journal can be silenced by an abuse of the confessional, the public has been very frankly told. And the journal, which was warned by a rival of its impending fate, has, through the interference of the clergy, ceased to exist: died of enforced inanition.

'If,' says the *Courrier du Canada*, a journalist in possession of the papal benediction extending to the third generation, ' a penitent does ill by reading your journal *(Le Bien Public*, a rival in business and an opponent in politics) do you imagine that, you can dictate to the confessor what he ought to do or not to do to this penitent? . . . . . He (the confessor) alone is judge whether he ought to *bind or loose*. It is God which has given him this power; he must account to God, not to the civil law, for its use.'

In this way the confessional may be abused; and if it be impossible, as it probably is, to attach responsibility to a priest for his conduct, on account of the secrecy which of necessity enshrouds it, any journal might be ruined without ever being certain whence the blow came. But it is permissible to take notice of any external act ; and as it has become known that certain priests threatened to refuse the sacraments to readers of the *Bien Public*, they might be called on to justify—that is, show good reason for menaces they had given—in an action for slander.

If the *Courrier du Canada* will examine its own file, it will find in its issue of May 25th, 1874, a letter from Vienna, headed *La discussion des Lois Confessionelles*, containing the statement that the Bishop of Stepischnegg had shown that 'la nouvelle loi mettrait l'Etat el l'Eglise sur le même pied de guerre que les sont actualement dans la plupart des Etats Européans.' M. Stremeyz, Minister of Public Instruction, said the Government intended strictly to enforce the law. This shows that when the confessional has been abused, the result has been the enactment of laws to afford citizens protection against that abuse.

The *Bien Public* was very far from being extreme in opinion or violent in tone. It neither professed 'Catholic Liberalism,' nor made itself the apostle of the doctrines of the 'liberal Catholics' of Europe. On these points it left no room for doubt. Its proprietor twice applied to the eccleiastical authorities for directing guidance. He even withdrew an election protest, where he believed the election must have been voided on account of the exercise of undue influence of which there was proof on the part of the clergy. But these acts of submission and tokens of good will did not prevent the clergy from continuing to abuse the influence of their holy office by unduly interfering in elections. Against that abuse the *Bien Public* continued to protest. This was its offence; this it was that brought down on it the opposition of the clergy, and the faithful were enjoined not to read the offending journal. The prohibition proved fatal: the *Bien Public* ceased to exist. In such a state of things, free discussion is impossible. The prerogatives of the press and the rights of the electors alike become the prey of clerical tyranny.

An attempt was recently made to find whether, in actual practice, a French Canadian journal which avoided religious questions could command liberty of discussion in the political sphere without falling down to worship the idol of party. With this view *Le Réveil* came into existence at Quebec. But no sooner had the prospectus appeared than the forthcoming journal was condemned before its birth, for its promise to avoid religious questions. That the clerical journals spoke by the book was afterwards evident from the fact that the Archbishop of Quebec repeated this criticism. In a circular to the clergy of his diocese (August 13th, 1876), that functionary characterized the promised abstention, in a writer calling himself Catholic, as a species of apostacy, on the ground that 'the very nature of political, social, and educational questions recalls the idea of religion.' In the very means which the founders of the *Réveil* took to escape the censures of the clergy—leaving the whole religious field in their undisputed possession—the Archbishop espied indications of an anti-religious tendency! With the official denunciation of *Le Réveil* expired the last hope of a French Canadian journal engaging in free political discussion without bringing down on it the wrath of the clergy. Their opposition soon proved the death of the *Réveil.*

The *Réveil* had made itself the advocate of secular education, in which the Archbishop saw atheism. It was charged with having copied, without protest, something which made in favour of the development theory, known in these days as Darwinism; it had copied a remark of Castelar which enshrined the error that it is possible for a man to be religious without being either Protestant or Catholic. But the real offence of the speech was its advocacy of toleration. Judged by a decree of the fourth Council of Quebec, *Le Réveil* had taken rank among *les mauvais journaux.* Nothing remained for the Archbishop to do but to instruct each priest to find out whether the offending journal was read in his parish; and, if any of the parishoners had, in the past, been guilty of reading it, to interdict them from repeating the offence.

Necessarily the interdict was confined to the diocese of Quebec. The proprietor of the interdicted journal at once made preparations for moving to Montreal; but not before making a courageous and masterly response, to which reference will be hereafter made. The tide of intolerance has hitherto run higher in the diocese of Montreal than in that of Quebec ; but, in spite of years of repression, thought is likely sooner to assert its freedom in the city to which *Le Réveil* moved than in that from which it fled before the anathema of the Archbishop. Only fifteen numbers had been issued when the denuncia-tion was made ; so short is the impunity allowed to free discussion by a Quebec journalist whose mother tongue is French.

‘ To a Canadian Bishop,’ says M. Buies, the condemned editor, ‘ for a journal to commit the crime of being born without permission, appeared so extraordinary, and even provoking, that you (addressing the Archbishop) could not fail to find in it an anti-religious tendency.’ Such a tendency it would not, we venture to say, be possible for an impartial judge to discover.

The writers and orators of the New School show their zeal in propagating *les bons principes*, by daily giving utterance to the most detestable sentiments. Even advocates whose minds are formed by the study of Gallican authors can sometimes be transformed into ardent Ultramontanes ; a fact which attests the growth of the New School.

M. Charles Thibault may be taken as one of the most brilliant examples.* ‘ The crime of our epoch,’ he finds to consist in many things : ‘ The want of union,’ presumably among French Canadians ; ‘ in indifference ; in

* Discourse de M. Charles Thibault, écr., avocat. En réponse à la santé des anciens élèves du Petit Séminaire de Ste. Marie de Monnoir, le 13 Octobre, 1875, a la fête des ‘ Noces d'Or ’ du fondatur de ce Petit Séminaire, le Rév. E. Crevier, V.-G., du diocèse de St. Hyacinthe.

entering into pactions with evil; in consenting to argue
with it, which is compromising ; in the toleration of error,
and placing it on a footing of equality with the truth,' as
it is in the Church of Rome ; 'in forgetting that liberty of
a creature consists, as Bonald says, in the faculty of reach-
ing the natural object of its being.   Finally, thĕ evil of
our epoch is that it has lost sight of the imprescriptible
rights of the Church, and the duties which the State owes
to it.'

The New School wishes to remedy all this.   And when
that remedy comes, where will modern civilization be?

Of soldiers necessary for the present combat M. Thibault finds a want, but he scarcely expects better from the
debased condition of modern society—of soldiers—yes,
soldats—writers, orators, *savants*, men of letters.   But why
soldiers?   Pontifical Zouaves to restore the civil power?
That is the dream of the New School ; a dream that tells of
nightmare.

While efforts are made to fasten on the minds of Italian
children, by the use of rhyme, the prediction that the
Pope will, in a short time, be at the head of an universal
monarchy,* our Canadian Ultramontanes are urged to
keep their armour bright.   A journal published at Montreal, and founded more than five years ago, the *Bulletin Mensuel*, is devoted to the restoration of the
temporal power.   It energetically opposed the enlistment
bill, on the ground that it would be an impediment to the
enrolment of Zouaves in favour of the Pope.   This journal
has a circulation of six hundred copies, and its writers
show their zeal by giving their services gratuitously.
Published with the avowed object of aiding the restoration of the temporal power, by inciting young French

---

* Mr. Gladstone (Speeches of Pius IX.) gives the following example :
    Poco tempo ancora, e Pio
    Regnerà sul mondo intiero.

Canadians to hold themselves ready once more to take up arms in favour of the Pope, the *Bulletin Mensuel* has had the extreme good fortune to receive the special blessing of Pius IX. It was founded by the members of the Union Allet, which is under the control of the Jesuits. The Pontifical Zouaves of Canada, who have already once gone to Rome with arms in their hands, and there joined the Papal troops in fighting against Italian unity, and to prop up the tottering temporal power, of which they witnessed the fall, are now ready to fight for the restoration. In an address intended to be presented to Pope Pius IX. on the golden wedding of his episcopate, and drawn up three months in advance, they recall the fact that, some years ago, they had the happiness to serve his Beatitude ; and they sigh for the time when they will be again called upon to put on their ancient uniform, ' pour le triomphe . . . pour la revanche!' And they pray heaven that their wishes, in this respect, may be granted.

When, in the year 1867, the recruiting of French Canadians commenced, with a view of forming a battalion of Papal Zouaves, some of the Bishops openly applauded the movement. The Bishop of Montreal commended the 'noble project ;' he showered upon it a heart-felt blessing and wished it complete success. The enrolment, in his eyes, shed glory on the country and brought a benediction on the inhabitants. The young men who were inveigled into this enrolment were told that they were going to fight for the principle on which humanity rested, and that they were giving ' an admirable example of devotion to the Catholic cause.'*

The true description of this setting on foot of an expedition to take part in an international quarrel in which Canada had no concern, is, that it was a flagrant breach of the duties of neutrality.

* Bishop Bourget. Lettre Pastorale, 3 Dec., 1867.

3

Religious women who spend their lives in Canadian
cloisters were called upon by the voice of episcopal authority, which conveyed something of a command, to furnish military clothing for the Canadian Zouaves. A promise was made, in the name of the Zouaves, that they
would honour and respect the habiliments made by the
virgin hands of the sisters of Christ, whom Bishop Bourget flattered with the title of heroines.*

This appeal was not without effect. In those cloistered solitudes, the walls of which are supposed to shut
out the news of current events, the fair fingers of religious
women were applied to the unwonted task of making soldiers' clothes. The filibusters were flattered with the title
of ' soldiers of Christ's Vicar,' and some of them were half
persuaded that they were so many pious pilgrims about
to set out for the tomb of the apostles with the view of
delivering the holy land from the presence of the infidel.
' Soldier of the Pope' would always be a glorious title
in the estimation of true Christians. They were going, so
they were told, to make charges brilliant and impe-
tuous enough to vie with those made at Sebastopol and
Solferino. They were conjured to devote themselves to
the Pope and defend him valiantly. ' Once more,'
Bishop Bourget concluded, ' go; but never forget that
religion and the country expect that you will prove yourselves, everywhere and on all occasions, worthy of Canada, which has produced so many good Christians and
valiant warriors.' Adding the benediction, in the name
of the Trinity, the Bishop dismissed the filibusters on
their sanguinary errand.†

The Pope expressed his lively satisfaction at the accession to his cause of the Canadian filibusters. Subscrip-

* Circulaire aux Religieuses, 8 Déc., 1867.

† Allocution aux Zouaves Canadien à leur départ pour Rome, 19 Fev., 1868

tions for the cause which they had espoused were taken up everywhere, commencing in the convents and colleges, the example being set by children of both sexes to their parents and fellow-citizens, under what influence need not be told.*

The appeals made to the Papal Zouaves of Canada to prepare to fight for the restoration of the temporal power is made to willing ears ; and when these disbanded filibusters tell the Pope that they desire nothing so much as to be again called upon to take the field, there is no doubt they are in real earnest. They have been taught to believe that the name Papal Zouave is a synonym for glory ; and the vanity which the belief implies has struck so deep that it will not be easily uprooted.†

The sovereignty of the Church, so loudly insisted upon, implies the subordination of the State. These Ultramontane writers affirm‡ that any law passed by the civil power, with a view of preventing an abuse of ecclesiastical authority, is null and void ; and that it would be the duty of the judges, if asked to interpret it, to refuse to recognize as a law what has no other than an imaginary existence. If we allow the premises, that the Church is superior to the State, we must admit the conclusion; but Ultramontanism has not yet been able to influence opinion sufficiently to obtain a recognition of a claim which implies the total destruction of civil liberty.

Abbé Bégin, a professor of the faculty of theology in Laval University, teaches the students who are to become the future priests, bishops, and archbishops of Quebec that the doctrine which makes every human being sub-

---

* Bishop Bourget. Lettre Pastorale 8 Déc., 1867.

† J'ai prononcé ce mot les *Zouaves pontificaux.* Quelle pure gloire il rappelle !— Mgr. Raymond, De l'Intervention du Prêtre dans l'ordre intellectual et social. Lecture prononcé devant l'Union Catholique de St. Hyacinthe, le 8 Déc., 1867.

‡ R. Lefranc, 15 Sept., 1875.

ject to the Pope is an absolute and eternal truth ; that the subordination of the temporal to the spiritual authority is clearly established ; and that of the two swords the spiritual is to be used by the Church, and the material for her benefit, and at her bidding.*

The New School has indeed travelled far from the old landmarks of the Gallican liberties, when it proclaims anew the monstrous maxims of Boniface VIII. ‘The Pope,’ Abbé Bégin tells the students of Laval, ‘is constituted, by Jesus Christ himself, head of the Church Universal, and pastor of its flock : whence it follows that all without exception, kings, princes, archbishops, bishops, etc., are subject to his spiritual authority.’ This professor of theology accepts the assumption of Boniface VIII., that armies as well as kings are to move under the direction of the Church; that the material sword ought to be subordinate to the spiritual, since the spiritual power is incontestibly superior in nobleness and dignity to every earthly power. ‘It is certain,’ he says, ‘that Boniface clearly established the dependence and subordination of the civil to the religious authority ;’ ‘that the secular power ought never to prevent the Church from attaining its end, and that it ought, in certain cases, to assist it in doing so ;’ that, in certain cases, ‘the Pope has the right, which it is his duty to resume, to excommunicate kings, and to release their subjects from their oath of fidelity.’

In the bull *Unum Sanctum*, which is the foundation of the claim of the Popes to depose sovereigns, Abbé Bégin finds an exposition of an ancient and divine right of the Roman Pontiffs, conformable to the teachings of the fathers of the Church : that the civil power is bound to defend and protect the Church.

But we are not living in the middle ages, and there is ample evidence that a king excommunicated by Papal

---

* La Primaute et l’Infallibilité des Souverains Pontifes.

authority may still retain the allegiance of his subjects. Nevertheless we are not entitled to conclude that to instil into the minds of students, who are hereafter to form the clerical army of Rome in the Province of Quebec, as an unquestionable and eternal truth, that there may be cases in which Roman Catholics are bound to obey the Pope in opposition to their own sovereign, has not a pernicious and dangerous tendency. And when the poison has once permeated the minds of the young clergy, what means are there of applying an antidote? Will they be likely to accept a refutation of these doctrines, or even to listen to it?

Dr. Fessler, Secretary-General of the Vatican Council, attempted to reduce the bull *Unum Sanctum* to the narrowest limits;* pursuing, in this respect, a policy in direct contradistinction to that of the Canadian Ultramontanes ; which shows that pretensions which would be rejected in Europe are expected to be readily accepted in Quebec. His reading of this bull is : ' And this we declare, we say, we define, and we pronounce, that it is necessary for the salvation of every human creature that he should be subject to the Roman Pontiff.' Fessler's book is issued with the express approbation of Pius IX.: it follows that the Abbé Bégin is more Papal than the Pope though the difference between saying that all are, and that all ought to be, subject to the Pope, is not great.

The Archbishop of Quebec seems to have had a suspicion that the abbé's work might possibly have its imperfections, as his qualified approbation, ' *nihil obstat quin typis mandetur*,' suggests. Fessler contends that the only words which contain a definition *de fide* in the bull *Unum Sanctum* are those quoted above. It follows that the New School which has been nursed into life in Quebec is more extravagant in its pretensions than the foremost defender

---

* The True and the False Infallibility of the Popes.

of Papal authority in Europe, or even the Pope himself. Father Braün also contends that 'the universal laws of the Church are obligatory on heretics;' and he holds it as a general principle 'that the Church has jurisdiction over all who have been baptized, and consequently over heretics;' for 'though they are rebels and apostates who are outside of the Church, yet of right they belong to the Church. Their rebellion and apostacy do not free them from their obligations of duty. The sheep which have strayed from the fold always belong to the master whom they have left. The soldiers who desert remain subjects of the prince whose flag they have deserted, and they will be judged according to the laws of the country.' Father Braün quotes from Suarez, a great authority with Ultramontanes, to prove that heretics are always under the obligation to return to the bosom of the Church.

Prudent Roman Catholic writers, in Europe, do not employ themselves in unceasing iteration of these revived pretenses. In Canada, the same prudential restraints which operate there are not felt. And yet the number of persons among us who are ready at an hour's notice to prove that the serpent which hisses so loudly has no poison in its sting is not small.

The absolute subjection of the State to the Church is a well worn theme by writers of the New School. ' To be taught by the Church and receive from her the baptism of salvation,' says one of these writers,* ' it is necessary that the nations should submit themselves to the Church ; that they accept with docility the pre-eminence of her teaching authority. Nations are, therefore, bound to receive and obey the dogmatic and moral decrees of

---

* Quelques Considérations sur les réponses de quelques théologiens de Quebec aux questions proposés par Mgr. de Montreal et Mgr. de Rimouski, etc., etc., etc., par la rédaction du *Franc-Parleur.* For the publication of this brochure Adolphe Ouimet says he takes the entire responsibility, but it is evidently from the pen of a theologian.

the infallible Church ; bound to listen to the teachings of
the Church and obey its laws. Now, if the nations are
bound to show this submission and docility toward the
Church, is it not because they are subordinate, or because
the Church has the right of pre-eminence over them ? If
nations are subordinate to the Church in matters of
authority, if the Church takes precedence of the nations
in matters of authority, does she not do so in virtue of the
fact that the Church is the head of the nation ? Jesus
Christ did not say to his apostles : Go teach a part, a
fraction, of the nation ; he said : Go teach the nations ;
that is to say, every human society and whatever it comprises ; the little and the great, the poor and the rich, the
ignorant and the learned, the plebeian and the patrician,
subjects and kings. Besides, the Church, the constituted
teaching authority, having in view the salvation of all,
kings and princes, chiefs of the civil power are bound
to attend to their salvation, and to acquire a knowledge
of eternal truth ; it is evident that they ought to submit
to the Church, the sole guardian of eternal truth and salvation. Besides, the Church could not fulfil its mission
towards the State if kings, princes, the State, were independent of the Church ; the State independent, means a
State which can obey or refuse to obey ; in not obeying
the Church, the State closes the way of truth and of
eternal life to its subjects.'

In another passage, this writer almost outdoes himself.
' All truth, moral or dogmatic, defined by the Pope with
the intention of teaching the Church, is dogma *de foi*, and
becomes obligatory under the pain of heresy. Now we
have heard the Popes teaching the Church this dogmatic
truth : the Church is the first among societies, that which
has authority over all others, over the peoples, over the
nations, over the sovereigns, over the governments, over
the State. Therefore, the children of the Church are ob-

liged to believe, under pain of heresy, that the Church has a sacred authority over the State.'

Verily, the New School can boast the inestimable treasure of a large number of apt pupils.

Concede to the Church all that is here demanded for her, and her right to control parliamentary elections and to dictate the laws, to which every one of Her Majesty's Canadian subjects must submit, would be unimpeachable.

These pamphleteers form the advanced guard of the Roman brigade; and they are privileged to say in a loud voice what bishops and archbishops as yet only say in a whisper. But the attempt to control parliamentary elections is only the putting in practice of the theory of the pamphleteers. When we consider that the doctrines which the above quotation exposes was emitted in reply to theologians of the old, liberal, Gallican school, we get some idea of how far we have drifted from the ancient land-marks since the Syllabus and the Vatican decrees were promulgated.

III.

LIBERTIES OF THE GALLICAN CHURCH.

It will be convenient, at this point, to trace, in rough outline, the ancient land-marks of the Gallican liberties, which have become obscured and nearly effaced by time. On the model of the national Church of France, the Church of Canada, under the French Dominion, was formed. The resemblance was not, and in the nature of things could not be, in all respects, complete. But the general features were in both the same. Ultramontanism was better held in check, under the French, than it has been since the conquest. Of what the Gallican liberties consisted, in the land of their birth, will first form a subject of enquiry ; and then will follow the consideration of the extent to which they were transferred to Canada. These liberties were not always the same in their scope and extent ; they varied with time and circumstance, and sometimes they were theoretical rather than practical. At one time they assumed the defiant aspect of the Pragmatic sanction ; at another, they were embodied in a concordat concluded between the nation and the Pope. But whatever their form, and whatever deductions may have been made from the full demands of the Gallican advocates, there always remained a valuable residuum of real liberty, on which the national pride of France could fix with real satisfaction.

The term Gallican Church is too wide an expression for what is meant to be conveyed. There were other Gauls besides those of France, whom this Church did not include : Cologne, Treves, and Mayence, were Austrian Gauls, and others belonged to *pays d'obéissance*

which received without distinction all constitutions and
rescripts from Rome.

Under this submissive name came the Pays Bas,
Loraine, Provence, and Bretagne.'

The French Church, by the command or leave of the
king, had the liberty of meeting in national council to
make regulations for its government, and the conduct of
the ecclesiastics. In this respect the French sovereigns
followed in the footsteps of the emperors, by whom general councils had been called.

For more than five centuries during which national
councils were held in France, Spain, and Germany, no
general council was held. At length the Popes forbade the
assembling of national councils, unless their leave was
first obtained ; and in France none were held for several
centuries. It would seem that France disdained to ask
leave to exercise her ancient liberties, and shrank from
the responsibility of acting without leave. But the law-
fulness of national councils, called by the king, was always maintained.

France accepted the doctrines of Rome, as laid down
by the Council of Trent and other general councils. But
there she stopped ; she never accepted the discipline of
the Council of Trent, either for herself or for that New
France which she founded on the banks of the St. Lawrence. But this fact does not prevent Ultramontane
writers from constantly appealing to the decrees of the
Council of Trent, as if they were, without exception, in
force in Canada. Rome, it is true, objected to councils
which were not called by the Pope ; but France perse-
vered, and refused to admit that the lapse of time between one national council and another could establish a
prescription in favour of the Pope. Again and again
the armies of France flew across the Alps to the succour
of the Pope ; but she refused to accept his bulls and re-

scripts as a matter of course, or to surrender the right of regulating the discipline of the national Church.

Urban II. presided at the National Council of France held at Claremont in 1097, which refused to interfere with lay tithes, though the existence of such tithes was not tolerated in Italy. On the appointment of bishops, the king had the right of *régale* and investiture, and each new bishop was required to take an oath of fidelity. It was formerly held, even by some Canadian priests, that these rights descended to the English monarch on the conquest of Canada; and they were exercised for some time with more or less rigour. The representative of the sovereign in Canada used to select the Roman Catholic bishops, not absolutely, but in a way that confined the choice to one of three persons whom he named. But this check upon the choice of Rome has been removed; and a foreign priest, on becoming a bishop in Canada, is not now required to give the pledge of fidelity which the oath of former times contained, and with which France has not yet thought it prudent to dispense. The bishops, having command of the consciences of the subjects of the sovereign, are properly required to swear that they will bear faithful allegiance to him, and not exercise their authority to his prejudice. There is the more need of this in Canada, where foreigners are sometimes sent to exercise episcopal functions, including the power of appointing and removing the inferior clergy at their pleasure. A wire pulled at Rome sets the whole machinery in motion; and the command is obeyed by a clerical army, which is the depository of the secrets of the Catholic population, and has in its hands, besides the power of the confessional, the more terrible powers of censure and anathema.*

* Le prédications, les confessions et avertissements, que les ecclésiastiques font au fait des consciences peuvent beaucoup aider nuire á l'obeyssance que les sujets dovient à leur roi. Coquille.

The French bishops had original jurisdiction in all ecclesiastical causes, in their own diocese, without the interference of the Pope, to whom such causes could only
come by what the French called *dévolution*, arising out of
the neglect of those whose business it was to have tried
them. But ecclesiastical causes did not include questions relating to the possession of benefices and ecclesiastical tithes: these came before the king's judges, and
the ecclesiastical judge was not allowed to hear them.
From the ecclesiastical courts appeals were made to the
courts of Parliament ; a proceeding which was known
as the *Appel comme d'Abus*, the assumption being that
the ecclesiastical judge had exceeded his powers.

Benedict XII. was the first Pope who seized the elective benefices ; and succeeding Popes made similar usurpations : French archbishops, bishops, abbés, and priors
were appointed at Rome, and selections made by the
accustomed means were declared null. The abolition of
the elective benefices deprived the ancient collators of
their rights. With instinctive greed of gain, the Popes
generally pounced on the richest benefices. The Pragmatic sanction put an end to the abuse. But the opposi-
·tion of Rome, which had won over the Bishop of Bale
by the bribe of a cardinal's hat, forced Francis I. to enter
into a concordat, by which the king obtained, by way of
bargain, the nomination of the bishops.

Under Pope Alexander III., the Council of Latran
laid down the rule that if the person who had the right
of presentation to a benefice left it vacant for six months,
the right of appointment would devolve on the next
superior ; and a succession of such acts of negligence
would finally give the appointment to the Pope. Benefices were declared vacant on charges, not always true,
of irregularity, simony, or heresy ; and the king, to put a
stop to the abuse, called the estates together at Orleans,

and decreed that alleged devolutions were not to be regarded as creating vacancies till the cause of the vacancy had been adjudicated upon.

The Pragmatic sanction, embodying a decree of the Council of Bale, had abolished references to Rome in cases of original jurisdiction; and when causes were appealed to Rome, the Pope was to send delegates to the country where they had been tried. The Courts of Parliament enforced this decree. The Pope once sent delegates to France to judge consistorially a marriage cause, in which a Grand Seignèur was concerned, no opposition being made. There is no regular Bishop's Court (*Officialité*) or other regularly organized ecelesiastical court in Canada. The Quebec Act gives the sovereign power to establish ecclesiastical courts, but it was never exercised, and what were called *causes majeures* are all reserved for adjudication by the Pope. And it has become the fashion to refer mere disputes, which could not be placed in any catalogue of reserved causes, between ecclesiastics, where the Ultramontane feels assured of success in advance.

Some of the Popes, notably Alexander III. and Innocent III., not infrequently judged causes without touching their merits, and sacrificed justice to formalities of procedure. In this way the canon law, which was intended only to apply to ecclesiastics, became a second civil law; and the judicial practice of the canon law became better known than that of the Roman civil law. Ecclesiastics contended that there was little use in studying the civil law, since there were scarcely any causes that could not be decided under the canon law; and the Popes, to give an ascendancy to the canon law, even in the lay courts, pronounced the sentence of excommunication against all by whom it was contravened. By these and other means, they succeeded in enforcing the observance of the canon law. But, in France, the liberties of the Gallican Church kept this abuse in check. The delays in the court of Rote, at Rome, were ruinous : Balde says that if a cause were decided within thirty years, good progress was made.

Though the Popes, after they had laid claim to almost absolute power, reserved many cases to themselves, and interdicted the Diocesans from granting dispensations, the French Church, retaining its ancient liberties, was not willing to recognize all these reservations ; and if she sometimes allowed them, she did not hold herself obliged to do so for all time.

The necessity for each nation to make rules of ecclesiastical discipline for itself was derived by Gallican writers from the circumstance that what would be beneficial to one might be prejudicial to another. The changes in the order and discipline of the Church had been numerous. The mode of appointing Popes and bishops had not always been the same ; the priests had not always been required to be celibates; the dispensation and distribution of temporalities had varied; the establishment and regulation of monasteries had been subject to no uniform rules ; the age at which persons had been admitted to holy orders had been different at different times; a secular had been changed into a sacred order ; the mode of conducting the service of the Church had not been immutable; the constitution of the chapter had not been uniform ; the mode in which fêtes had been commenced and the days on which meat might not be eaten had differed, at different times ; neither the amount of tithes nor the mode of collecting them had been invariable ; presentations and collations to benefices had not always been made in the same way.*

The French Church acknowledged the Pope to be the true successor of St. Peter; but it recognized in him no

* Coquille.

right to resort to the use of absolute power. The only exception to this rule was found in the *pays'd obéissance.* The Popes claimed the right to exempt monks from the control of the Diocesans and to make them directly subject to Rome ; but the National Council of Paris decreed that no one could be regarded as clerk or priest who was not subject to the correction of some bishop. The monks, it was held, could not declare themselves subject to the Pope without contravening the ancient discipline of the Church ; and the Pope could not, at the distance he resided from France, watch over the monasteries and colleges of that country. One of the motives for the multiplication of dioceses, was that the bishops might better understand cases requiring adjudication than a judge residing at Rome. Reservations of crime and cases of conscience, Gallican writers aver, were unknown in ancient times, and were first made about the time of Gregory VII. By the middle of the nineteenth century no cause was consistorily judged in France without having first undergone the preliminary stages; though the Popes did sometimes, not without protest, continue to interfere in cases other than of appeal and *dévolution.*

Special means were taken to protect the rights of the lay patron, which were originally due to his or his predecessors having founded a church and endowed it: as a consequence of such foundation, he and his successors retained the right of presentation. No provisions of the Pope prejudicial to the patron's rights were admitted. When a legate went to France, it was customary for the Parliament so to restrict his powers, that he could not exercise his functions prejudicially to the lay patrons.

The French Church could, without having recourse to Rome, create new bishoprics—though in more recent times the Pope exercised the power—unite two old ones ;. secularize a monastic church ; dispense with such proh bited degrees in marriage as were the creation of human law, in other words, the canon law;—when the impediment arose from the civil law no ecclesiastic had the right to assume to remove it ;—unite old and erect new parish churches and other benefices ; transfer a bishop from one See to another ; fix the age at which the monastic orders might be entered and holy orders conferred ; dispense with the rule which prohibited bastards from holding benefices, though the Pope had reserved this power from about the eleventh century; abolish the indults of cardinals ; provide for the government of hospitals ; regulate and confirm the election of bishops, and give coadjutors to such of them as, from age or infirmity, required assistance ; provide for the administration of a vacant cathedral church ; define the rank and power of Roman cardinals in France, and fix the age of marriage. The necessity of archbishops going to Rome to receive the *pallium* was contested ; the metropolitan, as patriarch, it was contended, could confer it ; but the general practice seems to have been in contradiction of this contention.*

Numerous were the decretals and bulls which were not observed in France, and which were not allowed to be published there. The Ultramontanes contended that French Catholics were not the less bound by these decretals and bulls, as their publication at Rome, the capital of the Catholic world, made them obligatory on the faithful everywhere. When it was customary to publish at Rome, every year, the bull *in coenâ Domini*, the Roman Court assumed that this publication was binding on the faithful in France, as well as in other countries.

By this bull, the Pope claimed exclusive power of absolution in certain cases ; but Gallican writers held that no

---

* Coquille. Traité des Libertés de l'Eglise de France, et de droits et autorité que la couronne de France a és affaires de l'Eglise dudit Royaume pour bonne et sainte union avec ladite Eglise.

one could be interdicted the communion unless he had voluntarily confessed his crime, or been condemned by name, in some Court, ecclesiastical or lay. Anathematization, or damnation to eternal death, was, in the French scheme of discipline, reserved exclusively for those who remained incorrigible, after repeated opportunities to give satisfaction had been rejected. In early times there were no reserved cases ; a simple priest could absolve for crimes of every degree.†

The French Government disregarded the publication of this bull at Rome, and refused to allow it to be published in France : it denied to the Pope the possession of that absolute power which the pretence of binding people under other governments assumed. The Gallicans held that, if a rescript from Rome had reference to faith solely, the bishops could judge of the matter as well as the Pope, and that they could revise his judgments ; if the rescript had reference to discipline only, each Church had the right to regulate its own, and the authority of the Pope was powerless to change it. When a question of dogma arose, and the Church met in council to decide it, the delegates were bound to express, not their own individual opinion, but the opinion of the Church they represented. Rules for the discipline of the Church, it was held, are made for the benefit of the people, and neither Popes nor Councils could be in possession of the knowledge necessary to form an opinion as to what rules would be best for any particular country, and no general rule could possibly be suitable to the people of every country.

These maxims had been held by the French Church

---

† Coquille has preserved the formula used : Notre Seigneur Jesus Christ, qui est le Souverain Pontife, te absolve, et moi de l'autorité qu'il mà octroiée je t'absous. If, after absolution had been pronounced, in the supposed article of death, a recovery took place, Boniface VIII. held that the person so absolved again fell under censure, as if by way of penalty for disappointing the expectation of his death. But, at an earlier date, there were great doctors who opposed this doctrine,

from time immemorial. The *procès-verbal* of an assembly
of French clergy contains these principles : 1st—That the
bishops have the right, by divine institution, to judge in
matters of doctrine ; 2nd—That the constitutions of the
Popes are binding on the whole Church when they have
been accepted by the pastors as a body ; 3rd—That this
acceptation, when made by the bishops, should be in the
exercise of their own judgment.

While the National Church claimed this power of accepting or rejecting, the French king constantly exercised
the same power, not as co-ordinate but absolute. No constitution of the Pope could be received in France till the
king had, by letters patent, ordered it to be put into execution ; and such order was not given till it was ascertained
that it contained nothing contrary to the rights of the
crown and the liberties of the National Church. For the
king was the head of the French Church, as the Pope
claimed to be of the Church universal ; and as they both
claimed to rule by divine right, the national as well as the
universal Church was a theocracy. When the Papal ·
nuncio presented a bull to the king, the king caused a
meeting of the bishops to be called, to deliberate upon its
acceptance. If the bull was accepted by the bishops, and
their judgment was confirmed by the court, the king
caused letters patent to be addressed to all the parliaments in the kingdom, ordering them to register the bull,
but not till after they had examined whether it contained
anything contrary to the rights of the crown or the liberties of the Church. Legates of the Popes were only
received after their powers had been examined.

Nor did France accept without question or modification
the decrees of General Councils. The Councils of Constance
and Bale were not received in France without modifications, and the disciplinary decrees of the Council of Trent
were not received at all. The Council of Bourges, at

which the Pragmatic Sanction was framed, regarded the Council of Bale as œcumenical, but it received its decrees only with such modifications as made them conformable to the manners and usages of the French. The Council of Trent was received in Holland, when the country was under the dominion of Spain, but not without modifications, which had for their object the protection of the rights of the sovereign and his subjects.

In matters of faith, the definitions of Councils were binding on all Catholics: their decisions had force in the *for intérieur,** but no law of the Church could go into effect without the consent of the sovereign. In matters of discipline the people of any country could abolish an ecclesiastical rule by non-observance and the introduction of another of a different character. Even in spiritual matters, no innovation was possible without the consent of the sovereign, as the head of the National Church. All the sovereigns of Europe have, at one time or another, exercised the right of examining ecclesiastical rules, with a view to their adoption or rejection; and this practice is one from which France never departed. An *arrêt* of the Parliament of Languedoc, in the fifteenth century, ordered Bernard, Archbishop of Toulouse, to, revoke or cause to be revoked the *monitoire* obtained from Rome on the subject of the property of the defunct archbishop, because it was necessary to obtain the permission of Parliament to give it effect. Indeed, the prohibitions of the kings of France and their officers to receive bulls or briefs from Rome without express permission of the sovereign, verified by the Parliaments, are counted by thousands.

And other countries besides France acted with the same precaution. The Emperor Rodolph II. prohibited the

---

* Il y a deux sortes de *for* intérieur, le for de la conscience, et le tor de la pénitence ou de la confession sacramental.—*Trevoux.* The word for, from forum, signifies a, public place in which justice is administered.

reception, publication, or execution of any bulls without his sanction. In Spain, Poland, and Naples, letters received from Rome were at once taken to the Council of the sovereign for examination. Philip II. of Spain made it a rule that the publication of a bull at Rome should count for nothing unless it was accompanied with the *exequatur Regium ;* and though this rule was not always rigorously enforced, Spain did frequently place itself in opposition to the pretensions of the Court of Rome. Naples acted on the same principle. In Austrian Flanders, all rescripts from Rome had to be presented to the Council and examined before they were allowed to go into execution. Even in some of the States of Italy, including Venice, the same precaution was taken. The King of Sardinia, in the Victorian Code, forbade, under severe penalties, the execution of any bulls, briefs, letters, or mandates, without the express permission of the Senate, whether they came from Rome, or any other foreign ecclesiastical court, or any court out of the jurisdiction of the Senate of Savoy. The same usage prevailed in Sicily. The rule may be said to have been general in all the Catholic States of Europe ; but this right of sovereignty was one which it was not always possible to maintain, in active force, against the hostile powers with which the Court of Rome was armed.

Hence arose the custom of the Church having recourse to the temporal prince for protection, which the prince refused or granted at will, or as might seem prudent. The emperors came in time to regulate by law the manner in which the royal arm should assist the Church, by ordering the judges to give effect to the sentences of bishops, without which their judgments would have been inoperative. At length it came to pass that all Catholic States lent or refused to the Church the secular arm according to circumstances.

Various means were taken in different States for the rejection of the bulls of the Popes. In France, there was the *Appel comme d'abus*, before the king's judges or to a General Council. Spain simply retained the bulls to prevent their being executed ; other countries refused to allow them to take effect till they had been scrutinized by the Secretary of State, or authorized by the sovereign, or the judiciary ; among them Germany, Flanders, Portugal, Naples, Milan, and Florence.

The Court of Rome pretended that the ordinances of the civil governments for the execution of the bulls of the Popes were useless formalities, injurious to the Holy See, since they made kings judges in matters of faith, and superior to the Pope in questions of doctrine ; that the usage was new and unknown to antiquity. But the scrutiny to which the bulls were subjected by the civil power was regarded as necessary, not for the purpose of passing judgment on the dogma, but for the purpose of ascertaining whether, under the pretext of dogma, they contained anything that menaced the public peace, which every sovereign is bound to preserve. It is for the civil power to ascertain whether a dogmatic bull contains anything which derogates from the rights of the State, anything which is contrary to local liberties and settled customs. The sovereigns, it was contended, did not decide on matters of faith ; they introduced no novelties when they refused to authorize the execution of new decisions of the Court of Rome ; they simply maintained the ancient laws of the Church, of which they were the protectors; they refused the aid of the royal arm to carry out decrees, the execution of which would, in their opinion, have been an abuse of power.

From the time of Clovis, the French took precautions to permit the publication of such rules only as were not contrary to the rights of the king, of the Church, and the people. Ecclesiastical rules on the subject of discipline were made to conform to the local laws ; whence resulted a right which each nation called its liberties. These regulations were made in pursuance of the principle that each nation has an inherent right to govern itself, and that no foreign power has a right to interfere in its internal affairs. Pope Alexander III. admitted that, on the question of the validity or the invalidity of a marriage, the rules of the Church of Rome ought to give place to the customs of the Church of France.

From the countries in which these customs existed must be distingued the *pays d'obéissance*, whose feebleness subjecting them to the Court of Rome caused them to receive without distinction all bulls and rescripts. The pretensions of the Court of Rome once admitted, and acquiesced in for a long period of time, were often regarded as conferring the right of prescription ; though it was a maxim of the Gallican Church that no length of time could constitute a prescription in opposition to the public good.

The relations between the Gallican Church and the Court of Rome were long regulated by the Concordat concluded on the 16th August, 1516, between François I. and Leon X. Previous to this the Pragmatic Sanction had, for more than three quarters of a century, caused great opposition between the Courts of France and Rome.

The Concordat took from the chapters of the French Churches the election of bishops ; instead of which the king was to name to the Pope a doctor of theology or of law, not less than twenty-seven years of age, six months after the vacation of the See, in order that the Pope might confer the benefice ; if this election had fallen on an incapable person, the king was to be notified to name another, and if he failed to do so within three months, the Pope might make the appointment himself. Where the selection was made *in curiâ*, the Pope was authorized to appoint the bishop without waiting for the nomination of the king, and the same rule was applied to abbés and conventual elective priories. . The second article abolished the *graces expectatives*, by means of which the Popes had virtually, disposed of Church patronage in France through recommendations to the bishops and chapters, even before the benefices were vacant. The poor beneficiary was sometimes killed in order to vacate his place.*

At the time when the Popes seized the collation to benefices, by what was called prevention, the exercise of this power, which was always odious in France, was subjected to many modifications and restrictions, and the rights of lay patrons were in all cases guarded against the encroachment. There were canonists who defended the usurpation, by saying that the Pope was the source of all power, and could at will resume a jurisdiction which he had remitted to the ordinaries; but the doctrine was never fully accepted in France. The term prevention signified priority in the act of appointment, and sometimes the Pope and the Ordinary ran a race against time and against one another. If the provisions of the Pope and of the Ordinary bore the same date, it was customary, in France, to give the preference to those of the Ordinary; the canonists, on the contrary, gave it to those of the Pope.†

The Concordat dealt a heavy blow at the liberties of the Gallican Church. By it *causes majeurs* were reserved for adjudication at Rome; the Pragmatic Sanction was in its main features abolished, and the Councils of Constance and Bale condemned. The nomination of bishops reserved to the king lost much of its apparent value, from the fact that the Pope had the power of rejecting the selection

---

* Dict, Univ. Art. Libertés des Eglise Catholigques.
† Du Cange.

made on the pretence of its unsuitableness; and where the right of election had previously existed, the king did not even obtain the privilege of qualified nomination.

The Concordat did not embrace Provence and Bretagne, *pays d'obéissance.*

Some of the most objectionable articles were modified, restricted, or abrogated by usage. Leon X. and his successors suppressed the privileges of election which certain Churches possessed. Leon accorded to François I. an indult for the nomination of bishops in Bretagne and Provence, which was believed to be in execution of a verbal agreement made and secret articles framed when the Concordat was signed. It was in virtue of similar bulls that the king nominated to bishoprics in conquered countries. From the time of François I. the French kings nominated the bishops and archbishops in every part of the country, and the Popes conferred the benefices on the persons so selected.

The unpopularity of the Concordat aroused opposition on all sides. The Parliament of Paris only consented to register it when the menace of dissolution had for two years been hanging over it; declaring that it did so because expressly commanded by the king, and not because its own judgment approved. The cognizance of questions relating to the title of benefices, which the Parliament had up to that time possessed, was taken from it and transferred to the Grand Council. The University of Paris joined in the opposition, by remonstrance, protest, and appeals to a future Council. On several occasions the clergy demanded the restoration of elections, notably at the Council of Rouen. Such of the articles of the Pragmatic Sanction as were not specially abolished by the Concordat remained in force.

François I. desired to obtain the nomination of bishops, for the purpose of being able to recompense the devotion or services of members of the noblesse; and it is a curious fact that while twenty-four Popes, from Gregory VII., had employed both temporal and spiritual arms against the emperors, and taken from them the appointment of bishops and abbots, for the purpose of giving the election to the chapters in Germany, seven Popes used their utmost endeavours to take from the chapters of France the right of election which certain Churches had possessed for centuries, for the purpose of transferring the right of nomination to the king.

It is an error very widely disseminated which assumes that the annates, or the first year's income, which became payable to the Pope in respect of all sorts of benefices, had their foundation in the Concordat. They seem to rest on no other authority than a bull of Pope Leon X., which, in several editions, has been added to the text of the Concordat, as have several other pieces which form no part of it. The bull is of a date posterior to the Concordat; it was not registered by the Parliament of Paris; it was not received in France in the only way which could give it legal effect; it was not approved of by the fifth Council of Latran, along with the text of the Concordat; it was, in fact, not then in existence.

That annates were collected under a bull which never obtained legal acceptance in France, is a proof of how inadequate the precautions taken by the French Government to guard the rights of the crown against the usurpation of Rome sometimes proved to be. This bull required every one who applied to the Court of Rome to have a benefice conferred upon him to accompany application with a statement of its annual value. It was worth while to collect the figures with care, for the amount sent annually from France to Rome in the shape of annates, was nearly six hundred thousand livres. The Popes refused to give a year's credit for the annates to the newly appointed bishops: letters of institution and provision were not issued till the money was paid. Some Popes went so far as to visit with the penalty of excommunication non-payment if continued beyond a given time.

The Gallican Church, as a national establishment, contained one very grave defect when it found itself constrained, contrary to law, to send these immense sums to Rome for a purpose which a National Church ought to have been able to fulfil. This recourse to Rome would have been unnecessary if the resolutions of the French Church passed at an Assembly called by Charles VI. at Paris had been adhered to. According to this plan, the archbishops were to confirm the election of the bishops within their dioceses, and the election of the Metropolitan by the oldest of the suffragans, or by the Provincial Council; and for the collation and institution to other benefices recourse was to be had to the bishop of the place.

Henry II. had forbidden his subjects to send money to Rome, whether for dispensations, provisions of benefices, or for any other purpose whatever. The French kings, in this particular, gave a license to the Popes of Avignon which they would not, in the first instance, have given to those of Rome. The annates formed one of the chief means of raising the Popes from poverty to riches. Those who objected to their payment stigmatized them as simoniacal. The French, at the Council of Constance, expressed a desire for their abolition, and the Council of Bale, declaring them simoniacal, did formally abolish them; the Assembly at Bourges modified this decree, by permitting the then existing Pope to draw one-fifth of the annates; but it was by favour that they accorded so much to this Pope personally, with the distinct understanding that it was not to go to his successors.

The liberties of the Gallican Church, so called from the

successful opposition to the efforts which the Court of Rome had repeatedly made to reduce the French people to servitude, were guarded by a triple rampart : the interposition of the authority of the sovereign to prevent obedience where obedience was not due; the accepted principle that the Pope is bound by the canons, and is incapable of derogating from such of them as have been accepted in France ; the principle that a General Council possesses authority superior to the Pope. These liberties were regarded as the precious remains of the first centuries, which France believed she had preserved more strictly than any other State. If Bossuet could rise from the dead and make his appearance in Canada, with all the sins of Gallicanism on his head, the New School would brand him with anathema, and would not even permit his title to rank among the faithful.

The Gallicans recognized the Pope as the chief of bishops, and allowed that he possessed the authority which the ancient Councils had attributed to him ; but they did not grant him the possession of that power which infallibility implies. For the limits which they placed to his authority, they pleaded the warrant of antiquity. The French made it a subject of pride that they had preserved, with greater integrity than any other nation, the liberties of the National Church without breaking the unity of the Catholic faith. The perseverance of the Church of Rome in sustaining its pretensions was nevertheless rewarded by the growth of some usages unknown in earlier times ; but on every important occasion the Parliaments brought against the innovations a strenuous opposition. The French kings, for special reasons, sometimes accorded to the Popes privileges which could not have been claimed of right ; and succeeding Popes, regarding these privileges as the appanage of the See of Rome, converted them into a common right and gave them the name of privileges.

The body of ancient canons which the French took for their guide was the Code approved by the Council of Chalcedonia, known under the title of *Ancien Code des Canons*, in which they professed to find the ancient common-law of the Church ; while they regarded the new canon law as binding only on the countries into which it had been introduced. To the pretension of Boniface VIII. that all the faithful are bound to believe, as necessary to salvation, that temporal governments are subject to the Pope, and that it is in his power to make and unmake kings, they contented themselves by replying that it was new, and that the ancient canons gave the Pope no such right. To the assumption of the Popes, that their constitutions had the force of law throughout the Church universal, the Gallicans, in reply, asked to be shown the titles by which Rome assumed to take away the liberties of a nation of freemen.‡

What may be called the great charter of Gallicanism is to be found in the declaration of the French clergy of the 1682 ; but it is sheer misrepresentation to say that this declaration is the origin of Gallicanism. The declaration was drawn up by Bossuet, and is comprised in four articles. Before examining these articles, it will be necessary to a full understanding of the subject to glance at the causes which led to the assembly of the clergy, and the framing of the celebrated declaration.

The *droit de régale*, which had existed from an early period in France, consisted of the enjoyment by the king of the revenue of certain bishoprics, and the nomination to the benefices from the time they became vacant to the appointment of new bishops. The Parliament of Paris, in 1608, declared all churches subject to the *droit de*

‡ Dict. Univer. Libertés des Eglises Catholiques.

régale which had not a special title of exemption; and this judgment was sanctioned, in 1673, by Louis XIV. In this enterprise, the king encountered the opposition of two bishops, notably the Bishop of Pamiers. This prelate refused to recognize the canonry whom the king had nominated, *en régale*. The Metropolitan put them in possession, and the Parliament assured them the enjoyment of the revenue. Innocent XI. came to the assistance of the bishop, and in several briefs attacked the declaration of the king as contrary to all laws, human and divine. The bishop then excommunicated the regalists and the officers who had seized the revenue.

In the midst of this agitation, the bishop, M. Caulet, died, and the Parliament of Toulouse ordered the entire chapter to meet within three days, to appoint Vicars-General. One of the Vicars-General, who had been named by the ancient canons, Aubarède, ordered the regalists out of the Church, and on their refusal to comply, declared them excommunicated and delivered over to Satan. This priest was sent into exile; but his colleague revoked the sentence of the Metropolitan, excommunicated the promoter and the Grand-Vicar of M. de Toulouse, by whom the vicars had been appointed, in pursuance of the *arrêt* of Parliament. The king selected M. de Barlemont for the bishopric of Pamiers; but the Pope, instead of granting him the necessary bulls, issued an acrimonious brief, in which he declared valueless all the confessions received and all the marriages contracted by permission of the Grand-Vicars named by the Metropolitan. The Parliament of Paris pronounced the suppression of this brief. The Pope, in turn, ordered the General of the Jesuits to address copies of this brief to the Provincials of the Society for circulation among the members of their order. The Advocate-General pronounced this manner of publishing briefs to be new, dangerous, and contrary to the

laws of the State. The Parliament issued an *arrêt*
forbidding not only the Jesuits, but all other religious
orders, to publish or circulate any briefs or bulls which
had not been admitted to registration.

On the death of the abbess of the monastery of Charonne,
an ill-governed institution, situated in the Faubourg St.
Antoine, the Archbishop of Paris made a temporary
appointment to the office. A year later, an unknown hand
carried to the abbé a brief from the Pope, which moved
the *religieuses* to elect a superior and assistants without
making an appeal to the Archbishop of Paris, their
immediate superior. Then came another brief praising
this act of obedience. The Parliament declared these
briefs an abuse of power, and ordered the seizure of the
goods of the monastery, on the complaint of creditors that
they were being clandestinely sold. The contest waxed
hotter and hotter ; a new brief proscribed the *arrêt* of
Parliament. The Ultramontanes ranked the affair of
Charonne among the *causes majeurs ;* they claimed for the
Pope the right to interpret the Concordat according to
his will and pleasure, and they treated as heretics all who
affirmed that the bishops held their authority immediately
from Jesus Christ.

The Assembly of the clergy of 1665 engaged Doctor
Gerbais to compose a treaty *des causes majeurs* which,
according to the Roman doctrine, could only be decided
by the Pope. Doctor Gerbais, on the contrary, undertook to prove that the bishops had the right to decide in
matters of faith and discipline, and to oppose the authority
which they received immediately from Jesus Christ to
the novelties which might be obtruded into their dioceses
and their provinces; that the bishops ought to be
judged, in the first instance, by their confrères in the province. Gerbais' book was condemned by the Pope, as
containing schismatical doctrine, being open to the

suspicion of heresy, and injurious to the Holy See ; and every one was forbidden to read it on pain of excommunication.

The causes of difference between France and the Court of Rome were constantly increasing. Father Buhy, a distinguished priest of the order of Carmelites, in a thesis read at the Sorbonne, had maintained the doctrine that there are laws to which the Pope is amenable ; that he cannot, in all cases, dispense with the canons; that he can neither depose kings nor impose tribute on the clergy of their kingdoms ; that the bishops hold their jurisdiction from Jesus Christ; that the Faculty of Theology of Paris neither regards the Pope as infallible, nor as above the Councils of the Church ; that the *droit de régale* is neither a myth nor an usurpation.

The Pope interdicted the book ; and on the very next day the Parliament of Paris forbade the execution of the order of interdiction. Buhy, regarding the interdict as suspended, went to preach at Lyons, and when the news reached Rome, he was declared incapable of performing any ecclesiastical function or having any voice in his order. The Procureur-General represented to Parliament that Buhy had been condemned contrary to law ; that the form of the condemnation was not less irregular than unjust, and that, as a French subject, he could only be judged in the first instance by a French Court ; that the case was one in which the Faculty of Theology of Paris had original jurisdiction. Buhy was ordered to continue his functions of lecturer in his convent, and the Carmelites and other religious orders whose superiors lived out of the kingdom of France were forbidden to execute any decree or letters patent of their orders which did not relate to the ordinary discipline of their houses, without having first obtained letters patent of the king, duly registered.

The Assembly of the French clergy of 1680, when about
to separate, learned that three briefs of the Pope on the
subject of the *régale*, in which the king was menaced, and
the bishops reproached, were being circulated in the
kingdom. They therefore assembled next year to the
number of forty, when they expressed the opinion that
' to remain silent under the briefs of Innocent XI. would
be to consent to the annihilation of the jurisdiction of the
ordinaries, and to renounce the inviolable maxims of the
discipline of the Gallican Church.' They remonstrated
with the Pope, and drew up a solemn, but respectful
protestation, and they unanimously resolved to ask the
consent of the king to hold the General Assembly, which
took place in 1682, which afterwards became famous.

At that Assembly, M. Coquelin raised the question of
the extent and the limits of the authority of the Sovereign
Pontiff, and there was a strong feeling in favour of bringing it under discussion ; but Bossuet, who was engaged
in controversy with the Calvinists, felt that this chord
should not be too rudely touched, and his opinion changed
the direction of the discussion. M. Coquelin recalled the
fact that, eighteen years before, the Faculty of Theology of Paris had protested against the six propositions
which attempts were then being made to propagate :
1st.—' That the Pope has authority, direct or indirect,
over the authority of kings ; that in certain cases the
Pope can depose kings ; that he can release subjects from
their oath of fidelity; that the Pope is not under subjection to the rules of the Church, and can depose bishops,
contrary to the dispositions of the canons ; that the Pope
recognizes no superior power, not even that of General Councils; that his decisions are infallible, independent
of the Church, and according to some, this infallibility
·extends to questions of fact.'

The school of theologians who preached these doctrines, the New School of that day, first stated as private opinions maxims which they afterwards aimed to erect into dogmas. A committee appointed to examine the six articles combatted by the Sorbonne, evolved from them the famous declaration in four articles which, as already observed, became the great charter of Gallicanism.*

* I subjoin a translation of these articles : 1st—' That St. Peter and his successors, vicars of Jesus Christ and the Church, as a whole, have received from God power only over spiritual things, which concern salvation, and not over things temporal and civil ; Jesus Christ himself said that his kingdom was not of this world, and in another place " render unto Cæsar the things that are Cæsar's, and unto God the things that are God's." That it is necessary to observe the precept of the apostle Saint Paul : " let every soul be subject unto the higher powers." ' Consequently we declare that kings are not subject to any ecclesiastical power by the order of God ; that they cannot be deposed directly or indirectly by the authority of the keys of the Church ; that their subjects cannot be exempted from the submission and the obedience which they owe, or released from their oath of fidelity ; that this doctrine, necessary to the public peace, and equally advantageous to the Church as to the State, ought to be held as conformable to holy Scripture, the tradition of the fathers of the Church, and examples of the saints.

2nd—' That the plenitude of the power of the Holy Apostolic See, and the successors of Saint Peter, vicars of Jesus Christ, have over things spiritual, is such nevertheless, that the decrees of the Holy Œcumenic Council of Constance, contained in the sessions four and five, approved by the Holy Apostolic See, and confirmed by the practice of the whole Church and the Roman Pontiffs, and religiously observed at all times by the Gallican Church, remain in their full force and virtue, and that the Church of France does not approve the opinion of those who attacked these decrees, or enfeebled them by denying that their authority is well established, that they have been approved, or that they had reference only to times of schism.

3rd—' That the use of the apostolic power should be regulated by the canons made by the spirit of God, and consecrated by the general respect of mankind ; that the rules, practices, and constitutions received in the kingdom, and in the Gallican Church, ought to have full force ; and that the limits placed by our fathers ought not to be overstepped ; finally, it appertains to the greatness of the Apostolic See that the laws and customs affirmed by the consent of this venerable See, and that of the Churches, should subsist without alteration.

4th—' That the Sovereign Pontiff has the principal part in the decision of questions of faith, and that all the decrees clothed with his authority address themselves, of right, to all the Churches and to each Church in particular ; however, his judgment is not irreformable if the consent of the Church has not been given. These are the maxims which we received from our fathers, and which we have formulated for the purpose of sending to all the Gallican Churches and to the bishops who govern them, with the assistance of the Holy Spirit, in order that we may all teach the same thing, cherish the same sentiments, and hold the same doctrine.'

5

The king, as head of the French Church, claimed a right not less absolute than that to which any Pope ever pretended, in respect to the teaching of the four articles. He ordered them to be registered by all the Parliaments and tribunals, by the Universities and Faculties of Theology and of canon law. Every one was forbidden to teach anything contrary to the doctrine contained in the declaration ; the bishops were ordered to cause it to be taught throughout their dioceses ; every one appointed to a professorship of theology was required to subscribe to the declaration and to promise to teach the articles ; and no one could receive the degree of doctor till he had, in a thesis, sustained the great charter of Gallicanism. The declaration was, in some sort, the work of the Sorbonne, since it contained the articles presented to the king in 1663, and the greater part of the bishops had been trained in Gallican principles in that famous school.

The stubborn temper of Innocent XI. had been irritated by the rejection of his briefs, and he was strengthened in his resolution to oppose the execution of the four articles by the intrigues of Austria and Spain, whose representatives assured him that if he yielded to Louis XIV. the right of *régale,* these countries could claim the same privilege. The French bishops excused themselves to the Pope for having consented to the extension of the *régale ;* and the latter, in an acrimonious reply, loaded them with every species of reproach, and said he had read with a shudder of horror that part of their letter in which they spoke of their deference to the king. He assumed to annul everything that had been done in the French assemblies regarding the *régale.* The bishops, in their turn, protested against the briefs of the Pope, as being contrary to the rights, usages, and liberties of the Gallican Church. Their action being made known to the nuncio, the Pope ceased to send briefs, and took refuge in the policy of silence and delay.

To the members of the clergy who had formed part of the Assembly of 1682, and whom the king had since named to bishoprics, the Pope refused the customary bulls. The idea of creating a Patriarchate in France, to which expression had been given under Richelieu and Mazarin, was renewed, and there was a disposition to demand the re-establishment of the Pragmatic Sanction. But Louis XIV., who had formed the project of extirpating Calvinism, discouraged these enterprises.

The wrath of the Pope was too fierce to be appeased by the fit of insane devotion which took the shape of the revocation of the Edict of Nantes. Two years after that event, the franchises of the French ambassadors at Rome were withdrawn. The Parliament pronounced against this bull by the *appel comme d'abus.* But the Jesuits, who had possession of the king's conscience, were not idle; and but for their efforts it is probable that the French Church would have obtained, from that time, absolute independence of Rome in matters of discipline. The impression which the Jesuits had made on his mind is fairly represented by the remark he is said to have made to the Procureur-General, Harlay, that it was impossible to have too great a regard for the Pope; to which Harlay is said to have replied : Oui, sire, il, faut lui baiser les pieds et lui lier les mains (yes, sire, it is necessary to kiss his feet and tie his hands).

Innocent XI., had nothing to do but to wait. The number of French bishops to whom was denied the power necessary for the discharge of their functions was constantly increasing. Cazzoni and other courtisans, whose ear the Courts of Austria and Spain had obtained, continued to confirm the Pope in his determination to refuse the bulls of provision and installation to the new bishops-

Innocent XI. died in 1689, and bequeathed the quarrel to his successor, Alexander VIII., to secure whose election France is said to have expended three millions of livres; but, whether this be true or not, the new Pope adopted the maxims of his predecessor. He demanded that the new bishops who had signed the Declaration should retract. The king replied that the execution of one of the principal articles of the Concordat could not be made to depend on this condition; the ancient formula of faith, he said, was sufficient; the Assembly of 1682 had not decreed a new article of faith, but made an exposition of the doctrines of the French clergy, which the demand for bulls could not be allowed to destroy; those questions were at least problematical, and there could be no reason for doubting the orthodoxy of the new bishops, as the Councils of Constance and·Bale had made the same decrees, and that of Trent had not made any contrary declaration; numbers of French bishops who had sustained similar propositions had obtained their bulls; the desire of the Popes to make new articles of faith was of dangerous consequence; finally, if the refusal of the bulls were persisted in, France would re-establish the condition of things which existed prior to the Concordat and supply herself with pastors.

The Pope lowered his demand so far as to express his readiness to accept from the bishops a letter stating that they had no intention to make any definition contrary to the faith, or to do anything that would be displeasing to the Holy See; and that the king ought to forego the execution of his edict on the subject of the four articles.

The king wished to come to an accommodation with the Pope, without a retraction on the part of the bishops; and while the form of letter to be written was under consideration, the Pope fulminated a bull concerning the four articles more heavily weighted with reproaches than that of his predecessor on the subject of the *régale.* Of this bull, which the Pope hesitated to publish, the cardinals sent some copies to France.

A second Pope had died since the rupture with France had taken place, and Innocent XII. appeared upon the scene. The number of French bishops awaiting bulls now reached thirty-five. The Papal nuncio at Paris frightened Louis XIV. into the belief that he was sustaining an impudent and impious doctrine of the Richerists, and was thereby imperilling his eternal salvation. '

Louis now yielded ; and Bossuet wrote the letter demanded from the bishops, which, though not intended for a recantation, might easily be taken for such, with the addition of voluntary self-abasement, which could scarcely have been necessary. 'Prostrated,' the letter read, ' at the feet of your beatitude, we declare ourselves penetrated with grief above all expression for things done in our assemblies which have highly displeased your holiness and your predecessors ; and everything which has been regarded as decreed touching the Pontifical authority we declare ought to be held as not decreed ; and we hold as not to have been deliberated everything that was regarded as deliberated to the prejudice of the Holy See ; for our intention was not to decree nor to do anything to the prejudice of our Churches.' Bossuet, interpreting his own letter, in his *Gallia Orthodoxa,* denies that the bishops intended to abjure as erroneous the doctrines of the four articles.

The king, on his part, wrote to Innocent XII. to say that he had given orders that the clauses of his decree which related to the Declaration should not take effect (n'ayant pas de suite). Nevertheless, the four articles did continue to be taught and defended in France.

St. Aignan, who in a thesis had applauded the four articles, on being named bishop by Louis XIV., was refused his bulls by Clement XI., to whom the king wrote to explain that 'if he had renounced the right of obliging his subjects to follow his edict, he did not thereby intend to prevent them expressing their sentiments on a, matter which was not one of faith.' And the Pope granted the bulls.

The Declaration being attacked by writers in the service of Rome as 'pestiferous,' and such of the clergy as adopted and upheld it as 'the ministers of Satan,' Louis XIV. engaged Bossuet to undertake its defence; which he did, in two folio volumes, on which ten years of his life were spent. 'We must not believe,' Ranke observes, that the king 'recalled the four articles, though the matter was sometimes looked on in that light at Rome. At a much later period he would not endure that the Roman Court should refuse institution to the adherents of the four articles. He declared that he only revoked the obligation of teaching them; but it was just as little reasonable that any one should be prohibited from acknowledging them.'

Among thousands of other arrêts to the same effect which issued from the Parliaments of France, one of the Parliament of Paris, 1773, specially enumerated some of the rights of the crown and the French Church. In ordering the suppression of some writings relating to the constitution *Unigenitus*, it forbade all persons to sustain, in public schools or elsewhere, anything contrary to the absolute independence of the crown in temporal matters, in respect to any other power on the earth ; to diminish the respect due to the canons received in France and the liberties of the Gallican Church; to assert the infallibility of the Pope and his superiority over General Councils ; to attack the authority of the Council of Constance, and especially the decrees contained in its fourth and fifth sessions, renewed by the Council of Bale. The authority of the Pope, it was further laid down, ought to be regulated by the canons; and it was admitted that these decrees were reformable by the ordinary means of appeal to a future Council, unless they had received the consent of the Church. To prohibit the expression of opinions instead of waiting to deal with acts is a rule which finds little favour among British English-speaking people ; still, some writings are treated by the English laws as treasonable, and it was against practices which were regarded as treason to the national sovereignty of France that this arrêt was launched.

Under the First Empire, the obligation of teaching the four articles was renewed by an organic law. The greatest opposition to them, at all times, came from the Jesuits. To-day, Gallicanism has scarcely more life in the country of its birth than in Canada.

After the death of Louis XIV., the great body of the French clergy either grew lukewarm in their defence of the four articles, or did not to teach them at all ; their principal defenders were now confined to the Parliaments and the persecuted Jansenists, against whom not less than fifty thousand *lettres de cachet* were issued.*

About one-fifth of the articles of the Syllabus are directed against propositions which Bossuet deduced from the four articles ; or constructed out of the floating *débris* of the Gallican liberties. This fact gives us the connecting link between the Vatican Council and the Assembly of the French clergy in 1682.

Our Canadian Ultramontanes have a jaunty way of stating of what the Gallicanism of the present day consists.† It consists, they tell us, ' in whatever tends to

* Origine, Progrès, et Limites de la puissance des Papes, ou éclaircissements sur les quatre articles du clergé de France, et sur les libertés de l'église Gallicane.

† Quelques considérations sur des réponses de quelques théologiens de Québec aux questions proposées par Mgr. de Montreal et Mgr. de Rimouski, etc., etc., etc., par la rédaction du *Franc-Parleur*

exalt the civil power to the prejudice of the sovereignty,
the independence, and the supremacy of the Church ; in
whatever tends to diminish the authority of the Pope,
his supremacy in the Church, his superiority over the
Councils ; in whatever tends to diminish the authority of
the bishops over the inferior clergy ; in the pretension
that the authority of the State is necessary to give effect
to the acts of the Popes, the bishops, and the curés ; in a
bishop pretending to be Pope in his own diocese ; in a
priest believing himself to be bishop in his parish.' The
modern Gallicanism so painted has two faces, one political, the other ecclesiastical. This writer described
Canadian Gallicanism, in 1873, as being confined to two
societies of priests, by which he no doubt intended to
indicate the Sulpicians of Montreal, and the allies of
Vicar-General Cazeau. Political Gallicanism the Ultramontanes find in the *Code des Curés;* in three letters
disavowing the principles of the *Programme Catholique,*
which asserted the sovereignty and independence of the
Church ; in the refusal of the demand that the unity of
the public school system of New Brunswick be broken in
the interest of the Church of Rome ; in the writings of
certain theologians of Quebec, who did not accept the
assertion that the creation of a new parish by a bishop
is a legal and binding act without the assent of the civil
power : a proposition sustained by the Syllabus, and
therefore not to be rejected by the faithful ; in the assertion of the right of the State to regulate and limit the
acquisition and possession of property by the Church,
an assertion condemned by infallible authority. In fine,
Gallicanism, in the mouths of Canadian Ultramontanes,
is the sum of all villanies.

IV.

GALLICANISM TRANSPLANTED TO CANADA..

The scheme of administration founded by the genius of Colbert, which combined administrative centralization with the separation of the spiritual and temporal powers, continued in force so long as Canada remained a colony of France. The colony, ceasing to be a mission under the rule of the clergy, came under the direction of a secular administration, carried on in the name of the sovereign. That turning point in history where the political succeeds the religious power had been reached ; a change against which the conduct of the Jesuits some- times formed a practical protest.

The edict of Louis XIV. giving effect to the Declara-- tion of the French clergy of 1682 was not registered by the Superior Council of Quebec ; but the Gallican liber- ties and franchises were enjoyed in Canada under the French dominion.* The ecclesiastical law of France extended to Canada.

* 'It is a principle of French law,' said Lord Brougham, 'that all ordinances not registered are void. They only take effect from the date of their registration.' This- was in obedience to the principle of legislation that a law only acquires force after it has been promulgated ; and registration was the only mode of publication known in France. This practice was introduced into Canada. But registration in France was- not sufficient ; it must be made by the Superior Council of Quebec, which was, except where the king ordered an instrument to be registered, the judge of the adaptability of any ordinance to the condition of the colony. 'The Superior Councils,' says the *Nouveau Denisart,* 'enjoyed in the colonies the same rights as the sovereign courts in France.' Edicts, réglements, and ordonnances made by the king expressly for New France, were invariably addressed to the Superior Council of Quebec, with an order to register them. But the necessity for registration did not apply to laws made pre- vious to the establishment of the Sovereign Council. It is admitted that the *Code Marchand* was in force in Canada, though never registered there. In the same way, the *Droit commun ecclesiastique* of France had force there without the necessity of registration.

Vicar-General Raymond admits that the principles embodied in the four articles were adopted in the colony. But the opposition of Rome began in time to tell. 'As discussion threw light on the question'—a lurid and blinding light—'and certain acts of the Pontifical See contained a practical disapprobation of the errors of Gallicanism, a reformation of ideas took place, and the doctrines taught came to resemble more and more those of Rome.'*

Gallican principles formed the guide of the civil tribunals in Canada under the French dominion;† and after the conquest they continued for some time to be more or less observed, along with an assertion of the rights of the sovereign, from which in France they were never separated.‡

One of the Intendants, Dupuy, in deciding a case against the pretensions of the Church, embodied in his judgment a summary of the four articles.§ 'These,' he added, 'are the principles which ought to be taught to the people here; rather than abuse the chair of truth, from which nothing ought to be˙preached but obedience to God and the king.' A difference had arisen between the canons of Quebec respecting the rights and dignities of one of them; and they took the ground that they did not recognize the right of any judge in Canada to settle the dispute; whereupon the Intendant found it necessary to define the powers of the Superior Council of Quebec.||
The Intendant claimed for the Superior Council the place which the Parliaments occupied in the different Provinces

---

* Vicar-General Raymond.

† Judge Baudry. Code des Curés.

‡ Dict. Univ.

§ *Ordonnance* 6 me. Janvier, 1728.

|| *Ordonnance* Janvier 4, 1728.

of France.* There was no order of men in the colony which was not subject to the correction of this tribunal. The contrary assertion was characterized as a formal disobedience and a seditious independence.

The chapter of Quebec wished to retain, besides the mortal remains of the late bishop, his cross, his mitre, and his other pontifical ornaments, contrary to the positive dispositions of his will, by which his body was to be buried in the Church of Notre-Dame-des-Anges. This church had been erected into a parish over which the canons had no control. They, however, resisted the order for the burial, and when the hour at which it was to take place arrived, they sounded the tocsin in their church, under the false pretence that the General Hospital had taken fire. This brought together a crowd, who rushed to the church where the burial was to take place, the baffled canons marching 'tumultuously and seditiously,' at their head. They threatened to depose the Superior of the general hospital and interdict the Church of Notre-Dame, which was connected with it. On being ordered to appear before the Superior Council, the chapter and canons refused. The Superior Council ordained that they should be constrained by the seizure of their temporalities both in France and Canada. Their pretension that the bishopric of Quebec had become vacant by the death of the late bishop, while M. Louis François de Mornay was coadjutor with right of succession was alive, was disallowed.† 'The people,' the ordonnance read, 'cannot know with too great precision that the power proper to ecclesiastics is only over the spiritual, and the things which concern

---

* And this accords with Garneau's estimate of that tribunal. ' Le Roi,' he said, ' fit organiser une cour Supérieure sous le nom de Conseil Souverain de Québec, qui fut l'image du Parlement de Paris. Le réglement suprême de toutes les affaires de la colonie, tout administratives que judiciares, fut déféré à cette cour, qui reçut les mêmes pouvoirs que les Cours Souveraines de France.'

† *Ordonnance* 6 Janvier, 1728.

the salvation of souls, the orders to be conferred upon
ministers of the Church, the administration of the sacraments, and whatever results from the sacrament of marriage and other sacraments; and that the other rights of
ecclesiastics and seculars between themselves are purely
temporal matters, subject to the power of the king, and
to the cognizance of the judges charged with the execution of his justice over all his subjects without distinction,
of whom the ecclesiastics ought to show themselves the
most submissive.'

The Church writers have ceased to deny that the Gallican liberties were introduced into Canada by France; and
they say it matters little whether the whole body of the
droit gallican was transplanted to the colony or not;
since, on the cessation of the French dominion, the relations which existed between the civil and ecclesiastical
authorities underwent a complete change.*

The Superior Council of Quebec was, by the edict
which created it, empowered to take cognizance of all
causes, civil and criminal, and to decide them, in the last
resort, according to the laws and ordinances. Pagnuelo
contends that the *appel comme d'abus* is a part of the
droit gallican which was never brought into Canada; but
it is certain that this form of appeal was received by the
Superior Council of Quebec from sentehces rendered in
the Bishop's court, (*Officialité*) of Quebec. This form of
procedure was used in the affair of the canons of Quebec
against an ordinance of the bishop (April 24 and June
30, 1693); against M. Deminiac, Vicar-General, the subject of contention being the position of a pew in the
church (April 21, 1738); and against the chapter of Quebec, only ten years before the conquest (June 30, 1750).

This court was at first composed of the Governor, the
Bishop, and five councillors; the number of councillors

* Pagnuelo.

was increased in 1675 to seven. The Bishop's court (*Officialité*), from which, according to M. Montigny, the Sovereign Council received *appels comme d'abus*, ceased to exist in 1759.

In France, the Official was an ecclesiastic to whose jurisdiction all the clerks of the bishopric or archbishopric were amenable, in purely personal actions. He also had cognizance of four kinds of actions between laymen : tithes *au petitoire*, the validity or invalidity of marriage, heresy, and simony. The Official also had cognizance of certain crimes committed by ecclesiastics, but he could impose no other than cánonic penalties; and when the crimes were of a nature to be punished corporeally or by imprisonment, they were always tried by the secular judge. The Official was obliged to observe a form of procedure prescribed by royal ordonnances.* The *Officialité*, in Canada, was presumably framed on this model ; though it seems to have seldom, some erroneously allege that it never, exercised its functions.

It is well established that, under the French dominion, the common ecclesiastical law of France was in force in Canada. But that this law has since been modified in many particulars, and always in favour of the Church of Rome, is equally indisputable.

The civil government interfered in the minutest details of ecclesiastical administration. The intention was to introduce a conformity to the practice and usage ' observed in the kingdom of France, where ordinary affairs are never decided but by a majority of the votes of the marguilliers in charge, and extraordinary affairs by calling in the aid of a sufficient number of marguilliers who have gone out of office, the curé being always present.'† When they neglected their duties they were sometimes ordered

* Montigny, Histoire du droit Canadien
† Ord. du Con. Sup. 12 Fév., 1675

to appear before the Superior Council to answer for their
default. They were repeatedly ordered to render honours in
the Church to those who were entitled, under the scheme
of ecclesiastical discipline in force in Canada, to receive
them. It was their duty to watch over the property of the
Fabrique. But sometimes the marguilliers were cowed by
the audacity of the ecclesiastics, and were afraid to perform their duty. Thus, when the ecclesiastics of the
Seminary of Quebec of their own authority emptied the
graves of a little cemetery adjoining the grounds on which
their building stood, annexed it to their Seminary, and
converted it into a garden ; when they built upon another
piece of ground which the piety of Sieur Couillard and his
wife had given for the use of processions round the
Church, Frontenac says the marguilliers were afraid to
oppose to the act so much as a remonstrance. The Governor told them it was desirable that they should demand
restitution of these lands. The marguilliers having been
ordered to attend before the Superior Council, explained
that the ground was all contained in the outer enclosure
of the Seminary, and that two large doors had been
left for the use of processions. The Governor replied that these doors served no other purpose than to
admit the passage of cordwood which the ecclesiastics
required, and that the carts occupied the ground required
for processions; that no processions had taken place
there for some time, and that there was an evident intention to discontinue them. This was prophetic ; in process
of time the religious processions filled the streets of Quebec. A hundred and thirty or forty years after this date,
Mgr. Plessis laid it down as a rule, that where the Protestants were in the majority the processions should be
confined to the church ; now they encumber the streets
of all our cities. The Council, Frontenac told the negli-
gent Marguilliers, should watch over the conservation of

what belonged to the Fabrique as a public thing, and
he added that the secular judges had the right to examine
the accounts of the marguilliers, and that it was their
duty to do so when there was reason to believe that an
abuse had been committed.* Two of the marguilliers
gave mortal offence to the Governor by remarking, one
of them, that the property of the Church would be en-
dangered if the secular judges could enquire into the accounts of these functionaries; the other, that were this to
happen, they would no longer depend on the bishop.
Frontenac complained of these expressions as disrespectful towards the magistrates; and suggested that it might
be necessary to prevent ecclesiastics coming from France
in future. When the marguilliers had first appeared before the Council, they sarcastically begged to be secured
in the right which the Governor ascribed to them, of performing the honours of the Church 'except on the days
when the Council should appear there in a body.' An
arrêt was passed,† ordering the marguilleirs to give the
officers of justice and the members of the West India
Company an honourable place in their church, after that
of the Council, and in other churches to local officers of
justice after the governors of the places and the private
seigneurs. Thus the first place was given to the Council,
of which the Governor was a member, and to which the
marguilliers had intimated their desire to be relieved
from the necessity of rendering any honours at all.

Endless disputes arose over the order in which honours
in the church were to be awarded, and there were numerous judicial decisions on the subject. The marguilliers sometimes evinced a reluctance to put others before
themselves. The clerk of the Royal Jurisdiction of Montreal had been in the habit of receiving the *pain-bénit* be-

* Ord. du Con. Sup. Mars 18, 1675.
† 26 Mars, 1675.

fore the marguilliers, whose jealousy made them resolve to put a stop to the preference. In vain this officer of justice pointed to the law which provided that the 'sacramental bread shall be presented to the Governor, the lieutenant of the king and the officers of the Royal Juris-diction, then to the marguilliers in charge, and indifferently to all who may be found in the church.' The case came before the Intendant, Hoquart, and he ordered the offending marguilliers to appear before him next morning, and that the clerk of the Royal Jurisdiction should continue to enjoy the honours annexed to his charge.

In numerous instances priority was ordered to be given to those entitled to it in the social hierarchy, conformably to the rules and ordinances of the king.*

The Intendant of Justice, sitting in the King's Court, decided causes according to the rules of the 'discipline of the Church and the ordinances of the king.'† By his judgments, which were called ordinances, the sisters of the congregation were forbidden to take vows, and any which they might take in future were declared null.‡ The Frères Hospitaliers of Montreal were forbidden to wear the distinctive dress of the Order ; were directed to doff the black *capot*, the girdle of black silk, and the muslin bands, and to confine themselves strictly to the rights accorded in their letters patent of living in community.¶

The nunneries were not free from fiscal supervision by the State. Sister Ste. Hélene, who had charge of the property of the Hotel Dieu, Quebec, was required by an ordinance in 1727 to render an account of her stewardship ; to furnish a statement of the goods and money she came

* Jug. Mars 23, 1737.

† Ord. Nov 26, 1706.

‡ Déc. 14, 1708.

¶ Ord. Déc., 1708

into possession of on the death of her predecessor, of what she had received afterwards, and of what was then in her possession, and, if required, to be prepared to swear to the correctness of the accounts.

The minimum *dot* which each religious was to pay on entering the General Hospital of Quebec was fixed by law at five thousand livres ; and the stipulations concerning the *dots* of young women who were to enter convents in New France were required to be presented to the Governor-General and the Intendant to be *visées* before the taking of the veil, and the superiors of religious houses were forbidden to receive and admit to profession any young women until the stipulations regarding the sum they were to pay by way of portion had been so *visées*.*

This restriction of novices to young women whose parents could afford to pay for each of them five thousand livres reduced in the short space of ten years the conventual communities to bands of aged and infirm females, and these institutions were rapidly sinking into decay. The high tariff rendered it impossible to fill up the gaps made by death, owing to the comparative poverty of the inhabitants.   As the convents then offered the only means of educating girls, and as it was thought the sick would suffer for want of the attention which the nunneries, if maintained in greater vigour, could afford, the amount of the *dot* was reduced to three thousand livres.†   The rules for enforcing the payment of this amount were the same as those previously laid down.   The number of nuns admitted into the General Hospital of Quebec was regulated by law,‡ and altered from time to time, as the Government conceived it to be desirable.

* Arrêt du Conseil du Roi Mai 31, 1722.

† Arrêt du Conseil d'Etat 15 Mars, 1733.

‡ Lettres Patentes, Avril 1737 ; Arrêt du Conseil d'Etat 1701 ; et Lettres Patentes Mars 1715.

6

The attempt to make the convents a sanctuary and a
refuge for criminals was forbidden. The pernicious habit
of making these places a shelter for criminals had been
formed by the indiscreet zeal of ecclesiastics and religious ;
and the civil law interposed to put an end to the abuse,
dangerous at once to the authority of the civil power and
the public security.¶ But the civil officers were to enter
the convents in search of secreted criminals only in case
there were good reasons to believe the law had been violated, and even then they were not to enter unless in
urgent cases till the authority of the bishop or one of the
Vicars-General had been obtained. The civil officers, on
entering a convent, were to notify one of the priests to
be present ; and the minute of the proceedings to be
drawn up was to state the fact of his presence.

Under the 289th article of the Custom of Paris missionaries were incapable of receiving wills, though fixed
curés were not under the same disability. This prohibition was removed by an ordinance of 1722. To wills
so received there must be three male witnesses, twenty
years of age ; and mention had to be made in the instrument that it had been dictated by the testator and afterwards read and re-read to him. So great were the precautions against fraud.

As seigneurs of Sillery, the Jesuits had, like the Sulpi-
cicions of Montreal,·been entrusted with the administration of justice in the higher as well as in the lower jurisdiction. Their powers over the higher jurisdiction were
withdrawn in 1707, not only in respect to this seignory,
but also in respect to lands they held in fief in Three
Rivers.†

Two priests, M. Rémy and de Francheville, on refusing to obey an order to appear before the Superior Council

¶ Ordonnance 19 Fév, 1732.
† Ord. Oct. 22, 1707.

of Quebec, had a fine imposed upon them. The Abbè de Fenelon, who had been a missionary to the Iroquois at the Bay of Kanté, attacked Governor Frontenac in a sermon delivered in the parish church of Montreal, in which, among other things, it was intimated that he did not pay due respect to the priests. Frontenac demanded a copy of the sermon, which Fenelon refused to give. 'I pronounced my discourse,' the priest said, 'before two hundred persons; inquire of them if you will. If I be innocent, there is nothing to be asked of me; if I be guilty, which I formally deny, no one has a right to ask me to supply materials for my own condemnation.' After refusing to give a copy of the sermon the priest, brought before the Superior Council, denied the competency of that tribunal. The Council stopped all parley by sending him to prison. The priest appealed to the ecclesiastical court, which he pretended was alone competent to deal with the case. Besides, he objected to be tried by judges who were friends of the Governor, and who had received their appointments from him. The Council having ordered the Vicar-General and Official, M. de Bernières, to appear before it, reprimanded him, and warned him not again to entertain requests of the nature of that addressed to him by M. de Fenelon. This priest was sent to France in the autumn of 1674, and when the case came before the notice of the king, Louis XIV. said: 'I blame the action of the Abbé Fenelon, and I have ordered him not to return to Canada.' But there were difficulties about proceeding criminally against Fenelon, or requiring the priests of Saint Sulpice to appear against him. The king, apparently moved by motives of prudence, temporized. He thought it would be best to allow the accused's bishop or Vicar-General to mete out to him ecclesiastical penalties. It may have crossed the mind of the king that neither of these ecclesiastics might adopt his view of the

complaint, or do what was required of him ; for he proposed, as the alternative of such punishment, which Fenelon was to be sent to Canada to undergo, that the offender should be arrested and re-conveyed to France.*
The civil authority assumed absolute power over the personal liberty of the accused, implying a legal right to
take cognizance of the complaint.

When M. Charon, founder of the General Hospital of
Villemarie, (Montreal), desired to establish a community of
Maîtres d' écloles, M. de Pontchartrain, Minister of Marine,
prohibited him from forming a religious community.
The Hospitalières performed their functions by the
authority of letters patent from the king.   On a dispute
between Bishop Laval and the Seminary of Saint-Sulpice,
M. Talon, Intendant-General, adjudicated.   M. de Saint
Vallier desired the Sisters of the Congregation to make a
vow of obedience to himself as bishop, but the Government forbade them to make any vows whatever.†

On the installation of Bishop Pontbriand, successor of
Laval, the king remarked that the bulls and provisions
conveyed by the Pope having been examined by his Council and found to contain nothing contrary to the privileges, franchises and liberties of the Gallican Church, he
would permit the new bishop to take the oath of fidelity.‡
This shows that if Louis XIV. had consented, contrary
to what he and the Parliament of Paris had contended
was the true intent of the Concordat, to allow the Pope
to appoint the first bishop, Laval, he now showed that
the crown would not forego its right of examining and
passing upon the bulls granted to a new bishop.   The
Canadian bishops, under the French *régime*, were re-

* Ferland. Hist. du Canada.

† Faillon. Mémoirs particuliers pour servir à l'Histoire de l'Eglise de l'Amérique
du Nord.

‡ Edmond Lareau.   Histoire de la littérature Canadienne.

quired to take the oath of fidelity to the crown ;§ a proceeding against which the Pope protested without effect.
No religious order could be created in the colony without the authority of the king, and the Sisters of the Congregation were at one time expressly prohibited from
being cloistered or taking vows. The amount of tithe
payable, instead of following the rule of the canon law,
was regulated by the Government, and was not always
invariable in amount. A multitude of edicts, ordinances, and arrêts of the Council of State regulated and
enforced the discipline of the Church. The decrees of
the Inquisition, under which, in New Spain, torrents of
blood were shed, were never admitted in Canada.

But there were other contrasts between the ecclesiastical discipline of Canada and of New Spain of a different
kind, which it may be convenient now to point out.

Excepting reserved cases, the Pope never had any
direct authority in the Spanish American colonies. Whatever pontifical authority was exercised there entered
through the prism of royal authority.‖ All bulls, briefs,
dispensations, indulgences, were required to be sent from
Rome to the King of Spain, who committed their examination to the Council of the Indies, and on the report of
that body their execution was permitted or refused. All
persons connected with the ecclesiastical administration,·
from the porter of the cathedral to the bishop, were appointed by the king. No cathedral, no parish church, no
monastery, no hospital could be founded within the Span-

---

§ The following is from the oath taken by Bishop Pontbriand:—'Sire,—I Henry-
Marie du Breil de Pontbriand, Bishop of Quebec, swear in the most holy and sacred
name of God, and promise your majesty, that I will be, as long as I live, your faithfu̧
subject and servant, that I will procure with all my power the good and the service of
the State, that I will not enter into any council, design, or enterprise to the prejudice
of the same, and if any such thing should come to my knowledge, I will make it known
to your majesty. So help me God, and the Holy Gospels by me touched.—Signed,
H. M. Du Breil de Pontbriand, Evêque de Québec.'

‖ Depons. Voyage dans l'Amérique méridionale

ish dominions in America without express authority from the king of Spain. If archbishops, bishops, and abbès were nominated by the Pope, it was only on the spontaneous presentation of the king. The canonries were disposed of in the same way. Pluralities were absolutely prohibited. It was the duty of the bishops to furnish the king an account of the vacant benefices in their dioceses, with a statement of their revenues and the names of the individuals most worthy to fill them. Candidates were required to apply to the viceroys, by whom the applications were forwarded to Spain. The representative of the king nominated to the cures; the bishop offered three names from which the selection was made. When, in the lapse of time, the nomination became a mere formality, from the practice of selecting the first name on the list, the jealousy of the crown prevented it from being formally abandoned. In 1770, the orders of the king made it obligatory on the viceroy to select the first name on the list, unless there were good reasons for not doing so. Native priests had the preference over Spaniards; and no foreign born priest, unless he had obtained letters of naturalization, was allowed to possess any benefice. All questions arising out of the exercise of patronage were referred to the Council of the Indies. To the Pope nothing was left but the barren privilege of granting the necessary bulls. The bishops paid annates to the king, not to the Pope. At first the amount was only a twelfth; but in time the bishoprics, like all other benefices, were required to pay the first year's income under the name of *annuidad.* As it would often be oppressive to exact the whole year's revenue in one year, the payment came to be divided into six parts and spread over as many years. The oath taken by the bishops on their installation obliged them to respect, in every particular, the royal patronage, and to oppose no obstacle to the exercise of the right of collecting the royal dues. Until he presented a *certifia* that he had taken this oath, the new bishop could not enter on his charge. Appeals to Rome were confined to reserved causes. The Bishop's Courts were each composed of the bishop, the fiscal proctor, and the provisor. Appeals from their decisions went before the archbishop, whose judgment, however, was not necessarily final except as against the appellant. The second appeal did not go, in the ascending order, to the Pope, but to the nearest bishop, and his judgment was definitive. These ecclesiastical courts of Spanish America came into collision with the civil tribunals ; and in the clash of jurisdiction the secular authority had a tendency to prevail. While the ecclesiastical jurisdiction embraced all purely spiritual causes, the secular tribunals had concurrent authority, even though both litigants were ecclesiastics. Causes arising out of the payment of ecclesiastical tithes were treated as *mixti fori*, and might come either under the ecclesiastical or the lay jurisdiction. The process in the ecclesiastical courts followed the forms of the secular tribunals. If the ecclesiastical courts were swifter in their action and less expensive, they were still far from perfection. The right of asylum, which the Popes made a point of maintaining, and which shielded from arrest the worst malefactors who took refuge in the churches, often paralyzed the arm of justice.*

I have dwelt at some length on this subject, because it is not generally understood that New Spain was nurtured in stricter ideas of national predominance than New France.

* If we are to credit Clavijo (Noticias de la Historia General de las Islas de Canaria), a similar right of asylum was observed by the natives of the Canary Islands, to whom Christianity was unknown: . . . . Ningun privilegio apreciaban tanto como al de hacer todas los dias à la Divinidad sus libaciones de leche en medio del Templo, cuyo sagrada era un asylo y lugar de refigio, que nadie violaba impunemente.

V.

THE JESUITS AND THE CIVIL POWER.

The early Jesuit missionaries in Canada were men to whom it would be impossible to deny the possession of many virtues. Their life, when in the depths of the forest, where they confined themselves to their proper vocation, was one of heroic self-sacrifice. The story of their missionary labours, the perils they encountered, the deaths they courted at the hands of savages whom they went to save—through famine and pestilence and fatigue beyond the power of the most robust to endure—have often been told, and well told, generally with a spice of allowable eulogy. But there was another side to their character; and of that side but very little is popularly known. When they emerged from the forest and took up their quarters at the centres of political power, they sometimes engaged in intrigues hostile to the Government, and propagated principles the reverse of Gallican, which struck at the root of civil authority.

In their attempt to make of Canada another Paraguay, in which their sway should be absolute and complete, they so far succeeded as to overthrow the tolerant policy of Sully, to chase the Huguenots from the colony, and to prevent the teaching therein of any doctrine contrary to that of the Roman Catholic Church. This prohibition is repeated in a number of public documents, issued under the authority of the King's Council and the Parliament of Paris. This prohibition accorded well with the policy of establishing a National Church in the colony ; for if Rome was an enemy of the king, New England Protestantism was an enemy of another kind, and there was the same necessity, it was then thought, for holding both in check.

Besides, though the Jesuits sometimes proved troublesome at the centres of colonial power, they were often of essential service to the French Crown when attending to their spiritual duties on distant missions. In the depths of the forest, along a border line of territory disputed by two colonizing nations, and surrounded by hostile tribes , to conciliate the good will of which each nation was trying, the Jesuit missionaries might so exercise their influence as to be of great service to the French Government; and that they did so exercise it, M. L. Dussieux,* after reading all the documents relating to Canada in the archives in the Marine and War Departments, avers.†

Charlevoix, himself a Jesuit, says the presence of a priest among the Indians was often of more value than a whole garrison ; and he cites the example of Illinois, which, since the year 1717, had been incorporated in the Government of Louisiana, as a proof of the great importance, in a political point of view, of sending missionaries among the other tribes. He points to the experience of two centuries in proof that the best means of attaching the Indians to France was to convert them.‡

As late as 1725, a priest of Saint Lazare, who had personal knowledge of the country, addressed to the French Government a programme for the civil as well as the spiritual government of the colony. He recommended that the Jesuits be maintained among the Iroquois

---

* Le Canada sous la Domination Française, d'après les archives de la marine et de la guerre.

† The military school of Saint Cyr, in which M. Dussieux is a lecturer, receives a large supply of scholars from a Jesuit college in Paris, a fact which may account for suppression of this statement in a second edition of his Work on Canada. But fact cannot so easily be blotted out.

Histoire Générale de la Nouvelle France.

for political reasons, since, in his opinion, they alone were capable of preventing them from becoming attached to the enemies of France.§

Frontenac has left it on record that the Jesuits did, in his time, make an attempt to grasp the whole authority of the colony in their hands. In every family they set a spy ; from every pulpit they denounced all who opposed their pretensions, not sparing even the Governor himself.

The ecclesiastical superiors, when remonstrated with, readily joined in blaming the preachers ; at the same time apologizing for conduct which they could not defend, by attributing it to an excess of zeal. The Governor affected to be satisfied with this explanation ; but he took care to state that, if the offence were repeated, he would ' put the preacher in a place where he would learn how to speak.'

This had the effect of restraining the license of the pulpit for a while ; but the Jesuits never abandoned the attempt to exalt, in the minds of the people, their own authority over that of the Government, even in secular matters. By means of hired spies and an abuse of the confessional, they possessed themselves of the secrets of every family. The use they made of this information was to tell husbands what their wives had confessed, and mothers the weaknesses of their daughters. ' They aimed,' says Frontenac, ' to establish a species of Inquisition a thousand times worse than that of Italy or Spain.' The Governor remonstrated against this conduct, but without effect. He at last threatened that the first spy who should circulate a scandal about his neighbour, without good proof, would be treated as a calumniator, who set public authority at defiance.

' These statements of Frontenac are in perfect accord with the evidence of Baron de Lahontan, who spent part

§ Ferland. *Cours d'Histoire du Canada*, Vol. II.

of the winter of 1684-5 at Montreal.* The all-pervading espionage of the Jesuits rendered life at Ville Marie miserable. No one could have or attend a pleasure party, engage in diversions, or visit ladies, without coming under the censure of the priest, who spoke of them publicly in the church and named the offenders.

A noble lady would be refused admission to the communion on account of the colour of her head-dress. In our day, Bishop Bourget has contented himself with crying down crinoline, without making the offence of wearing it a cause for refusing the sacraments.† The Jesuits made the wearing of a mask a cause of excommunication. They watched the conduct of the wives and daughters of the citizens with a vigilance greater than that exercised by husbands and mothers. They condemned to the flames all books which did not treat of devotion. Finding the *Adventures of Petrone,* the property of Baron de Lahontan, and which he professes to have valued more highly than his life, in the house of his host, the priest tore it up in a rage. Lahontan vowed that if he could have found the priest when he first saw the destruction he had made, he would have plucked out his beard. No one was allowed to play lansquenet, or to read a romance or a comedy, on pain of excommunication. In our day the priest Villeneuve writes a comedy of five hundred pages, which is a series of elaborate libels. The Jesuits desired to monopolize all the secrets of society themselves; and for this reason they denied the right of the Récollets to hear confessions.‡

A rupture had taken place between Bishop Laval and the Governor, on the subject of permitting or prohibiting

---

* *Nouveaux Voyages de M. Le Baron de Lahontan, dans L'Amérique septentrionale.*

† *Circulaire* 26 Novr. 1860.

‡ Pope Urban VIII., in 1635, gave the Récollets the necessary powers to resume their mission in Canada.—Faillon, *Vie de Madmoiselle Mance.*

the sale of brandy to the Indians. The Governor contended for a regulated traffic ; the bishop for a total prohibition of the commerce.* The Governor, however,
rigorously forbade any one to take brandy to the Indians
in the woods. The Jesuits, to whom Frontenac was
obnoxious, and who were glad of a pretext for assailing
him, took part with the .bishop in denouncing the traffic
and the Governor.

The Jesuits were powerful enough to make bishops,
and unmake governors. The bishopric of Quebec had
been founded at their suggestion, and the first bishop
was their choice. By their intrigues, three governors
had been removed in rapid succession. And now they
had turned their artillery upon Frontenac, with the same
design. But, being a relation of Madame de Maintenon,
his credit at Court enabled him to brave the fury of the
Jesuits for the period of ten years.

The bishop had gone to France to try to induce the
Court to accept his views on the brandy traffic ; and while
he was there, Frontenac wrote a letter to the king, in
which he describes the annoyance to which he was subjected by the Jesuit priests.† He describes the bishop
as being in a state of absolute dependence on the Jesuits,
and expresses the hope that, should that functionary resign, a successor would be appointed who was not under
that baleful influence.

The Jesuits denied the power of the sovereign to authorize this traffic ; it was, they said, one of the things over
which his authority did not extend ; it belonged to the
domain of the Church. These statements were made
in the pulpit, in the presence of the Governor. So great
was the annoyance he felt at being obliged to listen to
them, that he several times felt tempted to interrupt the

---

* *Histoire de l'eau de vie en Canada,* written by a priest at the time of the dispute.

† *Frontenac à Monseigneur* MS. Archives de Paris.

sermon by leaving the church with his guards. But he contented himself with visiting the Vicar-General and the Superior of the Jesuits, and complaining to them of the conduct of the offending priests.

Frontenac brought the powerful weapon of ridicule into play against the ecclesiastics who attacked his authority and endeavoured to thwart his policy. He is said to have employed, with questionable taste, actors and dancing girls in the castle of St. Louis, and even in some of the religious houses, in presence of the inmates, to perform comedies in ridicule of ecclesiastics whom he desired to belittle in the public estimation.* His quarrel was with the Jesuits and the bishop under their control. Partly out of rivalry, perhaps, but mainly on account of the difference in the conduct of the two religious orders, he favoured the Récollets. He stated, at his own dinner table, in 1678, in the presence of the bishop and Father Hennepin, a Récollet missionary, that he should make the Court acquainted with the zeal of the Récollets and the generous nature of their enterprises.† His will contained a direction that his body should be buried in the church of this order in the city of Quebec, to which, Miles says, he had granted the land on which their house was built, had materially aided other of their establishments, 'and professed to be a sort of trustee in their behalf, as well as a protector.'

What the Jesuits were then doing, under the French dominion, they are repeating to-day. Are they destined to meet a similar check? A like success they cannot have.

The age was intolerant. The New England Puritan, who had fled across the seas to secure an asylum in which he could exercise his religion in safety, became in

* Miles. The History of Canada under the French Régime.
† Hennepin. Description de la Louisiane.

turn a persecutor. But the malady passed away with the evil time. Not so with the Jesuit : his spirit is as intolerant to-day as it was two hundred years ago, and he is busy in repeating attacks which in the sixteenth century he made on the authority of the colonial government of France, of which Frontenac so bitterly complained.

When Nova Scotia passed, by the Treaty of Utrecht, under the crown of England, the priests persuaded the Acadians to refuse to take the oath of allegiance to their new master. ' I do verily believe,' said Lieutenant-Governor Doucette, in a letter to the Secretary of State, November 5, 1717, ' all would become subjects of His Majesty if it were not for the priests amongst them,' who made them believe that the Pretender would soon be placed on the throne, and Canada would again fall under the French dominion. There was nothing in the form of the oath to which any objection could be made. It only required the Acadians to ' declare and most solemnly swear before God to own him (the king of Great Britain) as our sovereign king, and to obey him as his true and lawful subjects.' No abjuration was required, and the free exercise of their religion was to be granted to the new subjects. One priest, with whom Governor Philipps had an interview, urged as reasons why they could not become subjects of England, that they had signed a paper which obliged them to remain subjects of France, and that such a declaration of a change of allegiance would render their lives insecure by arousing the wrath of the Indians, whom, far from having reasons to fear, they had reduced to the most submissive obedience. The king of France, had in the act of handing over these subjects to another sovereign, released them from their oath, which could only oblige them to serve him so long as their relation of subjects to him remained unaltered.

'It is a hard and uneasy task in my circumstances,'
Governor Philipps wrote to Secretary Craggs, May 26,
1720, 'to manage a people that will neither hearken to
reason (unless it comes out of the mouths of their priests)
and at the same time to keep up the honour and dignity
of the Government.' Unless the oath were taken or the
priests recalled, Philipps believed that, in the event of
war again breaking out between the two crowns, the
Acadians would be so many enemies in the midst of the
country. The priests may have felt the fear with which
they inspired their flocks : that if the Acadians took the
oath they would, in a short time, be reduced to the condition of the Catholics of Ireland ;'but that the former subjects of France could retain their allegiance to the nation
that had been obliged to cede their territory to a rival
was too grotesque a notion to be seriously entertained by
the men by whom it was instilled into the minds of the simple peasants. It was these misleading guides of the Acadians who forced them at last to choose between allegiance
to the new sovereign and deportation. If Basil, the
Blacksmith, with a face flushed and distorted with passion, cried :

> 'Down with the tyrants of England! We never have
> sworn them allegiance,'

the true reading of the history is that the Father Feli-
cians had inspired him with that passion, instead of
meekly praying for the new. masters : "O Father
forgive them!"* Admit that the deportation was a
mistake, a cruelty, and a wrong, what then ? It
still remains true that the real authors of it are the
men who induced the simple Acadians to believe that
they could continue to be French subjects in a British
colony. Those who took the oath were allowed to re-

---

* Longfellow. *Evangeline.*

tain their possessions.† The French of Cape Breton, who could still legally indulge their original allegiance, exercised a paramount influence not only over their countrymen in Nova Scotia, but also over the Indians. The Bishop of Quebec continued to send priests to Nova Scotia, to order the building of churches there and to exercise other acts of authority. Governor Armstrong despaired of seeing the people brought to obedience unless 'the insolent behaviour of these priests' could be curbed.* When the inhabitants asked to have the services of a priest, the British Governor seems to have had no other resource than to write to the Governor of Cape Breton to send him one who would be likely to prove inoffensive.† Sometimes priests were sent out of the Province for conduct 'tending to a jurisdiction of their own, independent of his majesty's authority' and the civil government ;‡ and when one gave in his submission, under circumstances which threw a doubt on his sincerity, he was required to find security for his future good behaviour, as a condition of his remaining in the Province.§

The use of the confessional as a means of restoring property wrongfully taken by the penitent has been much extolled. Governor Mascarene of Nova Scotia, June 29, 1741, complained that this power was sometimes greatly abused ; so much so that 'the missionaries often went so far as to make themselves sovereign judges of all causes.' Then follows the example of a parishioner who complains to a priest that his neighbour owes him a debt or detains something belonging to him. The priest examines witnesses, and

† The ' French Popish missionary is the real chief commander of his flock, and receives and takes his commands from his superiors in Cape Breton.' P. Mascarene 1720, in Nova Scotia Archives.

* Despatch to Lords of Trade, Nov. 16, 1731.

† Gov. Armstrong to St. Ovide, June 17, 1732.

‡ Minutes of N. S. Council, May 18, 1736.

§ Minutes of N. S. Council, Oct. 11, 1726.

then, deciding in a judicial manner, condemns the accused to make restitution ; the execution of the sentence being enforced by a threat to refuse the sacraments for noncompliance.* In New Spain, the confessors made a restitution of duties withheld from the king a condition of absolution. The confessor was generally the channel through which restitution was made., The Spanish Government, it was estimated, was defrauded of $400,000 every year in America ; and of this amount only $500 was restored. As a means of ensuring restitution, the confessional would seem to be a very inadequate instrument. When it does cause something wrongfully obtained or detained to be restored, if it makes the mere confession and disgorgement a condition of forgiveness, it is not likely to act as a spur to the performance of duty.

The absolute subordination of the missionaries to their superiors was found a cause of much difficulty.‡ The Vicar-General of the Bishop of Quebec, in Nova Scotia, promised obedience. Finally no priests were allowed to enter the Province without leave.§ None were to presume to exercise any ecclesiastical power of the Church of Rome therein ; the fourteenth article of the treaty of Utrecht granted Roman Catholics the free exercise of their religion, 'so far as the laws of Great Britain permit.' The rule came to be that no priest could exercise his spiritual functions until he received the approbation of the commander-in-chief and of the Council; and no missionary was allowed to remove from one parish to another without first obtaining leave from the Government.|| The Bishop of Quebec claimed the right of sending into the Province missionaries at discretion. For assuming the

* Governor's Letter-Book.
‡ Governor Mascarene to the Lords of Trade, Nov. 23, 1741.
§ Mascarene, June 16, 1742.
|| Mascarene, June 16, 1742.

7

title of Vicars-General two priests were ordered to leave the Province.* The missionaries of the French at Louisburg, acting in the conjunction with the priests, brought over the Indians of Nova Scotia to their side† at a critical juncture.

M. J. L. Le Loutre, a missionary priest, wrote, in the form of a petition and in the name of the inhabitants of Cobequid, to the inhabitants of Beaubassin, asking them to strike a blow with a view of driving the Rangers from his parish, after which he promised that his parishioners should go to Grand Pré and Port Royal and strike successive blows at these places. 'It is your brothers,' he assured them, ' who ask you for help ; and we think that the charity, religion, and union that have always existed between us will constrain you to come and rescue us.'‡ Another priest, Daudin, acted so badly that he had to be suspended from his functions for some time and placed under arrest.

These samples of the conduct of the priests justified the suspicion that when war broke out their influence would be used on the side of the French. It is reasonable to suppose that the priests did cling to the hope that the fortunes of war would one day restore Acadia to France. Even so astute a statesman as Talleyrand believed that the Canadians would of their own accord return to the French dominion.§ One of the first results of the persistent opposition of the priests to the English dominion was a resolution come to by the Government not to grant any unconceded lands to Roman Catholics ; and the deportation of the non-jurors, whatever we may now think of

* Gov. Mascarene to Sec. of State, Dec. 3, 1742.

† Gov. Mascarene to the Lords of Trade, Sept. 22, 1744.

‡ This piece is not dated, but it was written after the year 1749. Nova Scotia Archives.

§ Essai sur les avantages à retirer de colonies nouvelles dans les circonstances présentes, an V.

it, presented itself to the minds of the English as a measure of stern necessity which offered the only means of safety and self-protection.*

The future influence of the Jesuits in Canada depends in a great measure upon their being able to get control of the education of the young. Several years ago they formed the design of establishing an university at Montreal; and in order to show the necessity for such an in. stitution, they found it necessary to undertake to prove that the University of Laval did its work in an unsatisfactory way, and did only a small portion of what was required of it. It desired, they said, to limit the number of students to one hundred, while they alleged there were in the Province five or six times that number who were desirous of obtaining an university education. 'Large numbers of these, resident in Montreal, could not or would not go to Laval. The distance and the expense of attending it were obstacles in the way; the teaching was erroneous in more than one respect. The fury of the opposition to the teaching of Laval was sometimes carried so far as to describe it as atheistical. Five or six hundred young Canadians, it was pretended, who desired an university education, were either deprived of it or driven to Protestant universities or schools affiliated with them, where their faith and morals were exposed to terrible dangers.

Yet Laval, the criminatory argument continued, played dog in the manger; what she could not or would not do herself she debarred the Jesuits from doing. She was a

* Abbé Raynal's one-sided account of the treatment the Acadians received from the British Government evidently formed the groundwork of Longfellow's *Evangeline*, and Haliburton's *History of Nova Scotia* failed to reconstruct the facts, partly because he knew scarcely anything of the archives of the country whose history he was writing, and partly because his political success depended on the favour of a constituency in which there were French votes enough to defeat any candidate. What I have said, without attempting to justify the deportation, will serve to show that the measure was not resolved upon without great and long-continued provocation.

monopolist, an obstructionist, an enemy of progress, instead of being, as was hoped at her birth, the Sorbonne of New France.

The Bishop of Montreal was exceedingly anxious to promote the project of the Jesuits, but he was opposed by a majority of the Episcopate of the Province, including the Archbishop; and, what was worse, his scheme and the scheme of the Jesuits was twice vetoed at Rome, first in 1862, and afterwards in 1865. At a later period, 1872, the Bishop of Montreal represented that the opposition of Rome had ceased ; and though the necessary authority for the canonical erection of the projected university was still withheld, it was only withheld from motives of policy. The President of the Sacred Congregation suggested that much trouble might be avoided if the necessary charter were first obtained from the civil authority, and he sustained the objection by pointing to the difficulties which had been created by the canonic erection of the University of Dublin before the Government had granted a charter. The Bishop of Montreal, after the refusals he had met at Rome, had asked the President of the Sacred Congregation to be allowed 'to return to the charge;' and the granting of his request, which really meant no more than that he was not commanded to forego his importunity, was tortured by the Jesuits into an assent to their project. An assent it no doubt implied, but with conditions, and the problem was to obtain the charter. To this concession only two of the bishops were favourable, those of Montreal and Three Rivers. Against the opposition of the majority of the bishops and that of the University of Laval the charter could not be obtained.

If the Jesuits were busy at Montreal, at Three Rivers, at Rome, the Rector of the University of Laval was not idle ; he induced a majority of the bishops to pronounce against the design of the Jesuits and the Bishop of Montreal.

The letters in which they did so having been published by the authorities of Laval, were subjected to violent criticism, and treated with jeering ridicule and undisguised contempt by the Jesuits and their friends. In re-publishing extracts from them, these hostile critics interjected long passages in parentheses, much longer than the letters themselves, containing what they contended the bishops ought to have said ; a mode, scarcely polite, of saying that they told not the truth. Let us cite a few examples.

The Bishop of Ottawa having said : ' I believe, M. Le Recteur, that you are right, after having made all the sacrifices which you have not feared to impose upon yourselves in the past, in asking the Government to see that your rights are not sacrificed,' the critic* remarks : ' The thing, however, would be difficult, and it would require all your ability to succeed ; if your rights are not so certain and irrefragable that they may not be disregarded, as I had the honour and the advantage to do when I obtained an university charter for my college of Saint Joseph. I thank you for not having, at that time, put forward your present pretensions ; not that I should have been prepared to admit them, for it would have been easy to prove that other Catholic universities were possible as well as yours, even at Ottawa, that is in the ecclesiastical Province of Quebec, but your reclamations would have caused contestations and disputes, things for which I have little or no liking.'

Then the Bishop is allowed to speak in the next sentence of his letter : ' It seems to me that after the sentence which has been delivered at Rome, and not yet been revoked, which maintains the right of the University of Laval, it is not allowable for good Catholics to oppose, directly or indirectly, a decision which ought to be respected and followed, at least until it is revoked.' What

* *La Redaction de Franc-Parleur.*

the bishop ought to have said, according to the champion of the Jesuits, is : ' At least that the thing should not be regarded, as I believed myself entitled to regard it, when the university charter for my college of Saint Joseph was granted, in spite of the sentence of the Holy See in 1865, without my ceasing on that account to be a good Catholic ; that is to say, to be able to act thus, that the Holy See has several times expressed the desire that the civil power should remove all the difficulties, so that the Holy See would have no difficulty in permitting what it had at first deemed inexpedient.'

The Bishop of Rimouski having stated that he should see with extreme regret ' the rights of the University of Laval set aside, and the immense sacrifices it had made rendered useless by the legislative concession to other institutions, in the Province of Quebec, of the power of conferring degrees to Catholics,' the Jesuits' champion interjects, as what the bishop ought to have said : ' What is essential for your cause, M. Le Recteur, is to establish your right to exist alone, if I judge by your own memoirs, which I have under my eyes, and which irrefragably establish the contrary, and that in twenty different places; for example, at page 28 of the memoir of 1862, where you affirm that, contrary to the statement of the Bishop of Montreal, you have neither asked for nor obtained a charter for a Provincial university.' Never, surely, was so weighty an argument hung upon so slender a peg.

The Bishop proceeded to remark that the circumstances under which Rome had given its decision had not changed ; whereupon the Jesuits' champion interjects, as what the Bishop ought to have said : ' Before making use of this argument, it will be necessary to assure yourself whether Mgr. of Montreal had not been authorized one way or another, this circumstance being of a nature to act as a strong inducement to the Legislature to favour the creation of an university at Montreal.'

The Jesuits as little respect a decision come to at Rome, on a controverted question in which they are interested, as they would a decision of the Legislature refusing them the charter for which they ask. The Bishop of St. Hyacinthe had ' no difficulty or hesitation in affirming that the University of Laval has the right to be maintained in the position assigned to it by the sentence delivered at Rome.' On which, the champion of the Jesuits remarks that the Bishop ought to have said : ' That, in order to comply with this condition, you should not confine yourself to offering the establishment of university chairs for Montreal ; but that you should do so on acceptable conditions, without which the sentence of the Holy See has no longer its *raison d'être.'*

The Archbishop of Quebec made two voyages to Rome, one in 1862, the other in 1864, to sustain the rights of the University of Laval against the attempts of the Jesuits practically to supersede it by the establishment of a university at Montreal. Both parties were heard before the decrees of the Sacred Congregation were rendered. ' To consider oneself authorized,' said the Archbishop, ' to infringe upon these decrees, before they have been revoked by the high authority by which they were rendered, would be to reverse all the notions of the Catholic hierarchy.' It would naturally be supposed that such vehement advocates of the authority of Rome as the Jesuits and their friends are, on ordinary occasions, would have accepted this view of the Archbishop without question. On the contrary, he is told that he ought to have said : ' It is true that the Bishop of Montreal may have had permission to return to the charge, as he had after the sentence of 1862, and one could not deny this possibility without being blind and foolish. To consider

oneself authorized to deprive him of this liberty, if it has
been given him by the Cardinal Préfet of the Propaganda,
it would be necessary to reverse all the notions of the
Catholic hierarchy ; for we know that when the Préfet
of the Roman Congregations permits a thing to be done it
is not for the bishop or the archbishop to oppose it.'

But the Jesuit university is not yet. Let no one, however, suppose that the project is abandoned. At Rome,
the question was, five years ago, little more than one of
the prudence of taking the initiative. If a charter had
been obtained from the Legislature of Quebec, Laval
would have found itself deprived of support at Rome.
The sentiment which would protect Laval out of consideration for the sacrifices she has made, is feeble compared
with the advantages which the Jesuits represent as certain to result from the realization of their plan. The
immense difference between one hundred students receiving an university education and six times that number
enjoying the advantage, is one of those broad statements
which produce an unerring effect on the public mind.
The alleged fact must be more than half fiction ; for if
only a hundred students seek access to Laval, is it probable that six times that number are anxious to obtain
an university education ? The population is too small
and the Province of Quebec too poor to permit us to accept such a conclusion. The danger of allowing the sons
of Catholic parents to attend Protestant universities can,
by a little artful exaggeration, which is certainly not
wanting, be made to count for much.

The question of establishing a branch of the University
of Laval at Montreal has no longer an active existence.
Unless the Jesuits were permitted to control it, they
would not accept the arrangement as an accommodation
of their difference with the University of Laval. The
Bishop of Montreal notified the Primate that he could not

consent to the establishment of this branch, because
'the bishop would count for nothing in it.' The Archbishop replied that it was not necessary that the bishop
should interfere in this establishment. But Bishop
Bourget was not to be moved from the position he had
taken, though the opinion of the Archbishop differed from
his own. From which it is plain that, according to
Bourget, though the Pope hears Christ, and the bishop
hears the Pope, he does not hear or does not heed the
archbishop.

The Bishop of Three Rivers thought the objection
drawn from the decision given at Rome feeble and of little account, since he regarded it as certain that neither
the Bishop of Montreal nor the Jesuits intended to erect
a Roman Catholic university without the authorization
of the Holy See. And to prove the strength of his convictions and of his sincerity, he refused to attempt to
'induce the Government to beg the Jesuits to withdraw
their demand.' The experience of twenty years convinced him that the University of Laval could not attract
to her a majority of the Roman Catholic youth of the
Province who desire to obtain an university education.
He found that more than three-quarters of those in his
own diocese who desired to enter the liberal professions
pursued their preparatory studies at Montreal. He assumed that, beyond doubt, the objection made at Rome
seven years before had been withdrawn.

The question of the charter remains. The champion of the Jesuits is of opinion that the Government
must shape its conduct on this question entirely by the
desire of the Cardinal Préfet of the Propaganda ; and
that, knowing his wishes on the subject, it may ' without
fear grant what Montreal demands.' And he adds : 'Let
the members of Parliament choose : on one side are four
letters in flagrant contradiction with the facts in the

cognizance of their authors, and even with the acts of some of these authors. On the other side are two letters in perfect accord with the facts, and entirely conformable to the desires as well as the authorization of the Cardinal Préfet of the Propaganda ; to good faith, right, justice, equity, and good sense the choice is not difficult.'

This shows, at least, if nothing else, that the New School can proclaim, when it suits its purpose, that the bishops state that which is not. And the remarkable fact is that, by this mode of attack, they have at length succeeded in imposing silence on that moderate section of the Church of Rome on whom they made war. The Archbishop is told that, for the purpose of producing a deception at Rome, he disfigured the facts, and put a question in a way that was not conformable to the truth.

The Jesuits have taken towards the University of Laval the same line of attack with which, two centuries ago, they crushed Port Royal. The greater part of the young men who leave that university they have described as being imbued with very advanced Liberal and Gallican ideas, which they predict will shortly conduct us all into an unfathomable abyss. In nothing but name, its accusers are never tired of repeating, is this university Roman Catholic. It teaches its students the doctrines found in law books which Pius IX. has formally condemned ; and it is clear that it must continue to do so, because there are no other works that could supply their place. It is made a crime in 'this university that it does not compel the students to get such glimpses of physical science as might be possible by looking through the mists of Church dogma.*

Not till May 15, 1876, did the University of Laval receive canonic erection. By the bull of Pius IX., the Archbishop of Quebec is made Rector, and the University

* See *La Question de l'Université*, par l'Abbé Pelletier.

obtains a protector at Rome, in the person of the Cardinal
Préfet of the Propaganda *ex officio.*

In this recognition of Laval, its enemies see no honour.
In the natural order of things, they say, every Catholic
university ought to be canonically erected. Laval has
always been called a Catholic university ; and ' it is absolutely necessary, on account of this title, that Rome should
interfere, and with a·firm hand so exercise her authority
as to give this institution a truly official character.' The
latitude·which has hitherto been allowed to the teaching
of the professors is abnormal, and must in future be put
an end to. Over one thing, the most hostile of Laval's
critics rejoices : ' Rome no longer fears, as she feared
twenty years ago, to awaken the susceptibilities of Protestant England, by giving canonic erection to a Catholic
university in one of her colonies.'†

It is impossible to doubt that, at Rome, the sympathy
is with the Jesuits ; and if the Order met a check in
Quebec, the reason is that it had there scornfully rejected
the counsels of prudence. It requires no small fund of
perversity to enable any one to see a victory for the
Liberal or Gallican element in the canonic erection of
Laval University. The accusations which the Jesuits
had brought against Laval may have created the impression, at Rome, that the University needed to be kept
better in hand. That this will be the effect of the bull of
May, 1876, does not admit of a reasonable doubt. The
bull places the doctrine taught and the discipline enforced
therein under the surveillance of the Episcopate of the
Province of Quebec. This covers the ground of faith and
morals. In every other respect, the University is to be
regulated by the decision of the Congregation of the Propaganda, February 1, 1876. If what the Jesuits attacked
receives from the Pope the balm of an ample measure of

† Abbé Pelletier, in the *Franc-Parleur,* Sept. 8, 1876.

consolation and praise, we must not mistake the meaning of the fact. In practically taking the direction of the University, Rome could have no object in proclaiming that the past had not been satisfactory and that any great change was going to be made in future. Nevertheless the arrows of the Jesuits may not have missed their mark. Pius IX. extols the sagacity of the professors, several of whom studied in the Gregorian University of the Jesuits at Rome, and in the classes of St. Apollinaire; but he admits that Rome expects from Laval greater benefits in the future than she has derived in the past. Any desire to derogate from the royal charter, granted by the Crown of England, is judiciously disclaimed. The declared intention to leave the University to govern itself receives a disturbing commentary from the fact that the Episcopate of Quebec and the Congregation of the Propaganda at Rome divide the government between them.

Immunity from alteration is claimed for all the provisions of this bull. If the legislative authority saw cause to reject any of its provisions, it would find in advance that the presumption would 'incur the indignation of God and of Peter and the Apostles.'

Nothing contained in the bull is to be criticised, combatted, infringed upon, withdrawn, demurred to, restricted, lessened, or derogated from in any particular; no matter what necessity the civil Government, to which the right of establishing educational corporations belongs, might see for making any change. It is conceivable that the directions of the Congregation of the Propaganda might contain something which, on national grounds, it would be desirable to reject, and which might in fact conflict with the royal charter; and then the question would arise whether the civil Government or a Roman Congregation should win the mastery. The royal charter gave the 'University full liberty to govern itself; and though Pius IX. professes not to desire to derogate from this privilege, it is impossible not to see that the real control will be in the bishops and the Congregation of the Propaganda. The power of the former will be directory; that of the latter will be judicial, and will be exercised as an original jurisdiction.

When certain general edicts of previous Popes, which are not enumerated, are made to apply to this University with the same force as if they had been cited in the bull at length, ' anything else to the contrary notwithstanding,' the suspicion naturally suggests itself whether this may not be intended to be a fatal arrow shot at the royal charter. In other cases, we have to deal with the conflict of laws and jurisdictions ; here we flatter ourselves that the civil law must prevail. Is it possible this may prove a delusion ?

Twenty years before this bull was issued, M. Louis Jacques Casault, the first Rector of the University of Laval, to which a royal charter had then recently been granted, went to Rome to solicit the favour of canonic erection. He met with a refusal from the Pope. That refusal probably had a double motive : a desire to avoid what might be objected to by the British Government, as the Rev. Alexis Pelletier avers, though the danger from this source must have been very small, and a certain doubt may have hung over an institution which had just accepted a royal charter from a Protestant Crown. The canonic erection which was then refused, is granted only after the Pope has assured himself that several of the professors have received their education at hands of Jesuit instructors at Rome. If there be a prospect that Jesuit influence will become predominant in this seat of learning within a space of time which it is possible to estimate, it is easy to see why the decision at Rome against the establishment of an avowed Jesuit university at Montreal should have been followed by the canonic erection of Laval. There were two ways of taking the citadel: one by assault, which was the plan of the Jesuits; the other by gradually introducing into the professors' chairs teachers educated in hostility to the old order of things. This is the plan of the Pope, and an attempt is being made to put it into execution. The Congregation of the Propaganda may be relied on to do its share of the work; and in the Episcopate of Quebec it will find a willing backer. Cardinal Franchi and his official successors for all time are to adjudicate on all causes that may arise, in the shape of accusations or otherwise, against the University; by which the increasing volume of references to Rome will be still further swelled.

What the first Bishop of Canada did in this connection the present Archbishop of Quebec warmly extols. He was energetic in his endeavours to prevent the introduction of 'certain propositions' which the will of Louis XIV. had imposed upon the French seminaries of learning. These unspecified propositions were probably the four articles. He is also credited by the same dignitary with having compelled the Canadian clergy to accept the Roman liturgy, which was persistently rejected in France. He proclaimed, in short, *Ubi Petrus, ibi Ecclesia*: 'where Peter is, there is the Church;' another form of saying, 'the Pope is the Church.' This is the light which the Archbishop pledges himself to follow. He guarantees that Laval will, 'in all things, follow the direction that comes to her from Rome;'‡ and that 'she rejects what Rome condemns, and is always ready to submit her teaching to that of Rome.' This is what the Pope calls leaving the University that liberty to govern itself, which it derives from the royal charter. In the light of these facts, the

‡ Mandement promulguant la Bulle *Inter varias solicitudines*, Sept. 13, 1876,

refusal of Rome to sanction the erection of a Jesuit university at Montreal is intelligible. It does not follow that the Jesuits will, in the end, be losers by that refusal : on the contrary, they are morally certain to gain.

When the Archbishop claims for Laval the merit of having, at all times, maintained a position of strict neutrality between different political parties, we do not care to question his statement. This attitude, he hastens to assure us, has the approbation of Rome. The University, the Archbishop adds, recognizes in public men the right of freedom of opinion in all purely civil matters. Nevertheless, the bull *Inter varias solicitudines*, in giving to the Episcopate of Quebec supreme surveillance over all questions of faith and morals which may arise in connection with the institution, extends its jurisdiction over politics, which even Archbishop Lynch identifies with morals. The doctrine of intolerance taught by the theological professors of Laval, trained in the schools of Rome, cannot in the long run be without its influence on politics.

The University of Laval has done good service in the cause of education ; but a turning point in her history has been reached. In future she will listen only to the voice of Rome, and her teaching will be more and more an echo of that of the Gregorian University of the Jesuits. Are we wrong in saying that out of apparent defeat the Jesuits will know how to evolve substantial victory ?

The Catholic historian Garneau charges the Jesuits with having desired to make Canada a second Paraguay. This is a weighty charge, and one against which we do not think they have been successfully defended. Let us see what we escaped by their want of success. In Paraguay the Jesuits appropriated all the products of the labour of the Indians under their charge in excess of the small amount necessary for the subsistence of the toilers, which probably did not exceed in value $50 a year each. The labour of these virtual slaves, whose masters had the merit of not being brutal and ferocious, has been estimated at $1,500,000 a year;* but a doubt has been expressed whether even this sum, large as it is, does not fall far below the entire profit, mercantile transactions being added, which the Jesuits made out of these Indians. The wealth of a single mission, that of San Ignacio Mini, appears by the official inventory to have been nearly $27,000,000; and of these missions there were not less than thirty. The Jesuits and the Indians formed a community, the most extensive experiment in socialism the world has ever seen; but the Indians contributed the labour and the Jesuits took the fruits. The greatest equality was enforced among the Indians in the matter of dress; but it was an equality in which all were alike bare-footed; there was an equality of labour, which consisted of unceasing drudgery. The Indians under the Jesuits were absolutely cut off from all intercourse with the Spaniards. They lived in mud hovels; the Jesuits built palaces and were surrounded by every luxury. The priests constantly made forced matches between the two sexes, which led to the greatest indifference between husbands and wives, and parents and children.‡

But the day of reckoning was at hand. On the 27th February, 1767, Charles III. of Spain issued a royal decree, banishing the Jesuits from all his dominions. He defended the act in a letter to Pope Clement XIII. as 'an essential step of political economy,' taken after careful examination and profound reflection. The Pope remonstrated against the expulsion and vindicated the Jesuits. His Majesty's Extraordinary Council advised the king that to enter into controversy on the merits of

---

* J. D. Robertson. Letters on Paraguay.

‡ Memoria sobre las Missiones, by Don Pedro de Angelis, Buenos Ayres, 1836, an official report.

the case would be 'to incur the most greivous inconvenience of compromising the sovereign prerogative of His
Majesty, who is responsible to God alone for his actions.'
In Paraguay, the Council adds, the Jesuits had taken
the field with organized armies against the Crown, and in
Spain they had attempted to modify the government to
suit their own purposes, and 'to promulgate and put into
practice the most horrible doctrines.' The succeeding
Pope, Clement XIV., not only ratified the decree of expulsion, but gave at length, in a brief of forty-one articles
(Sept. 12, 1773), his reasons for approving. In this brief
many weighty charges against the Jesuits were insinuated.

Canada was not, thanks to the vigour of the French
Government, made a second Paraguay; the Jesuits were
not expelled by the civil authorities, but they lost their
property by the natural extinction of the Order. To-day
Canada is fast becoming the paradise of the Jesuits, and
the experiment of what they may be able to do in the
Province of Quebec is now being worked out.

On the occasion of the golden wedding of Bishop Bourget of Montreal, the Jesuits in connection with the veteran
prelate resolved to make a demonstration which could
not be otherwise than offensive to many of the ten bishops
and four hundred priests who were present. To perform
the most important part in the ceremonies, three priests
distinguished for their opposition to the late Archbishop
of Quebec were chosen. Two of them who had, on account of insubordination, been sent from Quebec had
found a ready welcome at the episcopal palace of Montreal, and one of them had publicly lectured the Archbishop in the cathedral church. The sermon was preached
by the Jesuit priest Braün, and proved extremely offensive to many who were present.* It was a pulpit manifesto of the Jesuits and their allies. This shows how

* Dessaulles.

8

completely the late Bishop of Montreal was in the hands of the Jesuits.

Loud murmurs of disapprobation followed the preaching of the sermon ; and the dissatisfaction of the mass of the audience was shared by the Archbishop and the Bishops of St. Hyacinthe and Ottawa, as well as the Seminarists of St. Sulpice. The protests against the extravagant Ultramontanism of the sermon were echoed by politicians and journalists.‡

The Jesuits have always made use of the confessional as an instrument of power to be wielded so as to bring about the accomplishment of their own ends. And it would seem that the Jesuits of Quebec walk in the well-worn track. We are told, for instance, by M. Dessaulles, that while the Roman Congregations were condemning the Institut Canadien and its little blue covered pamphlet, Jesuit and other New School confessors were exercising a terrorism at Montreal which might vie with the Spanish Inquisition. Upon wives and mothers they brought to bear the terrors of the confessional to induce them to use the influence of their tears and their fears to compel husbands and brothers to quit their connection with the Institute. Many, as a means of obtaining some measure of peace in their distracted families, did so. Many who went away, the same authority informs us, promised still to remain at heart true members, and freely to give their subscriptions to the institution they had, in effect, been compelled to abandon. The latter part of their promise, it is to be feared, many of them failed to keep.

The Ultramontane journals of Quebec defend the use of the confessional as a means of extracting from unwilling breasts secrets which the ballot-box was adopted as a means of guarding. They argue that the priest, having directed the elector how to vote, has a right to use

‡ See Dinan.

the confessional to find out whether he has been obedient and acted according to instructions. If this really be done to any considerable extent, the fact is probably traceable to the rapid increase of Jesuit priests. But, necessarily, the question is one on which it is difficult to obtain evidence. The law respects the secrets of the confessional ; and this form of undue influence, if it really exists to any great extent, cannot be made a subject of judicial enquiry. It is reasonable to infer that a priest who, from the pulpit, denounces as a mortal sin the voting for a particular candidate, would not hesitate to ask, in the confessional, whether that sin had been committed. In doing so, he would incur little danger of exposure or of being called to account for the exertion of undue influence; while for the direction openly given in the pulpit, backed with the menace of spiritual censures, he might be called upon to answer in the courts, the same as a layman would be if he had resorted to some other form of undue influence. But a willing witness might blurt out the fact that electors are asked in the confessional how they voted, as was done in the Bonaventure election contest. The practice is therefore proved to exist ; and it is probably due to the audacity and exertions of the Jesuits.

VI.

THE ANGLO-GALLICAN THEORY.

If the Ultramontanes could show that the conquest of
Canada by England had the effect of abolishing, in the
conquered country, the whole body of the common ecclesiastical law of France, and substituting the canon law
of Rome in its place, they would have made an immense
step towards the subordination of the civil authority.
Hence Pagnuelo's contention that that event completely
changed the relations which previously existed between
the civil and the ecclesiastical authorities.

We may allow, with Wheaton, that a conquest has the
effect of changing the political system previously in force
in the conquered country; with Lord Mansfield, that the
laws, especially the municipal law, which in such case
previously existed, remain in force till they are changed
by the conqueror; with Marshall, that on the cessation of
the relations with their old government, the inhabitants
enter into new relations with their new masters; with Lord
Stowell, that a part of the ancient laws is inevitably re-
placed by the change of government, and even that 'the
administration of justice in the person of the sovereign,
and the appellant jurisdictions and whatever concerns the
sovereign authority, must undergo alterations conformable to the change ;' but this would not prove that the
whole body of the common ecclesiastical law of France,
on which the French colonists had, up to that date, relied for the protection of their rights and their interests,
was at one stroke swept away.

The question is not whether the relations between the

Roman Catholic Church of Canada and the King could continue to exist, by an act of transference, after the conquest, but whether the common ecclesiastical law of France, which formed the guide of the civil tribunals previous to 1760, still continued to be in force. Before M. Pagnuelo can answer the question in the negative, he must be prepared to show that the tribunals have systematically taken a mistaken view of their obligations, their functions, and their duties. He must show that dignitaries of the Church as well as judges have been in error on this point. He must refute the opinion which Mgr. Déstautels‡ has expressed in a very confident tone. ' We cannot doubt,' says that ecclesiastic, ' that the common ecclesiastical law, which was that of France before the cession of Canada to England, is the special ecclesiastical law of Canada. Indeed,' he adds, ' the arrêt of the King's Council of State creating the Superior Council of Quebec gives to this Council the power to decide absolutely and in the last resort, according to the customs of the Kingdom of France.'

Chief Justice Lafontaine judicially expressed the same opinion, in 1860;§ but it is an opinion which requires such modification as is implied by the frequent alteration of the laws affecting the Church of Rome.

Between France and the Church of Rome there was no doubt a sympathy which could not exist between a Protestant nation and the Roman Catholic Church: but besides this what more was there ? The check which the French Government exercised over the French Church, as a means of maintaining the independence of the secular power, was political. When it nominated bishops, it

---

‡ Manuel des curés, 1864. This ecclesiastic, a Canadian, owes his title of Monseigneur to the fact of his having been named secret honorary chaplain to Pius IX., though he resides in Canada. Abbé C. Tanguay, Répertoire Général du Clergé Canadien.

§ L. C. Jurist.

did so to prevent a foreign court exercising an influence which might prove dangerous to its own security. When it provided secular courts to correct the abuses of the ecclesiastical tribunals, the object was to protect its subjects. When Frontenac threatened to send the Jesuit priests to prison for attempting, in their sermons, to weaken the authority of the king, of which the governor was the depository, he could not have derived the right to do so from the fact that France was a Catholic government. This right, whenever and in whatever manner it was applied, was the right of self-defence and self-preservation ; a right which is necessarily inherent in all governments, whatever be their complexion.

The penal laws of England regarding Roman Catholics happily did not extend to Canada. This opinion was given by the Crown law officers in 1765, Sir Fletcher Norton, Attorney-General, and Sir Wm. de Grey, Solicitor-General. Three years later, the Advocate-General and the other two Crown law officers reiterated this opinion. In 1774, Lord North had expressed the same opinion in the House of Commons. Whether the bishop's jurisdiction ought to be abolished he regarded as another question. ' I cannot conceive,' he said, ' that its presence is essential to the free exercise of religion ; but I am sure that no bishop will be there under Papal authority, because he will see that Great Britain will not permit any Papal authority in the country.' It was expressly forbidden in the Act of Supremacy.

Six leading universities of Europe, in Roman Catholic countries, in reply to three questions put by Pitt, in 1789, denied that the Pope had any authority, direct or indirect, over the temporal power and jurisdiction of foreign princes and States ;* and this was probably one of the causes

---

* I. ' Has the Pope or cardinals, or any body of men, or any individuals in the Church of Rome, any civil authority, power, jurisdiction, or pre-eminence whatsoever, within

which led Lord North to assure the House of Commons that no bishop, acting under Papal authority, would be allowed to exercise his functions in Canada. The puzzle was to know from whom the bishop was to receive authority to discharge the duties of his office. Solicitor-General Wedderburn pointed out that no ecclesiastic could derive authority from the See of Rome without directly offending against the Act of Supremacy.† Attorney-General Dunning held that the rights and dues secured to the clergy related to the maintenance which they had possessed before the conquest, and did not extend to their ecclesiastical functions. Fox could not comprehend on what principle the priest could be entitled to tithes. Their right to tithes was not, as Bishop Bourget erroneously states,‡ agreed to on the capitulation of the country; on the contrary, the answer given by General Amherst to this demand was that this was a matter which must depend on the pleasure of the king. That pleasure was never exercised till 1774, when the Quebec Act was passed; during the preceding eleven years there had, according to Maseres, been no legal authority to collect tithes, and he states that, as a rule, they were not collected.§ This right is derived from the Quebec Act. Some writers contend, we are aware, that the authority to collect tithes is derived from the French law which was in force when the country was ceded to England.‖ But at the time of the capitulation the question of tithes

the realm of England? II. Can the Pope or cardinals, or any individual in the Church of Rome, absolve or dispense his majesty's subjects from their oath of allegiance, upon any pretext whatsoever? III. Is there any principle in the tenets of the Roman Catholic faith, by which Catholics are justified in not keeping faith with heretics, or other persons differing from them in religious opinions, in any transaction either of a public or a private nature?"

† Cavendish's Debates.

‡ Lettre Pastorale, 31 Mai, 1858.

§ Canadian Freeholder.

‖ Montigny, Histoire du Droit Canadien.

was specially reserved by the British negotiator. After the conquest, and before the Quebec Act was passed, the law officers of the Crown delivered an opinion that the obligation to pay tithes remained in full vigour, and that those who had the legal right to demand them could exact them not less from Protestants than from Roman Catholics. If this opinion had been beyond dispute, the authority of the Quebec Act would not have been required for the collection of tithes. If, on the other hand, Protestants had been under an obligation to pay tithes to the Roman Catholic Church, the Quebec Act would have given them relief, since it confined the right of the Roman Catholics to collect tithes to their own flocks.

The question whether the British monarch, a Protestant sovereign, succeeded to the rights of France in the nomination of bishops is one that has been much debated. But there is no doubt as to what the practice was from the time of the conquest to the war of 1812. Immediately after the treaty of peace, the British Government formed the resolution to allow the chapter of Quebec to elect the bishop ; but Governor-General Murray, enjoying, it may be presumed, special opportunities of acquiring knowledge by his presence in the colony, raised objections. The chapter proceeded to make the election privately, without the consent of the Governor.* The

* This was a return to the practice in vogue in the elective bishoprics of France in early times. The canons of the cathedral churches, the abbés, and the heads of the collegiate and conventual churches, the curés of the episcopal city and the rural deans of the diocese, the chief dean of the chapter of the cathedral church, who presided on the occasion, caused to be made of an uniform shape and appearance as many ballot papers as there were persons present, on each of which were written the words, ' You are an elector.' Among the ballots, to be drawn by lot from a bag, there were only nine which gave the right of nominating the candidates for election, and the drawers of these prizes became the nominators of candidates. The nine nominators separated into three divisions, and if two of the divisions did not make the same choice, lots were again drawn, and the winner obtained the right of nomination. After the final vote of the three divisions, and when each division had named aloud the person of its choice, the whole body of electors proceeded to elect a bishop from among the persons nominated. Each elector had the choice of open or secret voting; he could

choice fell on M. Montgolfier, Superior of the Seminary of Montreal.

M. Montgolfier, deputed by the French clergy of Canada, went to the Court of London, in the hope of bringing it to some agreement on questions such as that which General Murray had raised. The Government agreed that M. Montgolfier should become Bishop of Canada, but only on the condition that he should be placed on the same footing as the Roman Catholic Bishops of London and Dublin ; that he should assume no other mark of dignity than that of Superior of the Seminary of Montreal ; and that the ecclesiastics who formed the chapter of the Seminary should in no way be distinguished from the other members of their community.

The Government imposed another condition, and one which proved fatal to M. Montgolfier's chances of being allowed to fill the office of bishop : he was required to present himself before the Governor of Canada and obtain his consent to the arrangement. The English Government feared that, if M. Montgolfier were allowed to become bishop contrary to the wishes of the Governor-General, trouble and divisions would ensue. To the refusal of his assent, Murray added the demand that Montgolfier should cease to exercise the functions of General-Vicar, and that the chapter should proceed to a new election. He even named Olivier Briand as the person on whom he was desirous the choice should fall. This advice was taken, and at the second election, Sept. 11, 1764, M. Briand obtained the suffrage of the chapter.

either give aloud the name of his favourite candidate, or write it on a slip of paper which appears to have been handed to the secretary of the chapter. A plurality vote was sufficient to elect ; and if an equal number of votes was cast for three different persons the Metropolitan, to whom the facts were reported, made a choice of one of them. Bishops were sometimes elected by the clergy, and sometimes by the clergy in conjunction with the temporal authority. Even in Spain, bishops have at times been chosen by the king.—See Coquille. *Mémoires pour la Réformation de l'Etat Ecclésiastiques.*

When the Bishop-elect arrived in London, with letters of recommendation from the Governor-General, he found that a difficulty had been put in his way by a letter which Abbé Lacorne had sent from Quebec, and in which he undertook to show the inutility of a bishop in Canada. At first, the Government refused to accept M. Briand ; and it was only after repeated solicitations on his part that he obtained the necessary recognition.*

In a memorial which he presented to the Court of London, Abbé Lacorne had represented that the way to attach Canadians to the Government was to make them Protestants. This was not to be done by force, but by leaving them without priests. Though the law officers had twice given the opinion that the penal laws did not extend to Canada, there were difficulties in the way of permitting the consecration of a Roman Catholic bishop. Indirectly the Government gave M. Briand to understand that if he received his bulls, they would allow the circumstance to be passed over without notice. M. Briand therefore went to France, where he received his bulls, March 16, 1766, and was consecrated by the Bishop of Blois.*

The new bishop now set out for his diocese, to give a practical contradiction of Lord North's assurance, which was only two years old, ' that no bishop would be there under Papal authority,' because 'Great Britain would not permit any Papal authority in the country.'

An attempt to compel the priests to take the oath of allegiance which had been made almost immediately after the conquest, under a threat of deportation, had failed. Under the French *régime* the Canadian bishops, as we have seen, had been required to take an oath of fidelity to the Crown. Though this requirement must be

* M. Faillon. Vie de Mme. De Youville.

† Abbé Ferland, Histoire du Canada.

more necessary where the bishop is of foreign birth, the value of the oath would be greatly lessened by the previous obligation which he must have come under, to help, defend, and keep the Papal authority and the royalties of St. Peter against all men, sovereigns and subjects; to endeavour to preserve, defend, increase, and advance the rights, honours, privileges, and authority of the Holy Roman Church, of their lord the Pope and his successors; to observe and cause others to observe the apostolic decrees, ordinances, reservations, provisions, and mandates.‡ This formula, which was formerly, and probably still is, used by the Irish bishops, differed in some respects from that used by the Italian bishops at the epoch of the Council of Trent.§ The latter could not take part in any deliberation which might be construed to be contrary to the authority of the Pope. The bishop who has taken such an oath to the Pope as either of these, cannot afterwards take an oath of fidelity to another sovereign without equivocation or mental reservation.

The election of bishops by the chapter was a form of proceeding not destined to be continued. The practice came to be that the bishop, with the consent of the representative of the sovereign in the Province, named the coadjutor with the right of succession, and the Court of Rome issued the necessary bulls. In these days, the Court of Rome made no objection to this arrangement, but on the contrary, approved of it, on several occasions.‖

On the 16th March, 1768, Cardinal Castelli, Préfet of the Sacred Congregation of the Propaganda, wrote to the Bishop : ' It is the wish of the Pope that you should ask a coadjutor, provided the English do not oppose any

‡ Quarterly Review, Vol. XXXVIII.

§ Bungener, History of the Council of Trent.

‖ Abbé Ferland. Observations sur un ouvrage intitulé *Histoire du Canada*, par M· l'Abbé Brasseur de Bourbourg.

obstacle thereto ; ' which was the same as saying that
the opposition of the Government would be fatal to the
proposal. But in this, as in many other matters, there
were always to be found people more Catholic than the
Pope. M. Briand, says Abbé Brasseur de Bourbourg,*
when told of the authority claimed for the British Crown
in the nomination of bishops, ought to have said that the
French king has never possessed the right attributed to
him except by the favour of the Holy See, and that it
was not a right which could be transferred to a non-
Catholic sovereign.

Two years later, Bishop Briand besought the Papal
Nuncio at Paris to ask M. D'Esgly for coadjutor ; at the
same time informing him that the choice had been agreed
to by the Government. The presentation thus made was
accepted by the Court of Rome, and the Cardinal afterwards thanked the Bishop for having so managed the
matter that the appointment had been made without any
encroachment upon the rights and authority of the Apostolic See.

The elections of the bishops by the chapter would probably have been the best solution of a question which
presented many difficulties. There are conceivable cases
in which the right of the Crown to concur in, or to veto,
the choice, might almost be a political necessity. The
unchecked nomination of bishops by the Crown, judged
by its fruits where it has been tried, was far from being an
unmixed good. The selections were often made from
motives to which religion is a stranger. Political services,
and at some periods and in some countries services of a
shameless character, were rewarded by the bestowal of a
bishopric ; and the vicious qualities which had won the
incongruous reward continued in active vigour, to the
scandal of the Church and religion. The richer the

* *Histoire du Canada*, de son église, et de ses missions.

benefice, the greater the means of indulging in a dissolute voluptuousness, the greater the scandal. While the bishop wallowed in wealth, of which he made so ill an use, the simple clerk was a mendicant. The daughter, says the proverb, suffocated the mother; the piety of the Church loaded her with riches, and the riches smothered the piety. . But this state of things did not exist in Canada.

The appointment of curés by the Government was frequently resisted by the bishops; though the Royal Instructions formerly required that no Roman Catholic ecclesiastic should exercise his functions without a license from the Government. M. Briand, who had submitted to the conditions imposed on the occasion of his own appointment, said to the Governor : ' I would rather submit to the loss of my head, than accord you the permission of nominating to a single cure.'

The instructions of the Governors, whether they were strictly carried out or not, at least show the aim of the Imperial Government, and what it considered to be its duty. These instructions contained things which it is impossible now to approve; and others which, though they had a harsh look, may not have been wholly unnecessary.

The instructions of Governor Murray forbade the exercise of the ecclesiastical jurisdiction of Rome in the colony. Those of Sir George Prevost, dated 1775, may be taken as the affirmation of a policy which was not formally abandoned for more than half a century. They show what were the relations which it was the avowed policy of England to establish towards the Roman Catholic Church ; and they are therefore worth examining somewhat in detail.

Though the free exercise of the Roman Catholic religion had been guarded by the stipulations contained in the capitulation of Montreal and the Treaty of Cession, the instructions explained, 'that it is a toleration of the free exercise of the religion of the Church of Rome to which they are entitled, but not to the powers and privileges of it as an Established Church, that being a preference which only belongs to the Protestant Church of England.' The supremacy of the Crown in all matters, ecclesiastical as well as civil, was asserted. Appeals to a correspondence with any foreign ecclesiastical jurisdiction, of what nature or kind soever, were absolutely forbidden under severe penalties. No episcopal or vicarial power was to be exercised in the Province ' by any person professing the religion of the Church of Rome, but only such as are indispensably and indisputably necessary to the free exercise of the Romish religion ; ' and even this was not to be exercised without permission from the Governor under the great seal. No person was to have holy orders conferred upon him, or to have the care of souls, without a license from the Governor. No person professing the religion of the Church of Rome was to be allowed to fill any ecclesiastical benefice, or to enjoy any of the rights or profits belonging thereto, who was not a Canadian by birth ; such only excepted as already filled benefices or might be appointed thereto by the authority of the Crown ; and all right, or claim of right, in any other person than the sovereign or his representative, to appoint to any benefice was absolutely prohibited, the rights of lay patrons being reserved.

No Roman Catholic was to be appointed incumbent of any parish in which the majority of the inhabitants might solicit the appointment of a Protestant ; and in that case the incumbent was to be a Protestant minister, and the Roman Catholics might have the use of the church at such time as would not interfere with the worship of the Protestants ; in exchange for which privilege, the Protestant inhabitants of any parish where the majority of parishioners were Roman Catholics, were to have the free use of the church at such time as might not interfere with the worship of the Roman Catholics.

For some time the clergymen of the Church of England, in the conquered colony, were appointed by the Crown. And these instructions contain a claim on the part of the Crown to appoint Roman Catholic priests; for they forbade anyone else besides the sovereign or his representative to claim a right to appoint incumbents. Where the majority of the parishioners were Protestants, even the Crown had not the power to appoint a Roman Catholic incumbent, but the tolerated Roman Catholic minority was to have the use of the public churches at convenient times; and the Roman Catholic churches were to be so far treated as public property that the Crown could authorize Protestants to use them at times not inconvenient to their owners. Anglican control of the Church, in its different branches, was intended to go beyond the utmost extent of Gallican pretensions. But, in practice, it soon fell far short not only of the claims made in these instructions, but of the rules which the Government had enforced under the French dominion.

Every Roman Catholic ecclesiastic in possession of a benefice was required to take an oath of fidelity to the sovereign;† an oath which was substituted for that of supremacy and allegiance. All incumbents of parishes professing the religion of Rome, and not being under the

---

† The oath was in these terms: ‘ I, A. B., do sincerely promise and swear, that I will be faithful and bear true allegiance to His Majesty King George, and will defend him to the utmost of my power against all traitorous conspiracies, and attempts whatsoever, which shall be made against his person, crown, and dignity, and that I will do my utmost endeavour to disclose and make known to His Majesty, his heirs and successors, all treasons and traitorous conspiracies and attempts which I shall know to be against him, or any of them; and all this do I swear without any equivocation, mental evasion, or secret reservation, and renouncing all pardons and dispensations from any power or persons whomsoever to the contrary, so help me God.’ 14 Geo. III, Cap 83.

ecclesiastical jurisdiction of the Bishop of Quebec, were to hold their benefices during good behaviour, but any conviction for crime, or proof of seditious attempts to disturb the peace, was to vacate the benefice. Any such ecclesiastic who might marry was to be released from the penalties which such a step might subject him to by the authority of the See of Rome. It is a curious fact, in view of the Guibord case, that freedom of the burial of the dead in churches and church-yards was to be allowed indiscriminately to every religious persuasion. The Royal Family was to be prayed for in all churches and places of public worship,* and the royal arms were to be put up therein.

The guarantee that the priests who were not under the ecclesiastical jurisdiction of the Bishop of Quebec should hold their benefices during good behaviour, would, if enforced, have contributed to their independence and weakened the episcopal authority. The restriction of this rule to such priests as were not under the Bishop of Quebec must have gone far to nullify it altogether, for it is difficult to understand who were the priests who were not under his jurisdiction previous to the creation of the bishopric of Montreal. The Government went very far when it undertook to stand between the wrath of Rome and any priest who should renounce his obligations of celibacy and enter into the marriage state. Few changes made by the Reformation gave such offence to Roman Catholics as the marriage of the clergy; and now the offer was made to Canadian priests, that if they chose to marry, the British Government would shield them from the ecclesiastical penalties which they might incur for doing so. It is difficult to see how this could be done; and I have seen no evidence that the Government was ever called upon to carry this guarantee into effect.

* This practice was till recently kept up in the diocese of Montreal, by order of the Bishop, but it had become entirely voluntary; and I am not aware of its having been discontinued.

There were also instructions regarding the receipt of tithes by Protestant and Roman Catholic .ecclesiastics. Acting on the recommendation of Governor Simcoe, the British Government formed the design of supporting the Church of England in Canada by means of tithes; but it was soon discovered that the levying of tithes could not be made acceptable to an English colony in America, and the attempt had to be abandoned. The Church of Rome, which it was intended only to tolerate, while the Church of England should be established, retains its tithes, though those of the Church of England were abandoned before the end of the last century. The same fate has not befallen the landed endowments of the two Churches: the spirit of the age caused the secularization of the clergy reserves, set apart for the maintenance of a Protestant clergy; while the Church of Rome, with the exception of the Jesuits' estates, and a few other small parcels which fell into the possession of the Crown, retains its extensive territorial possessions.

The more stringent clauses of the Governor's instructions gradually came to be disregarded; and though spasmodic attempts were from time to time made by the British Government, or its representative in the colony, to recover the leeway which had been made, they had very little practical result, and the Church of Rome was enabled in time to shake itself free from that supremacy to which it had been intended to subject it. Forty years after the conquest the Duke of Portland sent out instructions to the Local Government to resume the authority in virtue of which no one was to have holy orders conferred upon him, or be entrusted with the care of souls, without a license from the Governor. No means by which this object could be attained were to be left untried. If the Roman Catholic bishop could be brought to a yielding temper by an addition to his worldly comforts, the British

9

Government was willing to increase his allowance ' almost to any extent.' The Roman Catholic clergy had, at this time, become accountable to their bishop alone, and that clergy, to augment its own influence, discouraged the education of the people.* To prevent the Bishop becoming more powerful than the Government, the Duke of Portland was willing to resume an authority which had already fallen into disuse, and to bring him to terms by an addition to his income.

Four years later an interview took place, at the suggestion of the Governor, between the Rev. M. Plessis, coadjutor, and Attorney-General Sewell, in which a desire of coming to an accommodation was admitted on the part of the Government. Mr. Sewell said he had authority from the Governor to state his private opinion on the subject. ' It is highly necessary for you,' he said to M. Plessis, ' to have the means of protecting your Church ; to the Government to have a good understanding with the ministers of a religion which it has acknowledged and established by the Quebec Act, and at the same time essential to have them under its control. The Governor having permitted the free exercise of the Roman Catholic religion, ought, he thought, to avow its officers, but not at the expense of the king's rights or of the Established Church ; you cannot expect,' M. Sewell told the bishop, ' nor ever obtain, anything that is inconsistent with the rights of the Crown ; nor can the Government ever allow to you what it denies to the Church of England.' But in this he was mistaken.

M. Plessis admitted that this position might be correct, and he saw no objection to the bishop acting under the king's commission. The Attorney-General claimed that submission to the king's authority, on all mixed as well as temporal questions, was essential. The Crown would

* Sir R. S. Milnes to the Duke of Portland, Quebec, 18 Feb., 1801.

never consent to give up its power; the bishop's right to appoint c* curés could not be admitted, for it was one which the Church of England did not possess. Under the 1st of Elizabeth, which the Quebec Act had extended to Canada—but happily no persecutions followed in its train— the bishop was without power. But, objected M. Plessis, the claim was practically that the king should collate to every benefice, whereas the King of France had collated only to consistorial offices, not to cures. This statement was too wide to express the truth, for there were many cures to which the French king was collator. But then, pursued M. Plessis, the bishop ought not to be obliged to give a reason for refusing to induct the priests so presented.

On this point the Attorney-General and the bishop did not agree, any more than on that of the removability of the curés; Mr. Sewell contending that a rector was removable only for misconduct. He was willing to allow ' that the Government ought, in policy, to give the bishop a jurisdiction over his clergy; subject always to the controlling power of the King's Bench, and to the operation of the writ of prohibition and an appeal, to which the Courts of the Bishops in England are subject.'

And now the Attorney-General reached the 'seductive part of his argument: ' The Government,' he said, ' acknowledging your religion, and avowing its officers to be officers of the Crown, should provide for them as for all others. The bishop should have enough to enable him to live in a splendour suitable to his rank; and the coadjutor also in proportion.' To do him justice, M. Plessis had performed his share in leading up to this proposal, by remarking that Bishop Denaud was living in a state of ' poverty, holding a living, and acting as parish priest, in direct contradiction to the canons.' The offer to raise the bishop from this condition to one of splendour, and

the coadjutor to a condition of relative splendour, caused
the latter to remark, that though he did not wish to see
the bishop living in splendour, he desired to see him freed
from the pressure of want. The Attorney-General having explained that he only meant that the bishop's income
should be that of a gentleman, M. Plessis acknowledged
that they both meant the same thing.

But there were difficulties in the way ; if the relinquish-
ment of the bishop's right to nominate to the cures, were
coincident with the receipt of a pension, a scandal-loving
public would not hesitate to say that he had sold the
Church. As for public clamour, the Attorney-General
saw that that could not be stopped ; and as for relinquishing a right, there was none to relinquish. 'Surely this is
a sufficient answer to any vulgar declamation against a
bishop who makes terms highly advantageous for his
church, and must be satisfactory to himself.' On so deli-
cate a point, M. Plessis could not presume to speak for his
ecclesiastical superior. Hesitatingly he said, 'I do not
know ; it is his affair.'

There was no time to be lost ; the opportunity might
never occur again. 'There is one idea,' said the Attorney-
General impressively, and with a slight flavour of menace,
'which I wish to suggest ; that if you ever mean to fix
the officers of your Church upon any footing, this is the
moment. The present Lieutenant-Governor is a gentleman
of most liberal principles ; he has been long enough in
the country to know all that relates to it, and is well disposed to serve you ; he is on the point of going to England, where this matter must be settled.' On this point
the interlocutors fell into complete accord : 'I am well
aware of all this ;' M. Plessis agreed, 'whatever is to be
done must be done now.'

At eight o'clock in the morning the Attorney-General
would expect M. Plessis to breakfast. 'You may,' frankly
replied M. Plessis, 'something must be done.'

A little more than three months after this remarkable interview, M. Denaud petitioned the king to cause him to be civilly recognized as Roman Catholic Bishop of Quebec, with 'such prerogatives, rights, and temporal emoluments as your majesty may be graciously pleased to attach to this dignity.' The petitioner stated that neither he who had been at the head of the Church in Lower Canada for eight years, nor his predecessors since the conquest, nor the curés of the parishes, had received from the king the special authorization of which they often felt the want, to prevent doubts on questions which might come up for adjudication in the courts touching the exercise of their civil functions. The bishops had however, he said, always taken the oath of allegiance and exercised their functions, with the permission of the sovereign, under different governors. But the day was coming when no more such oaths would be taken.

Mr. Ryland, in a letter to the Earl of Spencer, May 10, 1813, speaks of Denaud having offered to the Crown the patronage of the Roman Catholic Church. Perhaps, he concluded, or may have known it to be a fact, that Denaud was willing, in consideration of having his official position recognized by the Government and an annual salary paid out of the Imperial Treasury, to surrender the patronage of the cures. If this be so, the interview between Coadjutor Plessis and Attorney-General Sewell, followed by the eight o'clock breakfast, had not been in vain. But Denaud died before any arrangement was completed.

When M. Plessis passes through the chrysalis state of coadjutor and becomes bishop, we shall see him take the shilling.* Nine months after this conversation, Bishop Denaud died ; and Mr. Ryland ran to the Attorney-Gen-

---

* This interview, reported by Attorney-General Sewell himself, is given at length in Christie's *History of Canada.*

eral, and wrote to the Anglican Bishop of Quebec, and brought that functionary's powers of persuasion to bear on Mr. President Dunn, 'to dissuade him from a formal acknowledgment of M. Plessis, as Superintendent of the Romish Church, till His Majesty's pleasure respecting that situation shall be declared.' But the President had decided that on the morrow, Jan. 27, 1806, M. Plessis should be admitted to take the oaths in Council. The negotiations of the previous year had not yet matured into an agreement ; and Mr. President Dunn excited much criticism by his resolution formally to acknowledge M. Plessis as Bishop of Quebec. Mr. Ryland thought it would greatly tend to promote the views of the Government if an assistant superintendent were sent out from England, and a French emigrant bishop of approved loyalty could be found, who would accept on the terms offered by the Government.

But President Dunn went farther. Without awaiting for instructions from home, he allowed M. Panet to take the oath as coadjutor. The Anglican Bishop of Quebec was greatly scandalized ; he had in his possession an affidavit, in which the brother of the new coadjutor was said to have declared at the door of the church of Charlebourg, that if he could get M. Berthelot elected to the Legislative Assembly, 'they would trample the English under their feet' (*'ils fouleraient les Anglais sous les pieds'*). Who could tell what might not be done when the whole patronage of the Romish Church in the Province would be wielded by the brother of one who uttered this contingent threat ?

A few months later, Sir James Craig was Governor of Lower Canada. Mr. Ryland, who had tried so hard, and without effect, to impress his views on President Dunn, had greater success with the new Governor. The question which they conjointly undertook to resolve was, in

what way the Crown could most successfully assume the
patronage of the Roman Catholic Church. Having hit
upon a plan, Mr. Ryland, who had gone to England, un-
folded it in a letter to Peel, then under Secretary of State.
The plan was that the Governor should receive instructions from England to inform M. Plessis, that His Majesty was disposed to accede to the petition of the late Rev. M.
Denaud, by granting the Roman Catholic bishop recognition in the King's Courts, and letters patent appointing
him Superintendent of the Roman Catholic Church of
Lower Canada, with a salary suitable to the dignity and
importance of the office; and that letters of induction or
confirmation would be granted by His Majesty to the
curés, in the same manner as they were issued in favour
of the clergy of the Established Church, without which
they had no legal title to the privileges and emoluments
of their respective cures.

Meanwhile, the new bishop issued a mandement which
the Governor sent home as a proof of the position of complete independence which that ecclesiastic had assumed.
In this mandement, M. Plessis styled himself, 'by the
grace of the Holy Apostolic See, Bishop of Quebec.' Ryland raised the question, whether the bishop, by circulat-
ing the mandement, and assuming the title and authorities therein set forth, did not render himself liable to a
criminal prosecution.

Peel referred to the law officers of the Crown the question whether, under the Quebec Act, the king had a
legal right to assume and exercise the patronage of the
Roman Catholic Church in Lower Canada, in the manner
prescribed by the royal instructions; and also asked them
to take into account the question raised by Mr. Ryland,
with respect to the powers exercised by the Roman
Catholic bishop.

The law officers, Robinson, Gibbs, and Plumer, gave it

as their opinion 'that so much of the patronage of Roman Catholic benefices as was exercised by the bishop under the French Government, is now vested in His Majesty.' If the right be supposed to have originated with the Pope, the same consequence would result from the extinction of the Papal authority in a British Province. But the notion that the Papal authority was extinguished in Canada was already a delusion.

The Governor was impressed by the suspicion that the Roman Catholic bishops of Ireland, with whom the correspondence was being carried on, would instigate Plessis to refuse to acknowledge the king's supremacy. 'The priests,' Craig wrote in a letter to Ryland, 'certainly do their endeavours to estrange the people more and more from us.' Thus it was always more or less a question of allegiance.

The writers who contend that while the four articles were not registered by the Superior Council of Quebec, neither were Gallican doctrines introduced into the country,* overstate the fact. It may be true, as M. Garneau remarks, that the contentions which arose in France regarding the franchises of the Gallican Church had less interest for the scattered population on the banks of the St. Lawrence; but he admits that M. de Villermaule, M. Thibaut, and M. Glandelet, dean of the chapter of Quebec, accepted the doctrines of the author of the *Lettres Provinciales.* M. Oscar Dunn is correct in saying that, after the conquest, the French Canadians naturally gravitated more than ever towards Rome, as they had no longer any motive for making common cause with the secular power to form a national Church. Having to deal with a Protestant power, they only gave it half their confidence ; and ' to-day,' this writer boasts, ' we are perhaps of all peoples that which is in the strictest communion with Rome; there is not to be found the least restric-

* Oscar Dunn. Introduction de l'interement civil en Canada.

tion nor the least ambiguity in the acts of faith and solemn submission of our Provincial Councils.' In our day,
the fullest liberty has been granted to the Roman Catholics, with no grudging spirit; and now the time has come
when that Church claims supremacy over the State, and,
theoretically at least, denies the right of any other Church
even to toleration. So far from the Papal authority being
extinguished in Canada, it claims the first place, and insists on the subordination of the State.

The civil courts, under the French dominion, constantly restrained the abuse of ecclesiastical authority. Similar restraints can still be enforced; though the Church of
Rome in Quebec has never, at any time, made the same
efforts to break loose from them that she is making
to-day.

Abbé Ferland has printed a conversation between
Bishop Plessis and Governor Craig, which the former
committed to paper immediately after it had taken place.
He had not hesitated, in 1812, to ask the Government to
authorize him officially to assume the title of Bishop of
Quebec. In respect to the appointment to cures, he had,
even when secretary to Bishop Hubert, combatted the
claim of the Crown. Falling under the suspicion of the
Government, he was looked on as a man whom it would
be prudent to keep at arm's length. Prince Edward wrote
from Halifax to General Prescott, Oct. 16, 1797: ' As
to the coadjutor, M. Plessis, I think it my duty to inform
you that he is not a man in whom it would be prudent to
repose too great a degree of confidence. I have known
him since he was secretary to Bishop Hubert; and it was
perfectly well known, during my residence in Canada,
that he controlled both the bishop and the Seminary, and
induced them to adopt opinions which were incompatible
with those we maintained regarding the supremacy of
the king in ecclesiastical affairs.'

Bishop Denaut had consented to send to the Governor a list of nominations to cures, and the fact being reported to Prince Edward, the latter in another letter stated that, during his residence in Canada, M. Plessis had always influenced the bishop to refuse to submit to such nominations. 'M. Plessis,' the Prince adds, 'could not be considered otherwise than as occupying a doubtful position regarding his loyalty towards Great Britain.' In the interview with Craig, the bishop took the ground that, as father of the family, it was for him to send workmen into the field. The Governor replied that if the bishop denied the royal prerogative on this point, he must refuse to discuss the matter further with him; adding that the bishop's refusal of institution would not prevent the priests appointed in the name of the king from being maintained in their positions. The bishop contended that they would be unable to fulfil their spiritual functions. The Governor made a remark which shows that, in several respects, the royal instructions had been departed from; and he said he was liable to be called to account and put upon his trial for neglect of duty in this particular. Another remark seems to show that none of the priests then filling charges had been appointed by the Government; otherwise it is difficult to see why not one of them could have maintained an action for the recovery of tithes, unless it were that they did not hold their cures by a title which made them irremoveable except for crime. And now the bishop threw out a sly menace : the Government, he said, had, since the conquest, left his predecessors at full liberty to rule the Church, and they had therein found a motive to be zealous for the interest of the Government ; the inference being that a different policy would have a contrary effect.

The dispute waxed warm, and things calculated to irritate were said on both sides. The Governor reminded the bishop that under the capitulation of Montreal he had a right to no more than a toleration of his religion. The bishop professed himself the most devoted of His Majesty's subjects ; but in matters of spiritual supremacy every Catholic must bow to the chief of the Church, not to the Parliament of England. When the conversation ended, the bishop and the Governor were as far apart as they had been at the beginning.*

No claim was yet made that the bishops could exercise anything but a spiritual authority over their dioceses. Sir George Prevost, who succeeded Craig in the Governorship, asked the bishop on what footing it would be convenient to put the Roman Catholic bishops in future. The reply was that their spiritual power ought to come from the Sovereign Pontiff; but he did not plead that they should be authorized to enter upon their sees without the consent of the Government; on the contrary, he admitted that, as the spiritual functions have certain exterior and civil effects, it was reasonable that bishops should, for that purpose, be required to obtain the consent of the Government.

The new Governor took the same ground as his predecessor. But, on the breaking out of the American war, the curés exerted themselves in raising the militia ; and the bishop, exercising the power which circular letters and mandements gave him, prudence suggested that he was too important an ally of the Government to allow the contest begun by Craig to be continued. 'I have to inform you,' wrote Lord Bathurst, 'that His Royal Highness, the Prince Regent, in the name of His Majesty, desires that hereafter the allowance of the Catholic Bishop of Quebec be one thousand pounds per annum, as a testimony rendered to the loyalty and good conduct of the gentleman who now occupies that place, as well as

* Ferland. Obs.

of the other members of the Catholic clergy of the Province.'

Every embarrassment into which the British Government fell was felt to be the opportunity of the Roman Catholic ecclesiastics. In turning the war of 1812 to account, Bishop Plessis was only following in the footsteps of a predecessor, who had extracted advantages from the French revolution. The British Government had strenuously insisted on a practical adherence to that part of the royal instructions which forbade foreign ecclesiastics to exercise their functions in Canada. The bishops pressed for a relaxation of this rule, the more vigorously because, after the suppression of the Jesuits and the Recollets, it was very difficult to obtain an adequate supply of priests. For thirty years their efforts failed of success. The French revolution produced between the French priests and the British Government a common feeling : both found themselves in opposition to the new order of things. More than thirty of the priests who left France readily got passports from the British Government to go to Canada; and there was thereafter no attempt to revive a prohibition that had once, for special reasons, been removed.*

Almost immediately after the title of Bishop Plessis had been recognized and he had obtained an allowance of one thousand pounds a year, the Colonial Secretary replied to a complaint of the Anglican bishop regarding the anomalous recognition of two titulars in the same diocese, that ' whatever opinions may be entertained with respect to the adoption of measures for restraining the Catholic Church in the Province or reducing its lately acquired superiority,' the present was no time for bringing forward changes.†

The objection that the demand of the Anglican bishop

* Tanguay, Rep.-Gen.

† Ferland. Vie de Mgr. Plessis.

was inopportune was founded on the existence of the American war. On the arrival of General Craig as Governor, it had been doubtful whether the Roman Catholic bishop would be allowed any higher title than that of Ecclesiastical Superintendent for the affairs of the Church of Rome in Lower Canada. The breaking out of the war solved the difficulty, to the advantage of the Church; and to the full recognition of the title was now added a gratuity of a thousand pounds a year to Bishop Plessis. Lord John Russell was afterwards, as Colonial Secretary, to send to Canada a dispatch ordering the qualifying word 'lord' to be put before that of bishop. By this act, the veteran statesman earned a doubtful title to figure before the world as the author of the Durham letter.

Of the instructions so long given to Canadian Governors some clauses were reasonable and necessary, while others seem to trench, in some degree, on the free exercise of the religion of Rome which had been protected by international guarantees. But the spirit of the times when the penal laws of Elizabeth were in full force in England is not to be judged by the standards of to-day. It is greatly to be wished that the mad policy of the Ultramontanes of Quebec may not be carried to an extent which may render necessary the revival of some of the guarantees which gradually fell out of use.

The Church of England has been disestablished, and if there be an established Church in the country, it is the Church of Rome. The declaration in the preamble of the Act secularizing the clergy reserves, that all connection between Church and State ought to be abolished, is one the assertion of which would now bring down anathema on the head of any member of the Church of Rome in Quebec.

The extent of the pressure which the bishops may be

able to put on the inferior clergy must depend, in a great
measure, upon whether the latter be fixed in their cures for
life, or removable at the pleasure of their ecclesiastical
superiors. Whether they are legally removable is a question which has been much contested. Sir L. H. Lafontaine, as an advocate, argued with great force in favour
of immovability;* and the fact of his afterwards publishing
his *plaidoyer* seems to prove that he felt a personal interest in propagating that view : as a judge, he is said not
to have adhered to that opinion.

The decision, in the case of Nau against Bishop
Lartigue, went off on a side issue, and determines nothing
for or against the immovability of the curés who are appointed otherwise than by simple letters of mission. An
arrêt of 1679 confines the right to receive tithes and
other oblations entirely to curés appointed for life ; but
those who wish to augment the power of the bishops,
argue that a law which has been disregarded for nearly
two centuries has become a dead letter. Bishop Lartigue, in a memorial published anonymously, laid down
certain rules, the observance of which was necessary to
cover the curé with the protection of immovability.†
Previous to presentation to a benefice the priest must
undergo an examination before the bishop. Two months
after the appointment he must, in accordance with the
Council of Trent—which, by the way, in a matter of discipline, such as this is, was never accepted in Canada
during the French dominion—and the civil ordinances,
make the profession of faith of Pius IV. The bishop
must state, in the instrument of appointment, in what
quality he has the power to appoint ; in the case of succession to an immovable curé in what way the vacancy
occurred : whether by death, resignation, or otherwise.

* Notes sur l'inamovibilité des curés dans le Bas-Canada, 1837.
† Mémoire sur l'amovibilité des curés en Canada, 1837.

The secretary of the diocese, or, in his absence, two other witnesses, must attest the execution of the instrument. All these formalities, Bishop Lartigue contended, were necessary to be observed to make a priest irremovable under the law. The bishop, by neglecting these observances, and making the appointment by a simple letter, could evade the law. That is the argument of Bishop Lartigue, and his practice in the contested case was in accord with it. The usual mode of appointing curés came in time to be by a letter in which the bishop states that the appointment is revocable at his pleasure or that of his successor.* It was reserved for the English dominion to witness the complete success of the attempt of the bishops to overthrow the salutary principle of the irremovability of the curés. But if, by resort to the artifice of evasion for a long period of time, the law can be made a dead letter, what becomes of the provision that tithes are to be paid only to curés having a life tenure of their benefices? The Gallicans had a maxim that there was no prescription against the public good; but Gallicanism is now more than ever rebellion against Rome.

If the curé Nau had lived in the year of grace 1877, he could not have appealed to the Court of Queen's Bench without incurring ecclesiastical censure. The Bishops of Quebec, Nov. 14, 1875, in a joint circular assume to take away the right which M. Nau was at full liberty to exercise, and did exercise, in 1838. The bishops go back to a Council where they find it defined, that if a clerk or religious person cites another clerk or religious person before a civil court, he incurs the censures pronounced by the ecclesiastical law; not the ancient ecclesiastical law of France, but the ecclesiastical law of Rome. They find that the Propaganda has denounced

* Droit administratif ou Manuel des Paroisses et Fabriques. Par Hector L. Langevin, avocat.

the same penalties for the same offence. The bishops then add: 'strictly ecclesiastical causes are those in which the defendant is an ecclesiastic or a religious person, or the object in litigation is a spiritual thing, or connected with the exercise of some function of the ministry.' But does it follow that the civil liberties of ecclesiastics can be taken away by circular letters without their consent? The Privy Council, in a recent case, seemed to imply that if an ecclesiastical encroachment be not resisted, it may come in time to have the force of law.

In the light of these facts, we may form some estimate of the influence that may be wielded by eight bishops in the Province of Quebec, acting upon orders from Rome, and transmitting them to one thousand and forty-two priests, three hundred and fifty ecclesiastics, and one hundred and fifty-one convents.* The number of priests had increased in one year forty-three, of ecclesiastics ten, of convents seven.

When Mgr. Plessis (1821), Bishop of Quebec, consecrated M. Lartigue Bishop of Telmesse, *in partibus infidelium*, and informed the clergy and their flocks in the district of Montreal that they must henceforth apply to the new bishop for dispensations, ordinations, etc., some of the Gallican clergy of that district contended that, though there might be bulls of the Pope which had not been published conferring the benefice, the appointment would not be valid without the consent of the King of England, who, by the Treaty of Cession, had succeeded to the rights of the King of France with regard to the erection of bishoprics.† M. Chaboillez argued that it was the interest of Catholics that nothing should be done in the way of innovation to diminish the favourable disposi-

---

* Rolland et fils. Almanach Agricole Commercial et Historique, Montreal, 1877.

† M. Chaboillez, Curé of Longueuil. Questions sur le Government Ecclésiastique du District de Montreal.

tion of the Government towards the Catholic religion; and that no step could be more calculated to excite the jealousy of the Government than to pretend to erect a bishopric in a country belonging to England without the consent of the sovereign. Unless the new bishop were recognized by the civil power, his authority, and even his quality, might be contested in the tribunals. Another reason why the consent of the king should be obtained was, that such an establishment was comprised in the edict of mortmain. It was an ecclesiastical establishment: an *arrondissement* was formed, to which it was proposed to appoint a superior, assign him a territory, and give him subjects to govern. On his part there must be rights, and on that of his inferiors obligations, in civil as well as in spiritual concerns. The edict of 1743 showed that such an establishment, call it a bishopric or an episcopal district, could not, any more than the College of Nicolet, have a legal existence unless it were authorized by letters patent of the king. French canonists had insisted on the necessity of a bishop being commissioned by the king as well as the Pope. M. Chaboillez pointed to an early Council, held at Paris, which had pronounced null the erection of a bishopric without the consent of the clergy and the people, who were interested in it.

Three lawyers, Jos. Bédard, B. Beaubien, and M. O. Sullivan, staked their professional reputation on the statement that the position taken by the curé of Longueuil was entirely conformable to the civil and canon law of Lower Canada. M. P. H. Bédard denied that these gentlemen were well versed in the canon law; but it did not admit of question that they were constantly called upon to plead causes in which the ecclesiastical law of France might have a partial application.

To M. Chaboillez's pamphlet three replies were made; and the controversy may be regarded as one of the early

10

contests between the Ultramontanes and the Gallicans in Canada. In opposition to M. Chaboillez, it was con-tended that the Pope has the absolute power of erecting bishoprics and appointing bishops. To his contention that the ancient ecclesiastical laws of France were still in force in Canada, his opponents replied that the nomina-tion and institution of Canadian bishops, as well as the mode of receiving the decrees of the Holy See in this country, had become as foreign to the canon laws of France as to those of Poland or Hungary.*

The priest who took this ground boasted that the eccle-siastical power in Canada was gradually changing its posi-tion towards the civil Government; that the bishop under whose administration they were living had, by pur-suing a wise and prudent policy, 'obtained more favours from the Government than any one of his predecessors had been able to get.' He admitted that when a new bishopric was erected in France, the bulls of the Popes continued to state that the act was done with the consent of the clergy and the people; but this, he argued, went for nothing, since the Gallican liberties would deny them registration by Parliament without this piece of harm-less condescension on the part of the Court of Rome.

But a lawyer who defended the creation of the bishop-ric of Montreal by the sole authority of the Pope, M. P. H. Bédard, did not venture to assume that the case was one in which the consent of the Crown was not necessary. He denied that there was anything to prove that the con-sent of the king had not in fact been obtained; † and the Bishop of Quebec had stated‡ that he had done nothing except in concert with His Majesty's ministers. M. Bé-dard did, however, in general terms, extend the authority

* Observations sur un Ecrit intitulé Questions sur le Government Ecclésiastique, du District de Montreal. Par un Prêtre du Diocèse de Québec.
† Réponse de Messire Chaboillez, Curé de Longueuil, à la lettre de P. H. Bédard.
‡ Mandement, 5 Décembre, 1822.

of the Papal power nearly as far as the New School now assert the right to carry it. 'We are,' he said, 'united by our obedience to the chief of the Universal Church, to the diocesan bishop, the prelate whom the Sovereign Pontiff has specially commissioned to govern us. "Orders," says Saint Augustine, "have come to us from the Apostolic See; the cause is finished."' This writer, who had a reputation to make at the bar, did not deny that the ecclesiastical law of France was in force in Canada. There was a suspicion that he had not written the pamphlet himself, and that Bishop Lartigue had had some hand in it.

It was a question between the ecclesiastical law of France and the canon law of Rome: that the principles of the former had been applied in Canada is beyond doubt. The edict of May, 1679, concerning tithes and the fixity of the curés, says that means were to be taken according to the canonical forms to ascertain the convenience or inconvenience of the proposed regulations. And after all interested had been heard, the facts were to be reported to the Bishop of Quebec and the king, 'in order that suitable regulations may be made conformably to the laws and the usages of the Church of the kingdom.' The judgments of the Superior Council were conformable to this requirement. An arrêt of July 1, 1695, ordered the Vicar-General and Sieur Dudougt at once to remit to the Council the titles of their pretended ecclesiastical jurisdiction; an arrêt of June 30, 1693, accorded to the dean, canons, and chapter of Quebec relief against an ordinance of the Bishop of Quebec which assigned to the grand-chantre in future the installation of the canons; an arrêt of June 30, 1750, gave relief to the chapter of Quebec against an abuse of ecclesiastical power; and an arrêt of October 16, 1750, confirmed Le Sieur Récher in possession of the cure of Quebec. In all these cases, and many others, a lay tribunal decided matters which one party regarded as purely ecclesiastical ; and the clergy, far from denying the jurisdiction, had recourse to it them-selves to secure their own rights.* The victory on the argument remained with the parish priest of Longueuil ; but Ultramontanism had shown what it was in future to attempt. In point of fact, the judges of the Court of Queen's Bench adjudicated upon all this class of questions : questions of tithes, of the concession of seats in the church, the affairs of the Fab-rique, and a thousand others. Some years previous to the erection of the bishopric of Montreal, the Bishop of Quebec had appealed to the ecclesiastical law of France in support of his claims in a question between himself and the Government.

A large number of priests in the district of Quebec openly sustained the views of M. Chaboillez. The Galli-cans of Quebec were only to be finally silenced after the publication of the Vatican Decrees.

The quality of priest in Quebec only detracts from the rights of the citizen in one particular : the priest can vote at parliamentary elections, and is eligible for elec-tion either to the House of Commons or to the Legisla-ture of the Province, but he cannot be elected a munici-pal councillor. He is exempt from military and militia service, and from serving on juries. He can be elected school commissioner without the ordinary qualification. He enjoys his tithes in virtue of an Act of the British Parliament. He is entitled to the fixed emoluments aris-ing from the celebration of masses for the repose of souls, from foundations and other casual revenues, which are supposed to be fixed by the bishops, but which are not always uniform in amount. It is his duty to read, after divine service, any proclamation or act which the Gover-nor may require him to read. It is his duty to keep a

* Réponse de Messire Chaboillez, Curé de Longueuil, à la lettre de P. H. Bédard, suivie de quelques remarques sur les observations imprimées aux Trois-Rivière.

civil register of baptisms, marriages, and burials, also the register of the deliberations of the parish and of the Fabrique, and to give, extracts from the same when required, which are *prima facie* evidence in a court of law. He has the right, which is not accorded to the curés in France, of presiding at the general assemblies of the Fabrique ; a right which has been secured to him by Act of the Canadian Parliament. He presides over general meetings of the parishioners, held for any purpose in connection with the administration of the affairs of the Church. He also presides over the meetings of the marguilliers, whose duties resemble those of churchwardens. Without his consent the Fabrique cannot accept any foundation. The parishioners are legally required to provide a suitable dwelling or presbytery for the curé. It is usual for the bishop to prescribe the dimensions of the house in which the priest is to be lodged, but there is no legal authority for his intervention ; and the commissioners charged with the erection of the building are not bound to follow the bishop's directions. Any extensive repairs that may be required have to be made by the parishioners. The curé has the exceptional right of sepulchre under the choir of the church, even in cities where all other intramural interments are forbidden.*

In a twofold character, the curé is amenable to the civil courts of Superior Jurisdiction. As president of the Fabrique and of meetings of the parishioners, he is regarded as a public functionary, and as such, can be compelled by *mandamus* to perform the duties that are obligatory on him in that capacity. He is an officer of a religious corporation, and over all corporations, civil and ecclesiastical, the Superior Court has jurisdiction.† A

* Le (Canadian) curé est le pouvoir incontesté, le magistrat suprême de l'endroit. Tous les membres de la société subissent docilement son contrôle.—I. Guérard. La France Canadienne, Paris 1877.

† Code des Curés, par L'Hon. J. U. Baudry.

priest who performs the ceremony of marriage to which one of the parties is a minor, without the consent of his or her parent, is liable to damages in favour of those parents whose authority he has disregarded ; and equally so if he performs the ceremony without the consent of the girl's parents, and without publication of banns, though he be able to plead the dispensation of his bishop. So the Court of Appeal has decided.* In the presence of a notary, or three witnesses, the curé can draft the will of any one residing in his parish, but only on condition that it contains no bequest to himself or any of his relatives. The witnesses must not be women, members of religious orders, or novices. The will so drafted becomes attainted with nullity if not deposited with a notary immediately after the death of the testator. There does not appear to be anything to prevent a will, drafted by a priest, and made in favour of the Church, conveying real estate, provided it does not sin against the laws of mortmain.

The Anglo-Gallican policy was destined to fail. It was impossible to make a national Church out of a religion which the nation had renounced. Control, even in matters of discipline, of an alien religion meant repression, against which the instinct of a conquered nationality, into the very texture of which the religion of Rome was interwoven, would rebel. If the discipline of Rome was distasteful to the Gallicans, could Anglican discipline have been made generally acceptable to them ? Whatever danger there is in the present attitude of Rome towards the civil power, greater evils would have arisen from the Government having the absolute control of the patronage of two Churches—the Church of England and the Church of Rome—in its hands. But the danger that now confronts us, arising out of the claim of the Church of Rome to a controlling voice in civil affairs, through the election of those by whom the laws are made, is real and urgent.

* H. F. Langevin. Droit admin.

VII.

THE PROGRAMME.

On the approach of the elections for the House of Commons in 1871, the *Programme Catholique** offered a very positive direction to Roman Catholic voters. Yet, except an extract it contained from a pastoral letter of the Bishop of Three Rivers, it was not a document which had the force of ecclesiastical authority. It came into the world without a sponsor ; it went about like a literary waif, and was apparently invested with no more importance than usually attaches to an anonymous newspaper article of the 'campaign' order, intended to influence the future of an election. But somehow men did attach to it an unusual importance. It carried with it proof that a new element in political elections had presented itself; and that henceforth the Church of Rome was to aim at political control. Before long, candidates of both parties were to surrender themselves captive to the concealed authors of the Programme.

The pastoral letter in question formed the text of the Programme. On it the authors of the Programme built as on a corner-stone. The bishop had reminded the electors that the representatives to be elected were charged to protect and defend the religious interests of the electors, in accordance with the spirit of the Church, as a means of promoting and protecting their temporal interests. The civil laws, he said, were necessarily in accord with religion on a great number of points. As a mere matter of prudence, the electors were to assure

* First published in *Le Journal des Trois Rivières*, April 20, 1870.

themselves that the candidate to whom they gave their suffrages was duly qualified in both respects, and that he offered, morally speaking, every guarantee for the protection of these grave interests. The full liberty which the Constitution accorded to the Catholic worship in Canada enabled it to be carried on conformably to the rules of the Church. By a judicious choice of legislators, the electors would ensure the preservation of this right, the most precious of all, which gave the bishops ' the immense advantage of being able to govern the Church of Canada according to the immediate prescriptions and directions of the Holy See and the Church of Rome, the mother and mistress of all the Churches.'

There was nothing very startling in this, beyond the bare fact that the Bishop of Three Rivers desired that the Church of Rome should use its influence to sway the elections in its own interests. But nothing was said in favour of one political policy or against another: no individual candidates were pointed out for approval or condemnation ; much less was there any hint of a resort to spiritual censures to coerce the will of reluctant voters. But there was in the pastoral enough to build a Programme upon. The authors of the Programme took the ground, that so close is the connection between politics and religion that the separation of Church and State—to which the Legislature had committed itself a quarter of a century before—was ' an absurd and impious doctrine ; ' and especially was this true under the constitutional *régime*, under which Parliament exercises the whole power of legislation, and which places in the hands of those of whom Parliament is composed a double-edged weapon, of which a terrible use could be made. For this reason it was necessary that those to whose hands the legislative power is committed ' should be in perfect accord with the teachings of the Church.'

For this reason it was the duty of Catholic electors to select for their representatives men whose principles are
perfectly sound and certain. 'Full and entire adhesion
to Roman Catholic doctrines in religion, in politics, and
in social economy, ought,' continued the authors of the Programme, 'to be the first and principal qualification which
the Catholic electors should require from the candidate.'
By observing this rule, they would best be able to judge
of men and things.

It was necessary, the Programmists went on to say, 'to
consider the circumstances in which the country is placed,
existing political parties and their antecedents.' The
writers belonged to what they considered the Conservative
party, the defenders of social authority ; 'a group of men
professing sincerely the same principles of religion, patriot-
ism, and nationality;' inviolably attached to Catholic doctrines and manifesting an absolute devotion to the national
interests of Lower Canada. Besides this, a decided preference for the political party which goes under the name
of Conservative was avowed. But the support to be given
to this party was 'to be subordinated to the interests of
religion,' of which the electors were never to lose sight.
If the laws contained aught which placed Catholic interests in peril, a pledge was to be exacted from the candidate
that he would do what he could to remove the defect.
The laws relating to marriage, education, the erection of
parishes and the *registres de l'état civil*—the register of
baptisms, marriages, and burials which the curés are by
law required to keep—derogated from the rights of the
Church, interfered with its liberty and put difficulties in
the way of its administration, or was capable of a hostile
interpretation. 'This state of things,' the Programmists
boldly averred, 'imposes on Catholic legislators the duty
of changing and modifying these laws, in the way in
which our Lords the Bishops of the Province demand,

to the end that they may be put into harmony with the doctrines of the Roman Catholic Church.' The electors were told that they ought to require from the candidates a pledge to this effect as a condition of receiving their support. 'It is the duty,' the Programme asserted in so many words, 'of the electors to give their votes only to those who are willing to conform entirely to the teachings of the Church in these matters.'

Where there were two Conservative candidates, or two Liberal candidates, that one which would accept these conditions was to be preferred. As between a Conservative and 'an adept of the Liberal School,' the former was always to be preferred; except where the Liberal accepted, and the Conservative rejected, the Programme, and in that case abstention from voting was recommended.

However objectionable the Programme might be, there was nothing in it which any number of persons wishing to produce an influence on the elections had not a right to resort to. But as a first essay, a tentative movement, it went to the utmost verge of prudence. The influence of the Programme belonged to the order of moral coercion. It carried terror with it as it passed from journal to journal, and gained conquests, on either hand, from timidity in the prospect of defeat. Next year, a step far in advance of the Programme was to be taken.

VIII.

THE ASSAULT ON THE OLD LIBERTIES.

The first war in which the army of writers journalists, pamphleteers, authors of comedies, anti-Gallican treatises and sermons, who acknowledged Bishop Bourget as commander-in-chief, was domestic: it was waged against all who refused, at once, submissively to accept the extreme doctrines of the New School; against the Sulpicians of Montreal, the late Archbishop of Quebec, and Vicar-General Cazeau; against Vicar-General Raymond, and all others who were suspected of the heresy of Gallicanism or Catholic liberalism.

In this army, the figure of one of the captains, who consented to lead the forlorn hope, attracts special attention. Alphonse Villeneuve scorns all danger, and contemptuously refuses to listen to the voice of discretion. He addresses Pius IX. as the 'infallible Pontiff and the supreme king of Christian kingdoms.' After bestowing a fulsome eulogy on the Pope, he proceeds to lead the onslaught on the Sulpicians. His soul, he tells the Holy Father, is desolated with a great desolation, because in the holy place, the Church of Montreal, the abomination of Gallicanism has appeared. The Sulpicians have become the unhappy victims of a diabolical illusion, and have implanted the germs of a schism which he cannot better designate than by comparing it to Cainism. Half a century ago, the peace of the Church was broken by the Sulpicians. The Levites were the first Catholics who attempted to free themselves from religious authority. They refused to recognize Bishop Lartigue, and tried to induce the Protes-

tant Government to deprive him of his powers. They contended that his nomination was null, because the Pope, in
instituting him, had violated the holy canons; 'as if the
infallible Pope was not above the canons.' Because the
Bishop of Montreal insisted on dividing that city into a
number of parishes, contrary to the civil laws as expounded by the best authorities, the Sulpicians committed the
sin of refusing to aid his operations, and had the temerity
to appeal to the Pope against the act; ' as if,' says Villeneuve, 'the Syllabus did not condemn a like pretension;
in case of legal conflict between the two powers, the civil
law ought to prevail.'

Then follows a catalogue of the crimes of the Sulpicians,
who contended that: without the intervention of the
bishops, the Superior of the Seminary could authorize
Sulpicians to preach, hear confessions, absolve reserved
cases, go beyond the limits of their diocese, name priests
to the care of souls, at the Lake of Two Mountains, and
do a number of other similar things. When the Bishop
of Montreal insisted on depriving them of a part of their
income, they were charged with the crime of having been
guilty of calling him a robber. Their dislike of the bishop's
encouragement of the Jesuits is set down as the jealousy
of Cain. They are charged with having recourse to lying
and false pretext. When the bishop threatened them
with spoliation, they attempted to induce the Fabrique
of Montreal to commit the crime of taking the cause before the civil tribunals. After being guilty of the scandal
of defending their property, they committed the additional
enormity of declaring themselves innocent.

In appealing to Rome, the Sulpicians might have seen
that they made a mistake: the Pope was certain to side
with the bishop.* The good man, says their calumniator,

* In his reply, Sept. 24, 1867, the Pope said : ' *Posu Episcop et non Sulpicianos
regere Ecclesian Dei.*

found it impossible to respect the Sulpicians. In their service, he adds, a school of able men had been found, ' deserters and renegades to our traditions, who in politics, in the magistrature, and in the press, emit the accursed principles of ancient Gallicanism.' The writer finds a striking similitude between Cain and the Sulpicians, between the sin of the one and the crime of the other. The Sulpicians, another count reads, ruin the ecclesiastical authority, and assist in submitting the spouse of Christ to the secular arm.

The writers of the New School determined on an open attack, and tried to persuade the public that they were combatting bad faith and the lying Gallicanism of the Sulpicians and their partisans. The contest must be carried on in the arena of public opinion, a contest which they determined to pursue with a savagery which, Villeneuve confesses, did not well become the character of a priest, but to which, nevertheless, he did not scruple to resort. In this battle he admits the episcopate and the clergy appeared like men exercising a stroke of vengeance.

Before commencing the onset, Villeneuve confesses that he hesitated and waited ; but as no one appeared to lead the attack, he opened fire ' upon the fortress of Saint Sulpice, the refuge of Gallicanism and Catholic Liberalism.' If his book took the form of comedy, it was that he might laugh down the satanic illusion under which these errors flourished. Our author makes it a new crime in the Sulpicians that, according to him, they did not allow themselves to be calumniated with impunity, but the gives no proof of their having made any reply.

Before the appointment of M. Lartigue to a somewhat anomalous position in the episcopacy the Sulpicians had had pretty much their own way. The disciplinary arm of the Bishop of Quebec was almost too short to reach them, and they scarcely felt his authority at all. M.

Lartigue gave early indications that he intended to govern
the ecclesiastics of the district of Montreal; and the
Sulpicians seem to have felt his presence to be an intru-
sion. Still, they did nothing to occasion an open rupture.
They did not even encourage the independent attack
which M. Chaboillez made on his appointment; on the
contrary, they induced him to refrain from publishing his
first pamphlet a whole year after it had been written,
The Seminary was rich, and the new Suffragan Auxiliary
was poor. His friends contended that the Sulpicians
should have made a provision for him; they exaggerated
his poverty and privations, with a view of exciting odium
against the Sulpicians. They told many similar stories
to the disadvantage of the rich corporation, such as
refusing to provide M. Musard the means, which he did
not himself possess, of making a voyage to Europe, on
which his medical advisers said his life depended. In
reply to his application, the Superior is represented
as having said to his suffering brother: ' My dear sir, it
is better to die in this manner than to go against the rules
of the House.' At the same time, other members of the
Seminary are represented as being allowed to spend large
sums on voyages to Europe.

The Seminary is charged with having refused to build
a church in the Faubourg Quebec, or to announce a collection which the bishop desired to have taken up for the
erection of the church of St. James'. The friends of the
bishop were uneasy because he could not control a part
of the revenues of the Sulpicians; and the latter is represented as having stated that the bishop desired to have
half the income derived from their estates handed over to
him. Sometimes matters were carried to an extremity
that caused the partisans of the bishop to represent that
the danger of a schism was imminent. Now and then a
Sulpician priest did ally himself with the bishop, and

against his own order. If he was ambitious he was not without motives for taking that course, for it was the only one that could lead to bishoprics and other high dignities. Twelve Sulpicians are reported to have left the Seminary in a few years preceding that of 1847.

As the members of the Seminary continued to be recruited from the Sulpicians of Paris, the corporation was attacked on national grounds. It was pretended that it had not become acclimatized, had not taken root in the soil. The necessity of prohibiting the importation of additional French priests was often insisted upon. The prohibition, which had some time before been made by the Bishop of Quebec, looked to a return to the policy on which, during the lifetime of a whole generation after the conquest, the British Government had, for other and national reasons, insisted, and against which the predecessors of this bishop had never ceased to protest. But while the hierarchy had swung completely round the circle, there had been consistency in its course. It had always, and while apparently pursuing the most opposite policy, had in view the increase of its own influence. The Seminary was reproached with having no influence in the city of Montreal but that which its money purchased.*

The jealousy which the Seminary excited in the other clergy was extreme. It continued to be a nursery of Gallicanism long after Gallicanism had become hateful in the eyes of the bishop.

On the first appointment of M. Lartigue the Government refused to allow him to take the title of Bishop of Montreal. It is insinuated that this fact was not without its influence in causing the Sulpicians to refuse to provide him with a shelter during a period of fifteen years, and

* Brouillon de notes envoyées a M. Faillon, en Avril, 1850, sur l'opinion du Diocèse de Montreal. Par M. Jos. Marcoux, missionnaire des sauvages du Sault St. Louis, Caughnawaga.

that when they did offer him quarters, he was no longer in need of them.*

The result of the division between the ecclesiastics was to divide the laymen into two parties which cordially hated one another ;† but all the writers who preceded him had not done one-half as much to inflame that hatred as Alph. Villeneuve. The truth is, the time had come when the New School felt strong enough to make a mortal attack on its ancient enemy, with the hope of extinguishing the last remnant of liberal Catholic thought in the Province of Quebec.

With this explanation, anyone who desires to turn to that work will be the better able to understand Villeneuve's *Comédie Infernale, ou Conjuration Libérale aux Enfers.* The scene is laid in the audience hall of the palace of Pandemonium, fortress of Satan, between two deep gorges in the middle of *l'enfers.*‡ Time, December 1st, 1870. Lucifer is seated on his throne. Astoroth addresses him : 'Prince of the dark asylum, this day will be for thy faithful subjects a day of ineffable joy. To celebrate thy recent triumphs over the Church, the infernal regions have come

* Mémoire de Mgr. J. N. Provencher, Evêque de Juliopolis, afterwards Bishop of St. Boniface, Red River.

† Messire de J. B. Ch. Bédard.

‡ The following are the *dramatis personæ* :—

Lucifer,	Prince des Démons.
Belzébuth,	Prince des Séraphins.
Leviathan,	Prince des Chérubins.
Astoroth,	Prince des Trônes.
Babel,	Prince des Vertus.
Carreau,	Prince des Puissances.
Belial,	Prince des Principautés.
Oliver,	Prince des Archanges.
Baalberith,	Prince des Anges.
Azaphat,	Général des Trônes.
Fume-Bouche,	Lieutenant des Puissances.
Perrier,	Duc des Empires.
Belias,	Amiral des Vertus.
Rosier,	Général des Principautés.
Baal,	Vieux Chef retiré du service.

to place their homage at thy feet, and to make these secular arches resound with their songs of joy.' Lucifer understands this enthusiasm ; Europe having definitively set out on the road to damnation. After much fatigue, Belzébuth discovers in America a Catholic people on the banks of a majestic river. Lucifer recognizes in the description the Canadian people, with whom he has been acquainted from their origin. Nearly twenty years before he had instructed Carreau (which some insist must be read Cartier) to resort to special *ruses*, by which he had more or less succeeded. Belzébuth is able to bear witness to the incomparable zeal of Carreau ; but he had been indiscreet in being too openly impious to deceive so profoundly religious a people. After a number of older errors had been broken down, Lucifer asked for, and obtained, Gallican Churches and Liberal Governments. By aid of the mitre and the mantle of religion, Belial bears witness, liberalism and Gallicanism everywhere obtained admittance. Those who professed the new error ' fell asleep in a pious delusion ; they believed they were serving the Church in denying its authority, its supremacy, and its rights over the State. The Catholic populations the more readily fell into these snares as they were allured on by the most religious of men.' (Lucifer retires.)

As Belzébuth had sojourned a whole year in Canada, Belial asks him for a description of the country. ' Willingly,' is the reply : ' In the first place, it is a country altogether Catholic, and entirely devoted to the Pope. These young men whom I have seen at Rome were the Canadian Zouaves.' ' A bad sign,' remarked Astoroth ; ' very bad,' chimed in Belial. Whereupon Belzébuth implored them not to despair. ' Lucifer,' he observed, ' seeing that impiety did not take in Canada, since l'Institut Canadien, in spite of the ability of the Dessaulles,

11

the Doutres, the Lanctots, and several similar celebrities, had been able to attract to its bosom only souls lost by anticipation, counselled Carreau to leave aside, for a while, the heavy artillery, and proceed to the attack with the light infantry of Catholic liberalism.' He explains that in Montreal, with a population of a hundred and sixty thousand souls, there is but a single curé. From Rome instructions had come to the Bishop of Montreal to divide the city into several parishes. This the bishop was most anxious to do; but the gentlemen of the Seminary, pretending to be perpetual curés of the city, interposed objections: they had always opposed the episcopal authority. ' No matter,' word came from Rome, 'do your duty, dismember the parish of Notre-Dame.' The bishop, as in duty bound, obeyed ; but not without foreseeing that he should meet with serious opposition from the *Perpetual Curés.* Belzébuth bears witness that it is not in the nature of Gallicans to submit. The Perpetual Curés protested, and carried their protest to Rome. They raised every possible prejudice, saying: ' The bishop desires to despoil and ruin us.' Other persons were heard to say, that the bishop was desirous to render himself master of the property of the Perpetual Curés. The entire rebellion was fermented by two or three of the Perpetual Curés. Carreau urged on the opposition of this rich corporation, which was strong by means of its political friendships. In order the better to succeed, the civil laws were studied, and in them some ambiguities regarding the division of parishes were found. The Perpetual Curés had always desired to form an independent power in the Church in Canada. The first Bishop of Quebec had proved, at Rome, that they were disobedient priests, opposed to the Holy See, and in fine Jansenists. When a late Bishop of Montreal gathered the Jesuits, the Oblats, and other religious orders around him, the

Perpetual Curés objected, at Rome, that he had no right to do so without their permission. Their present Superior went so far as publicly to announce that the bishop, in conforming to the apostolic decree of Dec. 22, acted without prudence, with injustice, and in opposition to the interest of souls. In spite of the immense revenue of the parish of Montreal, where the casual dues are very high, they affirmed that the parish owed them four hundred thousand dollars. They give a hundred and forty-four dollars per head to the Christian Brothers (Frères des Ecoles Chrétiennes), and something to the Sisters of the Congregation, to aid them in supporting a little class of the poor, in four different localities. For the sick, the infirm, for orphans, they give nothing, or next to nothing.

In contrast to this picture, Belzébuth gives one of the Oblats, whose knowledge and virtue he lauds. But their great virtue is that they bow submissively to the Pope, believe in his infallibility, are devoted to the Church, and everywhere submit themselves to episcopal authority.

The parishes being canonically erected, the Perpetual Curés caused the State to withdraw the civil registers therefrom, alleging that the bishop cannot canonically erect a parish without obtaining the suffrages of the majority ; that the curés of the canonical parishes, not civilly recognized, are incompetent to celebrate marriages ; that the curé of a parish, canonical and civil, has a territorial jurisdiction and duties which the ecclesiastical authority can neither affect nor diminish ; that the curé, canonical and civil, can be constrained by the tribunals to perform baptisms, marriages, and sepulchres for the parishioners of a canonical parish.

After this explanation, Astoroth breaks forth : ' I now comprehend the thoughts of Carreau in the whole affair; he desires to establish Gallicanism in Canada, for such pretensions are Gallican.' ' Thou divinest truly,' quoth

Belzébuth, 'these pretensions of the Perpetual Curés are condemned by the Syllabus of 1864.'

Sir George Cartier is represented by one of the demons as having inspired the *Minerve* to say that the law requires the observance of certain formalities in the formation of a parish which no power can set aside, and which, in the present instance, have not been complied with. And to support their pretensions, the Perpetual Curés induced a judge to write a code against the pretensions of Rome and of the bishop.

The demons who are made to espouse the cause of the bishop, represent the Perpetual Curés as being guilty of an incredible degree of bad faith, and making statements 'entirely false;' as persecuting priests who took part with the bishop; as entering into intrigues to carry their point; as being guilty of the enormity of discouraging persons engaged in getting up a bazaar for the benefit of the Jesuits.

When the Guibord affair came under discussion, Belzébuth confessed that he had blown the 'cannibal inspiration of Joseph Doutre against the Jesuits, as well as the historical dissertation of Louis Dessaulles.' The *plaidoyer* of M. Trudel, the advocate of the Church, in this case, was approved by two of the great theologians at Rome.

Before the opening of the seventh scene, Belzébuth resumes his throne, and makes a sign to the demons to take their seats. He tells Carreau, who is present for the first time, that he had been awaiting him with impatience; he had heard of his successes and his fears. He desired to receive him in the bosom of his council, and encouraged him to speak with confidence, as the hall was surrounded by legions of deaf and dumb demons. Being thus reassured, Carreau tells the illustrious monarch that he has followed his late counsel to the letter. 'I left aside impiety for a while,' he said, 'to occupy myself more specially with errors which had a Catholic look. I profited by the burning question of the division of Montreal into parishes ; a book, the *Code des Curés*, by Judge Baudry, appeared, proclaiming perverse doctrines, but possessing a certain Catholic mirage.'

Lucifer.—' What is this book at bottom ? '

Carreau.—'The author, while protesting his devotion to the Church and his respect for ecclesiastical authority, while affirming that he does not desire the separation of Church and State, nor the subordination of the Church to the State . . . .'

Several demons.—' Why affirm such doctrines ? '

Lucifer.—' Listen, wait to hear the end before blaming.'

Carreau.—' The author, while affirming these Catholic doctrines, employs his time and his pen in establishing those of an entirely opposite character.'

Lucifer.—' I know it well.'

Carreau.—' He establishes, in the first place : that, in Canada, the bishop is not at liberty to take the initiative in the formation of any parish whatever, canonical or civil ; that for this purpose, it is necessary to wait for a request from the majority of the people, even when the salvation of a whole town evidently requires this to be done, when the canons of the Church are clear, and the conscience of the pastor engaged.'

All in Chorus.—' Vive le *Code des Curés*.'

Carreau.—' Secondly, that the bishop is not at liberty to say that property consecrated to God, and which has come out of the common mass, for example the property of the Fabriques, is the property of the Catholic Church.'

All in Chorus.—' Long live the author of the *Code des Curés*.'

The debates of the Vatican Council had begun to alarm Carreau, and made him think of giving up the work which Lucifer had counselled him to do. ' I must avow,' he said, 'that it would perhaps be better to abandon the affair of the parishes, Gallicanism, and Catholic liberalism; for I have observed that, since the great debates in the Vatican Council, people have been on their guard against these doctrines.

Lucifer.—' Explain thyself.'

Carreau.—' Before the controversy on infallibility began, the liberal writings of Dupanloup, Montalembert, and others, were much lauded in Canada. The *Minerve*, the *Journal de Québec*, the *Echo du Cabinet de Lecture*, published and praised the speeches delivered at the different congresses of Malines by these celebrated Catholics. Even the *Révue Canadienne* vaunted Dupanloup's book on the encyclical of the 8th Decr.'

Lucifer.—' And since the Council?'

Carreau.—' These same journals have preserved an extreme reserve with regard to these illustrious writers.'

Lucifer.—' Are these journals in favour of Ultramontanism?'

Carreau.—' The *Journal de Québec*, no ;* but the *Minerve*, yes!'

Carreau is inclined to hope against hope, and comforts himself with the reflection that Gallicanism, which is the basis of Catholic liberalism, penetrated into Canada with the French law, and that it still possesses considerable resources in the education of members of the bar. Lucifer, in consideration of the fact that Canada is a profoundly religious country, the country on which heaven reposes, concluded that all the forces of hell must be concentrated against it; at which all approve by shouting bravo! bravo! bravissimo ! ' This affair,' he said, ' of the parishes of Montreal is founded on the liberty of the Church, on its supremacy, and those who oppose priests and seculars'

---

* The answer would now be yes, but with a disposition to prevent extreme encroachments on the part of the clergy.

can triumph only in subjugating the Church.' Everything, Lucifer admits, depends on the colour of the politics ; when these cease to have a Catholic complexion, the people soon follow the same impulses in other respects. A system of erroneous politics had enabled the demons to triumph in Europe, and now a commencement must be made in Canada ; success in that enterprise would render everything else easy.

Baal tells how this is to be done : ' Confine yourself to preventing the authority of the Church being accepted in politics : Proclaim that kings, civil powers, legislation, are independent of the Church ; that the family, marriage, education, are purely civil institutions, and that the Church has no control over them : by that means, you will deprive the State of that divine light and that borrowed force which it requires to enable it to march in the straight path. To separate Church and State is to sap the foundation of the work of salvation ; because it is to take from nations and governments the graces of state which are necessary to their salvation.'

In the eleventh scene, Belzébuth exposes the political error—Cæsarism—of which he declares himself the father. Evidently referring to the four articles of the Gallican liberties, he says ; ' I assumed the air of an apostle, and said, render unto Cæsar the things which are Cæsar's, and unto God the things which are God's. Only I made the division: I gave everything to Cæsar, and nothing unto God.'

Being asked what the Church says of the doctrine of the separation of the two powers, Lucifer answers, that she necessarily condemns it. ' She says that, having been established in the world without the aid of the throne, she ought to surpass the throne ; that the State can never surpass her, and thus can never separate from her. The doctrine of the separation of the two powers is therefore satanic.'

The *Programme Catholique* and its history become a subject of the infernal dialogue. The Programme is described as having been the work of six laymen, and its object, to assure for the future, by means of parliamentary elections, an exclusively Catholic policy. It in effect told the electors to vote only for those who promised to support the bishops in questions on which they might be called upon to legislate. The opposition of the *Minerve* to the Programme is represented as having been inspired by Sir George Cartier, whose opposition to the dismemberment of the parish of Notre-Dame had embroiled him with the bishop. The words put into the mouth of Astoroth represent very fairly the 'spirit of party: ' To be a Conservative,' the *Minerve* is made to say, ' it is necessary to be disciplined and obedient. When one joins a party, he comes under an engagement to obey its chiefs in everything.' No Conservative, the statement is ventured, could have been elected unless he had promised to support the bishops, a promise which, it is admitted, was never before exacted. Three bishops complained of the inconvenience which resulted from the Programme having been drawn up without consultation with the episcopate. In the discussion which the Programme provoked, the *Journal de Québec* rejected the doctrine of the subordination of the State to the Church ; conduct which Rosier qualifies as atheistical.

In the third act, the demons are in a state of consternation, when Lucifer announces that their deliberations of the first of December, 1870, and the second of August, 1871, have been laid before the Canadian public in the *Comédie Infernale*. The resolution is come to that the Perpetual Curés must be defended. It is of course intended that the defence shall prove a failure. The Seminary is represented to be in a state of rebellion against the Holy See and the bishop, and its right of appeal to Rome,

which is admitted to exist, is, in the exercise, treated as
an abuse. ' The poor Sulpicians desire to govern the
Church, but they have not received the graces necessary
for that purpose. It is the bishop who, for that end, has
received a special grace.'

The Sulpicians are made responsible for the opposition
of Chaboillez to Mgr. Lartigue, though the documents on
which the *Comédie* professes to be founded clearly show
this assumption to be false. They are represented as
carrying their zeal for the Government to an extreme
length. ' We must not,' says Baalberith, ' be astonished
at this monstrous conduct. The Gallicans, whether priests
or not, are capable of attempting everything, even excom-
municating the Governments which refuse to molest the
Church.'

There is no doubt that the suffragan, Mgr. de Telmesse,
was not a welcome guest with the Seminary, which would
have preferred that the seat of episcopal authority should
have remained as far distant from their establishment as
the city of Quebec. But if the marguilliers of the parish
of Notre-Dame refused the episcopal throne to Mgr. de
Telmesse, it must be remembered that he refused to
exhibit the bulls in virtue of which he claimed to be entitled thereto.

M. Olier, who founded the Order of Sulpicians, is represented as having expressed the most absolute submission
to the prelates, and as having gone so far as to say that
if the Order should ever place itself in opposition to them,
he should demand the destruction of the House, which
would become the object of anathema in the face of the
whole universe. It is unquestionably true that the Sulpicians of Montreal have so far departed from this rule as
to have been in a state of perpetual and chronic opposition to the bishops of Montreal, since the day of their
creation to the present time. But the antagonism was

mutual, and the bishops may fairly be credited with the larger share of the acerbity which the quarrel evoked. The appointment of Mgr. Lartigue was resented as being in opposition to the Gallican liberties : it had not been preceded by the inquest *de commodo et incommodo.* The Pope was charged with violating the canons to which he owed obedience. Villeneuve makes Lucifer expose this error, that the Popes have not 'received from Christ authority, plenary power, supreme and universal.' Such a power could not, of course, be subordinate and dependent. Lartigue was a Sulpician, and as the Bishop of Quebec had no revenue which he could allocate to his suffragan, it seems to have been intended that he should have continued to live in the House of the Sulpicians, and that they should have provided him a suitable revenue. But this was not their view of the matter : they thought that when the Bishop of Quebec procured the appointment of a suffragan, he should have been in a position to assign him a suitable revenue. The Sulpicians are much reproached for not providing a palace and an income for Mgr. Lartigue ; but the reproach is not just, for they were under no obligation to do, in this particular, what it is pretended they ought to have done.

The most fatal blow that could be dealt to the Sulpicians was to divide the parish of Notre-Dame. The Bishop of Montreal being at Rome, in 1854, had a conversation on the subject with the Secretary of the Propaganda, Cardinal Barnabo, when the later volunteered to authorize its dismemberment. At a later period, the Seminary demanded a hearing at Rome, but it was destined to be defeated. It then came to pass that, in pursuance of orders from Rome, the city of Montreal was carved up into a number of parishes, in defiance of the laws of the land, as interpreted by Judge Baudry and other respectable authorities.

Villeneuve divides the Conservatives into Ultramon-
tans and liberal Catholics : the latter he describes as being
deceived by the Sulpicians.   Lucifer apologizes for Sir
George Cartier, and says that he and the other Conservatives are submissive to the Church, and that the Sulpicians
have exercised a particular pressure on him in the matter
of the dismemberment.   There was, it cannot be denied,
a real anomaly in Sir George being the counsel for the
Seminary, when, as a public man, he had to decide between them and the bishop.

In the fifth act, the Jesuits, by contrast with the Sulpicians, are liberally bespattered with praise.   If the latter
engaged in worthy enterprises, the Jesuits, and after them
the Oblats, are represented as always leading the way.   In
the fourth act, the following dialogue takes place among
the demons :—

Belias.—' The Society of Jesus is the invincible fortress
of Ultramontanism.'

Oliver.—' The Society of Jesus is the mortal and sworn
enemy of Gallicanism and liberalism.'

All.—' The Society of Jesus ought to be the supreme
and highest object of our anger, of our combats, and our
vengeance.'

Lucifer.—' Ah ! Let us combat the Jesuits ! Chase
them from Canada and our cause is gained ! '

Babel.—' It is all very fine to talk, *mais que faire ?*'

Oliver.—' We have attempted everything since they
have been in existence.'

Babel.—' In Canada, we have scarcely done anything
against them since their return.   The wisdom of Lucifer
did not desire that we should.'

Lucifer (furious).—' Thou liest viper !   Thou liest !'

Babel (derisively).—' It is true I forgot that Big Jos. had
chanted the hymn of the cannibals, on the altar of their
generous martyrs !'

Belzébuth (sensibly piqued).—' And this hymn has had its effect.'

Babel.—' I do not desire to blame Belzébuth for having inspired it. I desire only to recall what has been done. They ought to have been persecuted, chased . . . .'

Several voices.—' Bravo ! Bravo !'

Baalbérith.—'Thus, then, it is agreed : war to the Jesuits !

All.—' War to the Jesuits !'

Baalberith.—' Only it is probable that we shall not succeed. They enjoy, in Canada, great consideration and high esteem. The people venerate them. The clergy and the bishops give them their protection. The Bishop of Montreal, especially, is their benefactor and devoted protector. He has already given extraordinary proofs of the special affection which he bears them. On their part, the Jesuits entertain for his eminence a respect, a veneration, and a devotion, which are. proof against everything.'

Lucifer.—' The Bishop of Montreal, is he not ill ?'

Baalberith.—' Very seriously.'

Lucifer.—' So much the better, if he went we . . .'

Several voices.—' Let him die! Let him die !'

Baalberith.—'Another senseless desire !'

Lucifer.—' What ?'

Baalberith.—' In dying the venerable Bishop of Montreal would not abandon his diocese. More than now he would be the angel . . . . . . (great emotion),

Baalberith.—' His blessed shade would hover over his town and his diocese.'

Here we see distinctly the author's attitude towards the different parties in the Church of Rome : mortal enmity to the Sulpicians, praise and encouragement for the Jesuits. Those countries which, in self-defence, have at different times been obliged to expel the Jesuits, were, if we accept the assurance of Villeneuve, inspired thereto by Lucifer. It is possible, looking at history, to imagine a contingency in which the suggestion put into the mouth of Lucifer, in the infernal dialogue, might become a prophesy.

Let us here recall the fact that *Le Comédie Infernale* was written in the interest of the Bishop of Montreal and to aid in the dismemberment of the parish of Notre-Dame; that this onslaught on the Sulpicians, vile in conception and malignant in execution, was accepted by that high dignitary without protest and apparently with gratitude; that the book was not consigned to the *Index* or received with disapprobation at Rome; and that to answer it was treated as a crime by the highest ecclesiastical functionary in the diocese of Montreal.

The Sulpicians may comfort themselves, if they can find any comfort in the companionship of misery or misfortune, by reflecting that they had not to bear alone the whole weight of the Ultramontane attack.

At the distance of a year from the appearance of the *Programme Catholique* came the celebration of the golden wedding of the priesthood of the Bishop of Montreal. And now that tentative *programme*, that literary *enfant trouvé* which was fondled with such deep affection, was left far behind, like a guide-post which had served the Ultramontanes on their march, and which now remained to mark the track over which they passed in their triumphant march. The ashes of Gallicanism still smouldered, like the remains of a sacred fire, on the hearth of the Archiepiscopal palace at Quebec. The 'venomous serpent' of Catholic Liberalism still glided about in forbidden places, making accursed that which ought to be holy. The golden wedding would attract a majority of the Episcopate and a large body of the inferior clergy. The occasion might be seized by the Ultramontanes for sending forth a manifesto in the shape of a sermon. The blow thus to be struck at the Gallicans could be made to tell with stunning effect. So it was arranged. The Jesuit Braün, whose principles had been revealed in his work on marriage, was selected to deliver the sermon. He would be glad of an opportunity to deal a nameless blow at the Archbishop and all who shared his views. This would at once avenge an old grudge and advance the good cause.

It is only on very special occasions that a simple priest, who can never be more than a simple priest, is permitted the distinction of preaching before a congregation embracing many high dignitaries, including archbishop, bishops, and priests. This distinction the Jesuit Braün now enjoyed. He began by saying that, in dispensing spiritual gifts to the faithful, their curés and bishops were to them other Christs. Their father, the bishop whose golden wedding was being celebrated, had gone about doing good; and they were to second his efforts by their docility and zeal. In enumerating the rights of the Church, which he undertook to defend against the ' errors ' of the day, he claimed for her the prerogative of making laws to bind the conscience, and to which the State is bound to submit; of making laws on the subject of marriage; of erecting parishes, without the intervention of the civil power; of superintending education in public schools. The State was bound to yield implicit obedience to the Church. The fashion of looking on the majority as the source of right, now in vogue, was a revival of the old Pagan despotism.

'Gallicanism and Liberal Catholicism,' said the Jesuit preacher, ' have powerfully contributed to the propagation of all these errors.' ' Gallicanism' he defined to be ' insubordination towards the Holy Father, servility to the civil power, despotism towards inferiors.' 'The Gallican,' he added, ' refuses to obey the Pope, against whom he arms

himself with the protection of the powers of this earth ;
while he grants to the civil power, which protects him in his
rebellion, all the authority which he refuses to the Sovereign Pontiff. Everywhere the Gallicans are the flatterers
of the civil power, to which they have recourse even in
ecclesiastical cases, in which the bishop or the Sovereign
Pontiff should have the right of adjudication. 'This insubordination towards the Holy Father, and this servility
towards the civil power,' the preacher reminded his
hearers, ' was stigmatized by Pope Innocent XI., in a brief
of April 11, 1682, to the bishops who formed the Assembly
of the French clergy' which adopted the four articles.

Gallicanism having received its due share of flagella-
tion, Liberalism next came up for sentence. ' Liberalism,'
said the Jesuit preacher, ' is a so-called generosity towards error; it is a readiness to yield on the score of
principles. Liberal Catholics grant to the State the
right of requiring that parishes, bishoprics, and religious
orders be civilly incorporated, as a condition of their
having the right to hold property. They grant that the
State has a right to limit the possessions of the Church ;
to make laws for regulating the administration of Church
property. They grant to the State the right of taking
possession of Church property and keeping it; thus
sanctioning the principle of communism. Speak to
these sacrilegious usurpers of restitution : their only answer will be a sneer. Liberal Catholics pretend that the
State can prescribe the form of marriage, define invalidating impediments, and pronounce upon the conjugal ties
in matrimonial causes. Liberal Catholics confide to the
State the superintendence and direction of primary schools,
to the detriment of the Church and fathers of families
They grant to the State the rights of intervening in the
erection of parishes, independently of any authorization
of the Holy See.'

These errors, Father Braün declared, were gaining ground in the country ; were causing the Church to lose its independence, and threatening ere long ' to place her on the same level as the so-called Church created by Henry VIII. All these fatal errors,' he emphatically declared, ' must be fought against : the State must be entirely subordinated to the Church,' must give its civil sanction to the decrees of the Church, and defend and enforce all her claims, both civil and spiritual. The Provincial Council of Quebec, he volunteered the information, had decided ' that apostolic constitutions, once published in Rome, become binding in this country.' Government did not concur in the erection of parishes: it simply legislated on the civil effects of their canonic erection by the Church.

Before closing, the preacher passed a strong eulogy on Bishop Bourget, the leader of the Ultramontanes in Canada, at whose golden wedding his hearers had come to rejoice, and reiterated the assertion of the complete independence of the Church, coupled with the absolute subordination of the State thereto.*

This declaration of war created indignation and consternation among such of the clergy and bishops as it was directed against. The attack was to be promptly followed up till victory was won.

Archbishop Baillargeon of Quebec found himself in sympathy with the Bishop of Orleans, when the latter wrote his celebrated letter on the Vatican Council. Of this letter the author caused to be sent a MS. copy to the Archbishop of Quebec, with the words *écrit de sa main.* This letter the Archbishop caused to be printed and distributed among his clergy, in the beginning of the year 1868.

The ' dangerous doctrines ' contained in this letter did not escape the vigilant eye of the emissaries of a foreign

* *The Witness*, Montreal.

power. An obscure journal, the *Gazette des Campagnes*, was made the medium of the censure. This paper was published under the auspices of the college of Ste. Anne ;* and as the letter had been published by authority of the Archbishop, the adverse comments, coming from Catholics, seem to have been construed as a defiance of episcopal authority. Vicar-General Cazeau, feeling it his duty to communicate the article to the Archbishop, who was then at Rome in attendance on the Vatican Council, first wrote to enquire whether it had been written with the consent of the members of the corporation of the college ; if not, desiring that they might announce the fact in the same journal, or, if they preferred it, send the disavowal direct to him. They were reminded that they were required to inculcate respect for their first pastor ; and a hint was given that, if this were not done, changes in the persons in charge of the college might be made : a threat which was afterwards carried into effect.

This sleepless surveillance belongs to the severity of ecclesiastical administration in the Roman Catholic Church under its most liberal phases, and tends to prevent criticism of any writing or opinion to which the stamp of episcopal approval, has been given ; but the consequences are more serious when the only opinions allowed to be expressed are those to be found in the *Syllabus* and the Vatican decrees. That M. Cazeau and the late Archbishop of Quebec were once liberal in the sense liberals were condemned by the Pope seems undeniable. The editor of the *Gazette* was sure of an easy triumph. An appeal to Rome in favour of Infallibility, and against

---

* At that time, the Rev. Alexis Pelletier was professor in the college of Ste. Anne (Abbé Tanguay) ; and there is little doubt that he was ringleader in this attack. He had previously been professor in the University of Laval ; and he carried away with him an undying antipathy to that seat of learning, which breaks out on every occasion. He has been a formidable ally of the Jesuits and Bishop Bourget in their attempts to discredit Laval and set up a Jesuit University in opposition at Montreal.

12

Bishop Dupanloup and his sympathizers, was certain to be successful ; and the placing of the sanctum of the *Gazette des Campagnes* above the throne of the Archbishop shows what the press can do in the Province of Quebec, when it ranges itself on the side of Ultramontanism.

The Bishop of Orleans published more letters ; and the *Gazette des Campagnes* thundered new censures. The *Journal de Québec*, which in that particular phase of its existence got credit for speaking the language of the Catholic liberals, was suspected of receiving the secret approbation of the Vicar-General; a suspicion which is laid to the charge of M. Cazeau as a crime.* The *Journal* claimed the right of believing or disbelieving in Papal infallibility. The visits of the editor to the Archi-episcopal palace were carefully noted, and became the cause of great scandal ; and Ultramontane spies observed that there was an established connection between these visits and each new vindication of Catholic Liberalism in the *Journal*. But time ever brings its changes ; and when Dupanloup had wheeled into line, why should a Canadian journalist be denied the privilege of repentance ? By steady persistence Rome gains her conquests in the domain of civil liberty.

Near the close of 1869 and the beginning of 1870, the Ultramontanes gained an accession of advocates in the press. Abbé Jos. S. Martel, curé of Ste. Julie de Sommerset, and M. Routhier of Kamouraska, a lawyer, began to proclaim aloud the truth of the doctrines promulgated at Rome, the admission of which meant death to the old Gallicanism. By the light of the *Syllabus*, Abbé Martel discovered that the conditions under which public education was carried on were deplorable ; and, taking the

---

* Il (M. Cazeau) encourager, au moin par une approbation tacite l'homme du *Journal de Québec* à le salir, quatre mois durant, de toutes les injures et les calomnies imaginables. Il (the editor of the *Journal de Québec*) soutenait qu'on etait libre de croire ou de ne pas croire à l'infalibilité pontificale.—Abbé Pelletier, *Lib. et Gal.*

canonist Bouix for a subordinate guide, he contended
that the choice of masters and of books for public schools,
purely secular in their character, belonged to the Church;
that the teachers should be 'profoundly Catholic,' and
under the obligation of following the rules which the
Church might lay down for their guidance.† The only
duty reserved to the State in this scheme, is obedience
to the behests of the Church, whose decrees it should consider it a duty to execute. This may serve to give us some
idea of the tenure by which the Protestant minority of
Quebec hold their educational rights, and the circumstances under which an attempt would be made to deprive
them of guarantees of which Abbé Martel, adopting the
doctrine of Bouix in all its rigour, thus early essayed the
destruction.

From a doctrine so startling as this, M. Chauveau.
then Superintendent of Education, shrank with alarm,
Vicar-General Cazeau resisted the innovation. The
French Canadian press, though divided on the subject,
generally refused assent. M. Routhier, the Kamouraska
advocate, now a judge, contended for the right of the
Church to take the absolute direction of the public schools.
Episcopal encouragement of a doctrine so agreeable to
Rome was not long wanting. Mgr. Birtha, who then
exercised the functions of bishop at Montreal, in the
absence of Mgr. Bourget, wrote a letter of encouraging
congratulation to Abbé Martel and another to M. Routhier.‡ Vicar-General Cazeau, who represented the Archbishop in his absence, wrote to Mgr. Birtha to express

---

† Ainsi, says this canonist, dans l'organization des écoles publiques, le pouvoir civil
est tenu, quant à tout ce qui vient d'ête enuméré d'obtenir l'assentiment du pouvoir
ecclésiastique, et il doit, en pareille matière, lui laisser pleine liberté d'exercer la
surveillance, de prescrire ce qu'il jugera convenable et de le faire executer.

‡ M. Pinsonneault, when he retired from the Bishopric of Sandwich, Canada West
(Ontario), received the title of Mgr. de Birtha. To the late Bishop of Montreal all
the leading Ultramontanes were attracted by an irresistible affinity.

.his disapprobation of the countenance the latter had given
to these innovators.*   He was anxious to prevent all discussion of the subject; and one of his complaints was
that M. Routhier had written in the journals in contempt
of ecclesiastical authority, so little latitude of freedom
do the most liberal Roman Catholic ecclesiastics in Quebec give to laymen.   Mgr. de Birtha, in reply, recalled
the fact that the Pope had often encouraged journalists
who, like Louis Veuillot, had placed their pens at the
service of the Church; and he could find no words sufficiently strong to laud 'the brave curé' who had so
valiantly combatted the encroachments of the laity in the
direction of education.   As for himself, he had only done
what the Provincial Councils and the Pope, in various
encylicals, had ordered to be done.   The Pope had, in
the previous January, in writing to the editor of a Rio
Janeiro journal, incited him to 'cry aloud, to sound the
trumpet,' as 'Catholic journalism is one of the most efficacious means of dissipating error.'   After fortifying himself with this quotation from infallible authority, Mgr. de
Birtha, addressing M. Cazeau, says : 'And you, my dear
Vicar-General, you say to the Catholic journalism of Quebec : Silence, silence ; no discussion ;' and this by way
of prudence.   These Ultramontane writers express ineffable contempt for everything that at all savours of prudence.

The Abbé Pelletier now claimed to have convicted
Vicar-General Cazeau of the double crime of Gallicanism
and Liberalism.   The orthodoxy of the views expressed
by M. Routhier was guaranteed by this priest : they had
'the merit of being qualified as Ultramontane, in opposition to those called Gallican and Liberal.'   'We have therefore,' exclaimed Pelletier, 'from the hand of Vicar-

* In this letter the Vicar-General said : J'ai regretté de voir un evèque venir donner
sa sanction à tout cela, et je n'ai pu empêcher de trouver sa demarche intempestive.

General Cazeau an authentic document attesting that at Quebec,' in the palace of the Archbishop, 'profession is made of Gallicanism and Liberalism.' The Gallicanism which had a vigorous existence at Quebec six years ago is now silent as the tomb. Is it dead beyond the possibility of recovery?

The college of Ste. Anne became a hotbed in which' the new opinions were forced. In the summer of 1870 the Archbishop of Quebec resolved upon the removal of all the teachers, and formally addressed them a letter to that effect. They refused submission, and threatened to appeal to Rome. Called upon to disavow the authorship of the articles in the _Gazette des Campagnes_, they replied, Jesuitically, that they regretted whatever had appeared in that journal which could reasonably offend the Archbishop. The organ of the Archbishop simulated satisfaction with an answer which was the reverse of satisfactory. So obnoxious were the new opinions that M. Cazeau did what he could to prevent their expression in the press. He is said to have succeeded, for a long time, in imposing silence on the _Courrier du Canada_, and to have discouraged to the utmost of his power the circulation of the _Nouveau Monde_, an Ultramontane journal, set up at the instance of the Bishop of Montreal. In the nomination of curés, it was charged against him that he favoured the old Gallicans and discouraged the new opinions; that he retained in high positions the Abbé Chandonnet, who shared his liberal views and defended them; while Ultramontane priests sometimes sought a refuge in expatriation from the vexation caused by what they considered a want of appreciation of their merits. The malice of his enemies charged that he sent M. Proulx to Beauce, as to a penal colony. Between him and the German Jesuit Braün, notorious for the extravagance of his Ultramontane views, there could be no sympathy. This

Jesuit found a natural ally in Bishop Bourget; and he found his true place when, leaving Quebec, he took up his residence in Montreal.   If M. Cazeau had not made him specially welcome in the ancient capital, the fact should redound to the credit of a Canadian of the old school, and not be invoked against him.

Nor do the writers of the New School confine their attacks to ecclesiastics of the Old School.   Whenever a case comes before the courts in which Ultramontane pre-tensions have to be passed on, the judge becomes the target of attack.   He is accused of partiality, of indulging forbidden sympathies, of holding the scales of justice un-evenly.   When Judge Mondelet, during the hearing of the Guibord case, became the target of these attacks, he said in open court: ' I have been calumniated, but happily I am above calumny; ' and he pointed out the evils that would result from the success of like efforts to destroy public confidence in the partiality of our judges: ' It would be a thousand times better,' he said, 'to have nei-ther judges nor tribunals, to suffer the loss of our consti-tution, to be condemned to helotism, rather than see the people lose confidence in the tribunals ; for, if these were once abolished, the *régime* of carbines and bayonets would commence.'   During, the course of the trial, he stated that he had received certain indirect admonitions, and he indicated that an appeal had been made to the Government in the hope of inducing it to make an attack upon his independence, an appeal which he justly char-acterizes as an insult to the Executive, which must have been thought, by those making it, to be capable of so un-worthy an act.   This attack on the independence of the judge he regards as indicating the sort of *régime* which the New School would place us under, if it had the power.

Archbishop Lynch, of Toronto, came, in turn, under

the fire of the Ultramontane skirmishers of the Province of Quebec. He had publicly stated* that in Ontario the priests are forbidden to turn the altar into a tribune from which to deliver political harangues or to menace electors on account of the votes they may give at political elections; though they might instruct their parishioners in their duty to vote for the candidate whom they believe best capable of advancing the interests of the country.

Several Ultramontane journals, published in the French language, expressed strong objections to this mode of managing matters. They reproduced the joint instructions of the Bishop of Quebec authorizing the priests to denounce the censures of the Church against electors who refused to vote as directed by their spiritual advisers. Among the critics of Archbishop Lynch's letter who argued the existence of unity on the strength of this difference, the *Courrier du Canada* was prominent.†

And the *Courrier* was not long in receiving its reward. Before the end of April, it obtained from the Pope a mark of distinction which is usually reserved for writers who are in special favour at the Vatican. The *Courrier* announces that : ' Our Holy Father the Pope has accorded to us, in our quality of Catholic journalist, the apostolic benediction for us and our family to the third generation, with permission to read the books in the *Index* without exception.'

The Rev. Alexis Pelletier, ranking Archbishop Lynch with the ecclesiastics of Quebec on whom the viols of his wrath had recently been poured, turned his arms for a moment, as if by way of warning, against the chief ecclesiastical dignitary of the Roman Catholic Church in Ontario. A pamphlet written by him under the name of *Libéralisme*,‡ elaborates, at great length, the views of Bishop Bourget.

* Letter to the Hon. A. Mackenzie, Jan., 1876.
† Feb. 2, 1876, and subsequent issues.
‡ Coup D'Oeil sur le Libéralisme Européan et sur Libéralisme Canadien.

In an article in *Le Franc-Parleur,* this writer, under his well-known *nom de guerre,* gave Archbishop Lynch a first warning. ' It is evidently impossible,' he says, 'to discover the slightest trait of resemblance between the Catholic Liberal, which Pius IX. has painted for us and that which Mgr. of Toronto shows us. Now the infallible doctor cannot err, and it is he to whom we must listen. When he raises the cry of alarm the danger is really where he signals it, and it is such as he sees it to be.'

It is evident from these indications that the turn of the Archbishop of Toronto had come. His assailants have, so far, succeeded in silencing every one in the Canadian Church whom they have attacked. But Archbishop Lynch would be in a measure protected by the barrier of a language foreign to the people with whom he has to deal. Still, his critics would fail in the faculty of invention for which they have hitherto been remarkable, and in the persistency with which they have invariably followed up their attacks, should they not find some means of making Archbishop Lynch exceedingly uncomfortable, or reducing him to that silence which they have imposed on so many others. It is a noteworthy coincidence that, soon after the appearance of this criticism, the Archbishop ceased to favour the public with his views on these questions, which had been given in a non-official shape, as a correspondent of a public journal, in which capacity, the complaint was made, his words could not be taken as those of a bishop.

The bishops of Quebec never interfere to check the violence of the clergy when it is directed against the common enemy, against the liberty of electors, against the rights of the civil authority. A priest may preach and teach that civil laws are to be disregarded, if the Church pronounces against them, with the absolute certainty of receiving episcopal approval.

IX

CATHOLIC LIBERALISM.

It is no part of my plan to attempt to solve the question: ' What is Catholic Liberalism; is it religious or
political, or partly religious and partly political?'
Nor does it matter whether Catholic Liberalism
has been dogmatically defined, as some contend, or
not, as Dr. De Angelis affirms. What is important to
know is in what way the bishops, the priests, and the
clerical press of the Province of Quebec treat the question ; for what they say will be believed by a majority of
those whom they are in a position to influence, and the
terrorism of pastoral letters, political sermons, and decla-
mations of the press will produce a deep impression on
the minds of the Roman Catholic laity.

It is the custom of the Ultramontane writers to treat
Catholic Liberalism as the synonym of Gallicanism.
There may be some resemblance between the two, but
they certainly are not identical. Article seventy-seven of
the Syllabus stigmatizes as Liberalism the toleration of
other modes of worship than that of the Romish Church;
and the next article denies that it is a wise provision of
the law to allow persons who take up their residence in
Catholic countries to enjoy the public exercise of their
own worship. Article seventy-nine denounces the civil
liberty of every mode of worship as of corrupt and immoral tendency, which leads to the propagation of
indifferentism.

Whether this be a dogmatic definition or not, it is certainly not identical with the principles of Gallicanism,

which, whatever their merits, did not object to the national
Church being the only tolerated Church in the State.
Neither in Canada nor in Louisiana was any other reli-
gion tolerated under the French rule.

The fifth Provincial Council of Quebec compares
Catholic Liberalism to the serpent that crawled in the
Garden of Eden, when it sought to compass the downfall
of the human race. But this hackneyed figure, which
constantly appears in this kind of literature, hideous and
repulsive as it is, does not contain a definition. One of
the objects of this error, we are told, is to alter the constitution of the Church, and to break the ties which unite
the people to the bishops and the bishops to the Vicar of
Christ. This statement involves the definition of the
limits between the civil and the ecclesiastical power.
This the present Archbishop of Quebec, Mgr. Taschereau,
in promulgating the decrees of the fifth Provincial
Council, admits, and he contends that the Church alone
has the power to decide. And this doctrine every Roman
Catholic is commanded to hold and proclaim, in journal,
book, and pulpit. The term ' Catholic writers ' is defined
by the Council as including those who treat on politics as
well as on religion.

' Pretended Catholics,' says the Archbishop, ' who in
the meantime call themselves Liberals, are more dangerous than declared enemies,' because, whether they intend
it or not, they favour those who design the destruction of
the Church. There is about them an appearance of pro-
bity and sound doctrine which deceive honest men.'

When, as happens in this case, the word Liberal is
imperfectly qualified, the bias of a party writer has no
difficulty in treating it as a disapproval of Liberalism,
pure and simple.

The eight bishops of Quebec unite in telling the faithful * that Catholic Liberalism, according to ' Pius IX.,

* Lettre Pastorale, 22 Sept., 1875.

is the most incensed and the most dangerous enemy of the divine constitution of the Church.' And the Pope has since, in a brief, approved of that letter. After alluding to the serpent in the Garden of Eden, the bishops add : ' It tries to glide imperceptibly in the most holy places ; it fascinates the eyes of the most clear-seeing ; it poisons the hearts of the most simple, that they may change their faith in the authority of the most sovereign Pontiff.'

The partisans of this error, we read further, ' applaud the civil power wherever it invades the sanctuary ; they attempt by every means to induce the faithful to tolerate, if not approve, iniquitous laws. Enemies the more dangerous, because they often, without even being aware of it (sans même en avoir la conscience), favour the most perverse doctrines, which Pius IX. has so well characterized in calling them ' a chimerical conciliation between truth and error.'

' The Catholic Liberal is reassured by the fact that he still possesses certain Catholic principles, certain pious practices, a certain fund of faith and of attachment to the Church, but he carefully closes his eyes to the abyss which error has scooped in his heart, and by which he is silently devoured. He still vaunts, to all comers, his religious convictions, and is displeased when he is told that he has embraced dangerous principles ; he is perhaps sincere in his blindness, God only knows ! But side by side with these fair appearances, there is a large stock of pride, which causes him to believe that he has more prudence and sagacity than those to whom the Holy Ghost has given the mission and the grace to teach and govern the faithful : he is seen to censure without scruple the acts and documents of the highest religious authority. Under pretext of taking away causes of dissension, and reconciling the Gospel to the actual progress of society, he enters the service of Cæsar and of those who invent pretended rights in favour of a false liberty : as if light and darkness could exist together, and as if truth ceased to be truth when violence had been done to it, by taking away its true meaning and despoiling the immutability inherent in its nature.'

The bishops conclude by saying : ' In presence of five apostolic briefs denouncing Catholic Liberalism as absolutely incompatible with the doctrine óf the Church, though it has not yet been formally condemned as a heresy, it is no longer permitted in conscience to be a Liberal Catholic.'

In the muffled sound of these words are conveyed to us with sufficient distinctness the idea, ever dear to the Church, of reaction, and a determination to suppress all independent opinions and action, even in the sphere of legislation.

The joint letter of the Episcopate of Quebec was thought by Bishop Bourget to require to be supplemented by a pastoral of his own.*   This bishop, as is his manner, dealt with the subject in a more pronounced way than his colleagues had done. ' Catholic Liberalism,' he defines to be ' a body of social and religious doctrines which tend to free, more or less, minds of the speculative order, and citizens in the practical order, from rules which tradition had everywhere imposed upon them.' In answer to the questions, ' What is Catholic Liberalism ? What is Liberal Catholicism ? ' he replies : ' It is a false and dangerous sentiment ; it is a party rising up and in fact conspiring against the Church and civil society. A Catholic Liberal is a man who participates, in any degree whatever, in this sentiment, or with this party, or in this doctrine, who is sick in proportion as he is liberal, and healthy in proportion as he is

* Feb. 1, 1876.

Catholic., Liberalism tends always to subordinate the rights of the Church to the rights of the State, by prudent and sagacious means, and even to separate the Church from the State, desiring to have a free Church in a free State.'† Liberalism contends that the clergy alone is called upon to defend religion, and that this mission has not been consigned to laymen; while the Pope declares, in his encyclical of 1853, that laymen, in taking this part, perform a filial duty from the moment that they combat under the direction of the clergy. Modern Liberalism pretends that religion ought to be confined to the sacristy, and not go beyond the limits of private life. But the Pope declares that Catholics can effectually defend their rights and their liberties only by taking part in all public affairs.'

By these characteristic traits, Bishop Bourget assures us, Catholic Liberalism may be known. But he still thinks it necessary further to heighten the colour of the picture, in which Liberalism is made to stand forth as ' nothing else than the demon which, hidden under the form of the ancient serpent, and armed with its rage, its malice, and its *ruse*, is found in our midst attempting our destruction.' But no cobra, no copper-head, no boa constrictor, 'is half so dangerous as the serpent Liberalism.' It is a serpent ' a thousand times more dangerous than all the other serpents in the world, because it poisons souls.' As a means of avoiding the evils of Liberalism, each one of the faithful is instructed to say in the inmost recesses of his soul : ' I hear my curé ; my curé hears the bishop ; the bishop hears the Pope ; the Pope hears our Saviour Jesus Christ, by whom he is assisted by the Divine Spirit to render him infallible in the teaching and government of his Church.'

Dr. De Angelis, who was called upon to pronounce an

† This is the expression of Cavour.

opinion on this pastoral, does not admit that Mgr. Bourget intended to proclaim the infallibility of the bishops and the curés. What De Angelis meant, if he had thought it prudent to be more outspoken, no doubt was that such a claim could not be allowed. That the bishop meant no less than this, what he went on to add seems to leave no doubt. The priests, his argument was, had merely reproduced the instructions given by the Pope and the bishops against Liberalism. 'It is therefore,' said the bishop, 'the whole clergy who speak by the mouth of each of its ministers. Thus disrespect shown to this organ of the clergy is disrespect for the whole clergy; it is disrespect of Jesus Christ, whose ambassadors they are; it is disrespect of the Eternal Father.'

'But what are we to think,' the bishop goes on to ask, of those who, on the hustings, at the polls, in the tribune or in the press, dare to make disrespectful allusions o the person or the character of the priest, to regard with disrespect or cause others to regard with disrespect his word and his conduct, with a view of depriving him, if possible, of the esteem and consideration which he enjoys among the people, and how ought they to be treated?' The answer was, in effect, that such conduct properly incurred the lesser excommunication.

The bishops, in their joint letter, and Bishop Bourget in his separate pastoral, tell us that the superstructures they respectively raised have for their base the several apostolic briefs in which Pius IX. has denounced Catholic Liberalism, and to which another specially relating to Canada has since been added. But, if we turn to these documents, we shall find that the *nuance* in which the question is enveloped does not entirely clear away. The truth seems to be that, in the absence of a dogmatic definition, much latitude is allowed in the definition of Catholic Liberalism. The Pope, in receiving a deputation of

French Catholics on the twenty-fifth anniversary of his Pontificate, said: 'What affects your country and prevents it meriting the benedictions of heaven is a *mélange* of principles. What I fear is not the wretches of the Commune of Paris, true demons of hell, who walk about on the face of the earth. No, it is not that; what I fear is this miserable policy of Catholic Liberalism, which is the real scourge.'

According to a brief of July 28, 1873, the condemned opinions are sometimes held by honest and pious Catholics. 'Liberal opinions,' we read in this brief, 'are accepted by many honest and pious Catholics, whose religion and authority easily draw men's minds towards them and incline them towards very pernicious opinions.' When there is no want of piety the fault would seem to lay in the politics ; not the politics of any particular party, but the politics of all parties which are opposed to reaction and sacerdotalism.

Abbé Pâquet bids us seek the definition of Liberalism in the Encyclical of 1864 ; 'that immortal monument of the wisdom, penetration, zeal, and courage of Pius IX.'* In the Syllabus of errors accompanying the Encyclical, Pius IX. denounced Liberalism.†

The occasions which gave rise to these propositions being characterized as errors may here be recalled. In

---

* Le Libéralisme.

† Article 77. 'In the present day, it is no longer expedient that the Catholic religion should be held as the only religion of the State, to the exclusion of all other modes of worship.

78. ' Whence it has been wisely provided by law, in some countries called Catholic, that persons coming to reside therein shall enjoy the public exercise of their own worship.

79. ' Moreover, it is false that the civil liberty of every mode of worship, and the full power given to all of overtly and publicly manifesting their opinions and ideas, of all kinds whatsoever, conduce more easily to corrupt the morals and minds of the people, and to the propagation of the pest of indifferentism.

80. 'The Roman Pontiff can and ought to reconcile himself to, and agree with, progress, liberalism, and civilization as lately introduced.'

1851, Pius IX. entered into a concordat with the King of Spain, which stipulated, among other things, that the Roman Catholic religion should be the only religion of the Spanish nation, to the exclusion of every other form of worship, and that this religion should enjoy all the prerogatives accorded to it by the canons ; that in all the schools of Spain the teaching should be entirely conformable to the Roman doctrine ; above all, that the bishops, in the exercise of their episcopal functions, as well as in whatever relates to the rights and the exercise of ecclesiastical authority, should enjoy the full liberty with which the canons invest them ; that the Church might acquire additional property in whatever way it could *(à quelque titre que ce soit)*, and that the rights and property of the Church should be inviolable.

In this world of mutable things and ever varying opinion, it was not strange that a change came over the Government of Spain; a change expressed in terms which negatived the stipulations of the concordat by the assertion that, in the present day, it is no longer expedient that the Catholic religion shall be held as the only religion of the State, to the exclusion of all other modes of worship. The Spanish Government went still farther: it decreed the sale of ecclesiastical property, forbade the bishops to confer sacred orders, and passed other laws of a similar tendency.

The questions thus dealt with were not exclusively religious : they were politico-religious. The annulling of the concordat was made a subject of complaint by the Pope; but concordats, being human things, are not eternal, and the Court of Rome has not hesitated to abrogate a concordat when its interest lay in so doing. Pius IV., to quote an example, annulled the concordat with France, on the ground that it was too favourable to the nation, as represented by the king. And it was not till the Pope was made to feel the inconvenience of being deprived of the annates and the revival of the Pragmatic Sanction, that he consented to renew the concordat in 1562.* One of the most unpopular things done by the Government of the Restoration was the new concordat into which it entered in 1817. It was regarded as anti-national, and destructive of the liberties of the national Church. The popular feeling was so strong and so unanimous that ministers soon ceased to defend the act they had advised; and the publication of the Pope's bull founded on the concordat, and making a new division of the dioceses, increased the public indignation.† A Government with Ultramontane leanings may sometimes agree to a concordat which it is impossible long to maintain.

The history of the seventy-eighth article of the Syllabus is this: The Government of New Grenada, in 1854, promulgated a law by which priests and bishops who had been convicted of crime by a lay tribunal were forbidden to continue to exercise ecclesiastical functions, and their charges were to pass into other hands. Gregory XVI. protested, but protested in vain. Two additional laws were proposed, one for the abolition of tithes, the other to guarantee to immigrants coming from every country the public exercise of their religion. Pius IX. protested, but without effect. The ball kept rolling: the suppression of religious orders was decreed, the expulsion of the Jesuits confirmed, the ecclesiastical law of Rome abolished. Bishops and archbishops were made amenable to lay tribunals, and the choice of priests was vested in the parishioners. Unrestricted freedom of discussion was legalized. The clergy, resisting the law, suffered the penalty of disobedience. In these acts, Abbé Pâquet tells us, is to be found that modern Liberalism which Pius IX.

* Abbé Millot. Histoire de France.

† Léonard Gallois. Histoire de France.

13

denounced in article seventy-eight of the Syllabus. Most of these acts were politico-religious; that which legalized free discussion was purely political.

The seventy-ninth article of the Syllabus was a protest against the proclamation of the freedom of worship and the free expression of opinion by the Spanish Government, and the restrictions under which the bishops were placed not to cause the publication of their pastorals in the churches. There were non-juring bishops, who showed that they were not of the nation in which they lived by refusing, at the bidding of the Pope, to take an oath of fidelity to the Republican constitution. And if they had taken the oath, what guarantee would there have been that the Pope would not, under the circumstances, have assumed to release them from its obligation? Such things have been done, even in Canada. This is a weighty charge, not to be credited on doubtful evidence. The evidence is not doubtful, admits of no doubt. The authority is contained in the permission given by Pope Urban VIII. to the Provincial of the Recollets of Paris, March 25, 1635, with power to communicate it to the missionaries that might be sent to Canada.* It is true that this authority was to be exercised only for just cause; but of what constituted a valid cause the ecclesiastic must be the judge.

If to forbid or permit the free exercise of worship has its religious side, it is not the less a matter of civil right; while freedom of discussion may be political or religious, according to the nature of the subject discussed. It follows that in condemning modern Liberalism, the Pope

---

* Relaxandi juramenta ob instas causas. . . . . Communicandi has facultates in toto vel in parte Vicario seu vicepræfecto, ac alys missionarys ejusdem orainis ad Canadam Americæ Septentrionalis Provinciam transmissis, et ab eodem Provinciali ejusque definitoris, cum acitu, et consensu Nuty [Nunti] Galliarum approbante transmittendis et concessas revocandi toties quoties opus fuerit.—See the document in Sagard *Histoire du Canada*, Paris 1636.

included in his catalogue of errors political as well as religious matters.

The Pope, after the loss of his civil power, was advised to reconcile himself with modern progress, Liberalism, and civilization. The eighteenth article of the Syllabus contains his answer to the invitation. The Pope was asked to place himself in accord with three things, and the demand that he should do so he stigmatized as an error of modern Liberalism. Modern progress and civilization include political amelioration, and by no fair rule of interpretation can they be assumed to have an exclusively religious aspect.

After years of dispute, in which rivers of ink had been shed and tons of paper polluted, Pope Pius IX. issued a brief, September 18, 1876, which was intended to put an end to the conflict. It was addressed to the Bishop of Three Rivers, and has been communicated by other bishops, presumably the whole of them, to the clergy of their respective dioceses. In this brief, Pius IX. applauds the zeal with which the bishops of Quebec, in the joint letter, warned the people against the errors of 'Liberalism called Catholic.' The effect of this is to adopt what they said under this head. What that is we have already seen.

Mgr. Birtha gives a definition of the question which it is not easy to reject, when he describes Catholic Liberalism as politico-religious.† 'Who does not see,' says this ecclesiastic, 'that it is necessary, at whatever cost, to unveil and combat the enterprise of those who desire to form a political party, in direct opposition to the teachings of the Pope, whose special mission seems to be to unmask and destroy this dangerous sect of Catholic Liberals? What frightful evils has not this sect, filled with the cunning and imposture of the ancient serpent, brought

† Lettres à un deputé.

upon the Catholic kingdoms of Europe? Shall we undergo a like fate? Yes, without doubt, if we do not combat this insidious sect, wherever it dares to raise its head.'

If Bishop Pinsonneault did not assist in framing the decree of the fifth Provincial Council in which Catholic Liberalism is condemned, he may be allowed to be a capable expositor of the language employed by his colleagues in the Episcopate. Practically, his is the interpretation which the term Catholic Liberal receives in Quebec. The result is, that the Church has taken the field on the side of political reaction, and as its teaching claims an infallible origin, there is danger that nearly the whole political power of the Province will soon be wielded by a clerical army. With the opposition which such a line of conduct has begun to invoke has come the opening battle in the inevitable conflict which has been predicted. The first clash of arms has been heard in the stern challenge which the exercise of undue clerical influence over elections has met in the courts.

On another occasion* Bishop Pinsonneault said: ' The Catholic Liberal professes to believe the true faith, the same as other Catholics; but while believing the Catholic dogma, he absolutely rejects the intervention of the Church in human concerns. He does not wish that the priest should occupy himself with temporal affairs. He is willing to tolerate the Church so long as it confines itself to the temple and the sacristy. He wishes to restrain it from expressing itself on questions which belong to human politics. Therefore the Catholic Liberal excludes God from civil affairs. It is an error condemned by the Popes and the Councils. Liberalism being an error, those who declare themselves Liberals ought not to be

---

Analyse du sermon de Sa Grandeur Monseigneur A Pinsonneault, Evêque de Birtha, prononcé dans l'Eglise de St. Henri des Tanneries, Dimanche, le 4 Juillet, 1875.

followed or encouraged. What,' he asks, ' is the remedy for the evils of which Liberalism is the cause ?' And he answers that, ' since the Liberal idea is an idea of revolt, obedience is the only means to prevent its proving contagious ; ' and that that obedience is due ' to the authority established by God, the Church.'

The statement of Bishop Pinsonneault that the Catholic Liberal absolutely rejects the intervention of the priest in human affairs is, like most of the statements which come to us with the flavour of infallibility, gross exaggeration. There are many human affairs which are not political ; and though the Catholic Liberal denies to the priest the right to interfere in parliamentary elections with his spiritual authority and spiritual censures, no one denies that the priest, as a citizen, is at liberty to exercise his political rights.

As speak the bishops, so speaks the priest. In the following strain M. O'Donnell berates ' the apostles of modern civilization: '† 'Your civilization reposes on a principle at once false, destructive, detestable. You desire to form the child in the pattern of your own heart and intelligence—to rob it of its faith, its soul, its God—and turn it into a brute. For you matrimony is a thing which the first caprice may rupture. You desire the destruction of the family. " No connection," you cry, "between the Church and the State, between the spiritual and the temporal ; " and it is for the purpose of loading the Church with chains, and rendering it the slave of the civil power, that you announce the monstrous error. Not only do you wish that God should be a stranger in the State, but that the State should serve as the pedestal for the satellites of Satan. Anarchy, intellectual, moral, and religious, seems to you the fitting complement of these diabolical doctrines. Your

† Sermon prononcé par M. O'Donnell à l'occasion du sacre de Sa Grandeur Mgr Moreau, 1876.

liberty of the press is the oppression of the mind and the heart, its weapons lies and immorality; liberty of conscience is equal liberty for truth and error; liberty of speech is anarchy, license, the right of rebellion, and your political liberalism is the liberal theory of the relation which the Church and State should bear to one another.'

Father O'Donnell's picture of modern civilization is a caricature, or an invention, painted unlike the reality, for the purpose of making his subject hateful.   ·

A sermon preached on the occasion of the consecration of a bishop would miss its mark if it contained nothing on the subject of the episcopal function. Father O'Donnell did not forget the principal part he was required to play. The bishop's mission, in the direction of consciences, he described as all pervading; it extended to the whole man : 'his heart, mind, will, his civil, religious, and domestic duties.' Could there be a more melancholy picture of a slave than a man thus bandaged by episcopal cords? If the duty of directing consciences extends so far, and were so far practically extended, the minds of the faithful would have room for nothing but the impression made upon them in the confessional ; and the power of the Church would be supreme, in the civil as well as in the ecclesiastical domain. Rome would then become an universal monarchy, all divested though she is of 'the patrimony of St. Peter.'

Is it surprising that such pretensions as these should fill men's minds with alarm, and that the alarm should be raised that a great contest between Ultramontanism and the civil power is at hand?

Much of the evidence adduced by Ultramontane writers to prove that Vicar-General Raymond was a Liberal Catholic, guilty of the high crime of Gallicanism, is utterly worthless. If he abstained from quoting Ultramontane writers, such as Veuillot, Morel, Maupied, Keller, it was held to be proof that he did not share their opinions. And if he did not write against the doctrines of the *Univers* or Mgr. de Tulle, private conversations—such is the system of espionage in vogue—in which he spoke against them were not held sacred. Where the Pope had given his blessing, as in the case of Louis Veuillot, the Vicar-General was not at liberty to refuse his admiration. So his assailants concluded.

Under pressure of the attacks of which he became the victim, there came a time when M. Raymond was obliged to deny the charge of Liberal Catholicism. He could not afford to be under the reproach that he belonged to a class of men whom the Pope had described as having inflicted greater injuries on French society than the Commune of Paris. ' When,' the indictment against him ran, ' he preached liberty of conscience, *comme fait*, when he strove to calm the fears which the perils of Gallicanism and Catholic Liberalism had excited, he grievously pained Catholic Canada.'* He protested his attachment to Roman doctrines ; but this, his enemies said, was a common refuge of Catholic Liberalism. Montalembert had admitted that Gallicanism had long been hopelessly dead, so utterly extinct that, in 1844, it would not have been possible to find, in all France, four bishops who would have signed the four articles of 1682 ; and yet withal Montalembert had the sin of Gallicanism on his head. Vicar-General Raymond denied the existence of Liberalism in Canada,† proclaimed aloud his abhorrence of the ' perfidious error ;' but he did not the less

* Binan.

† And for this avowal, in due time, came his fitting reward. On the 21st of July 1876, the Pope, by an apostolic rescript, appointed him domestic prelate of his house. The honour is for him ; the conquest may not the less be for the Ultramontanes who drove him to this confession. Abbé Pelletier says : Le St. Office, d'après les explications qui lui furent longuement données par M. l'abbé Raymond sur sa lecture intitulée : ' *L'action de Marie dans la Société*,' s'est abstenu de la mal noter.

teach Liberal doctrines in his lectures, for though he condemned liberty of conscience, *comme droit*, he defended
it, *comme fait.* Therefore, in the eyes of the Pope he was
worse than the Communists of Paris. When the Pope
pronounced against liberty of conscience, no good Catholic is at liberty to speak in its favour.

Such are the doctrines of the Ultramontane writers of
Quebec in the present day. To state them is of itself
sufficient to excite horror and execration.

If the Encyclical *Quanta Cura*, which condemned the
so-called errors contained in the *Syllabus*, left the Liberal
Catholics no standing ground, it did not, as M. Raymond
found it prudent to say, at once bring the submission of
all Canadian Catholics ;* but the peril of speaking against
it is exemplified in the fate of *Le Pays*, of Montreal, to
which it proved so serious a sin as to cost it its life. The
submission may in many cases have amounted only to
silence ; a silence which did not at once become, if it is
now, absolute and complete.

· But,' says the Vicar-General, ' as the state of men's
minds would not permit the denial *(ne permet pas qu'on
touche)* of religious liberty *(liberté de cultes)*, in certain
States, without detriment to society and to the Church
herself, it is permitted to tolerate, to defend, and to swear
to observe, in the constitution, which forms a fundamental
law,† and that in virtue of the principle that the toleration of an order of things or of evil, which under certain
circumstances is to be feared, is permissible if it be a good
relatively to an opposite order of things.'‡

The meaning of this is that it all depends upon the
power of Rome to deny religious liberty to others ; and
though the liberty which simply refrains from attempting

* Nulle parole n'est elevée de leur part en opposition à celle du Vicaire du Christ
† The Pope refused this in the case of Spain.
‡ *Revue Canadienne*, 1866.

what there are no means of accomplishing is not very deep, its assertion proved highly offensive to the latter day Ultramontanes.

One of the Vicar-General's antagonists§ argues: 'It is vain to say that, in Canada, we are obliged to tolerate the liberty of worship; that it is to this liberty we owe our Catholic franchises: we reply that there is an enormous difference between *tolerating* and *defending* an *abuse*. The Catholics are entitled to say: our Church is free because liberty of worship exists, but that it is not equally permissible to grant liberty of worship to dissidents by invoking the liberty of the Catholic Church; we further reply that the Catholic Church alone has the right to liberty, because she alone is in possession of the truth; we reply finally that if M. Raymond desires to remain within the bounds of truth, and not fall into the error of the Catholic Liberal, he ought to confine himself to teaching that it is allowable to tolerate, when it is impossible to do otherwise, liberty of worship, of conscience, of speech, and of the press, but not to defend it; for to defend a thing is to recognize its rights: but it is never allowable to recognize error, though it may be endowed with forces and powers that give it predominance. If this liberty cannot be restrained, it may be left in peace; but though tolerated it must never be defended, that is to say, cause made on its behalf. If it (error) proclaims liberty of worship, and silences (étouffe) you because you are Catholic, call, as is its constant habit, attention to the liberties she grants, even invoke them if necessary, but do not make the apotheosis of these liberties, that is to say, do not defend them or make cause in their behalf; for, let us say once more that to defend is to recognize their rights, which they can possess only in proportion as they are devoted to the exclusive service of truth.'

§ Binan. Broch. Anon. Montreal, 1872.

A want of candour is not the vice of this defender of intolerance. There is a terrible and startling frankness in what he says. The rules of conduct he prescribes may easily be recognized as old familiars in actual experience. The difference is, that the ordinary disguises are thrown away, and the policy of Rome stands confessed in its most repulsive form. It is an advantage to be in possession of the programme, pure and simple, of the party in the Roman Catholic Church which, in the Province of Quebec, has reduced the liberal and national element to silence.

The Liberal School of French Canadian Catholics was fairly represented by Vicar-General Raymond. His defence of religious liberty, under the circumstances and conditions already stated—where it had long been in existence—is ingenious, and, all things considered, not lacking in a certain element of courage. He found that, in many States, a large part of the people profess what he considers false religions. The liberty they are permitted to exercise is held by the right of possession, and sometimes by the right of the strongest ; and in spite of the errors which they profess, he charitably allows that the teaching of the divine morality had not been entirely lost upon them, and that what they have retained will aid in the conservation of society.

In this state of things, liberty to dissidents to worship God in their own way Vicar-General Raymond allows to be a relative good. To proscribe them, under a non-Catholic Government, would be impossible; and under such Governments, the liberty of worship is altogether in favour of the Church, and the best thing it can do is to profit by it.

Even in countries where the faithful are in a majority, repression, besides being odious, would violate civil rights long since acquired, would bring about great disasters, and would certainly increase the number of dissidents from the Church of Rome ; it would transmute into violent hatred feelings which do not possess a character of pronounced hostility ; it would retard or prevent conversions which, in a state of peace, would take place ; besides, it would lead to the persecution of Roman Catholics in all countries where they are feeble.

For these reasons, the Vicar-General argues, liberty of worship ought not to be disturbed where it has already been established. ' No doubt,' his orthodoxy or prudence, or both combined, make him add, this liberty ' is injurious to the salvation of souls ;' but as he did not ignore the forces of existing society, he held fast to the conclusion that ' the attempt to put the opposite principle into practice would be a great evil, therefore it ought not to be made.'

Vicar-General Raymond long represented the moderation, the caution, the wisdom of the old Canadian School· He knew how to wait when action would have been rashness ; and to move, when it was prudent to move, with caution. In mixed questions, which have a civil as well as an ecclesiastical side, he knew the danger of wounding the susceptibilities of the citizens of another faith ; and he was not willing to press inopportunely doubtful points, at the risk of a repulse or a defeat. With this temporizing and tolerating spirit, it is difficult to see why he was not as good a Catholic as the loudest brawler in the opposite camp. If his policy was safe for the Church of Rome, it was well fitted to lull opposition and put to sleep, outside of the Church, that vigilance which the opposite policy of aggression in arousing.

' Away with this parody of the gospel !' cry, in full chorus, the whole pack of Mgr. Bourget's ecclesiastical coursers. ' Out upon this prudence, miserable counterfeit of truth !' The true weapons of the Church, they

insist, are protest and anathema ; and the free use which
Pius IX. has 'made of them offers the only safe example
for imitation. 'The prudence of the Vicar-General is the
prudence of the flesh, and his infallibility is the infallibility of inopportuneness, which the Vatican Council has
thrust back into the abyss of fire, out of which it had
been vomited.' *

'Liberty of conscience'—when proof is needed of so startling a proposition as this, that it is the bounden duty of civil
governments to suppress the liberty of conscience in favour
of the Church of Rome, it is better to quote textually
—'Liberty of conscience then existed everywhere, by
law or in fact; in France, in England, in Italy, in Austria,
in Belgium, in Spain, in all the countries of Europe, of
Asia, of Africa, of Oceanica, of America, except the countries where the religion of the State was pagan, schismatic, or heretic, everywhere there was liberty of conscience. It was therefore liberty of conscience, existing legally or in fact, which Pius IX. condemned,
and which he called upon princes and people to abolish
for ever. It was not an imaginary evil, which had yet to
happen, but a real and present evil which Pius IX. combatted in liberty of conscience. It was therefore M. de
Montalembert and the whole Liberal School that Pius IX.
struck when he dealt that withering blow at liberty of
conscience. And when M. Raymond, in 1869, proclaimed
this same liberty of conscience, as Montalembert had
done before, it was a doctrine reprobated (reprouvée) by
the Holy See which he preached and celebrated. Now,
to preach that which the Chair of St. Peter condemns
and rejects is Gallicanism and Liberalism, or we know
not what it is.'

It is a fact of supreme interest to be noted that the

* The language used is stronger than this : *l'infallibilité de l'inopportunité*, cette
infallibilité que le Vatican Council a refoulé dans l'abime de l'enfer d'ou elle venait.—
Binan, p. 32.

Ultramontanes of Quebec openly proclaim that it is the duty of the civil government to obey the instructions of the Pope to suppress liberty of conscience and to deny the right of openly professing any other religion than that of Rome. Happily they do not possess, and in this country never will possess, the supreme power necessary to put this monstrous doctrine into practice. But the Ultramontane press, Ultramontane priests, and Ultramontane professors in the chief seats of learning, cannot unite in teaching the duty of intolerance without giving a tinge to future thought that may lead to disastrous results.

These are the doctrines which, in Quebec, are now gaining the mastery. Dr. Newman disavows them; the Secretary-General of the Vatican Council lacked the audacity to stand up in the face of Europe and defend them.

'True prudence,' we are further told, 'consists in desiring only what God desires;' and what this is the Pope alone can know. If the command of the ecclesiastic were to do evil, unhappy would be the lot of him who had promised unlimited obedience.

The last pamphlet on this subject is, in some respects, the most pronounced utterance that has been made. The Abbé Pelletier finds Liberalism hanging upon every bush and lurking in every stream.† He finds proof that Liberalism has more partisans in Canada than is generally supposed, in the signs of a determination to combat the undue influence of the clergy in elections; in the disposition to deny the right of the Church to take the initiative in political questions; in a tendency observable in certain journals to advocate the separation of Church and State in our legislation on the liberty of worship and of the press; on marriage and education; on religious corpora-

† Libéralisme Catholique en Europe et Libéralisme au Canada, 1876.

tions and their property; on ecclesiastical immunities. On all these questions, he finds that Liberalism has produced bitter fruits. The Abbé Pelletier finds further proof in the unfavourable reception which the *Programme Catholique* met; for though all Catholics, he tells us, are strictly bound, by their baptism, to follow the Programme, the majority of them, on one pretext or another, refused to accept it.

Burning proofs of Liberalism M. Pelletier finds in the refusal to give the Métis, who had only rebelled for the benefit of their country, a prompt, full, and complete amnesty; in the refusal of the Federal Parliament to destroy the common school system of New Brunswick, over which in fact it had no legislative jurisdiction, in the interest of sectarianism.

Practically, this is the exposition of Liberalism which is now so current as to be almost universal in Quebec. However forced and unreasonable such an interpretation may be, the intimidating effect on the electors is the same as it would be if it were true.

The charge of Catholic Liberalism was brought against Vicar-General Cazeau on the strength of the following facts :—When the agents of Rome at Quebec thought the time had come for putting into practice the prescriptions of the encylical on the subject of the education of the young, they concluded that the way to do this was to substitute as text-books the lives of the Saints for the lives of the principal figures in Greek and Roman history ; and essays on the lives of certain saints appeared in the *Courrier du Canada*, among others that of ' the heroic Christian virgin ' Febronia.   She was represented as being despoiled of her garments, in a public place, by ruffians who assaulted her with intent.   M. Cazeau, scandalized at the idea of placing such reading in the hands of the young, sent a *communiqué* to the *Courrier* stating that he had met with nothing in Pagan authors which sinned against modesty so much as this statement in the life of a virgin saint. In doing this, his enemies said, M. Cazeau wounded Christian truth for the profit of pagan error; as if Christian truth was synonymous with a narration of an indecent assault, and that in reading Greek and Roman history one runs imminent risk of becoming a pagan. For defending classical learning, he was treated as the most pestiferous of Catholic Liberals. Though the assailants have so far failed in the part of their attack which had for its object the substitution of the lives of the Saints for classical authors, they ultimately obtained success on all other points.

One French Canadian Roman Catholic, who was educated by priests and among fellow-students many of whom were afterwards to become priests, calls upon the Ultramontanes to pause in their headlong career. 'You wish,' he says, 'to organize all Catholics into a single party, without other tie, without other basis, than that of religion; but have you reflected that by that fact alone you organize the Protestant population as a single party, and that then, instead of peace and harmony, which now exist among the elements of our Canadian population, you will bring on war, religious war, the most frightful of all wars?'*

* Wilfrid Laurier, M.P. Lecture on Political Liberalism, June 26, 1877, in the Music Hall, Quebec.

X.

THE APOTHEOSIS OF INTOLERANCE.

Rome holds with a death grasp to the dogma of intolerance, and the New School teaches it, in a loud voice, and
with wearisome reiteration. Bishop Bourget, the priest
O'Donnell, the advocate Thibault, Abbé Pâquet, and a host
of pamphleteers and anonymous writers, descant at great
length, on the right and the duty of intolerance.

From the lectures of Abbé Pâquet, delivered to the students of the University of Laval,* let us see how the
rising generation is being prepared to fulfil its mission
and perform its duties: what thoughts it is being made
to imbibe, what conduct it is instructed to observe.

The students are told that it is not in France, not in
Spain, not in Germany, still less in the New World, that
the true doctrine regarding liberty is to be found but
at Rome; Rome, the only guide which Laval acknow-
ledges in the teaching of philosophy and theology. The
highest ambition which both the professor and the university have is to be the faithful echo of the Roman
doctrine.

The principal maxims of Liberalism, the students are
told, are : liberty of conscience, that is, to believe or not
to believe; liberty of worship *(culte)*, that is, to embrace
any religion we think proper; liberty of the press, that
is, to propagate and defend error as well as truth, evil
as well as good. Liberty of the press is stigmatized as
another name for license. The Abbé leaves the students at
liberty to think; but they are bound to think the truth as

* La Libéralisme.

it is expounded at Rome, on pain of being deprived of the right to think at all. To proclaim liberty of thought, in matters of religion, is an impiety: so teach the doctors at Rome; so teaches this doctor of theology at Laval. God has manifested the truth through the Roman oracles, and we are bound to accept it, and to believe it in the sole and only sense in which it has been revealed. 'Therefore, we are bound to believe what God has certainly revealed.' 'No man has the right or the liberty to believe or to refuse to believe what has certainly been revealed by the God of truth, or by the organ which he has chosen to promulgate and explain his law; this right does not exist.' 'Listen then to the voice of faith manifested by the mouths of the Sovereign Pontiffs, the infallible organs of revealed truth.'

This doctor of theology distinguishes two kinds of tolerance: one civil, the other religous; one political, the other theological. Civil tolerance consists in a government according to its subjects the permission publicly to profess whatever religion they please. 'To say that it is possible to find salvation in different religions, whether they be called Catholic, Greek schismatic, Lutheran or Calvinistic, this is religious or theological toleration.' In the mouth of an individual, this doctrine, the students are told, is blasphemous and absurd. On the lips of a sovereign or the administrators of a government, it is an error and an impiety; because a sovereign or a Government, of whatever form, cannot accord what it does not itself possess ; the right to do evil, to teach, to believe, or to profess error. . . .

'Civil laws may, and ought, in certain circumstances, to tolerate what God and the Church reprove; but to create it, to give it the right of action, never ; to this reason and faith are opposed.' 'Man has neither the right nor the liberty to refuse to believe, or to choose at his will, be--

14

tween the different religions ; ' and a sovereign or a government has not, any more than the individual, this right or this liberty.   The chiefs and leaders of a people ought, like all other men, to respect the inviolable laws imposed on the human will and intelligence, and to conform themselves thereto.

The Abbé does not think it necessary to use further arguments to prove 'that religious toleration is a gross error, an insult to reason, a blasphemy and an impiety.' ' Everywhere, and at all times, the principle of religious or dogmatic intolerance,' he confidently announces, ' will remain master of the position;' for the reason that ' it is the truth,' and 'truth is indestructible and eternal.' 'Those who reproach the Church with being intolerant of toleration, reproach her with nothing less than her right of existence.' ' As the Church cannot renounce her mission without renouncing her existence, she ought always to anathematize this teaching ' of toleration.

But even the divine intolerance of which Pius IX. and the Abbé Pâquet are enamoured may sometimes have to yield to the force of circumstances.   The Abbé admits that there may be circumstances in which the rigid application of the principle of intolerance would bring danger or lead to disaster; and then, we are told, on the authority of Mgr. Audisio, ' truth may cede its place, but not its right, to error.'   There is a scale by which the liberty of worship may be regulated, according to circumstances ; but it is a golden rule that nothing which can be withheld should ever be granted.   Liberty of conscience is assumed, according to this School, to be granted when no one is constrained to profess, in words or fact, a *culte* which in his conscience he, rightly or wrongly, regards as false. Liberty of worship may mean a worship which is confined to the family and in no way obtruded on the public ; it is relatively public when it is exercised in a place where several meet without external publicity, as Judaism and Protestantism have been in the habit of hiding themselves at Rome.

For reasons of social order, toleration may sometimes be permitted : ' To prevent evils which might disturb the peace of society, a government is authorized to permit civil liberty of worship, and it is even its duty to do so.' But it is bound, at the same time, to promote the ' true worship ' to the best of its ability. And much prudence and sagacity must be used to prevent this civil liberty degenerating into license. In a country where different religions are professed by considerable portions of the population, the government, for prudential reasons, may not insist on that unity of worship which in Spain, Italy, New Grenada, and Mexico it is bound to enforce. France, Belgium, Canada may allow some latitude ; Catholic Governments none. In a word, intolerance is to be enforced wherever there is power to enforce it ; a measure of toleration may be allowed where the government is not strong enough to withhold it. But the Church is to hold fast to the sheet anchor of dogmatic intolerance.

' To sum up,' says the Abbé, ' the Church never has been, and never will be, anything but reasonable.' And he adds, with unconscious irony : ' Reason necescessarily compels every fair-minded man to accept the principle of dogmatic intolerance. Would it not,' he triumphantly asks, ' be unreasonable to affirm at one and the same time the negative and the positive of a question, or to regard as true two contradictory propositions ?' And this shows precisely where the Church and its children are intolerant. And this intolerance ought to be avowed by every intelligent and reasonable being. For truth is one, and the Church is the depository of the truth.' The Abbé flourishes a double-edged sword ; and we venture to say he would be loud in his complaints if the weapon, wrested out of his hands, were turned against himself. If he cannot be commended for his liberality, he deserves our thanks for . his abundant candour, which comes as a warning and reads like a revelation.

No sooner has the Abbé finished his admission that the toleration of other religions besides that of Rome is sometimes allowable, to prevent social disasters, than he turns round and contradicts himself with proofs that the civil power has no right to grant what he had conceded it to be, under certain circumstances, its duty to grant. A government, he suddenly discovers, cannot proclaim civil liberty of worship, without usurping a right which it does not possess. ' It is not judge in matters of religion ; and when it allows civil liberty of worship, it usurps a right which belongs to the spiritual power ; it substitutes itself in place of the infallible tribunal of the Church.' ' To authorize the liberty of different forms of worship is to hide a profound indifference for religion under an appearance of equity and liberality : this is immoral ; the living faith is not so accommodating.' ' The supreme law of God, His will as manifested by reason and revelation, is unity of worship ;' a government, especially a Catholic government, should do nothing in the opposite direction : ' on the contrary, it is under an obligation to protect the true religion, to the exclusion of all false forms of worship ' *(cultes)*. The Abbé's apotheosis of intolerance embraces both kinds, dogmatic and civil.

Spain is instanced as an example of an entire nation opposed to allowing the open profession of any religion except the Roman Catholic, on which assumption the recent conduct of the nation in proclaiming toleration, in opposition to the protest of the Pope, affords a sufficient commentary. What was done under the Republic has, in this respect, been repeated, not without a suspicion of bad faith, under the Restoration. Neither at the one epoch nor the other could the entire nation have been in favour of prohibiting the profession of all but the Roman Catholic religion ; for it is impossible to conceive a government opposing itself to the unanimous wishes of a whole people.

Mexico, New Granada, Spain, and Italy are here represented as contesting God's superiority over man, ' since by the mouth of the Church God speaks and commands;' conduct which is characterized as ' the liberalism of the atheist, the persecutor, and the tyrant, the liberalism of Lucifer.'

Such is the teaching of the University of Laval, under the inspiration of the Vatican decrees.

The Abbé Pâquet, if we may believe his enemies, gave great offence at Rome for admitting exceptions to the rule of intolerance. The book, it is alleged, barely escaped the ban of the *Index.* If it received the commendation of the *Civittà Cattolica,* the Rev. Alexis Pelletier says, the article was inserted at the request of M. Pâquet, and by an officious person who escaped the vigilance of the R. R. P. P. editors.

The difference between the doctrines of the Old and the New School is, that the latter deny that there are any circumstances or conditions under which religious liberty is admissible. Even before the Vatican Council was held, Vicar-General Raymond took the ground that, ' considered absolutely, religious liberty is an evil, since it favours error to the loss of souls ; as an abstract principle or a supposed natural right, it ought to be condemned. Now, as in previous times, it is desirable that society should recognize only the one true religion.' So far his orthodoxy is unquestioned ; but when he proceeds to make exceptions he falls under the censure of writers who glory in the qualifying word Ultramontane.

Father Braün, a Jesuit priest of German birth, who lives at Montreal, and stands high in the estimation of Archbishop Bourget, is one of the great lights of the New School. In his work on Christian marriage, published with the express approbation of the Administrator of the diocese of Quebec, and of the bishops of Quebec and Three Rivers, he says : ' It is customary to regard Protestantism as a religion which has its rights. This is an error. Protestantism is not a religion ; Protestantism has not a single right. It possesses the force of seduction. It is a rebellion in triumph ; it is an error which flatters human nature. Error can have no rights ; rebellion can have no rights. Neither error nor rebellion can dispense with the obligation to perform a duty. Rebellion has a strict duty to fulfil ; this duty is to repent, it is to come back ; it is submission to the Church. Error ought to give up its obstinacy and make way for the truth.'

We have seen French Canada in past times, under the pressure of a strong impulse, act as a political unit ; and if the ascendancy of the New School should become complete, we should see it again. The Roman Catholics of Canada claim to-day to number 1,780,000 ; and if this were so, which we doubt, they would be nearly one half of the population. In the actual state of matters, it is idle to say that the teaching of the New School has no warning for prudent and thoughtful men.

The views I have quoted in favour of intolerance are neither accidental nor isolated. They crop up everywhere. Scarcely a lecture is delivered in the Province of Quebec by a Roman Catholic but they find a place in it. On a recent occasion,* Father Lory defined conscience as the practical judgment by which reason judges that a thing can or ought to be done, because it is good

---

* Union Catholique, Montréal. Séance du 28 Mai, 1876. This association is, I believe, entirely under the control of the Jesuits.

and just, or that it ought not to be done because it is bad. But he went on to say : ' Reason is not at liberty to embrace error ;' that is, what the Church of Rome regards as error. He undertakes to establish that : 'when truth is evident, either by means of a certain demonstration, or 'the testimony of an infallible authority,' that is, the Pope, the 'conscience is at liberty to embrace it ; when doubt exists, conscience is free to embrace one side or the other, saving always the rights of legitimate authority, to which cases of doubt ought always to be submitted ; ' ' error has no right to manifest itself.'

These, we are told, are the cases in which the conscience enjoys a liberty more or less extended : the liberty to believe what the Church of Rome holds to be truth. But, M. Lory added, this is not what is understood, at present, by liberty of conscience. ' What the Liberal School understand by this state of things, in which the State recognizes and accords an equal right of public manifestations to all religions whatsoever, to error as truth, and to citizens an equal right to practice and manifest them ; ' a state of things which he rejects as wholly unwarranted.

So far as the differences go, the truth of one Church is the error of another ; and the State has no means of deciding between them. It can only, in fairness and justice, secure to all the enjoyment of that common liberty which the Ultramontanes so fiercely denounce.

The Archbishop of Quebec, as we have seen, placed *Le Réveil* under interdict for the unpardonable crime of reporting a speech of Castelar on religious liberty.† The only words which he quotes˙ from the speech as objectionable are : Je ne suis ni Catholique, ni Protestant, mais religieux (I am neither Catholic nor Protestant, but religious). But this was not the real offence. Castelar

† Circulaire, 31 Août, 1876.

stated that, in early times, the Spanish Church had been
the most democratic in Europe, though it was orthodox
even to the admission of the Immaculate Conception. During the whole of the eleventh century there were only
about four appeals to Rome; the people named their
bishops and the king confirmed them ; liberty existed in
the national Councils of Spain, as was attested by the
annals of the Council of Toledo, where the ecclesiastica
discipline of the nation was regulated, without the aid of
Rome and against her opposition. He described how
the spirit of intolerance attacked, in turn, the Jews, the
Maories, the Protestants. Turning to himself, Castelar
remarked that he received his first education from ministers of religion, but that on his entrance on practical life,
at twenty-two, he soon came to see that 'true liberty cannot exist, unless it has the support of liberty of conscience. As professor, he taught this doctrine, and when
the Jesuits attacked him for doing so, he was sustained by
his university, which held that he was not bound to say
what was agreeable, but what was true.' But he was not
always so fortunate. Once, when the Jesuits had the upper
hand, they succeeded in driving him from the university.

So great is the crime of reprinting the speech in
which these things appear, that the Archbishop of Quebec issued an order forbidding the faithful to read the
journal in which it appeared. If *Le Réveil* had contained
an article in favour of intolerance and a denunciation of
religious liberty, it would have met a ready approval at
the archiepiscopal palace. If we escape from the practical danger of this doctrine, we owe it to the large proportion of the population who hold it in abhorrence. When a
man tells you he would take your life or deprive you of
your liberty if he had the power, you may thank him for
his candour, but you will deem it prudent to be on your
guard against his machinations.

There were at the time when this speech was re-published more appeals to Rome, from Canada, than were sent there from Spain in the whole of the eleventh century ; a fact which the Archbishop probably foresaw would create some unpleasant reflections in the minds of a people who passed through a grave crisis to obtain the right of self-government.

Ultramontanism, when it gets full swing, and is not under the influence of some local restraint, is everywhere the same.   Mgr. Gaume, a great authority in the Church, who follows in the footsteps of M. de Maistre, has published a catechism of the `Syllabus, which is much in favour in Quebec, and which is advertised as having received the approbation of the Pope.*   He defines modern Liberalism as a sect which pretends to conciliate the modern spirit with the spirit of the Church.   Having asked what are the special points on which Liberalism asks this conciliation, he replies : ' liberty of conscience ; liberty of worship ; liberty of the press ; the secularization of politics.'   To the next question comes the reply : the Church can never accept such conciliation, because ' in sanctioning liberty of conscience and equality of worship, the Church would lose her *raison d'être*, since it is apparent to the whole world that there is only one true religion.'†

In sanctioning the liberty of the press, Mgr. Gaume, by a perversion of reasoning, pretends that she would be sanctioning the liberty of doing evil as well as good.   The right to teach error—that is, what the Church of Rome does not teach—he places on the same level with the right to murder and to rob.

---

* Petit Catéchisme du Syllabus, par Mgr. Gaume.

† In the year 1869, Cardinal Antonelli, in a letter addressed to the Bishop of Nicaragua, Central America, on the subject of an attempt made to establish in that State 'freedom of education and worship,' said : 'Both of these principles are not only contrary to the laws of God and of the Church, but are in contradiction to the concordat established between the Holy See and that Republic.'

The catechumens are taught that Catholic Liberals are wolves in sheep's clothing, who compromise the gravest interests of society; and who (strange comparison) can no more be admitted to absolution than can a pestilence. Their favourite maxim, a free Church in a free State, is described as being without meaning, or as signifying 'the independence of the State towards the Church,' which the author of the catechism finds to be the essence of despotism, and an impossibility not less than the attempt to make a man live by separating his body and his soul.

If Rome is alone in possession of the truth, how is heresy to be dealt with ? ' Heresy,' says Father Giovanni Perrone, Professor of Theology at Rome, ' being a crime against the State, ought to be proceeded against by the civil power and the Inquisition.' This is the key to the meaning of Ultramontane writers when they anathematize all who advocate the separation of the Church from the State. The connection they desire is that of master and servant : the Church to direct, the State to put the directions into force. The spirit of the partnership between Pope Alexander VI. and Ferdinand the Catholic is invoked by one of the greatest living theologians of the Church of Rome ; and civil governments are asked to give to Rome the service which that monarch voluntarily rendered in Spain, and which Charles V. extended to the Netherlands, at the expense, as it proved, of a revolution, in which a gallant people released itself from the Spanish yoke and proved its right to breathe the free air of national independence. If the blood-stained crimes of the governments which aided Rome to establish the Inquisition are not likely to be repeated in our day, it is not because the emissaries of Rome would not do their best to bring about the revival.

XI

THE MARRIAGE RELATION.

The New School claims for the Church of Rome absolute power over all questions of marriage ; not only when
the contracting parties are both Roman Catholics ; not
only in mixed marriages—when one is a Roman Catholic
and the other a Protestant—but also over the marriages
of heretics. ' It is,' says Bishop Bourget, ' for the Church
and not the State to make laws concerning marriage ; '
and he contends 'that the civil power cannot, in any
way, render null a marriage contracted by the Church :
that it can neither control nor annul the dispensations
which the Church judges proper to give for the purpose
of removing the impediments which she alone can put in
the way of marriage.' He liberally allows that the State
may legislate on the civil effect of marriage, provided she
respects the knot the Church has tied, for with this it is
not, in any case, permitted to interfere. Civil marriage
is stigmatized as concubinage ; ' divorce, though allowed
by the civil law, is a crime to be punished with eternal
damnation.' All matrimonial causes, the bishop further
contends, ' ought to be taken before ecclesiastical judges :
to pretend the contrary is to incur censure.'* The Jesuit
priest Braün has written a book of a hundred and seventy-
nine pages to prove that the Church is everything and
the State nothing. Of this work a single sentence will
give the key note : ' The legislation of the Church on
marriage comprehends not only marriages between

* *Approbation des Instructions Dogmatiques sur le Mariage Chrétien.* Montréal, le
1 Mars, 1873.

Catholics, but also mixéd marriages and the marriages of heretics with one another.' He appeals to the Council of Trent to show that any one who states that marriage causes do not belong of right to ecclesiastical judges, by that fact comes under anathema. It is quite true that the Council of Trent did go to this extent ; but that all the decrees of the Council of Trent have the force of law in Canada is an assumption which has certainly not yet been proved. It would be about as pertinent to quote an Ukase of the Emperor of Russia to prove the obligations of Canadians on the question of marriage or any other question, as to speak of the Council of Trent being binding on a country in which its disciplinary decrees were never received. And yet three bishops gave their sanction to all the assumptions contained in Father Braün's work : the Archbishop of Quebec, the late Bishop of Montreal, and the Bishop of Three Rivers. The Archbishop recommended it ' as containing an excellent *résumé* of the doctrine of the Church on this great sacrament.' The Bishop of Three Rivers concludes that the science and the logic of the author will so well serve the cause of truth that the latter will ' victoriously resume those rights which prejudice and error have long since suppressed or overshadowed.' Bishop Bourget, who is never to be outdone by any rival, when on any question everything is claimed for the Church and everything denied to the State, particularly recommends the study of this book to the people of his diocese ; considering, as he does, that an imperious duty is laid upon him to raise a voice of warning against ' the fatal errors concerning marriage which cause such terrible evils wherever they are put in circulation.' The logic of the author, which the Bishop of Three Rivers estimates so highly, is a little misty. Take an example : ' The contract is the marriage, the sacrament is the marriage, therefore the contract is the sacrament.' If you allow a logician a major and a minor which directly contradict one another, what possible perversity is there which he could not prove ?

Here we have a definition of the true sacrament of marriage : ' Whenever there is a legitimate matrimonial contract between a man and a woman, there is a true marriage sacrament among Christians.' ' The sacerdotal benediction is not essential to the sacrament ; . . . the essence of the sacrament consists in the act of the celebration of the marriage by the consent of the parties ; . . . Christian marriages are valid though they have not been blessed by a priest.' ' The priest is not minister of this sacrament or of the contract, because he does not contract.'

From these ' principles,' it results that a marriage entered into with the accompaniment of any religious ceremony, and without any conformity on the part of the contracting parties to the law of the land, is valid, provided it does not contravene some law of the Church. In fact, we are told that clandestine marriages contracted with the voluntary consent of the parties are valid unless the Church renders them null, and that to deny their validity is to incur anathema. The Church, nevertheless, prohibits such marriages. The Jesuit does but here give a fair summary of the decrees of the Council of Trent on marriage.

Father Braün commands us all, including heretics, to see that we are married according to the formalities prescribed by the Council of Trent; and when he adds that marriages otherwise performed are mere concubinages, that the contract is null, the oaths null, and that the parties are bound in conscience to separate, it becomes very important to learn what these ceremonies are. Let all persons about to marry therefore understand that the marriage can be valid only when it is performed ' In presence of the curé, or some other priest with the permission of the curé or the ordinary,' and that if there be not three, or at the very least two, witnesses to the ceremony, the knot will not hold, and must be considered as not having been tied. But let them take comfort in the reflection that all this applies only to places where the decrees of the Council of Trent have been published; where they have not been published, even a purely civil marriage, our theologian admits, is binding. But how is it possible to know whether these decrees have been published in any particular parish? The Council seems to provide for a publication in each parish separately, and that its decrees shall be binding thirty days after the first publication has been made in any particular parish. This may be Roman ecclesiastical law, but the Privy Council does not admit that it is in force in Canada.

The marriage of two Roman Catholics before a Protestant minister is not a very rare occurrence in Ontario; many such marriages have taken place. Father Braün notifies all persons who have been so married that, though they have had no suspicion of the fact, they are living in a state of concubinage. And here, strange as it may seem, this Jesuit author relies upon 'the ancient legislation of France, which still forms the law of the French Canadians,' and which he assures us does not recognize this kind of marriage. But why appeal to the civil law, if the Church alone has the right to legislate upon matrimonial questions and to adjudicate upon matrimonial causes?

The French ecclesiastical law, which was in force prior to the conquest, we have the highest authority for believing is the ecclesiastical law of Quebec to-day. Only a few years ago Bishop Bourget, by his endorsation of a work of Mgr. Destautels,* did in effect make this aver-

* Mauuel des Curés. Montreal, 1864.'

ment. But twelve years seems a long period when we consider the rapid march which Ultramontanism has been making; and the late Bishop of Montreal is now very far from admitting that the ecclesiastical law in force in France in 1759 is still in force in Canada. The counsel for the Church in the Guibord trial took the ground that all these laws were swept away by the cession of Canada to England. It is true that this contention was not finally accepted as law, but it gained some adherents even on the bench. Judge Drummond said: ' Under the ancient French law the civil tribunals could interfere in similar matters. The nation and the sovereign were Catholics ; there was a close connection between the State and the Church ; and the sovereign, as a pledge of the protection accorded to the Church, thought himself entitled to interfere, in certain cases, to prevent or repress the abuses and encroachments which the ecclesiastics sometimes committed. The cession of Canada to England changed this state of things. The guarantee of the free exercise of the Catholic religion accorded to the Canadians, and the fact that the sovereign was a Protestant, rendered as impracticable as dangerous the intervention of the State in the affairs of the Church.'

Judge Badgley took the opposite ground. ' It would be easy,' he said, 'to fix the jurisdiction of our courts in matters of ecclesiastical abuse, especially as the Court of Queen's Bench has more than once declared that it inherited the whole superior authority of the highest jurisdiction, in Canada, previous to the conquest.' That the whole civil rights of a people could be taken away by the act of cession is a notion which Judge Mondelet emphatically repudiates. Such a change, he argues, the French sovereign had no power to make, and the English Crown would not desire to make it if it had the authority to do so.

Of the French civil law relating to ecclesiastical affairs, to which Father Braün here appeals, his whole party would be only too happy to be rid at once and for ever. Under that law, unless specially relaxed for reasons of State, the marriage of minors, though performed under the sanction of an ecclesiastical dispensation, was null.* The Superior Council of Quebec annulled the marriage of Sieur de Rouville, a minor, to Louise André, who was of marriageable age, on an *appel comme d'abus*, brought by the Procureur-General, though it had been performed under cover of a dispensation by the Vicar-General of the diocese. It also enjoined all Vicars-General to observe the ordinances and canonic constitutions concerning the publication of the banns, which could be dispensed with only on the consent of parents or guardians; all curés and priests, secular and regular, were required to note, in the record of the celebration of the marriage, whether the contracting parties had parents alive or were under guardians or subject to the control of some one else; to state whether the necessary legal consent had been given by parents or guardians, or whether judicial authority had been obtained where unreasonable opposition had been made. The priest was also obliged to call in four witnesses to the marriage, ' according to the ordinances edicts, declarations, and regulations;' not accordin the Council of Trent or the canon law of Rome. The Council also exacted conformity with the declaration of the king, April 9, 1736, that the marriage should be inscribed in the register of the church where the ceremony was performed, and if for good cause the marriage were celebrated in some other church or chapel than that of the parish in which the contracting parties resided, the register was afterwards to be taken to the proper church and there inscribed. The curés and priests were forbid-

* Arrêt du Conseil Supérieur 12 Juin, 1741.

den to enter the record of the marriage on loose sheets, which could be easily removed, and the contracting parties deprived of the benefit of all the advantages of the contract of marriage. So great were the precautions taken to have the civil laws enforced, and all attempts to override them by ecclesiastical encroachments frustrated.

The ordinance of the year 1742, and the declaration of the king four years before, bring us near to the period of the cession of Canada, and they make us acquainted with the lineaments of that civil law on the subject of marriage to which Father Braün apoeals, apparently without so much as suspecting how complete a reply it furnishes to his own contentions.

The civil ordinances forbade the priests to celebrate the marriage of minors on any less evidence of the consent of parents or guardians than their written authority.†
It sometimes happened that when a projected marriage to which one of the parties was a minor became matter of notoriety, all ecclesiastics were judicially warned not to lend the aid of their ministry to its performance.‡ But while the Government took the greatest precautions to prevent ecclesiastics celebrating marriages which the civil laws discountenanced, it had from an early period held out extraordinary inducements to young persons in Canada to enter into wedlock. As early as 1660 the French king offered premiums for large families.§ From that time every father of ten living legitimate children was to receive a pension of three hundred livres, and the merit of having reared twelve children was to be rewarded with a pension of four hundred livres a year. But there was a condition attached to these premiums which showed that, in the opinion of the king, an increase

† This fact is recited in Ordonnance de 6 Fev. 1727.

‡ Ord. 6 Fev. 1727.

§ Arrèt du Conseil du Roy, 1 Avril.

15

in the number of priests, monks, and nuns was not a proper object of national encouragement: if any of the children
belonged to any of these three classes, the parents were
not to be entitled to the royal bounty.

But if the Government refused to allow the ecclesiastics
to authorize the marriage of minors by a dispensation, it
claimed for itself the right to authorize and encourage
such marriages when public policy seemed to make
early marriages desirable. Not only was the marriage of
young men of twenty years of age and under at the date
just mentioned, and of girls of sixteen and under, authorized, but these marriages were encouraged by a bounty
which passed under the name of 'the present of the king.'
The present of twenty livres to each young man and young
woman was payable on the day of marriage; and as
French parents exercised the most absolute despotism over
their children in the article of marriage, the most important event in their lives, Canadian parents were expected to copy their bad example, and every father who
neglected to get his sons married at twenty years of age and
his daughters at sixteen ought, Colbert thought, to be
subject to a pecuniary fine. But I have seen no proof that
such fines were ever imposed.

What is certain is that, in the days of the French
dominion, the civil government exercised absolute control over questions of marriage, with which bishops and
Jesuits now join in denying it any right whatever to
interfere.

The Church of Rome, pretending to possess the sole
right of legislating on marriage questions, has not, Father
Braün contends, any need to receive the authority of the
State to celebrate a marriage. But if the laws of the land
were set aside in the celebration of marriages, we know
what would happen : invalidity of the marriages, and illegitimacy of the offspring. But the object of proclaiming

these extreme doctrines is that the State may so far give way to the Church as to abandon its own rights and concede all her claims, even the most extravagant. To tell two persons whose destinies have been bound together by the ties of a civil marriage that they are bound to separate, can hardly be passed over as a piece of innocent declamation. It might not be without its effect upon some persons in this position, and the effect must certainly be of a mischievous tendency. The same remark will apply to the declaration that: 'A law which authorizes civil marriage has no force to bind the conscience; it ought to be regarded with contempt, and accursed as the crime of a government.'* This doctrine strikes at the root of civil society, and its assertion cannot be read without a deep sense of abhorrence and detestation. The authority of five saints is invoked to prove that when there is a conflict between the civil and the ecclesiastical law no account is to be taken of the civil law; advice which, if acted upon, would certainly lead those who put their faith in it into trouble. Civil marriage incurs excommunication, and separation is made the condition of absolution. From this it follows logically, and Father Braün does not shrink from the conclusion, 'that the parliaments which authorize civil marriage, labour to bring about the damnation of souls.' These are modest assumptions for a foreign Jesuit priest to set up in Canada.

Father Braün claims for the Church a supreme, independent, and exclusive power, which she holds by divine right, over marriage; from which many important conse-

---

* Father Braün might have cited the authority of the present Pope for this monstrous doctrine. 'Hardly any greater outrage on society,' says Mr. Gladstone *(Speeches of Pope Pius IX.),* 'in our judgment has ever been committed than by Pope Pius IX. in certain declarations respecting persons who are married civilly without the sacrament. For in condemning them as guilty of concubinage, he releases hem from the reciprocal obligations of man and wife.'

quences follow; the first and most important of which is that the State can have no right whatever over questions of marriage or matrimonial causes. Soon after the conquest, the British Government promised its protection to any Roman Catholic priest, in Canada, who might be disposed to enter into matrimony. Father Braün tells us that, even if a priest were to turn Protestant and then marry, his marriage would be null; 'a sacrilegious concubinage, even though all the governments upon earth should proclaim it legitimate.' If ' all parliaments, all governments, pronounced valid a marriage contracted with *dirimant** impediment and without dispensation, their sentence would have no effect.'

Let no one imagine that the pretensions of the Ultramontanes concern only the members of the Roman Catholic Church. Let any one disposed to take that view of the matter go to Father Braün for information on the subject, and he will be told that 'the universal laws of the Church are binding on heretics, and the *dirimans* impediments annul the marriages of heretics.' The general principle of the ecclesiastical law, the same authority informs us, is that: 'The Church has jurisdiction over all who have received baptism; consequently over the heretics themselves, who are bound by the universal laws of the Church.' Let all Protestants therefore understand that, as they can read no book which the bishop or the Pope does not authorize them to read, so they can only be married in the way which the Church of Rome directs, under pain of nullity, illegitimacy if there be children, eternal perdition. Father Braün may probably live to learn that his doctrines are not likely to have practical application even in the Province of Quebec.

---

* Dirimant. Tèrme de Droit Canonique. On appelle *empêchement dirimans*, un défaut, qui emporte la nullité d'un mariage. *Impedimentum dirimens.* Il y a quatorze empêchemens *dirimans.*—Trevous.

But if every person who has been baptised is thereby brought under the control of the Church of Rome, how does it happen that the baptism of Protestants was, throughout Europe and the United States, so far regarded as invalid, that when any of them sought admission into the Church of Rome re-baptism was made an universal rule ?†

But much depends upon whether decrees of the Council of Trent have been published in a particular country, province, or parish. Popes have before now dispensed with the impediment of clandestinity, for the benefit of heretics, where these decrees had not been published. Benoit XIV., in 1741, performed this friendly act for the benefit of the heretics of Belgium and persons who had entered into mixed marriages ; and in 1764, the year after the treaty of cession, Clement XIII. extended the declaration of Benoit XIV. to Canada. At the same time, this Pope declared that the other canonical impediments were fully binding on heretics, and took from the Vicars Apostolic the power of granting dispensations in this respect. As we are asked to admire the logic of Father Braün it is curious to note the conclusion he draws from these facts. ' It therefore belongs,' he says, as if it were a matter of logical necessity, ' to the Church to pass judgment on whatever regards the substance of the sacrament of marriage ; she alone has the right to judge matrimonial causes : she alone has the right to make laws concerning the conjugal tie.'

The difficulty Father Braün will find to be that States are obdurate, and refuse to be convinced by this kind of logic, though it assume a form never so perfect.

Here is a picture which Father Braün paints as one which may, in a certain eventuality, be realized in Canada: ' Let civil marriage be established in Canada, and you

† See Abbé McGuire. *Recueil de Notes Diverses.*

will see pretended wives obliged to separate from their
pretended husbands on the bed of death ; or to have their
marriage celebrated in the moments of the last agony ; or
to die without receiving the sacraments and '—here the
Jesuit becomes facetious—' be legally damned.'

With a view of taking from the State all pretence of
right to legislate on the question of marriage, otherwise
than on its civil effects, Father Braün rejects the doctrine of those theologians of his own Church who separate the sacrament from the contract.   In identifying the
contract with the sacrament and the sacrament with the
contract, he leaves no room for the State to legislate on
the contract while leaving the sacrament to the domain
of the Church.

The chapter hea led ' Refutation of the Errors of
Pothier on Marriage' is a curious though not unique piece
of reasoning.   ' Marriage,' says Pothier, 'has two distinct
characters : the sacrament and the civil contract.   As a
sacrament it ought to be clothed with formalities prescribed by the Church ; as a contract it is subject to the
secular laws, the violation of which entails nullity.   The
quality of sacrament comes after the contract, and pre-
sumes its pre-existence.'   The refutation which the head-
ing of the chapter led us to expect consists of the statement that the doctrine of Pothier has been condemned by
the Pope in the sixth article of the Syllabus.   ' Therefore,' such is the logic of Father Braün which we are in-
vited to admire, ' to pretend that the civil government has
the right to judge of the matrimonial contract is to incur
anathema.'

After the same fashion, Pothier is refuted, at length,
through many pages, which are relieved from dulness by
the astounding assumption of the author.   The opinions
of the jurisconsuls, we are told, for our instruction,
ought to be rejected.   Still, Pothier is in the head of every

advocate and the hands of every law student in Quebec, and we fear it must continue to be a text-book at Laval, until that institution be supplanted by the projected Jesuit university at Montreal. But let the law students beware : the Sovereign Pontiff prohibits the reading of a thesis taught in the University of Turin, and in which are maxims identical with those laid down by Pothier. His Holiness first catalogues the errors, and then pronounces the sentence of condemnation, to which he adds a terrible penalty. If the Pope is to rule in Canada, after he has ceased to rule in the States once qualified as Pontifical, we really do not see how the gaps which time and death make in the ranks of the bar are to be closed.

The Italian professor Jean N. Nuytz, whose work the Pope condemned in 1851, denied each and all of the pretensions of the Church of Rome on the subject of marriage. He held that the sacrament of marriage is accessory to the contract ; that it consists of the nuptial benediction, and is separable from the contract ; that the marriage tie is not, under all circumstances, indissoluble ; that the Church has not the right to remove impediments, but that this right belongs to the State, which can alone remove existing impediments ; that matrimonial causes are properly cognizable by the civil tribunals ; that the forms prescribed by the Council of Trent are not obligatory, under pain of nullity, when the civil law has prescribed another form.

So audacious a heretic could not be expected to be allowed to teach doctrines so unpalatable at Rome, in the Royal University at Turin, without being visited with spiritual censures. Pius IX., having consulted ' the Congregation of the Inquisition, supreme and universal,' condemned these doctrines as false, audacious, scandalous, erroneous, injurious to the Holy See. The faithful were forbidden to read the condemned books—for it seems there was more than one—under pain of interdict, in the case of clerks, and of the excommunication major in the case of laymen.

As Pothier was long since subjected to similar treatment, it·follows that no one can pursue the study of the law in Lower Canada, and no judge can administer the law of marriage, without coming under the penalty of the excommunication major.

The Church of Rome bases its pretensions on the assumption that marriage is regulated by divine law, of which the Church is the administrator. But these administrators of this divine law, who are themselves very human, claim the right of dispensing with the divine rules laid down for their guidance whenever they think proper to do so.

The ground on which the Church of Rome claims authority, legislative and judicial, over marriage is, that she merely interprets and puts into force the divine law. Now, a divine law must be inflexible, unchangeable, eternal. But the impediments to marriage which the Church of Rome sets up have not always been the same. For instance, the impediment of affinity created by unlawful intercourse was reduced by the Council of Trent to the second degree inclusively.*

By the canon law *ad sedem*, cousins-german were of the second degree, and by the civil law of France they were of the fourth degree ; while the issue of cousins-german were respectively of the third and sixth degrees : by the Council Latran they were restricted to the fourth degree inclusively, according to the civil computation. The wider the prohibited degrees, the more frequent the necessity of dispensations. The Popes were certainly not

---

* Il en résulte que si *Pompée* a connu charnellement *Pauline*, il ne peut plus épouser ni la mère, ni la fille, ni la sœur, ni la tante, ni la cousine germaine, ni la nièce de *Pauline* ; et *Pauline*, de son côté, ne peut épouser aucun des parens de *Pompée* qui se trouvent dans les degrés qui viennent d'être mentionnés.—Abbé McGuire.

guided by the inflexible rule of any divine law. Philip II.
of Spain was enabled, by a dispensation of the Pope, to
espouse his neice. After this dispensation had been
granted, the King and the theologians of Spain had the
strongest motive to uphold this power in the Pope; but
the Faculty of Theology at Paris did not approve of it, its
objection being grounded on the fact that though the
Pope is head of the Church universal, and is clothed
with sovereign power, he must submit to the decrees of
the ancient Councils and the canons. A Papal dispensation enabled the Queen of Portugal to marry her uncle,
and the son of that marriage, the Prince of Brazil, was
by the same means allowed to marry his aunt.†

That the prohibited degrees in the Church of Rome
were not always uniform proved that the alleged divine
law, of which she claims to be the interpreter, was a law
alterable at the discretion of men ; and the whole super-
structure built upon the pretence of administering a divine
law falls to the ground, involving in the ruin the extravagant pretensions put forth by writers of the school to
which Father Braün belongs.‡

Pope Urban VIII. authorized the Recollet missionaries in Canada to grant dispensations to the third and
fourth degree of consanguinity or affinity, to cover
polygamy among the Indians with the same sanction, and
to declare legitimate the children of polygamous marriages.§

Paradoxical as it may sound, the motive alleged was
that after the savage polygamists had been converted and

---

† Rev. Charles Buck.

‡ Coquille.

§ Dispensandi in tertio, et quarto simplici, et mixto consanguinitatis, vel affinitatis
in matrimoniis contractis, nec non dispensandi cum gentilibus et infidelibus plures
exhores habentibus. . . . . . Declarandi prolem legitimam in præfatis matrimoniis de præterito contractis susceptam. The document, dated March 29, 1635, is
given at length in Sagard, *Histoire du Canada*, on the fifth (unnumbered) page, after
p. 1005 : Paris, 1636.

baptized, each of them might content himself with that one of his former wives whom he liked best.

The Church of Rome holds that, though there is one cause for which a husband may put away his wife, or a wife her husband, neither can marry again, since the marriage tie is perpetual. The civil laws of almost all countries permit a re-marriage in the circumstances supposed, and on this point the Church of Rome and the civil authority are in direct antagonism.

Though the Church of Rome pretends not to sanction divorces, she has found an excellent substitute in the long list of invalidating impediments. She has disguised the divorces she has sanctioned, though not calling them by that name, under the denial that there had been any marriage. If it can be proved that the marriage was performed without the consent of one of the parties, that is cause for separation. By this rule, ninety marriages out of every hundred that take place in France could be annulled; for it is notorious that they are nearly all made by the parents of the parties to be married, and that those most directly interested have often little or nothing to say in the matter. The annulling of a marriage for want of consent in one of the parties would be a divorce as certainly as if it were set aside for any other cause. But the Church of Rome rejects the word, and falls back on an antecedent impediment, which, when it consists of want of consent, might be collusive and fraudulent. But if the Church of Rome were allowed to declare marriages null on account of any of the impediments which she chose to set up, marriages would often be dissolved against the consent of the parties thereto. The right to exercise this jurisdiction would bring an enormous addition to the power and the wealth of the Church. But, as we elsewhere notice, the opposition of this Church to the establishment of a Court of Divorce, which for the sake of uniformity the British Government asked that of Canada to establish, has hitherto prevailed. The abuses to which courts of divorce give rise in some of the neighbouring States have not tended to recommend these tribunals to the sober judgment of the Canadian people. At the same time, Father Braün greatly exaggerates the immoral influence of the Court of Divorce in England, when he represents married persons as frequently seeking the means of severing the nuptial tie in a premeditated commission of one of the crimes for which divorces are granted in that country. In the same way he describes Queen Elizabeth as ‚a bastard, who was equally wanting in humanity and chastity ; he stigmatizes Cranmer as a bigamist, and says that Knox counted his sister-in-law among the numerous victims of his disorders. But it was part of Father Braün's business to show that Protestantism covered itself with a multitude of crimes when it departed from the maxims of Rome on the question of marriage.

The question of a Canadian legislator being allowed to facilitate a divorce, for the most legitimate of causes, was referred to Rome, a few years ago, by M. Hector Langevin. Anterior to the confederation of the Provinces, a Court of Divorce existed in New Brunswick. Afterwards, a case came up in which the judge of the court was interested, and being unable to sit, he wrote to the Minister of Justice, Sir J. A. Macdonald, asking him to appoint a judge *ad hoc* to hear the cause. M. Langevin, a colleague of Sir John, finding all the bishops absent at the Vatican Council, wrote to one of them, asking to be instructed in his duties as legislator. The Canadian bishops, finding the question too weighty for their decision, referred it to one of the Roman Congregations which has cognizance of such matters. The decision informed M. Langevin that, as a Catholic, he was not at liberty to vote for the bill.*

This is one of the numerous cases in which Canadian legislators feel themselves obliged to enquire at Rome what is their duty to their constituents and their country.

The Church of Rome, by her general opposition to divorce, has rendered a great service to society. But she has done much to neutralize this benefit by representing celibacy as a holier state than that of matrimony, and affecting to raise the priest and the monk, on account of their celibacy, to a higher moral level than those who live in wedlock. If monks and priests and nuns are equal to saints of the first order, as Count de Gasparin has well remarked,† it is because marriage is assumed to be a bond of dishonour and the family an inferior order.

Besides, the general opposition of Rome to divorce is enfeebled by numerous sinister exceptions; by the annulment of a large number of marriages contracted by persons in high life, and on that account the more certain to spread afar the contagion of an example which often rested on no better foundation than the accordance of the act with the Papal policy at the moment. When Rome brands all divorce as immoral, she only pronounces the decree of her own guilt. She may call the divorces she pronounced with unbounded liberality in the middle ages by another name, but they are divorces none the less.

In another way Rome did her best to dissolve marriages and bastardize the offspring. When she interdicted the exercise of worship in a State and forbade the priests to confer the sacraments, among which marriage was

---

* La congrégation donna sa décision qui me fut transmise et qui déclarait entre autres choses que, comme catholique, nous ne pouvons pas voter pour une mesure de ce genre.—H. L. Langevin's evidence in the Charlevoix election case, 1876.

† L'Ennemi de la Famille.

ranked, all the marriages celebrated during the time the interdict was in force were treated as null, the innocent wives as concubines, and the helpless children as illegitimate.

Father Braün lays down a rule which would give the priest the power of saying, in a very large number of cases, whether marriages ought to be permitted or not. The Church of Rome, he observes, has always blamed the marriage of children without the consent of their parents, unless where the cupidity of the parents in a measure compels the children to take that course. The opposition of parents may be either reasonable or capricious, and we are told ' it is for the pastor of souls to judge whether the opposition of the parents is legitimate or not.' In the Province of Quebec, where a very large proportion' of the marriages are contracted at a tender age, this rule would make the priest the arbiter of the destinies of the youth of his parish.

This a new doctrine, and is part of the general aggressive movement which the New School is making. Writers who undertook to instruct young curés in the performances of their duties used to tell them that, where the father and mother opposed unreasonable objections to the marriage of children who were minors, an application to the Court of Queen's Bench ought to be made, and that, if reason for doing so were shown, the judge would authorize the marriage.‡

Every one knows that mixed marriages are no rare occurrence. They are, however, according to Father Braün, ' generally disapproved by natural and divine law ; they are besides expressly prohibited by the canon law.' And yet it is well known that such marriages are frequently sanctioned and performed by Roman Catholic priests, and even bishops. In a western county of Ontario, where there is a mixed French and English popula-

‡ Abbé Maguire, *Recueil de Notes Diverses.*

tion, one Protestant, the other Roman Catholic, a regular rule was laid down and acted upon for the education of the offspring of such marriages: the girls were to be Roman Catholics, the boys Protestants. By the operation of the law of natural selection, it came to be demonstrated, after the lapse of many years, that a large majority of the children were male; and then the Church of Rome repudiated the rule which had, by its express consent, long been acted upon.

The difficulties connected with the education of the offspring of mixed marriages are generally smoothed by special arrangement, though they are liable to be aggravated by clerical interference.

Disparity of faith is an *dirimant* impediment between a Christian and an unbaptized person; but between a Roman Catholic and a heretic, for whose conversion there is always reason to hope, the impediment does not amount to a prohibition, or render the parties incapable of contracting a marriage, although no dispensation has been obtained. But here, as at almost every other point, the laws of the land clash with the prescriptions of the Church of Rome. In 1868, Judge Monk, of the Superior Court of Montreal, decided that the marriage of a Christian with a pagan Indian contracted according to the custom of the tribe ought to be regarded as valid in Lower Canada.*

The claim of the Church of Rome alone to possess the power of creating impediments to marriage and to be the sole judge in ecclesiastical causes is one which, Father Braün at their head, the New School seems inclined to press to extremity; but to suppose that it will be granted is to suppose Canada sunk into an extremity of submission to Rome of which the world scarcely now presents an example.

* Désiré Girouard, B. C. L. *Considérations sur les Lois Civiles du Mariage.*

It is gravely argued, even by some lawyers, that matri-monial causes ought to be judged by the ecclesiastical authority; and we have seen that in one instance Judge Polette referred a cause of this kind to Bishop Cook of Three Rivers, and founded his judgment on that of the bishop. But the rule seems to be that the Superior Court of Quebec decides such questions, as it decides others that come before it, and entirely ignores the alleged ecclesiastical jurisdiction.

Under the French dominion, the right of the Church of Rome to dispense with publication of banns was strictly prohibited by the ordinance of Blois; so that in this parti-cular, as well as in a hundred others, the Church of Rome in Canada claims to-day a range of power which was denied to her before the conquest. Certainly the ordinance of Blois is too plain to be capable of misconception : ' Our subjects,' it says, ' cannot contract valid marriages with-out precedent publication of banns ; ' and Pothier says : ' when a marriage is accused of clandestinity, if the pub-lication is not well proved, the want of publication of banns has great weight in declaring it clandestine, and consequently in depriving it of civil effects.' Neverthe-less such marriages publicly solemnized would not be set aside.† By a play on the words contained in the Quebec Act, relating to the ' free exercise of the religion of the Church of Rome,' Ultramontane authors contend that the civil law of France was swept away after the conquest and the canon laws of Rome on the subject of marriage took its place.‡ On this pretension, as we have already seen, the Courts have given conflicting judgments ; but the judgment given, in final appeal, by the Privy Council is, that the law of France relative to ecclesiastical mat-

---

† James Armstrong, Advocate. *A Treatise on the Law Relating to Marriages in Lower Canada.*

‡ Girouard.

ters which was in force in Canada at the time of the
conquest remains in force to-day, subject to such modifications as have been made by statute.

It is certain that the civil law of France did impose
impediments to marriage, and these impediments no
ecclesiastic was permitted to assume to remove. Two
other kinds of impediments were admitted : one arising
from scripture, the other from the canon law. When
the impediment proceeded from the canon law, the necessity of going to Rome for a dispensation was not admitted.*

Before France adopted the prevailing opinion of the
Roman Catholic Church, divorces *à vinculo* were permitted ; afterwards divorces *mensa et thoro* were allowed.
The Canadian Senate, which has power to grant divorces
of either kind, must, in doing so, be assumed to act judicially, and though its judgment takes the form of a legislative enactment, it practically exercises the functions of
a Court of Divorce.

The fourth Provincial Council of Quebec, at which the
Provinces of Toronto and Saint Boniface were represented, in its XII decree made a *résumé* of the reasons
which the Church of Rome opposes to the establishment
of a Court of Divorce. These reasons must be equally
intended to apply to the Senate exercising the functions
of a Court of Divorce. Pius IX., in an allocution of Sept.
27, 1852, describes the doctrine of divorce as treating with
contempt ' the dignity and the mystery of the sacrament
of marriage ;' as ignoring and destroying the institution ;
as treating with contempt the power of the Church
over this sacrament; as favouring errors already condemned as heretical; as contradicting the doctrine of the
Roman Catholic Church, by treating marriage as a purely
civil contract, and assuming the right of civil tribunals to
judge of matrimonial causes.

* Coquille.

Father Braün, going beyond this allocution of the Pope and the Syllabus of 1864, plainly involves in his anathema the Canadian Senate, when it undertakes to pronounce a divorce in a matrimonial cause legally brought before it and legally dealt with.

If we regard the doctrines of Father Braün merely as a programme which the New School is desirous of realizing, it will not be without instruction and warning for us.

The validity of certain marriages performed in Ontario by Catholic priests, but in which the requirements of the civil law had been disregarded, came before the tribunals on the question of the right of succession to property. But though they were elaborately argued, no judgment was pronounced ; and the Legislature was finally called in to cut the knot of the difficulty by declaring the disputed marriages legal.   It is always undesirable, and generally dangerous, to resort to *ex post facto* legislation, and it is doubly so when the effect is to decide questions which have been before the courts and on which no judgment has yet been pronounced.   The Church of Rome had for years clamoured in vain to have these marriages confirmed.   Still, it can hardly be doubted that it was better that they should be confirmed ; for the dissolution of families by a judicial decision resting on some technical informality in the marriages would have been a social calamity.   But Father Braün would possibly not admit that the civil authority may, in this respect, do what the Church importunes it to do ; and if he were consistent he would have to declare the Legislature of Ontario anathema.

The claim of Bishop Bourget for the Church of an unlimited right of dispensation is one which was not admitted when Canada was a French colony.

16

XII.

APPEALS TO ROME.

The nearer Canada draws to Rome, the more frequent are appeals to the Roman jurisdiction. The fifth Provincial Council of Quebec accepted, in the most absolute manner, the decrees of the Vatican Council. The Council, in the words of Archbishop Taschereau, accepted in the most absolute way everything that was defined by the Vatican Council and especially on the infallibility of the Roman Pontiff. This official act binds in a special manner the Church, already bound before, of which the Council was the local organ. To appeal to an infallible judge the temptation is of course very great.

Between the infallible and the fallible utterances of the Pope, Canadian Ultramontanes make no distinction; they do not even admit that a Pope who is infallible in his teaching office, on the subject of faith and morals, can be fallible in anything.

In accepting absolutely everything the Vatican Council decreed, the fifth Provincial Council of Quebec accepts and echoes the declaration ' that by the appointment of our Lord, the Roman Church possesses a superiority of ordinary power over all other Churches, and that this power of jurisdiction of the Roman Pontiff, which is truly episcopal, is immediate,' and to which all are bound 'to submit, not only in matters which belong to faith and morals, but also to those that appertain to the government and discipline of the Church throughout the world.'

This leaves no room for the operation of any guarantees for the protection of national or civil rights. The right to prevent discipline, wholly under the control of Rome, being exercised to the injury of the nation, which has at different times, and in nearly all countries been enforced, is, at one stroke, swept away.

In accepting, in a spirit of absolute submission, all the definitions of the Vatican Council, the fifth Council of Quebec accepts the declaration 'that it is permitted to no one to interpret the sacred Scriptures contrary to' the decree of the Council of Trent concerning interpretation, 'nor contrary to the unanimous consent of the fathers.' But what if such unanimous consent has no existence? The declaration is remarkable chiefly for its pronounced intolerance.

Further, the Provincial Council necessarily accepts the statement that the Church 'derives from God the right and the duty of proscribing false science,' of which the Church is the sole judge. Does the Church still hold that the science of Gallileo was false? If not, when did she acknowledge her error? Are we to stop our geological investigations, or hide the discoveries to which they lead?

The Provincial Council also necessarily accepts and echoes the declaration that the Pope 'is the supreme judge of the faithful, and that in all causes, the decision of which belongs to the Church, recourse may be had to his tribunal, and that none may re-open the judgment of the Apostolic See, than whose authority there is no greater, nor can any lawfully review its judgment.' And that no appeal from the judgments of the Popes to general Councils is lawful.

This declaration of the Vatican Council is already bearing abundant fruit. Appeals to Rome are heard of almost every day, and some of the judges evidently look with concern upon the possibility of their judgments being condemned at Rome. Judge Routhier recently stated, on the Bench, with evident pride and satisfaction, that it was not true, as had been reported, that one of his judgments had been condemned at Rome; that on the contrary, it had been greatly praised there; only one of the grounds on which it was based had been condemned. He had evidently made personal enquiries on the subject at the centre of Papal authority.

M. Langevin submitted to receive instruction from Rome as to what his duty was as a Canadian legislator in a particular instance. M. Tremblay appealed to Rome asking to have adjudicated upon a cause arising out of an election in which he was a candidate, and which he complains that the Archbishop did not decide with promptitude, or show any disposition to decide at all. Sometimes the priests are unable to tell the electors for which candidate they ought to vote till the question has been sent to Rome and an answer received. At the Montreal West election, 1876, his eminence Cardinal de Angelis was asked whether it was permissible for Roman Catholic electors to vote for one of the candidates who was a Freemason. When the question was put it was explained that the other candidate was out of the question, and that the interests of the Church seemed to require that the prohibition of Roman Catholics to vote for a Freemason should in this instance be removed. The response was that, under the circumstances, it was permissible to vote for a Freemason.* When a letter appeared in a Toronto journal, March 17, 1876, under the signature of 'An Ultramontane,' the same Cardinal being appealed to, gave an elaborate opinion on its merits from the Roman standpoint. The *Courrier du Canada,* rejoicing in the possession of the Papal benediction as a good Catholic journalist, is nevertheless not quite infallible. One day the editor, feeling the need of ecclesiastical guidance in the treatment of poli-

* *Le Nouveau-Monde* and *L'Union des Cantons de l'Est*

tico-religious questions having reference to the alleged undue influence of the clergy, wrote to the Archbishop of Quebec for instructions. The Archbishop replied, August 14, 1876, that the fundamental points in dispute having been referred to Rome for decision he could not properly interfere. But, as everything had been said on both sides, he thought the decision of Rome should be awaited in silence. Another Quebec journalist (*Le Canadien*), who is painfully and belligerently orthodox, threatened, September, 1876, to appeal to Rome if he should be condemned in Canada for his treatment of the same question.

Appeals to Rome come from all sides. A pastoral of the late Bishop of Montreal was recently appealed against. The violence of the Ultramontane bishops and priests was appealed against. The question how far the clergy are entitled to interfere in political elections was sent for decision to Rome. Questions concerning the Canadian Institute of Montreal were referred to Rome, both by laymen and ecclesiastics. Questions of University education, raised by the Jesuits, were referred to Rome. When there is a question of the canonic erection of parishes, an order from Rome is awaited as the signal for action; and when a Canadian bishop issues a decree of erection it goes to Rome for revisal, and when it comes back, such revised decree obtains, by a special legislative enactment, the force of law in the Province of Quebec. Deputations to Rome are constantly taking place. Authors, pamphleteers, journalists, who fall into the errors signalized by the Syllabus, are denounced to the Holy Office, or their writings are placed under the ban by a more summary act of some agent of Rome in the Canadian Episcopate.

When the Roman jurisdiction is invoked, it is not often by way of appeal; in the majority of cases the matter in contestation has not been previously decided in this country. Liberals and Conservatives alike rush to Rome, for redress which they could better and more speedily obtain at home. These appeals to Rome, by investing a foreign authority with a power and an influence it does not naturally possess, tend to repress the national spirit and un-Canadianize the people.

A Montreal priest* stands ready, if the Pope should disavow a literary performance of his *(La Comédie Infernale)*, to curse it himself. In a letter to the Pope, June 13, 1872, he says : ' You are the judge of consciences, the doctor of faith ; yours are the words of eternal life ; judge you my book. If you condemn it, I also will curse it. If, on the contrary, you do not disavow it, I will thank the author of all good for having given me courage, and armed me with truth and justice.' Surely there can be no more effectual way than this of saying that the Pope is the Church and something more than the Church : a God-man whose ' words are eternal life !'

And the Pope not unfrequently interferes, or authorizes the bishops to interfere, in the civil affairs of Canada. By an apostolic decree of December 22, 1865, the Bishop of Montreal was authorized to divide that city into as many parishes as he might judge necessary ; and each new parish, including that of Notre-Dame, which was already in existence, was to be administered, not by the Seminary, but by priests whom the Seminary might present to the Bishop for approbation.†

A few months later, Bishop Bourget announced his intention to act upon the pontifical direction.‡ He explained the nature of a parish, as consisting of an ecclesiastical *arrondissement*, formed by the spiritual authority

* Alph. Villeneuve.

† Bishop Bourget. Lettre Pastorale, 26 Avril, 1866.

‡ Lettre Pastorale, 23 Mai, 1866.

and added, that when this ecclesiastical division obtains the recognition of the Government for civil purposes, the canonic parish acquires certain civil prerogatives. But, as there was no probability that the Government would recognize the new parishes to be created in pursuance of an order from Rome, the Bishop added that this consent was not always necessary, and in certain cases it might even be considered inopportune.

The decree of Bishop Bourget erecting the new parishes in the city of Montreal was sent to Rome, to receive the assent of the Pope, with or without amendments. In point of fact, it was amended there, and in its final form was published, in each of the new parishes, in 1874.

The Legislature of the Province of Quebec, to make doubly sure that the work of Rome could not be open to question, passed an Act,§ the English version of which contained this marginal reference : ' Decrees amended by Our Holy Father the Pope are binding.' It has been alleged that this marginal reference is erroneous ; that there is nothing in the text on which it could properly be based. This is certainly not true of the French version. The nature of the bill is pretty good guarantee that it was drafted in French, and that the English version is a translation. The French text fully justifies the marginal note :

' Chaque paroisse, ainsi reconnue, l'est sujette aux dispositions exprimées dans le décret d'érection qui la concerne tel que amendé par le saint-siége et publié en 1874 dans telle paroisse.'

The marginal note is absent from what we must assume to be a new English edition ; and, strange to say, the text is now different from that just given in French. It reads : ' Each parish so recognized is so, subject to the provisions set forth in the decree of erection which re-

§ 38 Vic. cap 29.

spects the same.' This is very nearly, if not absolutely, nonsense. The chief alteration in substance is the omission of all reference to the decree having been amended by the Pope. But the fact that the decree was amended by the Pope remains, and the provisions of that decree are recognized. So that the facts, as avowed in the French version and in the English marginal note, still subsist in all their force.

The Ultramontanes pretend that the civil government is bound to recognize whatever parishes the bishops, acting in conjunction with the Pope, may choose to erect. Very important consequences would follow the erection of new parishes, where the right to collect tithes depends upon their existence. It might thus lie in the power of the Pope to say whether the people, in a particular section of the Province of Quebec, should be compelled to pay tithes or not.*

If we may judge by the difficulty of obtaining anything like reliable vital statistics in Ontario, it would probably be difficult to dispense with the practice of requiring the parish priests of Quebec to keep registers of baptisms, nuptial benedictions, and funerals, and to furnish a copy to the Government. In France, the curial registers were dispensed with in 1792, and civil registers were established. The French clergy appear to have kept *les registres de l'état civil* fairly well, though some signal exceptions have been pointed out.† The reasons for taking the registers from the French clergy and placing them in the keeping of civil officers arose out of a social complication to which the Revolution had given rise. The priests who had taken an oath to observe the new constitution fell

---

* ' Il ne peut y avoir dans le Bas-Canada de paroisse purement canonique, à moins qu'elle ne soit privée et des registres de l'état civil et des moyens de percevoir la dime.'—Judge Baudry, *Code des Curés.*

† *Revue des Deux Mondes,* 15 Mars, 1874.

under the suspicion of the reactionists. The latter considered a priest who had taken the oath to be incapable of administering a sacrament, and they took their children, clandestinely, to nonjuring priests. The result was a number of clandestine baptisms, of which no authentic record could be kept.

If the priests, in the Province of Quebec, were to refuse to give, for civil purposes, a copy of the parish register, on the pretence that they are not civil officers of the State, much embarrassment might be created. The Ultramontanes did raise this objection when Notre-Dame of Montreal was divided into a number of parishes, and it may be raised again. But the law makes the priests civil officers, in requiring them to keep the *registres de l'etat civil;* and as such they are universally recognized by the courts. At first, registers were refused by the Government to parishes erected in defiance of the civil law ; but an appeal to Rome gave a complete triumph to the Church. The example of this success has probably done much to increase the number of appeals to Rome.

XIII.

THE BISHOPS CLAIMING POLITICAL CONTROL.

The united Roman Catholic Episcopate of Quebec instructed the clergy, in a joint pastoral, dated September 22, 1875, how to proceed in obtaining control of Parliamentary elections, and thus practically make the State subordinate to the Church, and coerce it into obeying her behests.

The joint letter assumes that the Church is a society perfect in itself, distinct and independent of civil society, having legislators, judges, and power to enforce its laws. But, the pastoral proceeds, 'not only is the Church independent of civil society, she is superior by her origin, her extent, and her object.' 'A civil society embraces only a single people; the Church has received for her domain the entire world,' with the mission to teach all nations. 'The State is therefore in the Church, and not the Church in the State.'

More of this: ' By the nature of things, civil society finds itself indirectly but in truth, subordinate ; for not only ought it to abstain from everything that places an obstacle to the final and supreme end of man, but it ought to aid the Church in her divine mission, and if necessary protect and defend her.' Besides, is it not evident that even the temporal happiness of nations depends on truth, justice, morality, and consequently all those truths which are confided to the Church ? '

This subordination, the bishops in their liberality admit, leaves the State independent in its own sphere.

But what is its sphere? Where are the barriers which it is forbidden to overleap? It must not touch any question of morals.

Who are the legislators and judges in this independent society, which has the whole earth for its heritage, many parts of which it has cultivated so badly that it ought to be ejected therefrom for neglecting the duties of the husbandman which it undertook to perform over eighteen hundred years ago? The answer of the bishops is : ' The power of legislation exists in a supreme degree in the Sovereign Pontiff;' and General Councils possess the same power, provided they are convoked by the Pope, presided over, and confirmed by him. It is nevertheless true that the right of presiding over many General Councils was denied to the Pope.*

From the Pope to the bishop is but a step. They have, the bishops of Quebec say, been established by the Holy Spirit to rule the Church of God ; and in their respective dioceses they have the ' power to teach, to command, to judge ; a power which is nevertheless subordinate to that of the chief of the Church, in whom alone resides the plenitude of apostolic power and doctrinal infallibility. Priests and laymen owe bishops docility, respect, and obedience.'

From the bishops to the priests is the next and last step. Each priest, regularly appointed, ' has a rigorous right to the respect, the love, and the obedience of his flock; ' obedience without limit.

---

* At the Council of Nice, he had to take a fourth place ; at the first and second councils of Ephesus, Cyrillus and Dioscorus, the Patriarchs of Alexandria, presided, in presence of the Pope's legates; at the Second Synod of Constantinople, the Bishop of Menas presided, against the wishes of the Pope, though the ' Greek Schism ' had not then taken place ; at the Council of Agulée, a town of Italy, St. Ambrose, Bishop of Melon, presided ; the Archbishop of Carthage presided at the Council of Carthage, where it was decreed (says Coquille) quil n'etait permis à l'Evêque de Rome, de recevoir les excommuniez par les évêques d'Afrique, et que quiconque pourvoiroit audit Evêque Romain feroit excommunié.—*Discours de droits ecclesiastique et de l'Eglise Gallicane·*

The hierarchy, the theocracy, is complete.

It is the priest that must come in contact with the flock; it is he who must carry out the instructions of his ecclesiastical superiors, by reading and explaining circulars and pastorals at the altar, and by enforcing the instructions they contain through the confessional.

The refusal of the sacrament to a disobedient elector would, Ultramontane writers tell us, be announced in the secrecy of the confessional.

The sum of the directions in the joint pastoral of the bishops as to the part which the priests are to play in politics is, that they are, in certain cases, of which they are necessarily to be the judges, to direct the electors how to vote under pain of spiritual censures.

The priests are to do more. 'They may and ought to speak not only to the electors and candidates, but even to the constituted authorities.' And all this is to be looked on, not as converting the pulpit into a tribune, but as enlightening the consciences of the faithful. When the priests speak to the constituted authorities, they are, of course, to speak with the authority of an independent society which is superior to civil society.

Such is the pastoral letter of the united Roman Catholic Episcopate of Quebec, which the bishops themselves issued with misgivings and trepidation, their better judgment seeming to be overpowered by some mysterious influence.

Bishop Bourget, when he speaks alone, is always more himself than when his voice is mingled with the voice of the rest of the Episcopate. In promulgating the decrees of the fifth Council of Quebec, among some sensible advice, he gave the most arbitrary directions. He told the electors that they would have to render a rigorous account to God for all the evil which a bad representative of whom they made choice, though they knew him to be unworthy and incapable, may do. The Bishop remarks that an elector who sells his vote ought to be deprived of the franchise ; a reasonable suggestion, and one which he de-serves credit for having made before it became popular. He also tells the electors that they ought to consider themselves obliged to vote, since the right to do so is given to them for the good of the country; though he admits there may be legitimate causes for abstention. When money has been corruptly received for a vote, it is to be given to the poor, as an act of penitence. The choice of a candidate is to be determined without the bias of a party spirit, prejudice, or interest. The candi-date is to be independent of all parties, ' who are intent only on their own interests and not those of the country.'

But there are other parts of the pastoral in which Bishop Bourget betrayed the secret that he was thinking little about the country and much about his Church. The candidates to be elected are, after all, men who would prove inflexible in what are called the rights and liber-ties of the Church of Rome. No one who sustains what the Church calls errors is to be elected ; no one who challenges the right of the priests to interfere with the menace of spiritual censures in elections, or to instruct electors or candidates how they are to perform their duties; no one who desires a separation of Church and State ; no one ' who sustains propositions condemned by the Syllabus ;' no one who rejects ' the intervention of the Pope, the bishops, and the priests in the affairs of governments, as if these governments were not subject to the principles which God has revealed to the Church for the good administration ' of affairs.

The list of those whom the electors are forbidden to vote for includes : all who affirm that the Church has nothing to do with political questions; all who ' criticise and censure the mandates and circulars of the bishops and the instructions of pastors relative to elections, and who, in spite of their protestations in favour of religion, effectually and openly favour journals, books, societies, which the Church condemns; all who dare to say that the priests ought to confine themselves to the Church and the sacristy, and who form part of any organization which aims to prevent them from teaching in their instructions the principles of sound politics, as the Church herself teaches;' or that a Canadian Bismarck may arise to mete out to the clergy who interfere in elections the measure that has been meted to them in Germany and other countries.

It is not quite clear that any parliament could be elected at all under the restrictions here imposed. The Legislature of Canada, under the late legislative union, long since pronounced in favour of a complete separation of Church and State; and the declaration, occurring in the preamble to a bill, was, we believe, made unanimously. The adoption of the Syllabus for a political programme would be a very simple proceeding; but if the Government must receive its impulse from Rome, the forms of a constitutional government would cease to afford any guarantee for the preservation of civil liberty, and the empty ceremonial might as well be dispensed with.

The assumption contained in the joint letter of the bishops, that the State is in the Church, is a repudiation of an ordinance passed nearly half a century ago. It is entitled 'an ordinance forbidding the pretended Vicars-General of the chapter of Quebec, and all the curés, to publish any mandate or manifesto which emanates from the pretended Vicars-General, under pain of the forfeiture of their temporalities.'*

The Church of Rome has a long memory, and she lets pass no opportunity of pushing her pretensions. For nearly a century and a half it was not deemed prudent for the

Ordonnance des Intendans du Canada, Janvier 6, 1728.

Church to take up ground directly in opposition to this ordinance, in which we read : ' The Church being in the State, and not the State in the Church, it makes part of the State, without which it could not exist.'

But perhaps the bishops had more particularly in view some offending theologians of their own Church in Quebec, who, only three or four years before, asserted the contrary of the proposition contained in the joint letter. They said : ' The Church was received into the State for the good of the people of whom it is composed.'†

If the New School, to which the whole Episcopate of Quebec seems to have given a more or less hearty adhesion, can conquer the State on which it is now making war as easily as it silenced the recalcitrant within the bosom of the Church, the day of its temporary triumph—for it could only be temporary—is not far off.

The doctrines of the New School are extending to the other Provinces. New Brunswick, to which Bishop Bourget has sent a number of priests, has caught the contagion. Bishop Rogers, of Chatham, has gone as far as Bishop Bourget in claiming for the Church the right to an absolute direction in political as well as in religious matters.‡

An occurrence took place which obliged Bishop Rogers to speak, and he could only do so in one way without placing himself in direct opposition to the eight bishops

---

† Quoted in *Quelques considérations sur les réponses de quelques théologiens de Québec aux questions proposées par Mgr. de Montréal de Mgr. de Rimouski.*

‡ In a letter published by him, in the *Saint Lawrence Advance*, February 24, 1876. As I find this letter in a French paper (*Le Courrier du Canada*, March 15, 1876), and as a retranslation might fail to restore the exact words of the original, I shall, to prevent cavil, give the words as I find them :—' Chacun est tenu de se conformer à la loi de Dieu, en politique comme dans les autres matières, suivant que cette loi dicte à sa conscience qui est bien ou mal dans les différents cas, dans lesquels il est appelé à agir. Pour le catholique, c'est l'Eglise—par la voix de ses pasteurs légitimes et surtout de son premier pasteur, le Pape—qui est l'interprète autorisé de la loi de Dieu pour sa conscience, non seulement en matière de foi, mais encore dans la morale, qui comprend tout acte humain, comme nous l'avons vu plus haut.'

of Quebec. A correspondent of a Chatham journal, writing under the signature of 'Juan,' and calling himself a Catholic, criticised the conduct of the Bishop of Montreal in compelling the curè of Boucherville to read the joint letter of the bishops from the altar, and contrasted his conduct with that of the Bishop of Chatham, a compliment which the latter found it impossible to accept. 'Juan' had committed the offence of claiming for each elector the right to think and act for himself in political matters; for his own part, he was not prepared to obey the Bishop of Montreal or any one else in this particular. Bishop Rogers, in reply, tells him that he, like everyone else, is bound to conform to the law of God in political as well as other matters; and what that law is he is to learn from the Church, speaking through its legitimate pastors, and above all the Pope, the authorized interpreter of the law of God, not only in matters of faith but also in those of morals, in which every human act is comprised. If the Church is to direct and control every act of a man's life, there is an end of individual liberty.

The Bishop of Rimouski appeared on the political stage, with a timely letter to the clergy and faithful of his diocese, when the elections to the Quebec Legislature were about to take place, in the summer of 1875. He constructed a Syllabus of errors, which every candidate was to undertake not to fall into himself, nor to follow a party which defended them, orally or in writing. This Syllabus contained six articles which, translated from a negative to a positive form, sustained the assertion that it is not dangerous to introduce religious principles—that is, the interference of the clergy—in political contests; that the Legislature has no right to interdict the pastors of the Church from interfering, with spiritual censures, by way of direction to voters at legislative elections; that it is not allowable to practise moral independence in poli-

tical questions; that the civil authority has no right to limit
the ecclesiastical power; that the functions of the clergy
are properly not confined to the sacristy; that it is not
desirable to have mixed schools in which no religion is
taught, and to take from the clergy the control of education.

The object of the partisans of the condemned doctrines,
Bishop Langevin assumes, is to diminish the influence of
the clergy, to subject the Church to the control of the
State, and to favour the license—he will not allow that it is
a liberty—of free discussion. He admits that among the
partisans of the so-called liberal doctrines there are to be
found men honourable, peaceable, and exemplary; but he
is kind enough to regard them with the pity due to the
dupes of worse offenders. The faithful are warned not
to vote for anyone who sustains principles which the
Church has condemned, and the command is backed by
the assertion of divine power: 'I am judge and doctor,
divinely appointed.'

To such a direction so given, the only response is
obedience. The meaning of Bishop Langevin's assumptions, like that of his colleagues in the Episcopacy, is that
the whole political power of the country belongs of right
to the Church, a doctrine against which a whole people
will one day rise up to protest.

But is the bishop, even according to the Roman
theory, divinely appointed? The Pope, it is admitted by
the Ultramontanes, is the sole judge, and he says that,
though bishops are successors of the apostles, they hold
their dioceses by an ecclesiastical, not a divine title.*
The claim of divine right, which the French representatives put forward at the Council of Trent, was rejected in
favour of the Pope, whose influence would have been
lessened in France if French bishops held their dioceses
by a divine title.

* Gladstone. Speech of Pope Pius IX., p. 39.

17

ʹ Bishop Langevin fortifies his position by an extract from the fourth Provincial Council of Quebec, which contains the strange argument, that to separate religion and politics would be to banish God from civil society, and free the conduct of politicians from His holy law. This is to put the priest in the place of God, and it is easy to conceive what the effect of such teaching must be on the mind of the simple, docile, and well-intended *habitant.*

Bishop Langevin is a two-sided man. What he now commands, he not long since interdicted. The Bishop Langevin of 1875 and the Bishop Langevin of 1867 are wide as the poles apart. At the latter epoch he condemned the abuse of the pulpit in political matters, and absolutely interdicted the priests of his diocese: to apply general principles to a candidate, a party, or a class of electors; to wound the feelings of anyone by personal remarks; to name or designate the candidates in the pulpit, or to pronounce on their respective merits; to counsel or order the faithful to vote for one candidate in preference to another.*

Six years after the time when Bishop Langevin issued this interdiction to the clergy of Rimouski, no layman could repeat his affirmations except at the expense of being denounced as impious, an enemy of religion and the clergy.

The late Archbishop of Quebec, M. Baillargeon, at the same time (1867) is reported to have replied to a person who went to consult him on this subject : ' You ought to vote in accordance with your own conscience, and not that of another.'† Between Archbishop Baillargeon and his successor, M. Taschereau, there seems to be a gulf which a century would be consumed in digging. And yet, in the face of these facts, we should not have to travel far

---

* Quoted by Hon. L. A. Dessaulles in *Legrand Guerre Ecclésiastique.*

† Dessaulles.

to find a number of persons ready to maintain that the Roman Catholic Church of Quebec is to-day what it has ever been.

Even Bishop Bourget has made almost as great an advance. At the election of 1867 he instructed the clergy to 'remain neutral in questions which in no way touched religious principles;' for he added, 'there is a great difference between the direction: "vote or do not vote for such a candidate," and this other: "vote for him who in your soul and conscience appears to you qualified to sustain the interests of religion and of the country." This was, in effect, a notice to the clergy not to name or express a preference for any candidate, but to leave the choice to the cónscience and intelligence of the elector. So long as the bishop adhered to this position, his conduct was not open to unfavourable criticism. · He is now completely at the opposite side of the circle.

These pastorals produced the effect that was expected from them; they caused the parish priests everywhere to take sides, in elections, in favour of one party and against another. An appeal was made to Rome to stay this interference of the clergy in elections ; and it was reported to be so far successful as to cause a *monitum* to be addressed to the Archbishop of Quebec on the subject. That a *monitum* came from Rome, the Bishop of Three Rivers denies; but it is certain that the Archbishop was called upon for explanations, and a pastoral which he afterwards issued, May 25, 1876, shows that something had occurred to cause him to make a temporary change of tactics.

This pastoral was in direct opposition to the Joint Letter of September, 1875. It forbade the priests to discuss political questions in the church or at the church door; to volunteer any advice on the subject of elections, under any circumstances, and even to answer questions on the subject which might be put while the priests are on pastoral visits or in attendance on the sick. It went so far as to deny the priests the natural liberty of defending themselves from attack in the press; a degree of severity which is equally unjust and unreasonable.

The question was naturally asked, whether the pastoral of the Archbishop was intended to supersede the Joint Letter of September; a question which the Archbishop himself hastened to answer. His pastoral, he said, neither revokes nor supersedes the joint letter. He protested against the insinuation that he regretted having signed the collective pastoral. ' The principles there propounded,' he said, ' are, in my eyes, too true and too certain for me ever to regret having written and signed it.' And he enters into a further defence of this united act of the Episcopate. It is impossible to agree with him that there is no contradiction between the two documents; nor does his recalling the fact that the collective letter is addressed ' to all Catholics of the Province of Quebec,' while the pastoral of May 25 is intended ' to enlighten the electors on certain duties which they have to perform at elections, and to put them on their guard against certain disorders,' produce that harmony between the two pastorals which the Archbishop invites us to admire.

It is enough to know that the collective letter is still in force. It was necessary to do something, or rather to appear to do something, towards abating the scandal which the electioneering of the curés had caused, and of which complaint had been made. But until the joint pastoral is revoked, nothing effectual will be done; and there is no probability of its being revoked, for it was afterwards to receive the express sanction of Pope Pius IX. It will continue to be the duty of the priests to read the Joint Letter and act upon it.

Already it was known, though the Pope had not spoken

personally, that the Joint Letter had been approved instead of being condemned at Rome ; Dr. De Angelis, professor of canon law, to whom the pastoral of Bishop Bourget on Liberalism had been referred, declared it extremely moderate as compared with the Joint Letter.* This Roman doctor extols the Joint Letter as an exposition of the true principles of the Church; and he approves of its condemnation of political Liberalism.

'Who,' asks this doctor of canon law, dare 'rise up against the collective letter of the Bishops of Quebec? Who dare refute and reject the principles exposed in the paragraphs above mentioned, principles which enter into the polical arena ? '

Let us see what are the principles contained in these paragraphs. Paragraph three is a denunciation of Catholic Liberalism (libéralisme Catholique). 'The partisans of this subtle error,' we are told, 'concentrate all their forces with the view of breaking the ties which unite the people to the bishops and the bishops to the Vicar of Christ.' Which means that they are not willing that orders sent from Rome, which violate the rights of civil governments, should be carried into effect by the bishops, the agents of the Pope. The Catholic Liberal, it is admitted, is not wholly devoid of Catholic principles, and he observes certain pious practices ; he is not without faith or attachment to the Church ; but this goes for nothing when he censures without scruple the highest acts and documents of religious authority. ' Under the pretext of removing causes of dissension and reconciling

* Si même nous rapprochons ce mandement de la Lettre collective des Evêques de la Province de Québec du 22 Septembre 1875 nous verrons qu'il est fort et moin pressant qu'il diffère de cette Lettre collective en ce que celle ci dans les paragraphes 3, 4, 5 expose d'une manière ferme et vigour oureuse les vrais principes admise par l'Eglise, la condemnation de l'erreur libérale, et la condemnation de cette erreur même politiquement considéré, tandis que la Lettre Pastorale de Mgr. l'Evêque de Montréal se maintient dans la condemnation du libéralisme considéré comme erreur religieuse, et rien de plus.

the evangelists with the progress of society, he enters the service of Cæsar and of those who invent pretended rights in favour of a false liberty ; as if darkness and light could co-exist and as if truth does not cease to be truth when violence is done to it by taking away its true meaning and despoiling it of its inherent immutability.' Five apostolic briefs declare that it is not permissible to be a liberal Catholic.

Paragraph four contains only general statements, in no way objectionable.

The fifth paragraph objects to the exclusion of the clergy from politics ; and to the assertion that in politics the people ought to practice moral independence ; in other words, that morality, applied to politics, may exist independent of dogma.* Those who complain of the undue influence of the clergy in politics are denounced as the greatest enemies of the people. It is this paragraph that contains the menace of excommunication against electors who refuse to vote as the priest directs.

When the bishops found the policy of the Joint Letter arraigned at Rome by parties in Canada whose names were withheld, they resolved to defend their action, and for that purpose they sent a delegation to Rome, consisting of Mgr. Lafleche of Three Rivers, and Rev. M. Lamarche. The delegates carried with them a petition signed by a number of priests, in which an attack is made on certain professors of the University of Laval for having objected to priests exercising undue influence in elections. No one is named, but M. Langelier, professor of law, is specially aimed at; he having been retained by M. Tremblay as counsel in the Charlevoix election contest, the principal feature of which was that it was to test, for the first time, the right of the clergy to interfere in elections with all the authority of their sacred office. The petition

* See Mgr. Raymond, De l'intervention du prète dans l'ordre intellectuel et social.

was drafted by the Rev. Alexis Pelletier, *alias Luigi*. The petition makes it plain that the difficulty had arisen out of the Joint Letter. The petitioners claim that that letter and what has been done under it are justified by the decrees of the Provincial Councils. It describes 'fanatic Protestants and Liberals ' as the enemies of the petitioners. There seems to have been a suspicion that in the complaint made at Rome the University of Laval, or some of its professors, had had some hand ; for the petition declares that that seat of learning contains men whom the clergy have always combatted.

Armed with this petition, the Bishop of Three Rivers set out for Rome. On his return, he published November 1, 1876, in the form of a pastoral letter, a report of what he had done. The priests, he says, alarmed at the clamours raised against them for the exertion of undue influence in the elections for the Province of Quebec in 1875, and the judicial proceedings with which they were threatened, saw that it was necessary to enlighten the faithful on questions of so much gravity. They conceived that the liberty of evangelical preaching was in danger. This led to the issuing of the famous Joint Letter by the bishops. Its appearance made a profound sensation, and caused menaces of proceedings against the priests to be uttered. Secret opposition to the Joint Letter was made. Doubts as to the accuracy of the doctrine contained in the episcopal manifesto had struggled into being. The reports made to Rome, by persons unknown to the bishops, Mgr. Lafleche characterizes as ' greatly exaggerated and entirely false, against the clergy of the whole Province.' But when he comes to particulars, we find that the clergy were merely represented as interfering ' in a manner altogether inconvenient in political elections, and as acting with a degree of imprudence that would compromise the future of religion in the country.'

When, in response, Cardinal A. Franchi, Préfet of the Congregation of the Propaganda, wrote to the Archbishop for precise information on the subject, the bishops felt the necessity of defending themselves ; and the delegation was sent to Rome to reply, on behalf of the clergy, to these charges. Those by whom they had been preferred had sent to the eternal city no advocate to sustain them ; and Mgr. Lafleche found that he was not confronted by any one by whom his statements could be questioned. This greatly facilitated the work of justifying the clergy which he had undertaken to perform. He drew up a memorial, founded on official documents, disciplinary rules, pastoral letters, mandements, and decrees of Provincial Councils, the instructions which the bishops had for more than twenty years given to the clergy, as well on their duties as citizens and in the political arena as on their religious obligations, and on the rules of conduct traced for the clergy in respect to these duties.

The bishop obtained a victory. The Préfet of the Propaganda, after reading this memorial, told its author that the teachings which had been arraigned ' were perfectly conformable to those of the Holy See, of which they were the faithful and often the textual echo ; that the rules of conduct prescribed for the clergy as to the way in which they should instruct the faithful in the fulfilment of their political duties were also very wise, and that both had received the approbation of the Holy See in the decrees of the Provincial Councils,' which can only take effect after they have been sanctioned at Rome. In going back a period of twenty years, it would be easy for the bishop to exhibit a state of things quite different from that which now exists. The fidelity of the picture, as a representation of the present, can only be known by a careful inspection. But the scandal which the publication of these conflicting documents would occasion will, we may be sure, be avoided.

The emissary of the Ultramontanes, in his memorial, combatted the 'liberal doctrines' which attempts had been made to propagate amongst the French Canadians; and showed how the bishops, presumably by a rigorous censorship of the Press, had prevented their expression. In a separate memorial, the bishop went into an exposition of liberal doctrines since 1848, quoting from the journals and speeches in which they had been advocated, and pointing to the acts of the leaders of the party, with the view of showing that the bishops in combatting Liberalism had only performed a necessary duty. He brought before the notice of the Préfet of the Propaganda the attacks which the Joint Letter had encountered. His Eminence replied, the reporter tells us, that the doctrine contained in that document is 'perfectly sound, and conformable to the teachings of the Holy See.' As that letter orders the curés to instruct the electors how to vote, at political elections, and to visit the crime of refusal with spiritual censures, the See of Rome has placed itself in direct conflict with the civil law of Canada as interpreted by the highest court in the country.

Cardinal Franchi laid before Pope Pius IX. a brief statement of the case, which probably afterwards formed the substance of the brief which contains the decision of this infallible Pontiff. The pro-Secretary of the Propaganda also drew up an address to the same august personage, with the view of enabling him to pass an eulogy on the Canadian episcopate. Mgr. Lafleche had a long audience with the Pope, and drew up a written statement of the case for his information. It was in reply that the brief of the Pope was addressed to the Bishop of Three Rivers. In communicating this Papal document to the clergy of his diocese the bishop says: 'You will there see that the infallible head of the Church fully approves of the zeal of your first pastors in teaching you the holy doc-

trine, exposed by textual citation from their Pastoral
Letter of September 22, 1875, and that His Holiness
highly extols their zeal in combatting liberal errors,' besides renewing the condemnation of Catholic Liberalism.

The bishop ends with an exhortation to the faithful to
follow the instructions of the Joint Letter ; in other words,
to do what the Supreme Court and three judges of another
court, in their official capacity, have declared to be illegal, and which the law, as by the latter interpreted,
stigmatizes as a ' fraudulent manœuvre.'* The rescript
of the Pope is an invitation, a command, that the bishops
and the priests, acting in unison, shall trample under foot
the laws of the land. It was the knowledge that such
things were liable to happen which caused so many Catholic governments to submit to examination bulls, decrees and rescripts of the Popes, to ascertain whether they
contained anything which would make their publication
injurious to the State.

Archbishop Lynch took ground in direct opposition to
the joint pastoral. 'Priests may,' he says, 'instruct their
people on the conscientious obligation of voting for the
candidates whom they judge will best promote the interests of the community ; ' ' but they are not to say to the
people from the altar that they are to vote for this candidate and reject the other.'† He goes further, and says
' it would be very imprudent in a priest, whose congregation is composed of Liberals and Conservatives '—as all
congregations in both Provinces must be more or less—
' to become a warm partisan of either party,' as the priests
in Chambly, Charlevoix, and Bonaventure have certainly
done. The national spirit of the Irish Roman Catholics

---

* I shall not insinuate, as some have done, that Mgr. Lafleche inspired an article
in the *Journal des Trois Rivières*, in which the ground is taken that ' the duty of
voting, or of directing voters, falls under the exclusive jurisdiction of the Church,
though his pastoral goes far to warrant that conclusion.

† Letter to the Hon. A. Mackenzie, Jan. 20, 1876.

of Ontario would almost certainly cause them to resent a
degree of clerical dictation which should fall far short of
that exercised in Quebec.

The brief of Pope Pius IX. dated September 13, 1876,
and addressed to the Bishop of Three Rivers, shows what
might from the first have been foreseen, that the victory
remains with the Ultramontanes. It sets out by thanking
the Canadian bishops for their affection and submission
to the Apostolic See, and insists on the necessity of
union. ' We rejoice chiefly,' the Pope says, ' at the care
you take to inculcate among the Canadian people sound
doctrine, and to explain to them what regards the nature,
the constitution, and the rights of the Church; the conception of which it is customary to prevent with great
subtlety for the purpose of deceiving the faithful ; and we
have had to praise the zeal with which you have striven
to forewarn the same people against the crafty errors of
libéralisme called *Catholique,* the more dangerous that,
under an exterior appearance of piety, they deceive many
honest men, and that, tending to lead men away from the
true doctrine, especially on questions which at first sight
seem to concern rather the civil than the ecclesiastical
power, they enfeeble the faith, break the unity, divide the
Catholic forces, and furnish very efficacious aid to the
enemies of the Church, who teach the same errors, though
with greater display and impudence, and insensibly lead
men's minds to accept their perverse designs. We therefore congratulate you, and we hope that you will always
labour to unveil their snares and instruct the people with
a similar ardour, a like discernment, and with that concord
which shows to all your mutual charity, and proves that
each of you thinks and teaches only the same thing.
This will naturally happen if you carefully nourish in you
that devotion to the Chair of St. Peter, mistress of the
truth, which you profess in terms so strong and so
affectionate.'

By reading the penultimate sentence in connection with the text between the lines, a hint at a division among the Episcopate may be gathered ; though it is so gentle that it might easily escape the attention of a careless reader.

The Bishop of Rimouski, in communicating the brief to the clergy of his diocese, says much noise has been made about a pastoral letter of his own as well as the Joint Letter of the bishops. ' Various commentaries, more or less correct, numerous interpretations, more or less exact, have been made. Some have gone so far as to desire to find a contradiction between this bull* and the principles laid down in our pastoral letter or the consequences resulting from it.'† He appeals to this brief to prove that ' the supreme head of the Church formally approves the teaching contained in our letter upon the constitution and rights of the Church, as well as the nature and danger of *liberalism* called *Catholic.*' Bishop Langevin, on the strength of the brief he is interpreting, bids the faithful ' understand more than ever that in everything involving religious or social questions, you are to receive the teachings and direction of the spiritual authority, and to recognize as legitimate and salutary its intervention *(immixtion)* and influence : ' this,' he adds by way of admission, ' is what many obstinately refuse to admit.' In the bosom of the Church, ' among those who call themselves its children, who conform to the externals of religion, who approach the sacraments, there is a certain number who, whether wittingly or not, insist on submitting the religious authority to the civil power in mixed questions, on gagging its ministers and

---

* The bull canonically erecting the University of Laval.

† This probably points to some words spoken by M. Tremblay at Chicoutimi shortly before : Eh bien, cette vérité pour laquelle nous avons combattu tous ensemble, la possession de nos libertés politiques, elle nous a été annoncé, dimanche dernier, par Notre Saint Père le Pape luimême, par Mgr. l'Archevêque, dans la bulle et le mandement vous ont été lus.

relegating them to the sacristy; finally, all who, with hypocritical professions of respect and submission on their lips, aim at nothing less than the destruction of the action of the Church in the things that belong to public life.' This submission is demanded on the authority of the papal brief.

In France the interference of the clergy in elections has been much less marked than in Canada. Yet Gambetta, in a speech delivered at Lyons, after the Republican triumph, said: ' It has become apparent to our people, as well as to all Europe, that for five years, owing to our misfortunes to our disasters, and perhaps also to our weaknesses, under the pretext of withheld monarchical rights, and of the restoration of this or that dynasty, the true leader of the reactionary coalition, the authority and guide of all those dangerous combinations against the liberty and future prosperity of the country, was clericalism.' The ecclesiastical opinions of the reactionists of France are echoed with tremendous exaggeration among the French population of Quebec, as those of the Rouges of 1848—not one of the leaders of whom had then passed the age of 22 years—in the words of M. W. Laurier, ' were based upon those of the revolutionists of France.' Such is the inheritance which the sons of New France receive from their original mother country, whence their sires drew the maxims of a sturdy and independent Gallicanism.

XIV.

SPIRITUAL TERRORISM AT ELECTIONS.

At every election that has taken place since the joint pastoral was issued, the parish priests at Quebec have made the walls of the sanctuary echo with the praise of one candidate or party and the censure of the other. They commence, as instructed by their superiors, by reading the joint episcopal letter, and proceed to comment upon it at great length, returning to the charge on several successive occasions. Every sermon delivered between the issuing of the writ of election and the day of polling is a political harangue. Three striking illustrations of this procedure have occurred: in Chambly, in Charlevoix, and in Bonaventure.

M. Lussier, the curé of Boucherville, one of the first on whom this new duty fell, did his best to avoid the necessity of reading the Joint Letter; but he was at last obliged to act on peremptory orders of the Bishop of Montreal.

This priest reports one of the candidates, Doctor Fortier, as having announced himself a Rouge and a Moderate Liberal. The attention of the Bishop of Montreal having been called to this fact, he wrote to the curé in these terms: 'Our Holy Father the Pope, and after him the Archbishop and Bishops of this Province, have declared that Catholic Liberalism is a thing to be regarded with the abhorrence with which one contemplates a pestilence: no Catholic is allowed to proclaim himself a Moderate Liberal; consequently this Moderate Liberal cannot be elected a representative by Catholics.'

If the term Liberal Conservative had been used it would have been equally the duty of the bishop, as the agent of Rome, to denounce it. The *Courrier du Canada*, with the aroma of the papal benediction about it, has discarded as altogether unauthorized the qualifying word Liberal; and announces itself Conservative, pure and simple.

M. Lussier has reported at length the commentaries with which he accompanied the reading of the Joint Letter of the bishops.* From this explanation, we learn that the bishops did not issue their letter without some trepidation, foreseeing that it would excite hatred and passion (bien des haînes, bien des colères). For this reason, M. Lussier would have avoided the reading of the letter i he could. He personally visited the bishop and stated that he had read to the parishioners his lordship's pastoral letter; on which the bishop remarked, 'You have done well.'

The curé asked what more there was for him to do. The bishop replied, 'You are to read the letter of the bishops.'

'But,' resumed the curé, 'permit me to say that I fear to excite the murmurs of some of the parishioners.'

'We must not fear to speak the truth,' the bishop said, by way of command; 'in desiring to be too prudent we compromise ourselves.'

The letter was read, in pursuance of the bishop's direction. When the priest came to the phrase, 'The State is in the Church, and not the Church in the State,' he undertook to refute 'the maxim invented by Liberalism, " A free Church in a free State." He told the parishioners what would be the penalty of their refusing to obey his directions. ' I explained,' he says, 'how the Church deals with error; I said she commences by pointing out the

See the *Nouveau-Monde*, Feb. 1, 1876.

danger; she puts the faithful on their guard against
novelties; she instructs, enlightens, and exhorts them;
and if after this they remain in error and refuse to submit themselves, she launches her thunders against them
and declares them excluded from her bosom.' In this
way M. Lussier interpreted and carried out his instructions.* The sermon received the approval of the bishop.

These threats, instead of being received with the absolute docility and submission which the bishops demand
from the faithful, raised a storm of indignation: many persons, M. Lussier does not hesitate to state, went so
far as to stigmatize the letter of the bishops as a menda-
cious document; conduct which the priest denounces as
blasphemous. 'If,' he says, 'the bishops, speaking with
the Pope, deceive themselves and say what is not true, it
follows that the Holy Spirit deceives himself and is a
liar; for it is he who has appointed the bishops to rule
the Church of God.'†

This is here a hopeful sign. In the opposition of the
Roman Catholics themselves to the tyranny of the hierarchy lies the hope of a remedy: they alone can be the
saviours of their own liberty.

But M. Lussier, in obeying the commands of his superior, did not perform his task in a half-hearted or merely
perfunctory manner. With whatever reluctance, he
did his work thoroughly. He concluded his sermon in
these words: ' It is necessary to explain myself clearly,
for I see that many do not understand. The candidate
who spoke last Sunday called himself a Moderate Liberal.
As Catholics you cannot vote for him; you cannot vote
for a Liberal, nor for a Moderate Liberal for moderate
is only another term for liar. One must be either Pro-

---

* M Lussier is a doctor of canon law, a distinction not often conferred. He resided many years at Rome, and there thoroughly inbibed the spirit of the Vatican.
† Lettre de M. Lussier, Jan. 3, 1876.

testant or Catholic; you cannot remain Catholics without saying your prayers. When you recite the symbol of
the apostles you say, " I believe in God and in the Holy
Church, etc." Now the Church condemns Liberalism.
You cannot remain Catholics and vote for a Liberal.'*

What M. Lussier and the other parish priests of Chambly did the curés of Charlevoix were doing almost at the
same time, and doing with a will. In this case, the facts
have been disclosed by no less than one hundred and
fifty witnesses, in an investigation before Judge Routhier,
having for its object the annulling of the ·election, chiefly
on account of the undue influence exercised by the priests.
The trial lasted six weeks.

The Charlevoix election took place in the beginning of
the year 1876. The priests held a consultation to decide
upon their candidate. The choice fell on M. Langevin,
Conservative, the other candidate being M. Tremblay, a
Liberal, so-called. In obedience to instructions, the curés
read and commented on the Joint Letter; and sometimes
the personal influence of the Archbishop was mentioned.
The general drift of their remarks was that they were two
flags: one blue, the flag of the Pope, the other red, the flag
of Garibaldi and Victor Emmanuel. The red flag meant
revolution and damnation, the worst evils that could befall
anyone both in this world and the next. The blue flag
meant present prosperity and eternal happiness. At
least one priest terrified the electors by telling them that
to vote for the partisans of the red flag would be to incur
the guilt of mortal sin. Another told the electors that
he, not they, was responsible for the use they would make
of the elective franchise.

Some of the curés preached several times on the subject of the election; and all of them reserved their
greatest effort for the Sunday before the voting. M.

* See *Nouveau-Monde*, Jan. 25, 1876.

18

Sirois, of Baie St. Paul, stigmatized the candidate of the red flag as a false Christ and a false prophet. If he succeeded in getting elected, tithes would be abolished, the priests would have to be supported by the Government, and the pressure of the taxation would become intolerable. The parishioners were as much bound to listen to the priest when elections were in progress as at any other time. Refusal to listen to to the curé on the question of voting was disobedience to the Pope. Liberalism must be crushed. If the electors listened to the false prophets a terrible chastisement would fall on the country, perhaps in the destruction of the greater part of the harvest; if the electors failed to listen to their curé, chastisements would speedily overtake them. The electors were, after all, to vote according to their conscience; not simply according to their conscience, but 'according to their conscience, enlightened by the mandement of the bishops of Quebec.' The simple peasants saw and noted the contradiction. The intelligence of the electors had been rated too low.

A strange use was made of the word conscience. Not only was it represented that the conscience unenlightened by the instructions of the episcopate, was a conscience not at liberty to act; it was at liberty to act when it was bound by these instructions, and was no longer free. If a man's conscience is not his own, and if it is not free, appeals to it are a mockery and a snare.

The sermons of M. Sirois awakened many fears and changed many votes.

M. Langlais, curé of St. Hilarion, told the electors that to vote for a Liberal was to set out on the road to hell. Is it a matter of surprise that the simple peasants, who repose unbounded confidence in their priests, should have recoiled before so terrible a danger? One witness swore that, after he was made aware of this terrible fact, he did not see how he could vote for M. Tremblay, the candidate of his choice. 'My religious belief,' he said, 'as a Catholic, is that those who act in opposition to religion and their pastors go to hell when they die.' 'Of myself,' said the same witness, 'I knew nothing, and I relied on the instructions of one worthy of confidence.'

It was a common remark among the congregation, after they had left the church, that, according to the curé, the members of the Rouge party would infallibly be damned. Some who did not change their votes were frightened into abstention.*

Another witness, Zephirin Savard, thought one-third of the electors had been changed by the influence of the curé of St. Hilarion, exercised during a pastoral visit. This fact was probably not without its influence in moving the Archbishop of Quebec, in his pastoral of May 25, to prohibit the curés from discoursing on politics while on pastoral visits. 'I was afraid,' said one elector to another, 'that if I voted for Tremblay, I should be damned.' Whoever voted for the Liberals, said another priest, engaged in the service of hell. The fear of damnation, as the consequence of voting in a particular way, operated most strongly on the minds of the women, and they naturally influenced their husbands to avoid so great a danger.

Some evidence contradicting, on some points, what had been said by the witnesses for the plaintiff was produced by the defendant. The two points which the defence tried to make were, that the priests spoke as citizens and not in their official capacity of curés, and that they did not say that to vote in a particular way would be a mortal sin. On the latter point, the weight of the evidence was altogether against the priests.

* Octave Simard, a witness, said : Je ne sais pas si c'est pour avoir mal compris qu'à la sortie de l'église les gens en s'en retournant chez eux ont dit que le curé avait dit que les gens du parti rouge étaient tous damnés. Par parti rouge on voulait parler du parti de M. Tremblay. Il y a des électeurs qui m'ont dit qu'ils n'avait pas voté à cause de ces paroles du curé.

But whatever objections may be made to the evidence
for the plaintiff, there is a kind of evidence, the statements
of the priests themselves, which their defenders will have
to accept without question.   The curé of Ste. Fidèle, in the
justification of his conduct which he sent to the Archbishop, admits that he said : 'If I had to pronounce on
the present conflict, I could not, with my knowledge, do
so in favour of a Government which calls itself Liberal,
nor for any man who supports that Government.'

The curé of St. Hilarion also sent in his defence to the
Archbishop, in the shape of a statement of what he had
said in his sermons, and to which he procured the attesta-
tion of a number of his parishioners.   His word of
command was: 'Vote according to your conscience enlightened by your superiors.   Do not forget that the bishops
of the Province assure you that Liberalism resembles the
serpent which crawls in the terrestrial paradise, to procure
the fall of the human race.' 'According to your bishops,'
he further said, 'the Liberals are deceivers whom you
will not follow unless you wish to be deceived.   Liberalism is condemned by our Holy Father the Pope.   The
Church only condemns what is evil, and as Liberalism
has been condemned Liberalism is evil : therefore you
ought not to give your suffrages to a Liberal.   So the
bishops have openly declared.'   The bishops had said
that to vote in a certain sense was a sin, but that in following the direction of the bishops they could not sin.   It
was not enough that a candidate should be a Catholic to
merit their suffrages, for not only was the man to be considered, but also 'his political principles, as well as the
principles of the Government he supports.'   The curé
reminded his parishioners that they would have to give an
account to God, and he asked them whether in the hour
of death they would like to find themselves on the

side of Garibaldi and Victor Emmanuel or of the Sovereign Pontiff and his bishops.

One priest, and one alone, the Rev. M. Cinq Mars, curé of St. Siméon, was heard as a witness. He protested, as required by his superiors to do, against the competence of the tribunal. But as the Archbishop had waived the question of immunity and authorized the summoning of the priests before the court, M. Cinq Mars did not refuse to appear or to give his evidence. He swore positively that he had not made the remark imputed to him.

M. Cinq Mars produced the Joint Letter of the bishops as authority for what he had done and a command to do it. He had told the electors that the mandements of the bishops were binding *sub gravé*, that is, under pain of a grave sin. It is easy to understand that for a parish priest removable at the pleasure of the bishop there might be only the alternative of obedience or starvation.* The priests, therefore, when they reluctantly carry out the orders of their superiors, are deserving of sympathy ; but when, in the blindness of their zeal, they go beyond these instructions, and have to defend their conduct before their ecclesiastical superiors, they pass the line of innocence and of what they can reasonably consider their duty.

It is quite evident, from the effect which these sermons produced, that the priests in their political harangues from the pulpit went beyond the point to which they could carry their parishioners with them. What had happened in Chambly happened in Charlevoix. In his evidence regarding a sermon preached at Baie St. Paul, Boniface La Bouche said : ' The sermon made so great a tumult that several

---

* No less than thirty-four changes of priests were made in the diocese of Quebec, in September, 1876, eighteen in the diocese of St. Hyacinthe, and twelve in that of Three Rivers. One curé in the diocese of Quebec, J. S. Martel, refused to accept the parish ' offered to him in exchange. In September, 1877, between thirty and forty changes were made in the diocese of Montreal, twenty-seven in the diocese of St. Hyacinthe, and between twenty and thirty in the diocese of Quebec.

persons left the church, and four electors, heated by the
sermon of the curé, fell to fighting after they had engaged
in political discussion.' The sermon of the curé of St.
Hilarion was found equally distasteful to the congregation
before whom it was preached. Several persons, to mark
their disapprobation of the political harangue, left the
church before it was concluded. At the end of the sermon
the curé alluded to this tacit protest as a scandal, and
said : ' Woe unto him by whom scandal comes.'

A knowledge of the opposition which these sermons
provoked must have been a motive to the Archbishop to
call the halt in his pastoral of May, 1876, which was so
great a surprise at the time, when it was not understood.
The temper of the laity had been tested in two constitu-
encies, and it was evident that many electors were prepared
to resent the clerical repression that had been put upon
them.

A long statement, purporting to be an analysis of the
sermon of M. Sirois, curé of Baie St. Paul, which had
been sent to the Archbishop, was put in, on the part of
the defendant. The duty of the electors, the curé had told
them, was to follow his instructions. ' While I, preaching
sound doctrine,' he said, ' am in communion with my
bishop, you ought to listen to me and obey me ; I am here
your legitimate pastor, and consequently charged to enlighten, instruct, and counsel you ; if you disregard (mé-
prisez) my word, you disregard that of the bishop, that
of the Pope, and that of the Saviour, by whom we are
sent.'

The Canadian law on the subject of undue influence is
a copy of the English law. The principle of the English
law applicable to the exercise of undue influence by the
clergy was first laid down by Sir Samuel Romilly.
' Undue influence,' he said, ' will be used if ecclesiastics make use of their powers to excite superstitious fears

or pious hopes ; to inspire, as the object may be best pro-
moted, despair or confidence ; to alarm the conscience by
the horrors of eternal misery, or support the drooping
spirits by unfolding the prospect of eternal happiness.'

This precedent was followed by Baron Fitzgerald, in
the Mayo contested election, 1857, and the election was
annulled on the ground that spiritual intimidation had
been made use of. Speaking of what the priest may do
and may not do in this respect, the judge said : ' He may
not appeal to the fears, or terrors, or superstition of those
whom he addresses. He must not hold out the hope of
reward here or hereafter, and he must not use threats of
temporary injury, or of disadvantage or punishment hereafter ; he must not, for instance, threaten to excommunicate or to withhold the sacraments, or to expose the party
to any other religious disability, or denounce the voting
for any particular candidate as a sin, or an offence involving punishment here or hereafter. If he does so with
a view to influence a voter, the law considers him guilty
of undue influence. . . . . As priestly influence is
so great we must regard its exercise with extreme jealousy,
and seek by the utmost vigilance to keep it within due
and proper bounds.'

The Joint Letter of the bishops of Quebec instructs the
priests to do precisely what Baron Fitzgerald decided
that the priests of Ireland cannot do.

The judgment of Judge Routhier in the Charlevoix
case has a striking family likeness to that which he delivered in the cause of Derouin vs. Archambault, and
which was reversed on appeal. The same false principles
are encountered in both judgments. The second contains
a quotation from the first, to the effect that the free exercise of the Roman Catholic religion, stipulated for at
the time of the conquest, implies the operation of the ecclesiastical law of Rome in Quebec ; though the Privy

Council holds, and Mgr. Destautels has expressed the same opinion, that the ecclesiastical law in force in that Province is the ecclesiastical law of France as it stood in the year 1759. France never could have intended to stipulate that Rome should enjoy, in the Province which was changing masters, privileges which she had herself refused to her, both at home and in the colony. Judge Routhier denies that the Crown, from which he holds his commission, could confer on him any jurisdiction in spiritual matters; which means that he recognizes a higher law than the law of the land which Parliaments and Legislatures enact. He undertakes to say, what no one could know, that if the priests had not interfered at all, the result of the election would have been the same. That the priest should not be the only person in the community forbidden to instruct the electors in their duty will readily be conceded; and with ' the liberty of Christian preaching' no one, at this time of day, wishes to interfere. But there are many things which it is not permissible to do under pretence of exercising this liberty. What would be a libel out of the pulpit, is no way privileged in it ; and what would be illegal intimidation out of the pulpit does not change its nature when uttered in the pulpit. The priest is not denied the enjoyment of civil and political rights; but intimidation is not a right; it is always and everywhere exercised in derogation of the rights of others. Voting, Judge Routhier says, is a moral act; and we are asked to conclude that that fact brings the Catholic voter under the canon law of Rome, gives him over absolutely to the control of the Church in the performance of this act, and ousts the Legislature and the civil tribunals of their respective jurisdiction. The priests, according to this doctrine, in acting as they did, were within the limits of their own domain, accomplishing their pastoral duties, as the guardians of morality, and did not encroach on the rights of the State, which has neither the authority nor the competence to deal with the matter. If these assumptions be accepted, it follows that the law under which the Galway election was set aside was no law at all. Ultramontane writers, we all know, teach that what the Church chooses to stigmatize as unjust laws, 'are violences rather than laws, and do not bind the conscience.'* If a priest refuses the sacraments to an elector for having voted for the wrong candidate, Judge Routhier can only refer him to the bishop. But the priest had, in the whole, matter, acted in obedience to the orders of the bishop, or of the entire Episcopate of the Province. If you ask the wrong-doer to sit in judgment on his own act and that of his agent, what satisfaction do you expect ? Judge Routhier somewhat scornfully rejects English precedents as inapplicable to a country where the hand of Rome is much more felt than in England ; and he holds that the text of the law of Quebec does not include priests in its denunciation of intimidation and undue influence.

Let us see what would be some of the consequences of sustaining this judgment. The plain meaning of it is that the canon law of Rome, having superseded in this country the ecclesiastical law of France, must henceforth have unrestricted force and effect. Let us suppose the case of a person excommunicated for some alleged offence, in the civil or political order, over which the Church claims jurisdiction on the ground that a question of morality is involved ; let us further suppose that the victim remains under excomunication for a year ; he must then, by the canons of the Council of Trent, be regarded as a heretic, and be handed over to the tender mercies of the Inquisition. If this were to happen, the civil power would, if Judge Routhier be accepted as authority, be unable

* Brownson, Conversations on Liberalism and the Church. Rev. Alexis Pelletier.

to protect the subject whose life was menaced for what, in the eye of the civil law, might be no crime at all. This is only one example of the thousand monstrosities which might be perpetrated if the canon law of Rome had full and unchecked course in this country. Ecclesiastical immunities would extend not only to persons but to property ; the orders of the Pope would be binding on the faithful, whether they related to the spiritual or the temporal order. The civil laws would count for nothing, if the doctrine were accepted that the temporal power is subordinate to the spiritual power of the Pope; and short of this it is impossible to stop if the canon law of Rome is to be accepted as having unrestrained force in Canada. It would have been easy to find Italian priests who would have rejected with indignation these pretensions at a time when the League was spreading desolation through France, when Jacques Clement assassinated Henry III., and French priests refused to pray for the king.*

In the Supreme Court, judgments were delivered by Mr. Justice Taschereau and Mr. Justice Ritchie. The former said that he and the other Catholic judges of the court felt themselves in a difficult position in consequence of the decision of three eminent judges of the Superior Court of Quebec having been severely blamed by an eminent member of the Episcopate for a judgment which they had delivered in an almost identical case, a judgment which he regarded as an important precedent. If an Ultramontane bishop has already embarrassed the judges of the highest court in Canada, what may some future bishop not hope to achieve in the same direction ? Mr. Justice Taschereau held that the agency of the clergy whose conduct was complained of had been clearly proved. M. Langevin had only consented to become a candidate on an assurance, obtained through M. Gauthier, that the clergy of

* See Histoire de Venise, par le Comte Daru, livre XXIX., pp. 66-7.

the county would support him. After he entered on the campaign, and had held personal conferences with the clergy, he stated at public meetings that they were favourable to him, and that the electors ought to listen to the voice of their pastors. Many curés denounced the opposing candidate in their sermons. These ʹcurés, by taking part in the election with the consent of M. Langevin, became his agents.

These sermons, Mr. Justice Taschereau held, created in the minds of many electors a dread of committing a grievous sin and being deprived of the sacraments. ʻThere is here,' he said, ʻan exerting of undue influence of the worst kind, inasmuch as these threats and these declarations fell from the lips of the priests speaking from the pulpit in the name of religion, and were addressed to persons ill-instructed and generally well disposed to follow the counsels of their curés.' He thought these sermons, though they may have had no influence on the intelligent and instructed portion of the hearers, must have influenced the majority of persons void of instruction. Although the secret mode of voting made it impossible to point to more than six or eight persons who had been influenced to vote against their natural inclination, it was proved that a large number changed their views through this undue influence. But proof of a single instance of the exercise of undue influence was sufficient to annul an election, though the candidate in whose favour it was exerted should have had an overwhelming majority of votes. Taking the evidence as a whole, Mr. Justice Taschereau thought it was clear that a general system of intimidation had been practised, and as a consequence undue influence exercised ; the electors did not consider themselves free in the exercise of the elective franchise. The court was unanimously of the opinion that the four curés, Cinq Mars, Sirois, Langlais, and Tremblay, had exercised undue influence, and that being agents of the respondent their acts·bound their principal. The election was declared void, with costs against the respondent, less some part of the cost of printing.

On the question of clerical immunity, which the advocate for the respondent had raised, the court expressed a very strong opinion, to which reference will be made when we come to deal with the immunities of the clergy.

It had been contended, during the progress of this suit, that the Legislature, in adopting the English election law, never intended to debar the exercise of clerical terror and intimidation. To this objection Mr. Justice Ritchie replied. He said : 'On the principles of common law, on the construction of the language of the Act, of which we entertain no doubt, we cannot for a moment doubt that it is our duty to declare that undue spiritual influence is prohibited by statute.' The clergyman, like the layman, has the liberty of 'free and full discussion, solicitation, advice, persuasion ; ' but he 'has no right in the pulpit or out, by threatening any damage, temporal or spiritual, to restrain the liberty of a voter so as to compel or frighten him into voting, or abstaining from voting, otherwise than as he freely wills.' If he does so, the law regards the act as the exercise of undue influence.

These judgments settle the law. What then follows ? Seven of the bishops have expressed their confidence that they will be able to procure an alteration of the law ;* a confidence based on the readiness with which the Legislature of Quebec hastened, in a similar case, to yield to the demands of the Church. Nevertheless it is extremely improbable that the Dominion Parliament will be found to be equally compliant. This Act of the Local Legislature was intended to enable the bishops to inflict ecclesiastical

* Declaration de l'archevêque et des évêques de la Province ecclésiastique de Québec, au sujet de la loi électorale, Québec, 26 Mars, 1877.

punishment for a refusal to bow to the decrees of the Congregation of the Index and the Inquisition. An amendment to the election law, in these words, has been suggested: ' Nothing in the preceding provisions shall apply to the words of a minister of religion pronounced in the exercise of his duty as such.'† This is the new programme.

The conflict between the civil and the ecclesiastical authorities has taken a very definite shape. On one side is the highest judicial tribunal in the country, on the other the entire Roman Catholic Episcopate of Quebec, sanctioned by the express approbation of Pope Pius IX.

The judgment in the Bonaventure election case delivered by Judge Casault agrees in principle with that of the Supreme Court. The Provincial Act, under which these cases come, is copied word for word from the ' Corrupt Practices Prevention Act of 1854 ; ' and as it has several times been held to include this kind of intimidation, Judge Casault thinks it would be an insult to the Legislature of Quebec to assume, as Judge Routhier did in effect, that its members were ignorant of the facts. The argument, founded on the treaty of cession, that Roman Catholic priests may trample on the civil laws because the French Canadians were guaranteed the free exercise of their religion, 'as far as the laws of England will permit,' went for nothing. These words—' as far as the laws of England permit '— seemed to the judge ' to restrict, in a very formal manner, what the defendant pretends to be one of the freedoms of the exercise of the Catholic religion : that of being able, in preaching, to practise intimidation, and thus to limit, if not to destroy, the electoral franchise.' When the treaty was made, representative institutions had long existed in England ; and both ' the law of parliament and the common law consecrated absolute freedom in the ex-

† Programme of the *Nouveau-Monde*, in the *Minerve* Oct. 2, 1877.

ercise of this franchise. If it were possible that something in the Catholic religion could be an obstacle thereto,
this something would have been contrary to the laws of
England, and would have been within the limit found in
the treaty itself.' Attacks upon the liberty of the elector were prohibited at the epoch of the treaty. The
present law ' has not and cannot have the effect of restraining the exercise of the Catholic religion, or of rendering it less free.'

The intimidation proved to have taken place was practised by two curés, named Thiviérge and Gagne. To
what the first said there were fifteen witnesses, and to
what the second said eleven. The witnesses differed
much, but without contradicting one another. ' It is conceivable,' said Judge Casault, ' that the account given
by illiterate fishermen and farmers of a sermon they
heard a year before must be more than incomplete, and
may perhaps be incorrect.' When it is considered that
more than three-fourths of the French Canadians in the
rural districts can neither read nor write, the influence of
the priest must be almost omnipotent. Two priests
alarmed the electors by stating that if they voted in a
particular way they would incur the penalty of a refusal
of the sacraments. For this menace the authority of
the diocesan was alleged. But this authorization, if it
had really been given, would afford no warrant for the
menace.

Not only was the election annulled on account of the
undue influence exercised by these two priests : M. Beauchesne was disqualified because the judges conceived
they were obliged to report ' that these fraudulent
manœuvres were practised with his knowledge and consent.' What Judge Routhier called the liberty of preaching, three other judges denounce as ' fraudulent manœuvres.'

The court, comprising three judges, Messieurs Casault, McGuire, and McCord, unanimously declared that the clergy is at liberty to express its opinion on political questions ; but that the menace of spiritual penalties constitutes undue influence. Judge McCord held, that to escape disqualification for the words used by the priests in his presence it would have been necessary for M. Beauchesne to repudiate them in express terms on the spot.

The question whether Judge Cassault should be deprived of his chair in the University of Laval, for the offence of delivering this judgment was sent to Rome, and decided in his favour by the Sacred Congregation.* The reference of this question shows the liability of Canadian judges, who happen to be Roman Catholics, to be censured at Rome for judgments they may deliver.

The Bishop of Rimouski, in a mandement of the 15th January, 1877, denounced the judgment of Mr. Justice Casault with defiant energy. He never could have thought, he declares, that such a judgment could have been received in Canada otherwise than with universal reprobation. He finds that it sins by being in unison with several of the propositions condemned in the Syllabus ;† and he informs all concerned that Catholic judges cannot in conscience administer civil laws such as that‡ which controls parliamentary elections in Quebec ; i they find any difficulties about the oath of office they have taken, he is ready with authority to prove that, in such a case, it does not bind the conscience ;‡ and he calls upon the Legislature to disclaim ever having intended to say what the words of the statute clearly express. With

---

* Letter of Bishop Conroy, Apostolic Delegate to Canada, to the Archbishop of Quebec, Oct. 3, 1877.

† Props. XLI., XIII., LIV.

‡ St. Lig. 1, III., Nos. 146 et 176.

him preaching includes the right of coercion, in so purely
a civil matter as the choice of parliamentary candidates,
by a menace to refuse the sacraments to offenders. For
the Church alone he claims the right to say what limits
the priest may not overstep under the pretence of preaching. This claim, if conceded, would make the civil authority powerless to check one of the most dangerous
forms of attack on the freedom of the elective franchise, or
to punish libels uttered under the shadow of the sanctuary. Taking the expression 'undue' to be equivalent to
'illegitimate,' Bishop Langevin argues that nothing can
be undue which a priest has been commanded by his
superiors to do; and that the destruction of the freedom of
election, if effected under orders, is a pious duty. In the
priest, he sees not the master but only the dispenser of
the sacrament; and when the Church prescribes a refusal
of sacraments, his duty is to obey. The difficulty is that
the bishops have placed themselves in opposition to the
civil law, which restrains no man's conscience and re-
stricts no man's true liberty, and which is designed to
secure the freedom of election. If we may judge by the
tone and attitude assumed by Bishop Langevin, the Episcopate is prepared to carry the conflict it has evoked
to the bitter end. He is scandalized that we have arrived
at—he ought to have said revived—the *Appel comme
d'Abus*, though even this would scarcely be an accurate
description of the actual proceeding.

The question has been asked whether the clergy exercised an influence undue and condemnable when, in 1775,
they denounced from the pulpit the attempt of the American Congress, through its emissaries in the Province, to
seduce the French Canadians from their allegiance;
whether the pastoral letters of 1837, which had for their
object to keep the Canadians from joining in the insurrec-
tion, are to be placed in the same condemned category.

There is no sort of parallel between the two classes of cases ; between counselling the people to be true to the national allegiance, in a moment of public peril, and denouncing ecclesiastical penalties against electors for voting for this or refusing to vote for that candidate of this or that party. And though Bishop Lartigue, in his pastoral of October 24, 1837, said : 'He that resisteth the power resisteth the ordinance of God; and they that resist purchase to themselves damnation,' he denounced no spiritual censures against those who took part in the rebellion, and did not authorize the priests to refuse them the sacraments. Nor has it been shown that any such weapons as are now used to compel obedience—and there could then be no question of voting—were resorted to by the Canadian clergy in 1775.

Instances might be pointed to in which, under the reign of the oligarchy, a Lower Canada Governor, acting under the inspiration of the dominant faction, tried to compel a priest to prostitute his influence in favour of the Government candidate; in which, in Nova Scotia, priests were required to use the knowledge obtained, or which it was assumed they might obtain, in the confessional, to compel the restitution of stolen goods, in a particular case ; in which political parties sought the aid of bishops and priests in party contests. But though these things are not to be justified, it cannot be denied that the clergy, once being tempted into the political arena, would soon tire of the ancillary position assigned to them, and come to defend their right to use their influence solely on behalf of the Church, which more or less remotely means themselves. But no government or party which invoked the aid of the Roman Catholic clergy ever asked them to make use of ecclesiastical penalties in its favour.

Other sermons, respecting which there has been no question in the courts, have been quite as bad as those

19

regarding which evidence was given in the election trials. One such sermon was preached by the Rev. Alexis Pelletier, at Baie St. Paul, in 1876. It is necessary to salvation, he told the congregation, to accept all the teaching of the Pope without exception. He represented it as an act of grave culpability on the part of electors to criticize, censure, or treat with contempt, words addressed from the pulpit with a view of directing electors 'in the choosing of a candidate and of voting,' because 'these are the words of God.' That is, in plain English, a political harangue pronounced by a priest is to be taken as a message from heaven ! Still, Roman Catholic congregations do sometimes revolt against the priest when he delivers such a message, and what is more, 'treat him with a degree of rudeness, and even of brutality, which are no longer found among savages.' The lesson which a sensible man would draw from such an occurrence would be that the interference of the priest in secular affairs had been carried beyond the bounds of prudence. But this preacher claims that the Church has a right 'to interfere with sovereign authority, which all are bound to respect,' in questions of legislation connected with the laying of taxes, the framing of tariffs, with immigration and colonization. And if laws contrary to the laws of the Church, and which, according to her interpretation, clash with the divine law, are passed, it becomes a duty to disobey them (nous devons alors lui refuser obeissance). For 'the priest, however humble he may be, transmits ' to his hearers ' the teachings of Jesus Christ, and all, learned and ignorant, ought to receive them from his lips with profound respect and perfect humility.'* This has an important bearing on civil allegiance, and it raises the question whether we are to live under civil or ecclesiastical rule.

These pastoral letters and political sermons mark the

* Printed in *Le Franc-Parleur*, 22 Août, 1876.

strides which the Church of Rome in Canada has made since the conquest. Under the French *régime*, the ecclesiastics of Canada were forbidden to read, or to cause to be read, either in the churches or at the church doors, any other writings than such as related to purely ecclesiastical matters.   .

To the priest no one desires to deny the rights of the citizen. He is allowed to vote as well as to speak and write on political questions. When he oversteps the line of persuasion, and abuses the powers of his sacred office to constrain, by means of spiritual terrors, electors to vote against their natural inclination, he becomes amenable to the law which guards the rights of the citizen from undue influence and intimidation. The law was not made specially for him ; its terms are general, and apply to all kinds of undue influence. In not exempting the priest from its purview, the law places him on the same footing as the layman.

XV.

THE CLAIM OF CLERICAL IMMUNITY.

The Roman Catholic Episcopate of Quebec forbids members of that communion to have recourse to the civil tribunals when they have suffered injustice at the hands of an ecclesiastic. 'The Church,' they say, 'has its tribunals, regularly constituted, and if any one believes that he has a right to complain of a minister of the Church he ought not to cite him before a civil tribunal but before an ecclesiastical tribunal, which alone is competent to judge of the doctrine and the acts of the priest. For this reason Pius IX., in his bull *Apostolicæ Sedis* of October, 1869, declares to be under the excommunication major all who directly or indirectly oblige lay judges to cite before their tribunal ecclesiastical persons, contrary to the dispositions of the canon law.'*

When the priest converts the pulpit into a political rostrum, under the direction of the bishops, it is natural that the latter should attempt to shield him from the consequences of his conduct by making inadmissible claims of clerical immunity. In the Circular which accompanied the Joint Letter, they instruct the priests whenever called upon to answer, before a civil court, for an abuse of spiritual authority, to protest against the competence of the tribunal, and claim the right to have the case adjudicated upon by an ecclesiastical tribunal ; and this, as we have seen, was done in the Charlevoix election trial.

When the curés received these directions, they were at a loss to understand what was meant by the words

* *Lettre Pastorale des Evêques,* Sept. 22, 1875.

'against the dispositions of the canon law,' and they asked explanations.

This led the bishops to undertake to answer, in another circular,† the question : ' What, at present, are the dispositions of the canon law with respect to persons and things ecclesiastical ? ' The Church, they say, while maintaining the principle of absolute immunity, is nevertheless guided by the circumstances in which her children find themselves placed in different countries, and she tolerates what she cannot correct without exposing them to serious inconvenience. Benoit XIV. is quoted to prove that lay judges ought not to be permitted to hear spiritual causes ; and that while new usurpations of the civil power on ecclesiastical immunities are to be opposed, the attempt to correct existing abuses is not to be made when it is evident that to do so would be useless and imprudent.

The Quebec bishops define as strictly ecclesiastical causes those in which the ' defendant is an ecclesiastic or a member of a religious order, and the object in litigation is of a spiritual character, or is connected with something possessing that character, or with the exercise of some function of the ministry.'

The rule laid down by the Second Council of Baltimore is adopted : that in case of a difference arising between an ecclesiastic and a secular person, the former is not to cite the latter before a civil tribunal unless the difficulty cannot be otherwise dealt with. And that Council exhorts the faithful to refer ecclesiastical causes to the decision of the bishop, instead of bringing them before the civil tribunals. The Council adds that one ecclesiastic bringing another before a civil tribunal thereby incurs ecclesiastical censures.

The Quebec bishops instruct the priests to exhort, in a general way, the faithful not to commence processes of

† November 14th, 1875.

this kind without having consulted their pastor, their confessor, or still better, the bishop, lest they should fall under
the major excommunication fulminated by Pius IX.

It is important to understand in what consist the
'regular ecclesiastical tribunals' of the Church of Rome,
in the Province of Quebec, which, in the cases mentioned,
are to supersede the civil courts. The tribunal, in the
absence of a regular bishop's court (*Officialité*) must consist of the bishop or some person whom he has appointed
to act for him. 'A bishop,' the Lords of Privy Council
said in the Guibord case, 'is always a *judex ordinarius*,
according to the canon law, may hold a court and deliver judgment if he has not appointed an official to act
for him.' But the next sentence shows that the question
which the bishops can so deal with are confined to 'faith
and discipline.'

The Quebec bishops, however, go beyond these limits
when they lay it down broadly that a layman is not at
liberty to cite a priest before a civil tribunal. Their second
circular would seem to show that they found it impossible
rigidly to maintain this position, for they produce authority for making exceptions. In the fifty-four days that
elapsed between their first and their second joint circular,
they probably received hints from the clergy that it would
not be wise at present to bend the bow too far.

Whatever relaxation of the rigid rule laid down is admitted, it does not necessarily avert the stroke of the
major excommunication. The sum of the matter is this :
Her Majesty's Roman Catholic subjects in the Province
of Quebec who may have suffered injustice at the hands
of an ecclesiastic, cannot appeal to the civil tribunals for
justice, without being in danger of incurring the major
excommunication. Most certainly the law of the land in
no way countenances this pretension.

There is no doubt whatever about the law ; but there

is sometimes a difficulty in its administration. A slander uttered by a priest in the pulpit, if it be unmistakably directed against an individual, is no more privileged than a slander uttered by a layman on the street. The tribunals of the Province of Quebec have placed this matter beyond the reach of doubt.

In a recent case, the judges of the Court of Appeal were unanimous on this point, though they were not agreed on the weight which ought to be given to the evidence in support of the allegations made against the priest. A blacksmith residing at St. Ephrem, township of Upton, of the name of Richer, brought an action against the Rev. M. Renaud *dit* Blanchard, for slander uttered in the pulpit. The case was tried at St. Hyacinthe by Judge Sicotte, and was decided in favour of the defendant. Subsequently it was taken before the Court of Revision at Montreal, where it was decided against the priest, by whom, however, an appeal was taken.

The judgment of the Court of Revision was set aside, and the decision rendered by the Superior Court in the first instance sustained. The pretension was set up, that as the alleged injury committed by the priest consisted of words pronounced from the pulpit, he could not be held responsible for their utterance. This doctrine Chief Justice Dorion did not accept; he knew of no person who was above the law, or who could not be held responsible for his statements.

Judge Ramsay, who decided in favour of the priest, upon the evidence, admitted that there was a good cause of action, if the facts had been proved. The blacksmith complained of two different species of slander, one uttered by the priest in private conversations, the other in a sermon. ' The first question,' said Judge Ramsay, ' is, whether the curé designated Richer specifically or not, and if he did designate him, how far he was justified by the circum-

stances in doing so. The rule is, that the denunciation
must be general in its terms; but it comports with reason
that there should be a limit to this. It would be extremely inconvenient to name or designate a person from the
pulpit, but it does not follow that the priest ought to confine himself to evil in general, from fear that the offender should be recognized by the denunciation.' This is
certainly contrary to the principle of the law of libel. A
person libelled is entitled to recover damages, though not
named, if the general description given of him is such as
to enable the public to fix upon him as the person intended to be struck at.

Judge Monk said: ' As to the right of the Court to accord damages if malice had been shown, he had no hesitation in saying that compensation would have been accorded. Any words uttered by a minister in the pulpit,
having in view the suppression of vice, were permissible.
The priest could make general remarks, and even allusions
more or less direct; so long as he confined himself to his
proper functions of spiritual guide and preceptor, he was
not responsible. But if he went beyond what was permissible by his sacred mission, he became responsible before the tribunals for what he said.'

Judge Sanborn thought the allegations against the priest
were sufficiently proved. On the general principle, he
said: ' Without doubt a priest or a minister has great
latitude in denouncing vice or what he considers error,
culpable habits of life or conversation and evil compan-
ions. He is permitted to warn and put on their guard
his hearers, and particularly those of whom he has charge,
against whatever he believes to be contrary to good manners and religious life; but this must be done in general
terms. His sacred mission does not authorize him, any
more than any other man, individually to name and denounce a person as unworthy of confidence, or to order

his hearers under severe pains not to frequent or visit his place of business.'

Judge Sanborn referred to the case of Darreau, in which the curé, in a sermon, had held up the seigneur of his parish to the contempt of his parishioners ; for which offence he was suspended from his functions during a period of five years, besides being fined and obliged to make an apology. ' He was of opinion that the judgment of the Court of Revision, which awarded a hundred dollars damages and costs, ought to be confirmed.

Not only is the law plain : the directions given by the bishop are directly contrary to the law. The antagonism of the two authorities, of which this is an example, presents itself in numerous and increasing instances.

Formerly the excommunication extended to the civil judges who heard causes which the Church forbade them to hear. A modification has been made by the present Pope, and it was made on the ground that the bull *In Cœnâ Domini* would have excluded Roman Catholics from the judicial bench, while the interests of the Roman Catholic Church required that they should sit there.*

Some defenders of the Church laud the Popes for having resorted to dissimulation and concealment on the question of immunities, when their pretensions were rejected by the civil authority.†

Some Ultramontane journalists and pamphleteers give the rule laid down in the first of the two joint letters of the bishops on the subject the most rigid interpretation. They describe as having come under the major excommunication all persons who, on a question of what they are obliged to pay to the priest, have recourse to a civil tribunal, instead of addressing themselves to the bishop.‡

---

* See *Le Nouveau Monde*, December 28, 1875.

† *La Revue Théologique.*

‡ Abbé Pelletier in *Le Franc-Parleur*, Dec. 17, 1875.

Others admit that these immunities are limited by specific exceptions, including : feudal causes ; personal property given to ecclesiastics under the reserve of civil jurisdiction ; causes arising out of the exercise of a civil employment by the ecclesiastic. And they add that a clerk who has cited a layman before a civil tribunal may himself in turn be subjected to the same treatment by his adversary, and an ecclesiastic who succeeds to the position of a lay-man who was already before a civil tribunal is excluded from immunity. As part of the immunities claimed, these bishóps have given sufficient notice of their intention to oppose any tax on the property of the Church. It is dif-ficult to estimate what proportion of the immovable pro-perty of the Province of Quebec the Roman Catholic Church may not acquire. All experience shows that, wherever the power of acquisition is almost or wholly unchecked, the property held in mortmain rapidly in-creases.

In Italy every vestige of clerical immunities is being swept away, that of freedom from liability to serve in the army being the last to go.

Clerical immunities will spread over an infinitely wider space than that which we have indicated, if for a while the Roman Catholic ecclesiastics of the Province of Que-bec obtain that absolute control of political power at which they are aiming.

Let us see what would be the effect of admitting the claim of immunity for the exercise of undue clerical in-fluence in parliamentary elections. In their joint letter of September, 1875, the bishops contend that, in certain cases, ' the priest and the bishop may in all justice, and ought in all conscience, to raise the voice, to signalize the danger, to declare with authority that to vote in such a sense is a sin, that to perform such an act exposes to the censures of the Church.'

When a priest rigorously carries out these instructions, what chance of justice would the injured candidate have in an appeal to one of the bishops under whose directions the priest had acted? The bishop would, in fact, be deciding in his own cause; for as the instigator of the act of the priest he would be more responsible for it than the man who believed himself bound to obey the order of his superior. The only chance of justice, in such a case, lies in an appeal to the civil tribunals.

There is manifestly a strong dislike on the part of persons who have suffered under this form of injury to apply to the civil tribunals for redress. The Archbishop of Quebec was recently called upon to adjudicate in a case of this nature. M. Hector L. Langevin complained that, in the heat of the Charlevoix election contest, in which he was candidate, two priests, Revs. MM. Audet and Saxe, had done him great injustice. The charge was that they had written private letters which contained ' an odious calumny and an infamous libel.' These private letters were publicly read ; and M. Saxe, when asked by the Archbishop to explain, denied that he used the words attributed to him.

The Archbishop then applied to M. Tremblay, by whom the letter had been read in public, to forward the original for comparison; and receiving for reply that neither the original nor a copy had been kept, the Archbishop declared himself incapable of deciding upon the complaint, since it was impossible to ascertain the real facts.

Of this decision we see no ground for complaining. What is worth notice in connection with the case, is that one of the candidates voluntarily makes the bishop the judge of the alleged misconduct of the priest in an election contest, and the other candidate, before venturing to appeal to the civil tribunals, takes the case to Rome. In his letter to the Archbishop announcing his determination to appeal to Rome, M. Tremblay, who had also made complaints of the conduct of a number of the curés, the great majority of whom were opposed to him, states that he had in vain demanded to be heard before a regular ecclesiastical tribunal, where he could produce witnesses and plead his cause; but that after the lapse of a considerable time he had not received any reply. In these letters he asked permission of the Archbishop to bring his complaints before the civil courts, if he could not have the case heard before a regular ecclesiastical tribunal.

There is no reason in law why M. Tremblay should not, in the first instance, have cited the priests of whose conduct he complained before the civil tribunals. But he probably feared that in doing so he would incur the major excommunication; that penalty being denounced against those who have the temerity to seek to obtain redress for an injury done by an ecclesiastic by citing the offender before the civil tribunals. The references made to the ecclesiastical authorities in these cases—for there are two distinct complaints—are just what the Church of Rome would naturally desire. In the first place, the Archbishop is recognized as the proper judge to dispose of a case which the complainant had the legal right to bring before a civil tribunal; and then the other party to the election contest, who preferred a similar complaint, expressed a desire to be allowed to carry it before a regularly constituted ecclesiastical tribunal, presumably in the nature of the *Officialité.* There is an implied objection to the mode in which the Archbishop proceeded. He certainly tried to put himself in a position to test the accuracy of the complaint made by M. Langevin; but when he was informed that the original letters had been destroyed and no copies kept, he did not pursue the subject farther.

But this was not the point of M. Tremblay's complaint.

His complaint was, that to the three letters he had written he had received no reply. The delay may have been caused by a reference to Rome, and when M. Tremblay's complaint reached there he may have been anticipated. If candidates for parliamentary position who have suffered from an undue exertion of clerical influence, and to whom the civil tribunals are open, are deterred by the menace of ecclesiastical censure from having recourse to them, and are to be cowed into submitting their complaint to the arbitrament of a bishop, an archbishop, or the Congregation of the Propaganda at Rome, it is plain that the rights of a large class of Her Majesty's subjects in the Province of Quebec will be placed on a new and perilous footing. It would not, we presume, require many repetitions of the demand made by M. Tremblay for the constitution of a regular ecclesiastical tribunal before which to take such cases to cause the wish of the applicants to be gratified. Were such courts once established, the tendency would be to draw to them an increasing number of cases, including mixed as well as such as are of a purely ecclesiastical character.

The Chambly, the Charlevoix, and the Bonaventure elections illustrate what sort of justice might be expected in election causes from regularly constituted ecclesiastical tribunals. The parish priests were compelled to read from the altar the pastoral letter in which the bishops authorized the clergy to threaten with the censures of the Church those who should be guilty of voting for the wrong candidate. And the bishops would have to decide whether the act they had authorized, and in some cases compelled reluctant priests to perform, called for their censure or approbation!

M. Langevin admitted practically, and M. Tremblay in terms, the claim of ecclesiastical immunities which the bishops put forth in their joint circulars last year.

The appeal which M. Tremblay makes to Rome appears
to be somewhat in the nature of a case of 'devolution,'
the Archbishop having neglected to act. The case is not
one that could have been appealed to Rome when Canada was under the French dominion.

Nor could the intimidation which has since been
proved to have been practised have occurred while
Canada was a French colony, and if it had occurred it
could not have come before any other than a civil tribunal. The complaint of M. Tremblay is that he has been
the victim of slander, and if this be true, the same remedy
which the blacksmith of Saint Ephrem sought in a like
case was equally open to him. How the superior courts
would deal with offenders such as M. Tremblay describes he could from the first have had little reason
to doubt. But if men, smarting under injuries of this
kind, are deterred from appealing to the protection of
the law, Roman canonists will begin to revive pretensions which were never admitted in France, and we shall
hear once more that contracts confirmed by an oath and
questions of usury are properly excepted from lay jurisdiction.

At last the discovery was made that the question of
undue influence exercised by a priest at an election may be
enquired into without citing the offender before a civil tribunal. Thus a means was found by which an aggrieved
candidate could insist on his rights without fear of incurring the major excommunication. It was then that M.
Tremblay brought his complaint before a civil tribunal.
.The exercise of undue influence is liable to be visited
with a penalty of two hundred dollars; and a priest found
guilty of the offence may be punished by the imposition
of that fine. If there were a public prosecutor, whose
duty it would be to take the initiative in such cases, he
could not escape. ,But neither in the Charlevoix nor the

Bonaventure election did any punishment fall on the offending priests.

Judge Routhier, before whom the trial took place, had previously exposed his views on the main question when he delivered his judgment in the case of Derouin against Archambault, in which he laid it down 'that a layman who asserts that he has been defamed by a curé, in a sermon delivered from the pulpit, cannot sue for damages. in civil tribunals for defamation ; preaching being a matter essentially ecclesiastical,' There, could, therefore,. hardly be a doubt what ground his judgment would proceed upon in the Charlevoix contest.*

But the Court of Appeal corrected the omission, and overthrew the principle which Judge Routhier had set up. ' These principles,' said Judge Mondelet, 'or rather these pretensions,' speaking of Ultramontanism in the bulk, ' are in contradiction to the jurisprudence of the country, and should no longer be a subject of discussion.' ' Priests, bishops, and all ministers of religion,' he added,. ' must be subject and obedient to the law and respect the rights of citizens.' ' The pretensions of the curé appear to me exorbitant ; but the judgment which dismisses the action enunciates a doctrine subversive of all the rights of the citizen, and is calculated to put the priest above the law.' This priest had gone to the extent of telling the congregation to drive one of the inhabitants of the parish from his home. ' Here,' said Judge Johnson, ' is a man of high position, who, on a public occasion, injures his neighbour in what appears to me to be a gross and unnecessary manner ; and, instead of his situation shielding him, it may fairly be said to add to the injury, for the

---

* Judge Routhier inflicted three fines with the alternative of imprisonment on journalists—and one journalist, M. Tarte, of *Le Canadien*, was imprisoned for thirty days —for being too free in their comments on the Charlevoix election contest while the trial was in progress: No priest has yet suffered in that way for his too great license of speech.

influence and authority of a parish 'priest are and ought
to be considerable.'

The success of the crusade of the Roman Catholic
clergy against civil liberty would blot out the individuality
of the citizens as completely as it would have disappeared
in the imaginary Republic of Plato, in the Utopia of
Moore, or in the Phalanstère of Fourier.

Many illustrations might be given to show how clerical
immunity from the jurisdiction of the civil courts would
work in actual practice. When an election contest was
going on in Soulanges, in the summer of 1875, M. Doutre
wrote to an elector of the county to protest against the
Roman Catholics banding themselves together and taking
the Syllabus for their programme. To do so, he thought
would create a very serious public danger. 'The Syllabus,'
he reminded his correspondent, 'proscribes every form of
worship except Catholicism, and decrees that physical force
may be resorted to to arrive at an uniformity of worship.'

What happened? The Bishop of Montreal wrote a
letter to M. Doutre's correspondent, which obtained immediate publicity, and in which he characterized M.
Doutre's letter as 'blasphemy' against the Syllabus, and
intimated that the writer merited the censure of the
Church, and might expect to meet the frown of the
Sovereign Judge when he is taken from this world.

Under such encouragement as this, there is no conceivable degree of license which the parish priests would
not think themselves justified in using. If in their denun-
ciations they uttered serious and damaging libels against
M. Doutre, and his only remedy lay in an appeal to an
ecclesiastical tribunal,.what measure of justice could he
expect to obtain from the bishop's court?

But is the priest to be divested of his rights as a citizen? Is he not, as a citizen, and outside of the Church,
to be allowed to utter a word on politics? No one, so

far as our observation goes, has expressed a desire to detract from the rights of a priest in his character of a citizen. The objection is to his using the influence of his sacred office and the terrors of spiritual censures for the purpose of deciding a political election in favour of a particular candidate or of a particular party.

The bishops, in one of their joint letters of 1875, say : ' There are political questions in which the clergy can and ought to interfere in the name of religion.' They also say: ' It belongs to the Church,' presumably meaning thereby the bishops, ' to give its ministers such instruc· tions as it may think suitable.' The questions in which they may interfere are described to be all those which have any bearing on faith or morals. And candidates may be judged on grounds wholly separate from their expressed opinions. A candidate may be condemned by his antecedents, which no doubt fairly make an element in the estimation of character. But, under this rule, a man might be held responsible for opinions which he had long since discarded. He may be judged by the antecedents of the leaders of the party to which he is attached; by the opinions of its principal members ; by those of the press which speaks on its behalf. Here a wide and dangerous latitude is given to the clergy, in their dealing with candidates for political position. The practical effect is to treat all changes of political opinion as insincere, and all supposed political offences as unworthy of moral amnesty.

An army of over a thousand priests now acting under the inspiration of these instructions, and having it in their power to make and unmake the political fortunes of the majority of the candidates in the Province of Quebec, might, if the immunity contended for were granted, inflict upon individuals serious injuries, for which there would practically be no remedy.

20

In Ontario, the question of ecclesiastical immunities is permitted to lie dormant. The Ultramontanes of Quebec, however, tell us that that Province is subject to the canon law of Rome, and point to the renewal of the major excommunication by the present Pope as proof that this penalty hangs over the head of any Roman Catholic who does not respect these immunities. And this, though it is true that the United States, by special authority of the Pope, were, in 1837, exempted from the penalty of excommunication for the refusal of clerical immunities.*

The Supreme Court, in the Charlevoix election case, the judgment being delivered by Mr. Justice Taschereau, met the claim of clerical immunity which had been set up by saying that ' the tribunal which is to take cognizance of the contestation of an election is indicated by law.' As for the ecclesiastical tribunal, he added, ' for me it is intangible, non-existent in this country, being incapable of existing effectively therein but by the joint action of the episcopacy and of the civil power, or by the mutual consent of the parties interested, and in the later case it would be only in the form of a conventional arbitration, which would be binding on no one but the parties themselves. If this tribunal exists, I am not aware that it has any code of law or procedure; it would have no power to summon the parties and the witnesses, nor to execute its judgments. And if it existed, it would be very singular to see the Jew seeking at the hands of a Catholic bishop the justice he can claim from the civil tribunals, and submitting to corporeal punishment adjudged by that tribunal; and the same might be said of any other individual belonging to a different religion.' What was aimed at in the Charlevoix contestation was that the election should be declared void on account

* *Le Franc-Parleur,* Jan. 7, 1876.

of the exertion of undue clerical influence ; and no ecclesiastical tribunal could either have annulled or confirmed the election. After forty years' practice at the bar
of Quebec, and sitting as a judge, Mr. Justice Taschereau
said he had now heard for the first time what he signalized as the ' extraordinary opinion ' that a Catholic
priest, speaking from the pulpit, may defame whomsoever
he pleases, and then shelter himself from responsibility
by pleading immunity. ' Such,' said the judge sententi-
ously, ' is not the law ; such it was not up to the time of
the judgment (Routhier's) in question. The most ancient
as well as the most modern authors repudiate this doctrine.' ' As for me,' he added, ' my oath of office binds
me to judge all matters which are brought before me according to law and the best of my knowledge. The law
expressly forbids all undue influence, from whatever
source it may arise, and without any distinction. I must
carry out this law fully and entirely conformably to the
Act.'*

Therefore the bishops and their organs in the press demand the alteration of the law ; they seek to import into
it that principle of clerical immunity which, in the words
of Mr. Justice Taschereau, ' the most ancient as well as
the most modern authors repudiate.' The wishes of the
bishops are equal to a command to the faithful ; and if
necessary this command can be reinforced by a direction
from a Roman Congregation to do or not to do a particular
thing.

* Mr. Justice Taschereau is brother of the Archbishop of Quebec, the author o
Joint Letter.

XVI.

THE CONGREGATION OF THE INDEX AND THE INQUISITION.

More than half a century ago, the parish priest of Longueuil foretold, in a voice of solemn warning, the calamities that would fall upon Lower Canada if the Roman canon law were substituted in that Province for the ecclesiastical law of France; and much of what he said has been realized to the letter. 'You would then,' he says, 'be obliged to recognize the authority of the Inquisition, and the power of the Pope to establish a similar institution in this country; you would recognize the authority of the Congregation of the Index, and when that took place multitudes would be excommunicated for having read without permission prohibited books ! You would admit the famous bull *In Cœnâ Domini*, though it has ceased to be published at Rome since the advent of Clement XIV. to the Pontificate ! You would admit the bull *Unam Sanctum* of Boniface VIII., which asserts the spiritual and temporal sovereignty of the Popes over the empires and kingdoms of the earth. You would admit without exception all the decrees of the Council of Trent which have reference to ecclesiastical discipline, though many of them were never received in France, because they were in opposition to the royal authority and the laws and usages of the kingdom.'

The members of the Institut-Canadien, against whom Bishop Bourget launched a general excommunication, have realized, in their own persons, the truth of that part of the prediction which refers to prohibited books. Owing to a defect of form, the excommunication was not legally valid ; but it was not, on that account, without effect on the fortunes of the institution against which it was directed. The fear of remaining under a condemnation which presented frightful terrors to the Roman Catholic mind caused numbers to quit their connection with the Institute. The effect was to cut off a large part of its revenue, impair its energies, and lessen its influence. It is now struggling under a load of debt, for the cancelling of which no efficient means has yet been provided. It has been stated, on authority which there is no reason to dispute,* that not a single Catholic member of Parliament was, in April, 1876, a member of the Institute.

Bishop Bourget found no difficulty, till the question came before the tribunals, in substituting the Roman for the Quebec ritual in the diocese of Montreal ; but his attempt to replace the ecclesiastical law of France by the canon law of Rome in the Province of Quebec has not been successful.

After a book has been put in the Index, 'from that moment no one, not even a bishop, is allowed to read it without special permission, which no one but the Pope can give.'†

There have been Catholic authors who could console themselves under the weight of this censure. 'If,' said Pascal, 'my letters are condemned at Rome, what I condemn is condemned in Heaven.' The President of the Institut-Canadien, in his address delivered, in 1868, in favour of tolerance, would, if interrogated, no doubt say the same thing. No distinction is made between Protestants and Catholics : the former have no more right than

---

* M. Oscar Dunn.

† Bishop Bourget. *Lettre Pastorale*, 30 Avril, 1858.

the latter to have in their possession a condemned book.*

Let us take a look into the Holy Office at Rome, and see the machinery by which books are condemned. The Congregation of the Holy Office is composed of several cardinals, a prelate of the Roman Court, called an Assessor or Reporter, a Dominican Brother, who is the *Commissaire-né*, an unlimited number of doctors of canon law called Consulters, and several learned theologians, to whom the name of *Qualifiés* is given. All the members of the Holy Office are appointed by the Pope.

When a book is denounced to the Holy Office, one of the Consulters is charged to examine it. If the reputation of the author is great, the work is examined by a second censor, to whom the name of the first is unknown, but the result of whose examination is communicated to him. Naturally, these doctors, like other men, sometimes differ as to what is good or bad, moral or immoral, dangerous or harmless ; and then the fate of the work is committed to the arbitrament of a third censor, from whom the names of the previous two are concealed. The report being made, is presented to the Consulters, who in the preparatory Congregations express their opinions on the work, of which their knowledge is wholly derived from the statement before them. Some member of the congregation goes through the mockery of defending the work ; but it is not probable that any author was ever benefited by such a defence. If the author were entitled to defend his work before the Congregation, he would scarcely choose for that office a member of the society whose special business it is to put books under the ban of the Index.

* Encore si, à l'Evêché on se bornait à interdire aux Catholiques seuls la lecture des livres de la bibliothiéque de l'Institut Canadien, mais on reclamé jurisdiction même sur la conscience des Protestants :—*Jugement rendu par son Honneur le Juge Mondelet in re Guibord, Lundi le 2 Mai,* 1870.

When judgment has been pronounced, it requires the approbation of the Pope before it is put into execution. To obtain the assent of the Pope, the prelate called the Assessor acquaints his Holiness with all the proceedings that have taken place. Frequently the Pope himself presides at the Congregation of the Holy Office, and listens to what the cardinals have to say on any book brought before them. But it is obvious that the real fate of the book is in the hands of the censor or censors by whom it is examined.

Considering the enormous multiplication of books throughout the world, and the proportion of them likely to be denounced to the Holy Office, that institution has plenty of work on its hands. When it was found necessary to divide the labour, to which the Holy Office was unequal, the 'Sacred Congregation of the Index' was created; its function is confined exclusively to the examination of suspected literature. Its organization and procedure are nearly the same as those of the Holy Office.†

The *Annuaire* of the Institut-Canadien for 1868 fell under the censure of the Congregation of the Index. By this decretum the faithful were forbidden to be members of the Institute while it taught what were condemned as pernicious doctrines, or to publish, read, or possess the *Annuaire*. Bishop Bourget, in a pastoral letter dated at Rome, in the August of 1869, gave warning that if any person still persisted in keeping in his possession the condemned book, or continued his connection with the Institute, he would be deprived of the sacraments, even in the article of death.

The Institute staggered under this blow, and by a formal resolution declared its unconditional submission to the decree of the Congregation of the Index; but it denied the accuracy of the alleged facts on which its condemna-

† Bishop Bourget. *Lettre Pastorale*, 30 Avril, 1858.

tion had been based. It declared that its objects were purely literary and scientific; that there was no doctrinal teaching within its walls, and that it carefully excluded the teaching of pernicious doctrines therein.

The Institute gained nothing by this act of partial submission, and it sacrificed logic to a desire to bring about an accommodation. If the alleged facts on which it was condemned were not true, the Institute yielded too much by a submissive acceptance of the decree. Bishop Bourget is of too unyielding a temper to accept, in such a case, anything less than the most absolute submission. It was he who had first opened fire upon the Institute; it was he who had secured its condemnation, and the condemnation of the *Annuaire*, at Rome; and he was not now likely to be satisfied with a half victory, which would have left upon him the stigma of having misrepresented the facts. He had been storming the fortress of the Institute during a period of twelve years, and he would accept nothing less than an unconditional capitulation.

In the spring of 1857, an attempt had been made to conquer the Institute by force of a cabal among its own members. A minority of the members had proposed to amuse themselves and gladden the heart of the bishop by a literary *auto da fé;* but the majority, having less respect for the decrees of the Inquisition and a greater regard for literature, objected. At the same time, they resolved: ' That the Institute has always been, and is, alone competent to judge of the morality of its library, the administration of which it is capable of conducting without the intervention of foreign influences.' The bishop pronounced this to be grave error, and referred to a decree of the Council of Trent to prove that he was the proper judge of the moral character of the books, and that any one who should read or keep in his possession heretical books would incur the penalty of excommunication. The Church having, as the bishop assumed, pronounced an excommunication, he was saved the trouble of performing that act.

This appeal to a decree of the Council of Trent was an attempt to set aside the Gallican liberties and the civil law in favour of Rome. ' It is,' said the Lords of the Privy Council in the Guibord case, which arose out of the excommunication of the Institute, 'a matter almost of common knowledge, certainly of historical and legal fact, that the decrees of this Council, both those that relate to discipline and to faith, were never admitted in France to have effect *proprio vigore*, though a great portion of them have been incorporated into French Ordinances. In the second place, France has never acknowledged nor received, but has expressly repudiated, the decrees of the Congregation of the Index.' And again : ' No evidence has been produced before their Lordships to establish the very grave proposition that Her Majesty's Roman Catholic subjects in Lower Canada have consented since the cession to be bound by such a rule as it is now sought to enforce, which, in truth, involves the recognition of the authority of the Inquisition, an authority never admitted but always repudiated by the old law of France. It is not, therefore, necessary to enquire whether, since the passing of the 13 Geo. III., c. 83, which incorporates (s. 5) the 1st of Elizabeth, the Roman Catholic subjects of the Queen could not legally consent to be bound by such a rule.'

This is the judgment of the highest judicial authority in the British Empire. A different opinion had, however, been expressed by Judge Mondelet in one of the long series of trials to which this case gave rise. ' The Council of Trent,' he said, ' is received in Canada. The Church, though universal, has not been able to get the authority of this Council admitted either in France or the United

States.' That it is not admitted in Canada is now settled
beyond the possibility of recall.

There is no reason to conclude, however, that this
Council will cease to be appealed to and quoted as an
unerring guide by the New School. Their argument is
that the secular power cannot reject the universal laws of
the Church which relate to matters within her cognizance ;
that beyond question the decree *Tametsi* has been published either in France or in Canada, as may be seen by
reference to the Quebec ritual, page 342.* But even if
the publication of this decree were of such a character as
to give it the force of law, it would not follow that all the
decrees of the Council of Trent are in force in Quebec.
The Court of Rome decided, in a rescript addressed to
Bishop Plessis, that this particular decree is in force in all
that part of British North America which was previously
possessed by the Crown of France: in the two Canadas,
the North-West Territory, Nova Scotia, and Newfound-
land. The neighbourhood of Lake Champlain was
excepted, on the ground that previous to the conquest of
Canada the possession of this territory was continually
disputed between the English and the French, and that
apparently the decree had not been published there.†
From this it is evident that it was not pretended, even at
Rome, that all the decrees of the Council of Trent were in
force in Canada.

There is one legal decision which seems to recognize
the decree *Tametsi* as being in force in the Province of
Quebec. M. Vaillancourt, by means of false representa-
tions, induced the curé, not of his own parish, but of the
parish of Three Rivers, to perform the marriage ceremony
between himself and his deceased wife's sister. Judge
Polette declared this marriage null : because it had been

---

* Abbé Maguire, *Recueil de Notes Diverses.*
† Abbé Maguire.

contracted before another priest than that of the parish in which the parties lived, and because it was within the prohibited degrees. The decision was made in accordance with the ancient law, the Code not having then been in force.

Before pronouncing on the validity of this marriage, the court sent the case before the ecclesiastical authority to have the canonical validity of the marriage decided. The Bishop of Three Rivers pronounced the marriage null for the reasons stated. The bishop's decree was reported in the civil court, March 23rd, 1866, when Judge Polette said : ' Seeing that the said sentence of the said bishop declares the said marriage radically null, this court declares and adjudges that the marriage contracted between the plaintiff and the defendant is null and without civil effect.'‡

The reference of the case to the bishop to have the canonical validity of the marriage pronounced upon was not without precedent, though there seems to have been only one other similar reference to which it is possible to point. Judge Polette was thought by some to have taken a step that tended towards the revival of the ancient *Officialité ;* but no such result followed. Under the Code of Procedure, it would appear that this reference cannot be repeated, for by the 28th article the Superior Court has cognizance, in the first instance, of all actions which are not within the exclusive jurisdiction of the Circuit Court or the Court of Admiralty; though the question is not beyond doubt.

It is certain that in most of those parts of British America in which the Court of Rome holds that the decree *Tametsi* is in force, questions of the validity of marriage are decided entirely by the civil laws, and these laws are not everywhere uniform.

‡ *Considérations sur les Lois Civiles du Mariage, par Désiré Girouard, B.C.L., avocat.*

Even by the admission of the Court of Rome, no other part of the Council of Trent than the decree *Tametsi* was ever alleged to be in force in Canada ; and the Bishop of Montreal was not authorized to appeal to that Council as a means of proving that to him belonged the right of deciding the morality of the books belonging to the Institute.

The bishop refused to accept the submission of the Institute, because that submission was contained in the report of a committee unanimously adopted, in which was a resolution 'establishing the principle of religious toleration, which,' he is candid enough to admit, 'was the principal cause of the condemnation of the Institute.' This confession is as important as it is startling. Let it be well understood that Rome makes the teaching of the dogma of intolerance in Canada obligatory, and treats as a crime adhesion to the opposite principle.

Let us turn to the condemned *Annuaire* and trace the language which the Congregation of the Index forbids us all, Protestants as well as Catholics, to read. On the 17th of December, 1868, the Hon. L. A. Dessaulles, President of the Institute, in a speech afterwards printed in the *Annuaire*, said : ' We form a society of students, and this society is purely laical. Is an association of laymen, not under direct religious control, permissible, speaking from a Catholic point of view ? Is an association of laymen belonging to various religious denominations permissible from a Catholic point of view ? What evil is there, in a country of mixed religious opinions, in men of mature mind belonging to different Christian sects giving one another the kiss of peace on the field of science ? What ! Is it not permissible, when Protestants and Catholics are placed side by side in a country, in a city, for them to pursue together their career of intellectual progress ! There are certain men who are never quiet except when they have made enemies both in the domain of conscience and of intelligence. Where do these men get their evangelical notions? Where then are prudence and simple good sense? There are those who, themselves a minority in the State, cannot endure persons of opposite opinions, and in whose mouth the word ostracism is always to be found. But we have no difficulty in enduring you, with all your perversity of mind and of heart. Imitate therefore a good example, instead of setting a bad one. We therefore form a literary society of laymen. Our object is progress; work our means; tolerance our connecting tie. We have for all the respect which men of sincerity never withhold. There are hypocrites who see evil everywhere, and who fear it because they are acquainted with it.

'What is tolerance? It is reciprocal indulgence, sympathy, Christian charity. It is mutual good will: the sentiment which men of good will ought to entertain for one another. The noble words: " Peace on earth, good will towards men," is at once a precept of charity and the expression of a desire that they may enjoy peace of mind. Tolerance is the practical application of the greatest of all principles, moral, religious, and social: " Do unto others as you would that they should do unto you." Tolerance is therefore fraternity, the spirit of religion well understood. Charity is the first of Christian virtues, tolerance is the second. Tolerance is a respect for the rights of others; it is indulgence for their error or their fault; it is Christ saying to the accusers of the woman taken in adultery: " Let him that is without sin among you cast the first stone at her." Tolerance is at bottom humility; the idea that others are not worthless; that others are as good as ourselves. It is also justice, the idea that others have rights which it is not permissible for us to violate. But intolerance is pride; it is the idea that we are better than others; it is egotism, the idea that we owe others nothing; it is injustice, the idea that we are not bound to respect the rights of God's creatures. Tolerance is always a virtue, because it is the expression of goodness; intolerance is almost always cruel and criminal, because it is the destruction of those sentiments of which religion r· - ι : the presence in the heart of man.'

These are the sentiments the expression of which the Bishop of Montreal, with an abundance of frankness, admits formed the principal cause of the Institut-Canadien being condemned. Their reproduction in the *Annuaire* was the cause of that little publication of thirty pages being prohibited by the Congregation of the Index; and their transfer to the present work would at Rome be a reason why no one, Protestant or Catholic, should be allowed to read, possess, or retain it, if the question were brought before the Holy Office.

Before the decision had been given at Rome against the Institute, its members had appealed to the judgment of the Sacred Congregation to decide this question: 'Can a Catholic, without rendering himself liable to ecclesiastical censures, belong to a literary association, some of the members of which are Protestants, and which possesses books condemned by the Index, but which are neither obscene nor immoral?' No answer to this appeal was made; and the Institute was condemned on a ground entirely different from that raised in the appeal: that it had passed a resolution establishing the principle of religious toleration. But this ground of condemnation, as the Lords of the Privy Council remark, 'was entirely new, does not appear in any former document, and further, it would seem could not have been known by Guibord.' The Institute was not heard on this point, it was condemned in its absence, some one member of the Congregation presumably going through the usual mockery of defending the *Annuaire* against the report which would, in the ordinary course of proceeding, be made against it. The Institute appears not even to have known, before it received the decision, that it had been accused of the crime of detesting intolerance.

Joseph Guibord, a printer by trade, a Roman Catholic by baptism and education, was a member of the Institute at the time when it was condemned at Rome, and when the Bishop of Montreal gave warning that any person afterwards continuing to remain a member of that body, or to keep the *Annuaire* in his possession, would be deprived of the sacraments, even in the article of death. Some years before his death Guibord, being dangerously ill, received extreme unction from a priest by whom he was attended, but he refused to purchase his right to receive the Communion at the price of relinquishing his connection with the Institute.

When Guibord died, the curé, who appears then to have known for the first time the position which the bishop had taken with regard to the members of the Institute, refused to give him ecclesiastical burial, and decided that the deceased could only be buried in that part of the cemetery set apart for persons who are not within the pale of the Church at the time of their death. The widow of the deceased offered to accept burial in the consecrated part of the cemetery without religious services ; and the rejection of the offer led to a long series of legal proceedings, which ended in a judgment of the Privy Council granting precisely what the widow had at first been willing to accept.

The decision turned chiefly upon the construction of the Quebec ritual on the subject of burial. The ritual gives a catalogue of persons to whom ecclesiastical sepulchre is to be denied. Under the head of ' Public Sinners ' five different classes are named, and to this enumeration the abbreviated words 'etc.' are added. But the Privy Council did not feel justified in sanctioning an arbitrary enlargement of the categories in the ritual in such a way as ' would not have been deemed to be within the authority of the law of the Gallican Church as it existed in Canada before the cession; and,' they added, ' in their opinion; it is not established that there has been such an alteration in the *status* or law of that Church, founded on the consent of its members, as would warrant such an interpretation of the ritual, and that the true and just conclusion of law on this point is, that the fact of being a member of this Institute does not bring a man within the category of a public sinner, to whom Christian burial can be legally refused.' The decree pointed out the danger which a discretionary enlargement of the categories named in the ritual under the head of public sinners would cause : ' For instance, the *et cetera* might be, according to the supposed exigency of the particular case, expanded so as to include within its band any person being of habits of intimacy or conversing with a member of a literary society containing a prohibited book; any person visiting a friend who possessed such a book ; any person sending his son to a school in the library of which there was such a book; going to a shop where such books were sold ; and many other instances might be added.   Moreover, the Index, which already forbids Grotius, Pascal, Pothier, Thuanus, and Sismondi, might be made to include all the writings of jurists and all legal reports of judgments supposed to be hostile to the Church of Rome ; and the Roman Catholic lawyer might find it difficult to pursue the studies of his profession.'

If the time should ever come when our judges will have to recognize the legality of the substitution of the Roman for the Quebec ritual, made by Bishop Bourget in the diocese of Montreal, judicial decisions of very startling import may have to be given. Will the Roman ritual, in that diocese, come in time to have the binding force of law upon all who have, by implication, tacitly consented to be placed under it?

During the Guibord trial Judge Mondelet asked the very pertinent question : 'How has the Roman ritual been introduced into this country? By what authority are the decrees of the Index in force in Canada?' M. Jetté replied, with characteristic nonchalance, that the Roman ritual was the code of ecclesiastical discipline, and that the Bishop of Montreal had made the change.†

The Privy Council, which decided both these points against the bishop, took the Quebec ritual for authority, and made no reference whatever to that of Rome. Judge Mondelet points out the difference between the Roman and the Quebec ritual on the question of burial. The Roman ritual omits the rules which ought to be observed with regard to 'criminals who are condemned to death, and executed in accordance with a judicial condemnation, if they die penitent.' The ritual of Quebec allows ecclesiastical sepulchre to be given to them, 'but without ceremony, the curé or vicar saying the prayers in a low voice and not having on his surplice.'

Judge Mondelet, still anxious to penetrate the motive for the substitution of one ritual for the other, asked

---

† It is surprising that neither Judge Mondelet nor M. Cassidy knew at what time nor in what way the change of ritual had been made. The Judge had had no special opportunity for learning ; but the counsel for the Church ought to have been instructed on the point by his clients. The Roman ritual is said to have been expressly recognized by the first Provincial Council of Quebec, held in 1851 ; (Supplément aux Réflexions d'une Catholique à l'occasion de l'affaire Guibord, 1871,) but recognition, even supposing this to be the exact term that should have been used, is not adoption. 'The curé ought not to be unable to distinguish whom the common law excludes from the right of sépulchre ecclésiastique,' *(Acta 1, Conc. Quebec ; Decretum VI., de Rituali)* and in the list enumerated are heretics, those who are notoriously under the major excommunication, and public sinners who have given no signs of penitence. But this does not identify a public sinner with more certainty than the ritual of Quebec.

21

whether the omission in the Roman ritual of what is contained in that of Quebec induced the Bishop of Montreal to introduce into that diocese a number of changes, among others the chanting at the funeral of the ' infamous Marie Crispin, who, with her paramour, expiated on the scaffold the horrible murder which they had committed, a solemn service which many honest and respectable persons fail to obtain.'

The priest who attended these criminals on the scaffold assured them, M. Dessaulles informs us, that the fall of the drop would open to them the gates of heaven. The popular comment upon this comforting assurance which the priest gave to the condemned assassins was that the ' best means to enable a person to die with public honours was to commit assassination.' The assassins were assured of a direct convoy to heaven, but for a man who reads Montesquieu, or Grotius, or Sismondi, all hope of salvation is for ever shut out.

The attempt to substitute the Roman for the Quebec ritual affords another proof of the desire of the New School to leave behind it the old landmarks. Mgr. de Saint Vallier, Bishop of Quebec, in an address to the curés, missionaries, and other priests of the diocese, Oct. 8th, 1700, said : ' In order that no person should have cause to pretend ignorance of our intentions we prohibit the use of every other ritual ' than that of Quebec.

The change of the ritual, if valid, the attempt to change it if the attempt be without legal effect, shows the growth of a Romeward disposition, and is one indication of the distance travelled in that direction since the days of Mgr. de St. Vallier.

Against the decree of the Privy Council ordering the burial of Guibord in the consecrated part of the cemetery, the Bishop of Montreal, by means of inflammatory pastorals, raised a fanatical opposition which threatened a breach of the peace. Once the remains of Guibord, and the *cortège* by which they were attended, were driven back by the menaces of an infuriated mob ; and finally, after days and weeks of delay, the decree of the highest court in the empire was only carried into effect under the protection of a strong guard of militia. At the last moment, the bishop recoiled from the precipice to which temerity had carried him ; yielding only when he became convinced that the arm of the civil power was prepared to carry into effect the judicial decree which had excited his wrathful opposition.

But the resort to *ruse* and subterfuge was still possible ; the bishop set his invention to work to find out some plan by which the decree of the Privy Council could be practically nullified. Guibord was to be buried in consecrated ground: it struck the bishop, as a happy thought, to interdict and separate it from the rest of that part of the cemetery set apart to receive the bodies of persons having a right to ecclesiastical burial, and thus make the final legal decision in the case of no practical effect. This threat was carried into effect, and so far with seeming impunity ; but the trick of evasion caused a heavy loss of moral strength, of which the bishop seemed to be unconscious, but which has its effect on the public mind. What he gained was only in appearance ; what he lost was real, enduring, and irrecoverable.

The act by which the Bishop of Montreal interdicted the grave of Guibord necessarily extended the censure to the body of his innocent wife, over whose coffin that of the husband was superimposed. She had died in the faith, and received ecclesiastical burial.

According to the Quebec ritual, Article X., ecclesiastical censure necessarily supposes a sin of considerable gravity. One guilty of venal sin cannot, according to the ritual, be punished with a censure greater than the excommunication minor. Does the fact of belonging to a literary society which has prohibited books in its library constitute a sin of considerable gravity? Judge Mondelet answers this question by saying: ' No sensible man will pretend that to disobey the bishop, especially when he is in the wrong, is a sin of considerable gravity: it is not even a venal sin.'

The *appel comme d'abus* could, in France, be invoked against an excommunication pronounced for improper or inadequate cause. When the Official of Toulouse had excommunicated the Seneschal of Toulouse, on account of his refusal to give up a prisoner to him, the Official was condemned to revoke the excommunication. The same result would follow if the excommunication were fulminated against the sovereign, the nation, or public officers for acts done in discharge of their duty.

It was in these words that the bishop cut off the grave of Guibord from the rest of the cemetery : ' We declare by these presents, in order that no person may be able to pretend to be ignorant thereof, that that part of the cemetery in which the body of the late Joseph Guibord may be buried, if ever it be, shall be in fact and remain *ipso facto* interdicted and separated from the rest of the cemetery.'* And recalling the fact, after the burial, he said :† " We have truly declared, in virtue of the divine power which we exercise in the name of the pastors, that the place in which the body of this rebel child of the Church has been deposited is in fact separated from the rest of the consecrated cemetery, to become henceforth nothing but a profane place.'

Bishop Bourget had a free and easy way of doing things. According to the *Dictionnaire de Trévoux*, which Abbé McGuire says ought to be in the library of every

---

* *Lettre Pastorale,* 8 Sept., 1875.

† *Lettre Pastorale,* 16 Nov., 1875.

curé in the Province of Quebec, an 'interdict *doit être pro-noncé avec les mêmes formalitez que l'excommunication*' (the interdict ought to be pronounced with the same formalities as the excommunication). Excommunication, the same author says, ought to be preceded by public notice, three times repeated, at intervals of two days each; and this, whether it be the major excommunication, which inflicts the penalty of separation from the communion of the faithful, or the minor excommunication, which merely implies a denial of the sacraments. In the alleged excommunication of Guibord, no public notice was given. The old formalities of pronouncing the excommunication, with maledictions and anathemas, amidst the ringing of bells and the trampling out of lighted candles, is one that might, one would think, be very well dispensed with. Sometimes excommunication was extended to the lower forms of animal life ;‡ but an insect or a rat could not be excommunicated without the formality of assigning it an advocate for its defence being gone through. Guibord was allowed no such privilege.

When a kingdom was placed under interdict for the assumed fault of the sovereign, the innocent suffered with the guilty. But who was the guilty party in this case? Who ordered the burial of Guibord to take place in the consecrated part of the cemetery of Côte des Neiges? The Privy Council. It is against their act that the ecclesiastical censure is directed. This act of the bishop bears an unpleasant analogy to those ecclesiastical censures on the decisions of lay judges against which the Gallican liberties guarded the rights of the French people when Canada was a colony of France.

‡ Il a y eu des évêques qui ont prononcé des excommunication contre des chenilles et autres insectes, après une procédure juridique, et après avoir donné à ces animaux un avocat et un procureur pour se défendre. Févet raporte divers exemples des pareilles excommunications, ou contre des rats qui infectoient les pays, ou contres les autres animaux.—*Trévoux.*

The inflammatory pastorals found a ready echo in the Ultramontane journals, when the question was gravely asked whether Guibord should be allowed to be buried, or whether—such was the implied alternative—violence should be used to prevent it ; and a torrent of contempt was poured on the decree of the Privy Council, in wretched rhymes, the work of ignorant fanaticism, or of disguised cunning bringing itself down to the intellectual level of the mob by whom the burial had once been forcibly prevented.

The spot in which Guibord was buried had been consecrated only as the result of a fortuitous circumstance. Even the part of the cemetery in which the faithful are buried is not consecrated in bulk : at each burial a benediction is pronounced upon the grave.*

If the fiat of a bishop can cut off a grave from that part of the cemetery in which the highest court in the realm directs a burial to take place, and if it can do so before the law is complied with, it is plain that he can in effect exercise the power of annulling judicial decisions. The pretended act of separation, . accompanied with the interdict, in this case preceded the burial. Is then a Roman Catholic bishop enabled at will to prevent the execution of the judgments of the civil tribunals ? For it is certain that he aims at, and claims to have accomplished, nothing less. The exercise of such a power in France would have been followed by the *appel comme d'abus.*

When the mob had been excited to oppose the burial by violence, and it had become evident that this first success against the cause of order would not be allowed

---

* Témoignage de Messire Victor Rousselot in the Guibord trial. There is no doubt about the correctness of this statement ; and yet Bishop Bourget, while pretending to use his influence to appease the fury of the mob, after its violence had prevented the burial of the remains of Guibord, in pursuance of the decree of the Privy Council, informed the mob *(Lettre Pastorale,* Sept. 8, 1875) that it had merely shown its religious sentiment 'for the holy place which the Church has consecrated.' It is notorious that there had been no general consecration at the time of the Guibord trial.

to be repeated, the Bishop of Montreal recoiled. While excusing the peace breakers, he assumed the *rôle* of peace-maker. The mob, it was gravely hinted, had even been obliged to make a public demonstration to prevent the profanation of a sacred place. To describe as a peaceful demonstration the outrage of a mob which prevented a burial ordered by the Privy Council from taking place attests a lamentable confusion of ideas. This spontaneous demonstration, which, according to the bishop, the hearts of the mob had inspired, he now, like a good citizen, advised them not to repeat.

Who, it is time to ask, was responsible for all the violent and tyrannical proceedings against the Institut-Canadien which finally excited the violence of this mob? Let Judge Mondelet answer. In no less serious a document than his judgment in the Guibord case, this functionary says: 'The responsibility of all this affair, the bad passions which are the fruit of ignorance and fanaticism, raised and fanned into activity as well by the pretensions of the bishop as by the inconsiderate sallies of the coterie who appear to have made themselves the organ and the reflection of his will; this responsibility, let it once more be said, belongs neither to the worthy clergy of the Seminary, nor to our estimable fellow-citizens, the Marguilliers; it belongs principally to the exaggerated pretensions of the Bishop of Montreal and his immediate *entourage.'*

The origin of all these difficulties was the attempt of the bishop to curb and destroy that growth of independent opinion in literary and political matters to which the Institute had given an impulse. A Protestant journal published in French, the *Semeur Canadien,* indicated the appearance of an influence which must at once be crushed. The Institute, having Protestants as well as Catholics among its members, committed the sin of placing on its files the *Semeur Canadien*. If the Institute would exclude all journals which treated of religious topics, it was given to understand, it might be allowed to continue to exist undisturbed. But the resolution proposing this exclusion was voted down. Then the time had come for making the attack general, and the bishop, as we have seen, claimed the right to judge ot the morality of the books. In vain was he told that the Institute did not consist exclusively of Roman Catholics, and that it did not depend altogether on them to say what books should be used. The members were not afraid that he should examine the catalogue, and note his objections to any books found therein.* This the bishop undertook to do. For this purpose he received the catalogue, which he finally returned without having pointed out the objectionable books.†

In this contest, the Institute was not without the support of many of the more reasonable and moderate of the clergy, by whom its members were advised in the very matter in which the bishop brought an accusation of hypocrisy. The identical words in which the Institute declared its submission to the decree from Rome were written and sanctioned by those members of the clergy.

Vicar-General Truteau, who administered the diocese of Montreal in the absence of the bishop, which was sometimes continued for many months at a time, when interrogated on the point, swore that he had never seen a list of the books in the Index, and that he did not know whether it was to be found at the bishop's palace. He could not, therefore, have known when he was reading a prohibited book, and whether he was or was not rendering himself liable to ecclesiastical censures which entailed, as he himself contended, refusal of the right of ecclesias-

* Déposition de Joseph Emery Goderre.

† Témoignage de L'Hon. L. A. Dessaulles.

tical burial. Can it be that the want of a list of the Index was the cause of the bishop not fulfilling his promise to point out what were the objectionable books contained in the catalogue of the Institute?

But if the Vicar-General was innocent of all knowledge of the Index, he could lay down with great precision those ecclesiastical laws which relate to the possession of prohibited books. As an administrator of the diocese, it is easy to conceive that it might have been inconvenient to him, in some possible emergency, to point out a single condemned book, or to say whether the perusal of any particular book was allowable or not. In these lucid terms, the administrator laid down the law : ' M. Joseph Guibord, from the fact of his being a member of the Institut Canadien, belonged to a body which was and still is under the censure of the Church, for the reason that it possesses a library containing books prohibited by the Church under pain of excommunication *latæ sententiæ* incurred *ipso facto*, and reserved to the Pope by the fact of the possession of the said books. This species of excommunication is incurred by the simple fact from the time that the persons in question understand the law of the Church which prohibits thenceforth the reading and possession thereof.' If Vicar-General Truteau had only been possessed of a list of the Index, and had taken the trouble to read it, what a multitude of evils might not have been prevented.

When the Guibord case was before the Superior Court of Lower Canada, the presiding judge, Mondelet, stopped one of the counsel, M. Cassidy, who was giving utterance to very extravagant Ultramontane pretensions, and said : ' I wish to ask you a question, M. Cassidy. Is a person excommunicated from the moment he reads a book in the Index ?' *M. Cassidy*—' He is, or at least his sin will be according to the nature of the book.' *The*

Judge—' Do you pretend to say that if, to-day, I should have occasion, in studying a cause, to open Montesquieu, for example, that I should by the mere fact of doing so be excommunicated ?' *M. Cassidy*—' It is easy to reply, your Honour; the laws of the Index exist or do not exist; if they exist, they bind all Catholics. When one is in doubt it is easy to apply to his spiritual adviser. The bishop could grant a dispensation.' *The Judge*—' Then there are a great many people out of the good road.'

Unless M. Cassidy be a better authority than the Bishop of Montreal, he is mistaken in supposing that if Judge Mondelet, or any other judge, found it necessary in studying a cause to open Montesquieu, the bishop could authorize him to do so by dispensing with the prohibition. The Pope alone could grant the dispensation.

We fear that M. Cassidy is but an indifferent canonist, for he seems to imply, though he does not say so in express terms, that the prohibition to read condemned books is confined to Roman Catholics. Vicar-General Truteau, though by some mischance he has never seen a printed list of the Index, is a better authority on the point to which Rome carries her pretensions. Being asked, when under examination, whether the Church in Canada claimed jurisdiction over public bodies composed of persons professing different religions, he replied: ' The jurisdiction which the Church of Canada exercises is a part of the universal jurisdiction of the Church. The Church regards as those over whom she can exercise jurisdiction all persons who have been baptized. There are, therefore, only non-baptized persons belonging to the Institut-Canadien who are not subject to the authority of the Church; all others are subject to that authority, whether they be Catholics or Protestants. And on this principle I consider that the entire body of the Institute was bound to conform to the exigencies of the Church.' To the objection that this doctrine made all Protestants members of the Roman Catholic Church, the Vicar-General replied that the Church had cast them from her bosom, and did not regard them as members; but claimed that, in virtue of the baptism they had received, they were subject to her jurisdiction, from which they could not release themselves, though she had the right to deprive them of all advantage of connection with her.

This doctrine, so comforting to Rome, offers a melancholy prospect for the stray sheep.

The question which the extreme assumptions of Rome raises is not a question of Roman Catholic and Protestant; it is whether that Church can deprive the people, without distinction, of their civil rights, without their consent and against their will.

But, in truth, was the Institut-Canadien really condemned by the Inquisition? Judge Mondelet does not admit that it was; the Bishop of Montreal having, the judge contends, drawn from the decrees of Rome inferences which were not justified. Some laymen have taken the same view; but it does not appear to be concurred in by the Privy Council. The *Annuaire*, it may be admitted, is an official document, in the nature of a yearly report of the Institute. It contains, besides the balance sheet for the year, and the constitution and rules of the Institute, a speech of the president, a lecture of Horace Greely, and a speech by M. Geoffrion, all delivered on the twenty-fourth anniversary of the foundation of the society. The Institute was clearly responsible for the publication of its own report, paid for out of its funds; and so far it seems to be fairly open to the charge—what a subject of complaint!—of having combatted the principle of intolerance, and of having defended that of toleration. It is true that M. Dessaulles afterwards stated on oath that his object was not, in the part of the *Annuaire* for which he was responsible, to write in favour of dogmatic toleration, but that he only contended for personal tolerance, in a society composed of persons of different religious creeds.

The Institute, situated in the midst of a Roman Catholic population, and depending for its support, to a large extent, on the good-will of that denomination, had a strong motive for attempting to efface the impression that it had come under the censure of the Congregation of the Inquisition. And though it is true that the *Annuaire* is not the Institute, it cannot well be denied that the doctrines contained in that report were accepted and published by the Institute; and if bigots say so much the worse for the Institute, liberal-minded men do not the less say so much the better for the Institute.

But why go to Rome when books obnoxious to the New School require to be condemned? Villeneuve* has let us into the secret that the ten priests who formed the *entourage* of the late Bishop of Montreal were charged, among other things, with the examination of new books in view of their possible condemnation. If the Vicar-General, who was at the head of this council of ten, has never, as he confesses, seen a list of the Index, what may be the qualifications of the inferior clergy who form his assistants for this office? Certain it is that Bishop Bourget, by the aid of the council of ten, did assume to exercise the functions of the Congregation of the Index. We have already passed in review *La Comédie Infernale* of Villeneuve. When the reply of M. Dessaullęs to this libel appeared, Bishop Bourget, as we have seen, issued a circular to his clergy forbidding any one 'to keep, for any purpose whatever, except to refute,' this pamphlet, 'unless the consent of the bishop has been obtained.'

* La Com. Inf.

What is the nature of this pamphlet, the reading of which is so peremptorily forbidden? It is a philippic more or less—more rather than less—*amer* against the local Ultramontanes of Quebec. It was written at a time (1873) when the press which had previously opposed the aggression of thé New School had been cowed into silence, and when an attempt was being made to gain a like conquest over the Archbishop of Quebec, the University of Laval, and the Seminary of Montreal. It would have been surprising if the author had not caught something of the tone of the controversy in which he engaged. A writer at whose head every odious epithet which the French language supplies had been thrown, did not feel called upon to measure and curb the force of the blows which he struck back. When an attempt is made to stifle all discussion, even the calmest and most moderate men who assert their right to the freedom of opinion are not likely to do so in a whisper. The cause of the Secularists in Quebec may have been injured by the acrimony of its advocates; but it is better that men should assert their right freely to express their honest convictions with something of the bitterness which the attempt to rob them of their rights has a natural tendency to engender than not at all. It was not so much what M. Dessaulles said, as what he professed to have in reserve, that made the clerical party anxious to crush him. By what he said he irritated his opponents beyond measure; by what he threatened to say in future, he alarmed their fears.

'It is,' he said, 'long since I came to understand, from the rapid development of a tendency towards domination in the clergy, that we are advancing towards a grave contest, in which perhaps many will succumb before they gain strength to go against the tide; but here, as elsewhere, it will necessarily end by the victory of laicism, that is to say, the national sovereignty, over clericism, which is the

final *résumé* of the despotism of one man. And foreseeing
this contest, I prepared to enter on it not simply with
declamation, but with tangible facts sustained by undeniable proof. I therefore made a special study of the
social action of the clergy in this country; I followed
them not only in the public arena, where they appear
irreproachable to those who judge with their religious
sympathies,.but also outside the scene where they are so
much flattered, and there,* Mgr., I saw many black spots,
many a rent in the sacerdotal costume caused by walking
in a thorny and dangerous path. . . . . It it should
ever be necessary for me to render an account of certain
ecclesiastical inquests that have come to my knowledge,
I shall reveal some strange things.'

M. Dessaulles announces his determination to put an
end to the practice of denouncing calumnies against individuals in the Church; a practice against which only
the laws of the land require to be invoked to crush it out
effectually. He went further: he demanded that the
priests should cease to make the pulpit the arena of political propagandism. Numerous instances of such clerical
interference in politics are given; in some of which the
priests went so far as to declare that to vote for the candidate of a particular party would be a mortal sin.

' That the intervention of the clergy in political contests, especially within the walls of the Church,' we read
in the prohibited pamphlet, ' is a grave abuse, there exist
so many mandates of eminent bishops, in various parts of
the Catholic world, which so define it, that it is not necessary to resort to the use of logic to prove the fact.
And those who think so, are truly the wise and thoughtful
men of the episcopate, while we too often find those who
are neither wise nor thoughtful speaking otherwise. Common sense says that the pastor estranges from him those

---

* The pamphlet is in the form of letters, addressed to the Bishop of Montreal.

with whom he places himself in antagonism, and whom he violently blames, in public, for not consulting him as to how they should exercise their rights as citizens, or for acting contrary to his wishes. When the blame is not violent in form, it is still reprehensible, from the point of view of canon law ; for from the moment that any one is publicly designated in a church, the attention of his neighbours is fixed upon him in an unfavourable manner. This point is too elementary in canon law for your lordship not to admit it. And it is evident that the undue influence of the clergy exercised over temporal affairs, in the name of religion, vitiates the whole constitutional system, practically nullifies free institutions, in some sort puts the whole political system in the hands of the clergy; and there are a hundred examples of what the clergy will do with people whom they control. They are not satisfied with their work till they have caused the people to stagnate in ignorance and superstition.'

The writer points out the weak point in the system which our Ultramontanes are building up : 'The Ultramontane founds his power on the abasement of character; he agrees only with the intelligences which he has fashioned in his own mould ; and when the people have been reduced to nullity and to slavery, he triumphs in the completion of his work. There is only one weak point in this beautiful system : when the Ultramontane has need of energetic characters to defend him, in times of peril, they are not to be found, because he has reduced them to nullity by prohibiting them from thinking outside of the narrow sphere in which he has immured them. This is why he is always sure to be beaten in a time of crisis : because he has always enfeebled, in advance, the moral force of his defenders. And it is fortunate that his system of universal abasement thus carries within itself its own antidote.'

One of the reasons for condemning this pamphlet was that the author had shown himself hostile to Ultramon- tanism. The charge is true, and to our mind it consti- tutes the chief merit of the work. ' The infallibility of a man in all questions of morals, that is to say, in matters social, political, legislative, legal, or scientific, over all subjects of the temporal order, is the most terrible aberra- tion in history. " It is," as an illustrious priest who died in the bosom of the Church said, "the most stupendous insolence that has yet been offered in the name of Jesus Christ." This principle of infallibility, in temporal mat- ters, can only mean the exercise of arbitrary power in its worst form ; the absolute and unlimited power of one man who has no sort of responsibility in this world.' If the powers attributed to the Popes were admitted, 'govern- ments would become the slaves of sacerdotalism; the people only a troupe of animals, to be told off to ungrateful labour without any right to enquire into the condition that is prepared for them or to watch over their adminis- trators ; human reason loses all her rights, because she can only receive her direction from the Pope in every order of things ; and there is but one sole sovereign master of society and of states, who, according to the abominable pretension of the commentators of the canon law, " can make just what is unjust, and unjust what is just." '

Another reason for condemning this pamphlet was be- cause the author, so the Bishop of Montreal said, 'out- raged with revolting insolence the Sacred Roman Congre- gations, those supremely august tribunals which command the respect of the entire world.' It is true that M. Des- saulles' estimate of these Sacred Congregations was not high. He said : ' There does not exist a man worthy to enter a government who would consent to act under the direction of the Roman Congregations, some of which have been so decried by their arrêts or their opinions of decisions, at different epochs. It would not be necessary to have studied much, Mgr., to be able to cite a hundred decisions of the Roman Congregations which would make even the clergy of to-day laugh ;' . . . . when intelligent travellers have discussed the 'public law of the members so vaunted here of the Roman Congregations, they have been stupified with their inability to compass the simplest questions of public law.' M. Dessaulles accounts for this, by saying that they have read nothing which has been published during the last fifty years, and that they still seek in St. Thomas the solution of social, economic, and industrial questions.

Whence did Bishop Bourget obtain the right of prohibiting not only Catholics, but also all other persons who have been baptized, from reading this or that book? Did the Pope authorize him and the ten priests who acted conjointly with him in such matters to form themselves into a local Congregation of the Index ? Or did he invest them with the powers of the Holy Office of the Inquisition? We know that the bishop sighed for a Canadian Sorbonne. Did he, in conjunction with the ten priests, undertake to discharge the functions of a Canadian Sorbonne? But does not the idea of a Canadian Sorbonne, which the bishop certainly did at one time encourage, belong, in some sort, to those Gallican errors against which he and his troupe of writers can *au besoin* declaim so loudly? Did not St. Louis, of Pragmatic Sanction fame, favour the foundation of this famous faculty of theology ?

The Faculty of Theology of Paris was accustomed to deal out its censures without stint, but it did not confine itself to mere denunciation; and though it made use of hard words, it did not feel at liberty to dispense with criticism and bid adieu to reason. Its method of pro-

22

ceeding was at least intelligible. When it censured a
book, it let the world know why. It extracted the passage to which objection was taken, and then gave, by
way of commentary, the grounds on which its censures
were based. I have one of these performances before me
which extends to one hundred and seventy pages.* It is
a criticism marred by the anger of theological disputa-
tion ; but to the method on which it is based no objection can be taken. On the contrary, it presents some
decided advantages. The author knows precisely why
his work is censured, and it is open to him to reply on
any and every point. In this way, the public could
judge between the disputants. But the Sorbonne, while
condemning the book, does not undertake to prohibit its
use or possession. In addition to receiving the censure
of the Sorbonne, the book had been ordered by the parliament of Paris to be burned by the hand of the hangman.
After these two sentences had been passed, the Archbishop of Vienne issued a mandate forbidding it to be
read within his diocese. The Bishop of Montreal, without even obtaining the consent of the primate, assumed
to exercise the power of saying authoritatively what
books might and what books might not be read. What
is important to be known in this connection, is whether
the rights of citizens, even of such as have not given him
any right to control their acts in any way whatever,
can be arbitrarily taken away by a stroke of a Roman
Catholic bishop's pen ?

But while the Bishop of Montreal confined himself
merely to denouncing M. Dessaulle's pamphlet and forbidding it to be read, one of the pamphleteers in the service of that functionary set to work to decry it under

* Censure de la Faculté de Théologie de Paris, Contre une Livre qui a pour titre :
Histoire Philosophique et Politique des Etablissemens des Européens dans les
Deux Indes par G. T. Raynal.

colour of answering its arguments and refuting its opinions. Than this division of labour nothing could possibly be more convenient. The pamphleteer, though he be the Abbé Pelletier, who was in close connection with the bishop, can make statements which a grave monseigneur might not think it prudent to venture, and when, as happened in this case, he writes anonymously, nobody is responsible ; he may act as the mere amanuensis of a high ecclesiastical dignitary, and in that case also nobody is responsible. In the *rôle* he undertook it was the duty of the abbé to decry liberty of conscience. If all men are not indiscriminately allowed to use fire-arms, to sell intoxicating liquors, to keep and distribute explosive materials, and to circulate poisons, the abbé concludes that it is equally proper to prohibit the expression of all opinions which have not been approved at Rome. False and erroneous opinions he classes as moral poisons, destructive of morality and religion, while ' the books and journals to which they have been consigned are infinitely more pernicious than physical poisons.' Whence it follows that the Church not only may, but ought to, proscribe their use, under severe penalties, if necessary. If men were as generally agreed as to what opinions are dangerous and what are safe as they are on the deadly qualities of physical poison, this analogy would go for something ; but in the divided state of opinion on questions of dogma, it goes for nothing.

To the objection that there are excellent books in the Index, the Abbé Pelletier thinks it sufficient to reply that there are plenty of worthless people who contend that the penitentiaries and *bagnes* are peopled with very honest personages. What are we to think of reasoning which admits no moral difference between the speculative opinions of Montesquieu, Grotius, or Buarlamaqui, and the acts of the burglar and the highwayman ? ' To pretend,'

says the abbé, 'that one has the right to read bad books'
—everything is bad which the Congregation of the Index
or the Inquisition has condemned—' because he belongs
to a literary society which has placed itself out of the
religious sphere, is the extreme of folly. As well might
it be said that one has the right to kill, because he belongs to a band of brigands. To join such a society or
association is the first crime; to act conformably to its
spirit is the second.' A member of a literary society incorporated by Act of Parliament possesses rights in connection with that society, and of which, let us be thank-
ful, the Congregation of the Index or the Inquisition has
not yet, in this country, the power to deprive him.

But let us not be too certain. When Guibord was
burried, bishops had not the power to deprive members
of a literary society, in whose library are books condemned by the Index, of the right of civil burial in that
part of the cemetery which is consecrated, either as a
whole or when each burial takes place. An Act since
passed by the Provincial Legislature, which contains only
a dozen lines, invests the bishop with this power of exclusion. Practically, therefore, he can give effect to the
decrees of the Congregation of the Index and of the In-
quistion, unless he be debarred from doing so by the
operation of English statutes which are in force in this
country, and which it may not be in the power of the
Local Legislature to repeal.

It is impossible that any large public library can exist
without having on its shelves many prohibited books.
On the same principle that the Institut-Canadien was condemned every legislative library in America offends, and
all are liable to the same condemnation: the only thing
that is wanting is some bishop with a sufficient stock of
indiscreet zeal to denounce them to the Holy Office.

No future Guibord case can ever come before the civil

tribunals of Quebec, the bishops having obtained absolute power over burials from the Provincial Legislature. These functionaries can give full effect to all the consequences of the major excommunication pronounced in punishment of the sin of reading, possessing, or belonging to a literary association which possesses, books under the ban of the Index. Legally, the decrees the Inquisition and of the Congregation of the Index are not in force in Canada ; practically they are in force in the Province of Quebec.

In New Spain, the tribunals of the Inquisition, which held their sessions at Mexico, Lima and Carthagena, spent most of their energies in examining and anathematizing books. No books, wherever produced or in whatever language, were permitted to go into circulation till they had been examined by the commissioners of the Holy Office. The crime of selling a forbidden book incurred for the first offence prohibition to the seller to deal in books for two years, banishment from the place where the business had been carried on, and a fine of one hundred ducats. A repetition of the offence brought a heavier punishment. As the fines went into the coffers of the Inquisition, there was a strong temptation to find in the books examined heresy, immodesty, or disrespect of the government. No one was at liberty to use a catalogue of books which he received from abroad till he had sent it to the Holy Office, which was not bound to restore it. Private individuals were liable to domiciliary visits from the commissioners of the Inquisition, in search of prohibited books, at any hour of the day or night. Permissions to read condemned books were most generally given to priests and monks, but this liberty did not extend to all books. The Spanish *Index expurgatorius* might vie in comprehensiveness with the Roman : in 1790 it contained no less than five thousand four hundred and twenty authors.*   Is it any wonder that a people whose intellect was thus stunted and repressed has, even to our time, shown a deplorable incapacity for self-government ? The narrow spirit of intolerance which has practically caused the ruin of the Canadian Institute, and restricted the reading of nearly a million of people in Quebec to books which the Roman Index has not prohibited, is a survival of what in many parts of the vast country which formed New Spain no longer finds legal manifestation.   In some of the Republics of South America, Ultramontanism has, from time to time, met resolute checks ; in Quebec, it has steadily been gaining ground for more than a century. What may be the relative position, in this respect, of the offspring of New France and New Spain in the future, is a question which is closely connected with one of the problems of Canada's destiny.

* Depons, Voyage dans l'Amérique

XVII.

THE WEALTH OF THE CHURCH.

The twenty-sixth article of the Syllabus, when transformed from its negative to a positive form, asserts the innate
and legitimate right of acquisition and possession in the
Church. Civil governments have, however, hitherto, and
will in future, find it necessary, for their own protection
and the good of society, to place these alleged rights under
many restrictions. If, in spite of the statutes of mortmain, the English monasteries once got within their grasp
a fifth part of the lands of the kingdom,* what might not
have been done in Canada, before a like restraint was put
upon the acquisitions of the French clergy? An arrêt of
the Council of State, Nov. 26, 1743, gives us the answer. In the Declaration of Louis XIV., prefixed to the
arrêt, the king, after stating what he has done for the Religious Orders, proceeds to tell what they had done for
themselves. In virtue of their privileges, they had acquired such considerable properties that it became necessary to put a limit to their acquisitions. And, in the
year 1703, instructions were given that each of the Religious Orders in the French West Indies should not be
at liberty to possess more land than would employ a
hundred negroes. But this restriction, the king distinctly states, was disregarded, and a new prohibition was issued in the form of letters patent, August, 1721, that no
acquisition, either of houses or lands, should be made by
these Orders without the king's express permission in

* Hallam.

writing, under penalty of escheat to the domain of the
Crown.

And now a state of things existed in Canada which
made it necessary to extend the regulation to that colony.
Whatever favour might be merited by establishmen'.
founded on motives of religion and charity, the king declared the time had come when efficacious precautions
must be taken, not only to prevent the formation of new
establishments without the royal permission, but also to
prevent those which already existed from making new acquisitions. The Religious Orders were drawing money
from commerce, lands, and agriculture, and a state of
things contrary to the common good of society was being
introduced.

The prohibition extended to religious communities,.
hospitals, congregations, brotherhoods, colleges, and
other communities, ecclesiastic or lay. All testamentary
dispositions in favour of these bodies were to be null. No·
new foundation was to be permitted, unless on the advice
of the Governor, Lieutenant-Governor, and Intendant.
The letters patent were to mention the extent and char-·
acter of the endowment, and no other was to be acquired
without further authority. The Procureurs-General were
to examine the letters patent, and if they found reason
for objecting to them, the letters were not to take effect.
The prohibition extended to all immovable goods, and
all revenues derived from the property of individuals, an
exception being made in favour of certain revenues (*rentes
constitués*) derived from the Crown or the clergy of France.
The whole arrêt is of the most sweeping character, and
it placed the right of future acquisition entirely at the op-·
tion of the civil government.

The provisions of this declaration were renewed by the·
edict of mortmain of 1749, which was not registered in
Canada, and for that reason it became a question whether

it was in force there. The decisions of the courts on the point have been conflicting.* However this may be, the religious communities have never possessed, since 1743, the unlimited right to acquire immovable property without the express authority of the civil government. Still, immense additions have been made to the wealth of the Church of Rome in the Province of Quebec,

Of all the lands granted, exclusive of islands, by the French Government previous to the conquest the Church had managed to clutch about one-fourth. The total of these grants was a little less than eight millions—7,985,-470—of acres, and of those held in mortmain the quantity was over two millions—2,115,178—of acres. The Ursulines had obtained 195,525 acres; the Recollets 945 acres; the Bishop and Seminary of Quebec 693,324 acres; the Jesuits, who received a larger quantity than any other order or corporation, 891,845 acres; the Sulpicians, 250,191 acres; the General Hospital of Quebec, 28,497 acres; the General Hospital of Montreal, 404 acres; Hôtel Dieu, Quebec, 14,112 acres; the Sœurs Grises, 42,336 acres.† A large proportion of these lands was situated at points to which population would first tend, and round which it was finally to centre. The Jesuits, besides receiving a booty altogether disproportionate to the other orders, managed to get gifts in positions where lands were best worth having. The Sulpicians, and the General Hospital of Quebec, were also both fortunate in this respect.

It may reasonably be assumed that the whole, or nearly the whole, of the grants in mortmain had been made at the time when Louis XIV. intervened to put a stop to the acquisition of real estate by the Religious Orders. As the arrêt could not have been required for the mere

* Abbé Maguire. Recueil de notes diverses.
† Smith's History of Canada.

purpose of tying the king's hands and limiting his bounty large acquisitions must have been made from private persons. That profuse grants were made by such persons is notorious.

The grants were not always made directly by the Crown to the Religious Orders, but sometimes came through a third party, who may not have designed, when he obtained the grant, so to dispose of it. When the grant was not made directly by the Crown, the king generally confirmed the title, and his consent that the land should go into mortmain was always necessary, as it had been in France.

The Jesuits, before the suppression of their Order in 1773, had been banished from Spain and other countries. Before these events happened, the Jesuits had conspired against the safety of every throne in Europe. Their doctors had openly proclaimed that no faith should be kept with heretics ; that an excommunicated king is deprived of the right to his throne ; that an ecclesiastic is independent of the government of the country in which he lives, and owes obedience only to the chief of his Order: doctrines, many of which they are reviving in Canada to-day with as much fervour and boldness as in times when the Order was considered most dangerous. For, like some other Religious Orders, which were abolished only to reappear, the Jesuits were restored by Pius VII. in 1814. The spirit of peace and reconciliation which Clement XIV. evoked in the preamble of his brief of abolition they again contemn with the violence of former days.

By the Treaty of Paris, 1763, all the property of the Jesuits in Canada devolved by right of conquest to the Crown ; but the surviving members of the Order were, from reasons of policy, allowed to occupy and to enjoy the rents and profits of portions of the estates during their natural lives. In the year 1801, Joseph Cazot, the last of the Order, died, and the Sheriff of Quebec seized, on behalf of the Crown, all the property which had belonged to the extinct Order. Attempts, backed by the English population, were made soon after the conquest to get those estates applied to the purposes of education, but without avail. It was natural, perhaps, when the revenue of the Crown domain in Canada was disposed of at the will of the central authority in Downing-street, that the colonists should make this demand; and it was equally natural, all things considered, that the demand should be refused. The Jesuits' estates were managed by the British Government till 1831, when they were handed over to local control.

To obtain a restoration of these estates was long—has perhaps always been—a design, seldom openly avowed, of certain leading Roman Catholics, by whom their appropriation to the uses of the Crown was denounced as spoliation; and it was pretended that to place them under the control of the Roman Catholic Bishop of Quebec, to be applied to the instruction of Indians and the subsistence of missionaries, would be to conform to the intention of the donors. But the bishop was not the Jesuits, and the Jesuit Order had become extinct by an act of the Pope. Its subsequent revival was no reason for restoring the property. Fortunately for Canada, this enterprise has not succeeded. But it is certain that it has not been abandoned.

By the order of their institution, the property of the Jesuits at no time belonged to the individual members who happened to be missionaries in the particular country in which the property was situated. By bulls of Gregory XIII., the whole property of the houses of missions was vested in the Father General.

The means taken by the Jesuits to increase their land-

ed possessions was sometimes such as will not bear scru--
tiny. Once, at least, they were compelled to restore to
the French Crown lands of which they had illegally possessed themselves, with all the seignorial dues they had
received therefrom.* These lands were situated in the
town and *banlieu* of Quebec. The Jesuits had conceded
them to a number of persons, from whom they had received seignorial dues to the amount of £3,026 18s. 6d. They
pleaded twenty-five years' possession, but the validity of
this plea was denied on the part of the Crown. The
same *ordonnance* condemned the community of the Hôtel
Dieu to restore property of which it had become illegally
possessed, and from which it had derived seignorial dues
to the amount of over 3,300 livres, which, like the Jesuits, they had to restore along with the lands.

The first two Jesuits, Biard and Massé, who visited
New France, attempted to obtain possession of a large
extent of domain in the neighbourhood of Port Royal
(Annapolis). Poutrincourt, who had ruined himself in
colonization adventures to New France, had received assistance from the wife of the Marquise de Gourcheville.
Father Biard, who with his fellow priest had brought
her into the partnership, counselled her to obtain from the
Sieur de Monts all his rights and title to lands which
Henry IV. had granted to him. The object of this advice
was, according to Lescarbot,† that the Jesuits should
themselves get possession of the property. He adds that
they had taken care not to tell the Marchioness the extent
of the lands covered by the titles of de Monts, which
embraced 'Port Royal and the lands adjacent and so far
distant as the land may extend:' that is, to the other
side of the peninsula. These two Jesuit priests resolved
to go into a trading adventure before they set out for

* *Ordonnance* 15 e. *Mai*, 1758.
† *Histoire de la Nouvelle France.* Ed. 1618.

Canada, and they bought half a cargo which Biencourt and Robin had put on board a vessel at Dieppe. Lescarbot prints the contract, drawn up by a notary, between the Jesuit priests and their partners. There are other instances of Jesuits engaging in trade in Canada, and it became necessary to prevent them doing so by a positive legal prohibition.

The way in which the Island of Montreal was obtained from the original proprietor affords a remarkable illustration of the influences the religious corporations sometimes exerted in the acquisition of property. The island had been granted to Jean de Lauson, Intendant of Dauphiné, on condition that he should plant a colony upon it. He had, however, neglected this part of the contract. M. de la Dauversière had received a command from heaven, so he said, to establish an hospital on the Island of Montreal, and to carry out this command, the design of obtaining a cession of the Island from M. de Lauson was formed. The acquisition was at first to be made in the name of the associates. M. de la Dauversière and M. de Faucamp went on a mission to Dauphiné to ask from the proprietor the cession of the island. The demand that he should, without equivalent, give up a property from which he had expected his family would derive great benefit, was one to which he could not listen with patience. The envoys, however, insisted on arguing the point with him.

The failure of the mission was not taken as a final refusal. M. de la Dauversière and M. de Faucamp, reinforced by P. Charles Lallement, the director of the Jesuits, went a second time to Dauphiné to induce the proprietor to make a cession of the island. This time they succeeded. Of the nature of the arguments by which they overcame the opposition of M. de Lauson some idea may be formed from the circumstances under which they were acting. The necessity of complying with a demand from heaven would naturally be insisted on. M. de Lauson was not likely to be left in ignorance of the apparition of the Holy Family, Jesus, Mary, and Joseph, which had been made to M. de la Dauversière in the Church of Notre Dame; when the Saviour said: *Où pourai-je trouver un serviteur fidèle ?* ' (where can I find a faithful servant?) In response to which the Divine Mother, taking M. de la Dauversière by the hand, presented him to her Divine Son, saying: ' *Voici, Seigneur, ce serviteur fidèle*' (here is that faithful servant). The Saviour received him kindly, saying: ' You shall henceforth be my faithful servant; I will invest you with force and wisdom ; you shall have a guardian angel for guide. Engage energetically in my work ; my grace shall be sufficient for you, and you shall not want.' The Saviour then put a ring on one of the fingers of M. de la Dauversière, on which were engraved the names, *Jésus, Marie, Joseph*, and recommended him to give a like ring to each of the women who would consecrate herself to the Holy Family in the congregation which he was about to establish.

In this vision, M. de la Dauversière became acquainted with all the persons who were to assist him in establishing the proposed community on the Island of Montreal.*

We have the solemn assurance of M. Faillon that this is veritable history.

The ' Associates for the conversion of the savages of New France in the Island of Montreal,' being now seized of the property, made it over, by a deed of gift, to the Seminary of Saint Sulpice, Paris. In the same indirect way, the Jesuits Biard and Massé, as we have seen, attempted to obtain for their Order a large part of the peninsula of Nova Scotia.

---

* Faillon. *Vie de Mlle. Mance*, et Histoire de l'Hotel Dieu de Villemarie dans l'île de Montréal, en Canada.

The motives alleged for the grants to the Jesuits are only less numerous than the grants themselves. Did a proprietor wish to mark his friendship for the Jesuits, he declared the fact in a grant of land to the Order. Did some one wish to contribute to the spiritual aid of the country and the support of missions, he made a grant of land to the Jesuits. Did one of the several companies which the Government of France created for the purpose of colonizing Canada wish to aid in the support of the Jesuits, it granted them a portion of its estates. Persons wishing to aid in the propagation of religion by the conversion of the savages did likewise. Indeed, there was hardly any motive capable of moving a charitably disposed person which might not be excited to swell the estates of the Jesuits.

To the acquisitive appetite of the Jesuits, whetted by long years of abstinence, or of secret and partial indulgence, full rein can now be given. There is nothing to prevent them from resuming their zeal in heaping up wealth. Over the barriers of mortmain they will leap, if they cannot break them down; if they make acquisitions without the authority of law, they may safely depend on their ability to obtain an Act placing the whole under mortmain: the dead hand of a never-dying corporation will be enabled to hold their property in its grasp.

Already there are indications that the Jesuits are bent on securing a restoration of the estates which bear their name, and which came into the possession of the Crown on the extinction of the Order in Canada. That the Church has a right to the whole of the Jesuit estates is now asserted with an air of confidence which has, at no previous time since the conquest, been equalled. The bull of the Pope suppressing the Order, we are told, directed in what manner the estates which had belonged to them should be employed. ' So long as there is a Jesuit

in the country,' says a writer, whose language makes it
morally certain that he belongs to the Order, ' he ought to
have the absolute control of this property and the power
of disposing of it.' The English authority in Canada,
the argument proceeds, was bound to follow the directions
of the bull of Clement XIV. regarding the destination of
the property; but that as this was not done, and the
Jesuits were not dispossessed of these estates in a legal
manner, it became, if it was not before, the property of
the Church *(biens de l'Eglise)*; that the Government cannot employ it for other objects than those for which it
was given.* This claim purports to be based on the
treaty of cession, from which in fact it does not derive the
least countenance. The audacity of tone in which this
claim is now put forward, seems to indicate that henceforth the Jesuits will exert all their energies to secure
the restoration of these estates.

In 1845 a pamphlet was issued in Montreal anonymously, but which was known to be written by a gentleman
who does not object to have the designation of lay Jesuit
applied to him, in which it was contended that these
estates are still the property of the Church of Rome.

The Legislature of Lower Canada did, at different
times, address the Imperial Government with the view of
getting these estates devoted to education; and under
the late union an appropriation of them to that purpose
was even made. When a transfer of the Jesuit barracks
was asked by the Legislative Assembly in 1831, Lord Goderich, then Colonial Secretary, replied, that the request
might be complied with on one condition: That the
Assembly should secure, in substitution, other barracks
that would be sufficient for the accommodation of His
Majesty's troops. This was, in fact, to answer the de-

---

* See an essay in the *Journal de Québec*, October 2, 1877, on the Premier projet de
la foundation d'une université mixte à Québec.

mand for a cession of the property with a proposal to exchange it for other lands with convenient barracks erected thereon. At the same time, Lord Goderich announced the determination of the Crown to resign to the Colonial Legislature those estates, to be used as an educational endowment.† This statement cannot be supposed to have carried greater weight than the order, which was twice sent from the Colonial Office to the Government of Upper Canada, to endow rectories out of the clergy reserves. It was even enacted‡ 'that all moneys arising out of the Jesuits' estates then in, or that might thereafter come into, the hands of the Receiver-General, should be placed in a separate chest,' ' and should be applied to the purposes of education exclusively.'

The intention of the British, as well as of the Colonial Government, from these documents, is clear. Nevertheless the amount at the credit of that fund was almost immediately afterwards transferred to the general fund of the Province, with which subsequent revenues derived from the same source afterwards continued to be mixed. The question is, what was meant by education. Was it an education which should be placed almost entirely under the control of the Catholic Church? As the Catholic clergy of Lower Canada are fast becoming Jesuits, the law passed by the Quebec Legislature last session means little short of the absolute control of all education, the dissentient schools excepted, by the Jesuits. That this is not what was meant by education at the time to which we are referring, is proved by the fact that authority had been given to erect a corporation in Lower Canada, to be called ' the Royal Institution for the advancement of learning,' to which ' the entire management of all schools and institutions of royal foundation in the

---

† Despatch July 7, 1831.

‡ 2 Will. IV. c. 41. A statute of Lower Canada.

23

Province, as well as the administration of all estates and property' which might be appropriated for their support, was committed.* This Royal Institution lingered on for some time, through a feeble existence, owing to the opposition it met from the Roman Catholic Church. This opposition was, according to Buller, 'founded on the exclusively British and Protestant character by which, it was asserted, its organization and management were distinguished.' I am not enquiring whether the establishment of such an institution was wise, reasonable, or proper; but only undertaking to show, that at no time since the conquest would a proposal to give these estates to uphold a system of education controlled by the Jesuits have been listened to.

The Lower Canada statute of William IV., which was never acted upon, and which has been a dead letter for over forty years, cannot be invoked in support of the claim which there can be scarcely a doubt the Jesuits intend to push.

The Legislature of Canada, in 1856, assumed to appropriate the whole of the Jesuits' estates, and the funds arising therefrom, to the support of superior education in Lower Canada. The fund was to be administered under the control of the Governor in Council. Over twenty years have passed since this Act was put on the statute book; and like the one previously noticed, it has remained a dead letter.

The rest of the religious communities retained their estates, with trifling exceptions, which may be here stated.

Soon after the conquest, the chaplain of the garrison of Quebec made a formal proposal to the Executive Council to take possession of the palace of the Roman Catholic bishop, with all the property belonging to it, for the bene-

* Arthur Buller. Report of the Commissioner of Enquiry into the State of Education in Lower Canada, 1838.

fit of the Anglican Bishop of London.† The Imperial Government seems to have been of the opinion that it would be justified in taking possession of the property of the religious communities, on condition of granting a life pension to the possessors by arrangement. The Lords of the Treasury (1765) sent to Receiver-General Mills instructions which seem to have contemplated the practical carrying out of a policy based on this conviction. The ground was distinctly taken that these properties form or ought to form a part of the revenue of the Crown. Next year the Government took possession of the Church of the Recollets, Quebec, and converted it into a Protestant church. Some land belonging to the Ursulines was also taken without any indemnity.‡

These appear to be the only exceptions to the rule that all the religious communities other than the Jesuits were permitted to retain their estates after the conquest.

The Church of Rome had, to commence with, when the colony came under the dominion of the British Crown, 1,223,333 acres of land, the Jesuits' estates, which had become the property of the Crown, being deducted. The title to the estate of the Sulpicians was not always unquestioned, but it was finally confirmed. Sir James Marriot, the King's Advocate-General, in a report on the state of Canada, 1765, expressed the opinion that the title was invalid, and Lord John Russell arrived at the same conclusion when Secretary of State for the Colonies. In the year previous to Marriot's report, the British Government is said to have shown a disposition to buy these estates.§ But the Council of the Seminary of Paris, after frequent deliberations, refused to part with the property, on the ground that the suppression of the establishments of Saint

† Garneau.

‡ Pagnuello.

§ Archives du Séminaire de Paris. Assemblée du 21 Janvier, 1764.

Sulpice in Canada would have rendered it necessary to recall forty ecclesiastics who were connected with them, and that it would have been impossible to replace and retain so large a number of priests. Nearly all the members of the Society of Saint Sulpice resided in France, and the question was whether, under the capitulation, they were entitled to sell or retain their property. The thirty-fifth article provided that if the priests of St. Sulpice exercised the option of leaving the colony and going to France, they should be at liberty to sell their estates. Sir James Marriot was of opinion that the Sulpicians, 'who as principals at the time of the conquest were not resident in person, did not fall under the privilege of the capitulation, nor come within what is termed by civilians the *casus fœderis*, so as to retain the property of their estates under it.' And the reason of this was that they were not in a position to accept a favour as a condition of ceasing their resistance, or objects of distress, or persons who had shown a courage which merited some special mark of favour. Nor could they retire from a country in which they did not live. The Sulpicians at Paris transferred to their brethren in Canada what, it is argued, they had no right to transfer. Attorney-General Sewell, in 1828, gave an elaborate opinion against the claim of the Seminary to the estates which bear its name. This opinion embraces several points which it may be interesting to recapitulate. The motive of the gift of the Island of Montreal to the Seminary of St. Sulpice, Paris, in 1663, by an association for the conversion of Indians in that Island, created a trust which was never fulfilled, and the title was bad for *non-user*. The French king afterwards authorized the establishment of a Seminary at Montreal to carry out the grant. The ownership was in the Seminary of St. Sulpice, and the Seminary of Montreal did not subsist as a separate corporation. The deed of gift, April, 1764, by which the Seminary of Saint Sulpice, Paris, assumed to convey the property to the Seminary of Montreal, is void. The Island of Montreal being vested in a foreign community, incapable of holding lands in Her Majesty's dominion, the right of property would devolve to the Crown. The estates were public property held by the Seminary of St. Sulpice, Paris, under trust for a particular purpose, and they fell to the Crown by right of conquest. The absence of a right to transfer the property must make the deed of gift null. The right of property in the Seminary was only that of administrators, and not such as would entitle them to convey. The grantees not being a distinct corporation, were incapacitated from taking under the deed. Without a new charter, the Seminary could not be prolonged after the death of such of its members as were alive at the time of the conquest. The Attorney-General was of opinion that the rights of the Crown to the property could be enforced in the courts.

But this colourable title, however doubtful it may have been, was confirmed by ordinance of the Special Council of Lower Canada in 1840.

For the purposes of this ordinance, the ecclesiastics of the Seminary are erected into an ecclesiastical corporation (*Communauté Ecclésiastique*). It does not follow that the title which this ordinance confirms is absolute, for there is no pretence that it is other than that which the Seminary of St. Sulpice, Paris, had in the year 1759. According to the opinion of Sir James Marriot, the Sulpicians of Paris had no title at all. ' By the French law,' he says, 'it is clear that no persons, aliens, not being naturalized, can hold lands ; so that by the right of conquest, these estates may be considered to have fallen to the Crown, in sovereignty.' The objects of the confirmation of title were specific and limited : ' The cure of souls within the parish (*La Desserte de la Paroisse*) of Montreal ; the mission of the Lake of the Two Mountains, for the instruction and spiritual care of the Algonquins and Iro-quois Indians ; the support of the Petit Séminaire or Col-lege at Montreal; the support of schools for children within the parish of Montreal ; the support of the poor invalids and orphans; the sufficient support and main-tenance of the members of the corporation, its officers and servants ; and the support of such other religious, charit-able, and educational institutions as may from time to time be approved and sanctioned by the Lieutenant-Governor,' and ' for no other objects, purposes, or intents whatsoever.' The corporation came under an obligation to commute the seignorial tenure of its estates at specified rates. The total amount which the Sulpicians might re-ceive in commutation was limited, and any overplus was to go to the Crown. These were the conditions of the confirmation of a title which is probably now indefeasible.

There was one clause in this ordinance which may hereafter require to be extended to many other religious corporations. The right of visitation which the French Crown possessed before the conquest, and which the Special Council was careful to state is now possessed by the British Sovereign, is specifically preserved.

The political motives for a confirmation of the title, which Bishop Plessis had urged on the Imperial Govern-ment in a memorial to Earl Bathurst (1819), had proba-bly not been without effect. If there were any doubt about the validity of the title, the Sulpicians were pre-pared to give irrefragable proof of its legality. As to the greatness of the wealth so much talked about, there was, he said, very little left after the cost of administration had been paid and the support of the community provided for. But even if the Government could derive a profit from the seizure of these estates, was that to be put in the 'balance against the discontent and disaffection which such a proceeding would excite in the minds of the Catholic subjects of His Majesty in the Province, and principally in the district of Montreal, which was a daily witness of the exemplary and honourable uses to which the property was put ?' His Majesty's Government had always treated his Catholic subjects with unexampled consideration (*une bonté sans example*), even before their loyalty had been so manifest as it had become in the late war. Surely, at such a time, so rigorous a measure, and one that would cause general alarm, ought not to be expected. If one religious community were despoiled, the *habitans* would regard it as the signal for despoiling all the others. To attack the revenues of the clergy would be to paralyze their influence over the people; an influence which for sixty years had been constantly used to inspire the faithful with the duty of submission to the king and his government. This influence could not be enfeebled without loosening the strongest tie that attached these people to His Majesty's government.'

This is the language of diplomacy, and it may have saved the estates from forfeiture at the time ; while further political considerations probably led to the confirmation of the title in 1840. Bishop Lartigue, of Montreal, a relative of Louis Joseph Papineau, the leader of the rebellion of 1837 in Lower Canada, came to the aid of the Government in that crisis. The Church seems to have reaped the reward of these services, in having had secured to it the estates of the Sulpicians.

A Church in possession of vast estates is liable, like individuals, to have its title to some portion of it contested. A regrettable affair, arising out of rival claims to property at the mission of Oka, Lake of Two Mountains, occurred in 1875. The Indians claimed some property on which a Methodist chapel was built, and the Seminarists of St. Sulpice, who also claimed the property, brought the matter before the Superior Court. Judgment was rendered in their favour, and they proceeded, as proprietors of the land, to demolish the Methodist chapel, through the agency of the sheriff. The benches were first removed, and the materials of which the chapel was composed were, by order of the sheriff, carried within the enclosure of the Seminary. A few days later some Catholic Indians and the missionary priest caused them to be conveyed to the grounds of the Protestant school. The demolition of the chapel occupied only three hours.

After the chapel had been removed further legal proceedings were commenced on behalf of the Methodist Indians against the Seminary, and the case is still before the courts. The proprietary rights have in the meantime been decided by the Superior Court in favour of the Seminary. Whether it was judicious for the Seminary, standing on its extreme rights, to proceed to an extremity that would be sure to create a great scandal and enlist the sympathies of a portion of the population in favour of its antagonists, is more than doubtful. It would have been better to make an arrangement by which the ground occupied by the chapel should have been conveyed to the opposite party, if the latter had shown a disposition to enter into an arrangement to that effect.

Some outrages were at a later period committed by the Indians, on both sides, first by those under the charge of the Seminary, and afterwards by those opposed to it, in which a Roman Catholic Church was (1877) burnt down. Such outrages are generally committed by the less responsible hangers on of one side or the other ; and their adoption by the principals would discredit any cause, however sacred.

The appointment of M. Lartigue, Suffragan Auxiliary and Vicar-General of Quebec, for the city and district of

Montreal, in 1822, caused some alarm among the Sulpicians for the security of their property. The danger came this time from an exertion of episcopal or extra-episcopal authority ; and M. Roux, Superior of the Seminary, was sent to Rome to obtain the permission of the Holy See to sell the estates of the Order to the British Government. The authority was given, but the Bishop of Quebec refused his assent, and sent two agents to Rome whose arguments induced the Pope to recall it.* It was necessary to protest, on behalf of the bishop, that he had no design to seize upon the property of the Sulpicians, The disclaimer did not altogether quiet the fears of the latter, and the breach then made between them and the episcopal authority was never healed. Mgr. Provencher admits that the idea that the bishops of Canada were capable of robbing the Church of its immense property is one that became generally accepted by the Catholic world of Europe : he characterized the accusation as ' a lie and a calumny.' It seems, however, to have been believed even at Rome ; and this belief made the Pope willing to sanction a sale of the property to the British Government.

M. Bédard, the Sulpician priest who had deserted the cause of his Order and espoused that of the bishop, had, we have seen, used the language of menace. Montreal, he suggested, could be wrested from the hands of the Sulpicians and served by a curé and priests who did not belong to the Seminary, and they might be displaced from the control of the missions of the Lake of Two Mountains, Sault St. Louis, and St. Regis. Against this danger the Sulpicians appeared afterwards to be guarded by the ordinance of 1840, which, as before stated, made it a condition of the confirmation of their title that they should continue to have the cure of souls in the parish of Mont-

* Mém. de Mgr. J. N. Provencher.

real, and the charge of the mission of the Lake of Two
Mountains for the instruction and spiritual care of the
Algonquin and Iroquois Indians.

But the Bishop of Montreal, if he could not drive a
coach and four through the ordinance, was one day to
become strong enough, by the aid of the Pope, to treat it
as waste paper. There were besides three episcopal
decrees and one arrêt of the French king which gave the
cure of souls, in the parish of Montreal, in perpetuity to
the Sulpicians.. The guarantee of perpetuity Bishop
Bourget afterwards treated as nothing, and found, in the
fact that episcopal decrees had been rendered, that authority to take away the rights of the Sulpicians was vested
in him.* The argument is a dangerous one, because it
might easily be turned in the other direction. The civil
government has twice passed laws and regulations regarding this property, and has several times done so on
the subject of tithes. The argument that this proved
that both were at the absolute disposal of the Government
is not less legitimate than that used by the bishop.
When the decree came from Rome, December 22, 1865,
authorizing Bishop Bourget to divide the city into as
many parishes as he might judge necessary, and each of
these parishes, as well as the cure of Notre-Dame, was to
be administered, not by the Superior of the Seminary,
but by priests whom the bishop might appoint, the
assumption was conveyed that Bishop Bourget and the
Pope united could set aside one of the conditions of the
ordinance of 1840. The Government, through Sir George
Cartier, protested that this was an invasion of the rights
of the civil authority. The bishop replied that his intention, as well as that of the Pope, was to erect canonic
parishes.† Sir George Cartier, representing the civil

* *Lettre Pastorale,* 26 Avril, 1866.

† *Lettre Pastorale,* 23 Mai, 1866.

authority, was brushed aside like a cobweb, and victory perched upon the united banner of the Pope and the bishop. The ordinance of 1840 was treated as of no account.

If the wealth of one portion of the Church excites the envy of another portion, is there not danger that if it should increase beyond all bounds, it may excite cupidity in other quarters?

Starting with 1,223,333 acres of land in 1763, the Roman Catholic Church of Quebec must now be in possession of an enormous mass of wealth. Its acquisitions may have been somewhat checked by the operation of the laws of mortmain; but the quantity of land that has legally been placed under mortmain during the last twenty years has been very considerable. It would be an interesting inquiry to attempt to find by what means the bishopric of Montreal had, in fifty-five years, become the largest holder of real estate in the city of Montreal, with one exception. If anything like a similar accumulation of wealth has taken place in other places, the domain of the Church must be extending at a rate that may well give cause of uneasiness.

The immunity from municipal taxation which large masses of Church property enjoys puts a yoke on the neck of lay proprietors which already begins to sit uneasily. The question of putting an end to it has recently been raised in Montreal. The municipalities are unable to make any change, for the exemptions are contained in laws which they do not make, but only administer. A change in the law has already many advocates; but in the present state of things they cannot hope to succeed against the predominant power of the Church of Rome in the Province of Quebec. Already the episcopate is on the alert, and has made a sign which shows that it intends to resist the change with all the power it can command. In a circular issued in November, 1875, the seven bishops, on the strength of their united authority, instruct the priests that if the municipalities or other civil authorities speak of taxing the property of the churches and of the religious communities, the priest is to communicate the fact to the bishop under pain of excommunication. To be logical, the bishops would have to pursue with the terrors of excommunication the members of the Legislature who should venture to touch this sacred immunity; and that they would do so we can hardly permit ourselves to doubt, in presence of the attitude the New School has assumed.

It is easy to foresee what the line of defence will be, when the attack upon the immunity from taxation becomes serious. We shall then be told, though the contrary is often asserted, that the rule observed in France at the time of the conquest must be our guide. Luckily for the bishops, the French clergy, shortly before the conquest of Canada, were able to defeat the attempt of the Comptroller-General to obtain a statement of the value of the ecclesiastical property in France, with a view of making it bear a due proportion of public charges with the property of the rest of the nation. Up to that time, the French clergy had been in a position to dispute the amount of taxes demanded from them, and what they paid went under the name of a free gift (*don gratuit*).* The triumph of the French clergy was odious to the more enlightened part of the nation. Of this triumph they were to pay the penalty in the storm of the coming revolution. The temper they were then in is shown by the fact that, in obedience to the Bull *Unigenitus*, they were pronouncing excommunications, and, contrary to an arrêt of Parliament, were refusing the sacraments to such as could not produce tickets of confession. Coffin, successor of Rollin in the University of Paris, and several others, were deprived

* D'Anquetil. Histoire de France.

of spiritual consolation in the article of death. In the quarrel between the clergy and the parliament, the king took sides with the former. Clergy and king were heaping up wrath which was one day to overthrow both the throne and the altar.

But if the tax be withheld, will the *don gratuit* be offered? No: it will then be in order to plead the prescription of over a hundred years, and to prove that when a precedent is cut into halves, one half is equal to the whole.

But if we must go to France to find rules for our conduct, we must at least be permitted to bring back with us the fact that the French Church did, in another way, contribute largely to the public burdens. The tithes were almost everywhere charged with *rentes constituées*, part of which went to private persons. These charges amounted at one time to fourteen hundred thousand livres.†

No doubt it may fairly be argued that whatever the Church contributed to the maintenance of the State, unless under constraint, belongs to the category of *don gratuit*. One Pope, while forbidding the clergy to pay a tax demanded by the State, made the cheap vaunt that in case of necessity, of which he was to be the judge, he would sell the sacred chalices to aid the civil power. As the power of the Popes increased, the immunities of the Church were so enlarged as to exempt it from all contributions, except in cases of extreme necessity and when the revenues of the laity proved insufficient. The transfer of the heritage of the nobles and *routuriers* to the clergy tended to impoverish the State. But the French king had a right to require the Church to dispossess itself of newly acquired property, unless it had, by his authority, been placed under mortmain. Private persons were not always at liberty to alienate and transfer to the Church

† Coquille.

lands they possessed without leaving it subject to the ordinary contribution to the State. The French Church, in the matter of temporalities, was subject to the king and owed him service. All the temporal revenues which the Church of France possessed were held in fief or in *roture* of the Crown. The seigneurs held in fief of the king, unless the king and the seigneurs had placed such revenue under mortmain. When the heritage was held of some seigneur in fief, the seigneur could compel the Church, within a given time, to vacate the property, and in case of refusal could seize it and *gagner les fruits.*

But there are precedents for taxing Church property in Canada. When the French were masters of the country, the civil government levied a tax on the property of the Sulpicians of Montreal, as well as on the other religious communities, to meet the expense of enclosing the town within a wall of masonry. Of the six thousand livres a year to be raised for this purpose, from the whole of the inhabitants, religious and secular, two thousand, or one-third of the whole, was payable by the Seminary. When the fire of June, 1722, had destroyed half the town, including the best houses, and diminished the revenues of the ecclesiastics, the amount payable by the Seminary each of the next three years was reduced to a thousand livres a year; and the payment of the other four thousand livres, during these three years, by the rest of the inhabitants of the city, including the other religious and secular communities, was allowed to cease altogether. One wealthy religious community was, during this interval of time, alone of all the inhabitants, taxed for this object.* It is certain that, under the French *régime* in Canada, the scandal of so enormous an amount of untaxed property as is now held by the Church in Quebec would not have been permitted.

* Arrêt 24 Mars, 1728.

The sweeping into mortmain of all the lands of which the Church of Rome had become possessed, by an ordinance of the Special Council of Lower Canada, 1839, confirmed the title to an immense mass of property which she had had no legal right to acquire. It included all the real property then in the possession of every parish, mission, or Christian society, whether acquired for churches, chapels, public buildings, cemeteries, presbyteries, school-houses, and the houses of the founders of Religious Orders. Every parish, mission, or Christian society, which did not form a parish recognized by the civil law of the Province, was authorized to acquire real estate through agents ; and so far as these parishes, missions, and societies were concerned, the last remnant of the salutary safeguard which Louis XIV., in 1643, had placed against the acquisition of property by the Roman Catholic Church was swept away. There was no provision that this property should contribute, like the property of laymen, to local improvements. The amount of property which might thus be acquired was not unlimited ; but it might practically be made so by the indefinite increase of Religious Corporations. Parishes, missions, and Christian societies, corporations not previously recognized as parishes by the civil law now received such recognition. The means for erecting churches and presbyteries, and providing a cemetery, may be obtained either by voluntary contributions, or a local rate which the majority can constrain the minority to pay.† In this respect modern legislation but follows the traces formed by the early edicts of the French kings. In 1663, it became obligatory on the faithful to provide churches, and sixteen years later the obligation was extended to presbyteries and cemeteries.

Contrary to the provisions of the edict of mortmain

See Pagnuelo, *Lib. Relig.*, and Judge Baudry, *Code des Curés.*

which bears the name of Louis XIV., a Religious Corporation can now, under the 352nd article of the *Code Civile* of Quebec, be formed by prescription. A mission becomes a corporation by the mere fact of its existence, and it possesses the same rights as any other religious society or congregation whatever.* Under the French dominion no religious corporation could be created otherwise than by letters patent.

Similar legislation took place in Upper Canada (Ontario). At the request of Bishop Power of Toronto, and Coadjutor Phelan, administrator of the diocese of Kingston, an Act was passed erecting them severally into corporations sole and perpetual, with the right to possess real estate without restriction either as to quantity or the revenue it produced, and making them proprietors of all the churches and chapels which might in future be erected in the diocese. The old way of defeating the law of mortmain was to place real property which the Church could not receive in the hands of trustees. All property held so was, by this Act, made to pass to the bishop, and he was empowered to alienate it, if a good chance for a speculative sale offered, with the consent of the coadjutor and the oldest Vicar-General, or two ecclesiastics selected by the bishop, in case of the absence or illness of the other functionaries. All new bishoprics to be founded in future were to enjoy these unbounded privileges.†

It is always difficult to find out the amount of the wealth of a Church which is subject to no annual assessment, and not bound to make an annual return to the Legislature.

In 1854, the late Anglican Bishop of Toronto, Dr. Strachan, estimated the average value of the livings of the Roman

* Cap. 9 Consol. Stat. Lower Canada.

† 8 Vic. cap., 82.

Catholic clergy of the Province of Quebec at $1,000 a year each. If this estimate be correct, though it is probably too high, those clergy are at present in receipt of a million dollars a year, for their number is, as we have seen, over a thousand. At that time, Bishop Strachan estimated the endowments, tithes, and other dues of the Roman Catholic Church in that Province at a capital value of twenty millions of dollars, which at five per cent. would yield a million dollars a year. He stated the number of the clergy, exclusive of those employed in colleges and shut up in monasteries, at four hundred, which is much less than half their present number. If the increase of property has kept pace with that of the number of priests, it would amount to-day, in value, to fifty millions of dollars. Where the endowment originally consists of lands in a state of nature, the increase in value as population and wealth augment is very great. A religious corporation which never dies, and never sells its real estate, cannot, when it early acquires a wide extent of domain, help becoming wealthy.

A great difference between the mode of dealing with the Protestant Clergy Reserves and the Roman Catholic endowments is, that at a comparatively early date it was decided that the first, instead of being held in mortmain, should be sold, and the proceeds alone should form the endowment. The advantage of the increase in value would have been lost, and the fund to be realized from sales would probably have been not over a twentieth part of what the revenue might have been, if the lands could have been retained. The Roman Catholic Church, by holding her estates in mortmain, has added enormously to her wealth.

The great majority of the Religious Corporations are restricted in their rights of acquisition and possession of real estate ; there is a definite limit to what their charters

24

allow them to hold. The measure applied to them is a money value. Many of these corporations must largely have exceeded the legal limit. When this happens, the question might arise whether they have a legal right, even as the law now stands, to exemption from taxation on that surplus which they have no legal right to hold.

One great source of wealth is the unparalleled power of absorption which the Church of Rome possesses. There is nothing which she cannot turn to account. She finds the means to enable her to pick up every bargain, and to utilize every species of substantial building which is no longer applied to its original destination, and which is passing through that transition stage in which it is wait-ing for a new employment. No pressure of bad times, no degree of commercial depression, seems to affect the purchasing power of that Church: she can command funds at all times, and for all the bargains, in the way of improved real estate, that offer. Her acquisitions are alarmingly great, not in Quebec alone, but in some of the other Canadian Provinces, including Ontario. It is now beginning to be understood that every piece of property which goes into mortmain increases the burthens of the laity. The present generation is spelling out a lesson which every layman could repeat but too easily in the middle ages.

The exercise of an extraordinary power of raising money and amassing wealth is as old as the Church in Canada. No difficulty in the shape of debt disheartens the Church. When Madame Youville undertook the administration of the General Hospital of Montreal, in 1752, it was bur-thened with a debt of 48,486 livres, the whole of which she undertook to find the means of discharging.

Another source of wealth for the Church of Rome is found in lotteries. Into the morality of lotteries, taken in the lump, it is not necessary to enter. The prevailing, laws of most countries have, beyond a doubt, given a colour to the popular idea of morality. Governments have, with a singular approach to unanimity, voluntarily renounced their right to the exploitation of this source of revenue, and what they have denied themselves they have forbidden to their subjects. But in the Provinces of Quebec and Ontario the end is held to sanctify the means. What laymen may not do for secular objects, the Church may do in the name of religion. Lotteries are legal only when money is wanted for pious uses. Lottery tickets to the amount of millions are offered to the public in Quebec, and apparently they find purchasers. Here is one, the *Grand Loterie du Sacré Cœur*, in which the prizes offered amount nominally to over a quarter of a milllion of dollars ($272,782). Some of the prizes are of undoubted value, but they comprise only a small portion of the whole. There are seven purses of gold, which make altogether $15,400. This is not subject to any discount: the whole amount must be paid. But the very next item, figuring up to no less than $250,000—round numbers are exceedingly convenient—is one which allows the utmost latitude to the imagination. It is divisible into five hundred building lots, of which the average value is set down at $500 each. Whether they are in Eden or in the moon, the advertisement does not tell. What is their real value? But why should we be sceptical? Have we not the guarantee of a long array of names, including those of high ecclesiastical and civil dignitaries, with the Bishop of Montreal at their head? Then there are precautions for the honesty of the drawing. The committee of direction comprises a priest, the Provincial Visitor of the Frères des Ecoles Chrétiennes, and several respectable citizens, and the managing director gives 'considerable security.'

Eleven of the prizes would properly come under the name of church furniture, including chasubles, chalices, censor and altar garniture, and would be useless to any lay winner for any purpose but to convert into gifts. Hence, lose who may, the Church has a double certainty of winning.   ˄

Lotteries of this kind are announced every few months, and they must bring heavy showers of gold into the treasury of the Church.

If lotteries for pious purposes are to be continued, they ought, strange as it may sound, to be placed under the regulation of law, to ensure honest management. The methods followed in State lotteries offer the best models for imitation. The scheme adopted in France by the Council of State in 1776 seems to be very complete. The whole theory of the doctrine of chances is elaborately worked out in detail.* It is perhaps not difficult to account for this form of gambling having been retained for Church purposes after it had been discarded by governments as a means of revenue and denied to laymen as a dangerous pastime. People half disposed to give money for Church purposes can be induced by a remote chance of gain to do so; and there is much less anxiety to win than when the object of the venture is simply the hope of gain delusively indulged against certain odds. In the streets of Mexico, a familiar sound is, or was not long ago, a cry that the last ticket of some favoured saint was for sale.†

The tithes of which the Roman Catholic Church in Quebec enjoys the possession are not the same in amount or in the number of objects on which they are levied as those collected in countries which follow the canon law of Rome, according to which they should be exactly a

See Dic. Univ., mot Loterie, t. 24.

El ultimo billeto de Sor San Jose que me ha quedado para la tarde tenth, and should be paid in respect to all products whether industrial or natural. Nor do they coincide with the tithes formerly paid in France, where they were restricted by custom, and varied from a twelfth to less than a thirteenth part. The Popes tried in vain to collect the full tenth.

Tithes were first instituted in Canada in 1663. They at first comprised one-thirteenth part of all kinds of produce, whether of the labour of man or the spontaneous growth of the soil. The burthen proved to be too great, and the amount of the tithes was reduced in 1667 to one twenty-sixth part; payment was made obligatory, to the discontent of many of the *habitans*. Men were not slow to recall the fact that the Capucins had, some years before, offered their services in the cure of souls, without the exaction of compulsory tithes in payment. The offer was refused, and their church at Montreal, probably through the influence of the Jesuits, was placed under interdict.

The grains on which tithes are paid are wheat, Indian corn, rye, barley, oats, and peas. The tithes are payable at Easter; but no tithe is payable in respect to crops raised on new land during the first five years. They are payable in kind, and the farmer is required to take the grain, threshed and winnowed, to the presbytery at his own expense.

When a Roman Catholic ceases to belong to that Church, and wishes to avoid the obligation of paying tithes, he must make a formal declaration of apostacy, or show that he has joined some Protestant denomination. It has been decided that a Protestant, occupying as tenant the lands of a Catholic proprietor, is bound to pay tithe. Lands which had become free from tithe by falling into the possession of a Protestant, become again subject to it, though they had been in his possession

thirty years, on once more becoming the property of a
Roman Catholic.*

It has been contended that the right of the Roman
Catholic priests to tithes existed, under the British
dominion, before the passing of the Quebec Act.† But
it is certain that the articles of capitulation made the
perception of tithes subject to the king's permission, and
that the question remained in a state of suspense until
the passing of the Quebec Act. No doubt the power of
the sovereign to alter the laws of a country by proclamation is limited ; but these are the articles of capitulation to
which both conqueror and conquered are parties ; and
if ever they can be appealed to, they can in this
case. It is felt, no doubt, that if the right to collect
tithes depended on a British statute passed twelve
years after the conquest, they would rest on a less enduring foundation than if covered by the guarantee of a
law which the cession of the country did not for a moment suspend. But, in a self-governing country, the
permanence of tithes must ultimately depend on the
bent of public opinion. Some years ago there was,
among the Catholics of Quebec, a party, small indeed,
but energetic and enthusiastic, which, among other de-
vices, inscribed on its banner 'the abolition of tithes.'
This 'plank' has, for the time being, been submerged
in the ocean of Ultramontanism; but more unlikely
things than that it should again rise to the surface have
come to pass.

An Upper Canada member of the Legislature about
the time to which we refer, gave notice of his intention to
move a resolution looking to the abolition of tithes ; but
the motion was not proceeded with ; and it may safely be

---

* See Garneau, *Histoire du Canada ;* Judge Baudry, *Code des Curés;* Langevin,
Droit administratif, ou Manuel des Paroisses et Fabriques.

† B. A. Testard de Montigny, Avocat, Histoire du Droit Canadien.

said, that if tithes are ever to be abolished, the movement will come from those who are interested in their payment.

A neglect to pay tithes before the end of Easter subjects the delinquent to spiritual censures ; the exception being, where the payment by that time would have been very injurious to him (*dommage considérable*).‡ Sometimes the majority of the inhabitants of a parish refused to pay their tithes till compelled by legal process;§ sometimes the proportion of defaulters was less ;|| sometimes the judicial order to pay extended to all the inhabitants of a parish, without naming the number or proportion of those in arrears.¶ The fine, where a refusal to pay was persisted in, appears generally to have been ten livres.

This sin is placed among the reserved cases, for which the bishop alone can give absolution, unless the person under censure be in probable danger of death.

As late as 1839, the Roman Catholic clergy asserted a right to collect tithes in Upper Canada ; and making a merit of their forbearance to do so, they claimed by way of compensation the right to become stipendiaries of the Government. They had already been in receipt of a small annual grant, which had been made for a purpose about to be described, and they now asked an increase of the amount.

To make a National Church out of an alien religion was, from the first, hopeless. The Imperial Government, as we have seen, conceived the idea, soon after the conquest, of transplanting the National Church establishment to the new colony, and endowing it with an authority which would enable it to overshadow the Church of

‡ Extrait du Nouveau Rituel de Québec.

§ *Jugement des Intendant*, 3 Juillet, 1730.

|| *Jugement de Begon*, 27 Avril, 1716.

¶ *Jugement de Begon*, Mai 21, 1717.

Rome. While Roman Catholics were to pay tithes to their own clergy, the lands held by the rest of the population were to be subject to tithes for the support of a Protestant clergy. The theory of establishing a National Church in the colony was, that the political attraction of the colony to the parent state could in this way be best secured. Colonel Simcoe, who was regarded as an authority in colonial matters, for no other reason than that he had served in the American war, recommended a Church establishment as the best counterpoise to the democratic influence which pervades colonial society. Dundas regarded a Church establishment as a political necessity and a means of curtailing the influence of 'enthusiastic and fanatical preachers' on the minds of the multitude.

A commencement was made by providing that a proportion equal to one-seventh of all the land granted should be reserved for the support of a Protestant clergy, which Simcoe was no doubt correct in assuming it was intended to treat as a national clergy. A bishopric of Quebec was created, and a bishop appointed. But it was soon found that the tithes intended for the Protestant clergy would have to be abandoned; and the discovery was promptly acted upon. The Anglican ministers sent to Canada were at first promised temporary salaries by the Imperial Government.

The Presbyterians in connection with the Church of Scotland claimed a right to share in the Clergy Reserves; and as the legal meaning of the term 'Protestant clergy' comprised the clergy of the Church of Scotland as well as those of the Church of England, their claim could not be denied. The Imperial Government, however, anxious to preserve the whole of the Clergy Reserves for the Church of England, resorted to the policy of paying small annual sums to quiet the Scottish claimants. But before long the Local Legislative Assembly assumed an attitude of hostility to the scheme of establishing a National Church ; first, by proposing an equal division of the endowment among all sects, and next, by advocating its alienation to secular uses. In time, five denominations other than the Church of England were allowed to receive slender· stipends from the State.

Forty years after authority was first given for setting apart these reserves, the failure of the object they were designed to attain had to be confessed. At the sugges- tion of the Imperial Government, a bill was introduced into the Local Legislature of Upper Canada to reinvest these lands in the Crown. But whether the recommenda- tion was merely made for the sake of appeasing public opinion in the colony, or whether the local Oligarchy intended to defeat the measure, in defiance of positive in- structions from England, certain it is that the bill, of which the draft had been prepared in the Colonial Office, did not get beyond its first stage. If the Clergy Reserves· were to be abandoned, the Church of England might be aided out of the Crown Lands revenue, which was still under Imperial control. Lord Goderich sent out instruc- tions to the Lieutenant-Governor to apply six thousand pounds, in the year 1832, towards the maintenance of the bishop and ministers of the Church of England in Upper Canada. This seems to attest the sincerity of the de- clared intention of the Imperial Government to abandon the Reserves. Next year came a private letter to the Lieutenant-Governor from Lord Goderich's successor in the Colonial Office, recommending the endowment of a rectory in every parish or township out of the Clergy Reserves, and the application of a portion of the funds· under the control of the Local Government, to the build, ing of rectories and churches. To quiet the most clamor- ous of the other denominations, four thousand pounds·

was to be taken from the proceeds of the Clergy Reserves. In this way it was hoped that the balance of the territorial fund might be retained for the Church of England. The difficulty was to find money enough to satisfy the cravings of the five other denominations, which had, on a small scale, become stipendiaries of the State.

Five years after the Imperial Government had declared its intention to abandon the Clergy Reserves as an ecclesiastical endowment, Lieutenant-Governor Colborne erected and endowed forty-five rectories, patents for twelve more having been left in an incomplete state. This act, betraying an intention to give the Church of England the position of dominancy which it had been at first intended it should occupy, excited the alarm and jealousy of other denominations. The Church of Scotland called for the revocation of the patents; founding her objection, not on the ground which other denominations took, but on the assumption that by the treaty of union between England and Scotland she was entitled to an equality of privileges with the favoured Church. While the creation of the rectories caused other denominations to insist on the secularization of the reserves, the Church of Scotland insisted on her right to share in the booty.

The Roman Catholic bishop and clergy repeated their claim for pecuniary assistance from the State, exaggerating their numbers with a hope of increasing the amount. But it was becoming more and more evident that the whole scheme of ecclesiastical endowments by the State would crumble to pieces. The Imperial Government, which, from the first, had authorized the Local Legislatures to vary or repeal the provisions of the Act under which this appropriation of lands was made, now took the matter into its own hands. By the Act now passed (1840), the interest and dividends arising from the investment of the money previously received from the sale of these lands was divided into three equal parts, two of which were to go to the Church of England and one to the Church of Scotland; the interest and dividends arising from future sales were divided into six equal parts, two of which went to the Church of England, and one to the Church of Scotland; the remaining three-sixths was to be at the disposal of the Governor and Council, to purchase the acquiescence in this arrangement of the other denominations.

But just when to the Imperial Government fancied an ample sum had been set apart to purchase, for the Churches of England and Scotland, the quiet immunity of the revenue secured to them, a new difficulty which had not been anticipated cropped up: it was found impossible to satisfy the public. The fate of secularization, to which these endowments had, in fact, long been doomed, was soon to overtake them. The resistance to secularization continued in active force in Lower Canada long after it had ceased in the Upper Province. The resistance of M. Lafontaine, a representative French Canadian, and a public man of great influence, was probably due to the fear that, if the Protestant endowments were swept away, those of the Church of Rome must, sooner or later, share the same fate. When secularization came, the Protestant population of Lower Canada, which had never objected to the Clergy Reserves, found itself shorn of that endowment. The life incomes of the stipendiaries on the reserve fund were commuted; and the savings represented by a capitalization of the commutation fund represent all the endowment that now remains out of an original appropriation of 3,329,739 acres of land, except the small amount of land assigned to the rectories.*

Thus, while what was intended to be a National Church

* See my *History of the Clergy Reserves.*

was, in course of time, stripped of almost all its endowments by the force of public opinion, the Church of Rome
was able to retain almost everything it ever possessed,
except the Jesuits' estates; and it had been allowed to
accumulate, under the British dominion, vast amounts
of property, which the French laws forbade it to hold in
mortmain.

M. Morin, that member of the double-headed Coalition
of 1854 who represented the French Canadian population, approached the work of secularization with fear and
trembling. Literally, on the second reading of the bill,
he wept at the success of his own measure. Hints had
been thrown out, and even menaces made, that if the
Church of England were despoiled of her property, the
Church of Rome would not long be able to retain hers.
When the Imperial Act of 1854, which recommitted to
the Local Legislature the final destination of the Clergy
Reserves, was under discussion, remarks were made which
may have had a disquieting tendency on the usually
placid mind of M. Morin. But it was not the first time
that he acted like a man impelled by destiny; and in this
instance he would have been wholly incapable of resisting
the force of public opinion, by which he allowed himself
reluctantly to be borne along. Peel, in introducing the
bill of 1854, reinvesting the Canadian Legislature with
control over those lands, took the ground that the Clergy
Reserves rested on the same footing as the endowments of
the Roman Catholic Church. The Duke of Argyle thought
the Roman Catholic endowments were equally under the
control of the Colonial Legislature. The Roman Catholics, Lord St. Leonards remarked, were in favour of the
measure, because it menaced the property of the Protestant clergy; but, he predicted, the time would come
when the Canadian Legislature would attack the Roman
Catholic tithes and endowments.

The Anglican Bishop of Toronto, Dr. Strachan, while pointing to the sinister omen with which these suggestions were pregnant, uttered, on his own account, very emphatic menaces.* He argued, that the religious endowments of what he called the three National Churches ought not to be dealt with separately, but as a whole. Together, the Churches of Rome, of England, and of Scotland, being a majority of the population, could repel any attacks on their property ; but if the Church of England was to be the first victim—and her endowments could not be taken away without Roman Catholic votes—the Church of Rome would be the second. ' It is true,' said the Bishop of Toronto, addressing M. Morin, ' some of your adherents have been heard to say that they would fight for their endowments, and rather risk a civil war than give them up. This would be the height of madness ; for, no longer having the Protestant Churches of England and Scotland to stand with you in the breach, you would soon be overcome by numbers, and your total defeat embittered by the thought that you might have prevented such a calamity, and blessed the Province with a longer period of peace and happiness, had you adopted a truer and more just course of action.'

The population of Canada, the Anglican bishop argued, would be essentially English, embedded among people of the same race, Our Republican neighbours dislike all religious establishments. In a short time the people whose Church property was menaced would be three times as numerous as those whom M. Morin represented ; ' and then,' Bishop Strachan continued, with a menace intended to carry dismay into the heart of his correspondent, ' the evil you have done to us will be returned to

* A Letter from the Bishop of Toronto to the Honourable A. N. Morin, Commissioner of Crown Lands.

you ten-fold, and the besom of bitter retaliation will sweep away your magnificent endowments.'

This prediction may prove true; but at present there is no sign of its fulfilment.

There were Roman Catholics in Lower Canada who were already more or less affected by the fears which the Bishop of Toronto wished to excite. One of them described the Clergy Reserves as the outer wall that protected the Roman Catholic endowments. Secularization was a declaration of war against all that Roman Catholics held sacred; its meaning was 'a temporary forbearance to the Roman Catholic Church and future proscription.'

Bishop Strachan was right in saying that the 14th George III. excepted the religious orders and communities from the rest of His Majesty's subjects who were entitled 'to hold and enjoy their property and possessions.' This prohibition was the starting point of British legislation after the conquest, but it has long since been removed. In the capitulation of Montreal it was stipulated (Art. XXXII.) that 'the communities of nuns shall be preserved in their constitution and privileges; that they shall continue to observe their rules, and to be exempted from lodging any military; that it shall be forbid to trouble them in their religious exercise, or to enter their monasteries.'

The same privileges were demanded (Art. XXXII.), but refused, with regard to the communities of Jesuits and Recollets, and of the house of the priests of St. Sulpice. (Art. XXXIV.) Yet the communities and all the priests were to preserve their movables, and the property and revenues of the seignories, and other estates which they possessed in the colony; and the same estates were to be preserved in their privileges, rights, honours, and exemptions.

The definitive treaty of peace left untouched the ground covered by these articles ; and it is a question whether they continued to have force after the treaty was signed. The British Parliament assumed that the treaty alone was obligatory, when it excepted the religious orders and communities from those subjects who were entitled to hold their property and possessions. We have nowhere seen it stated that France took any exception to this practical interpretation of the international engagement.

An agent of the French Government at the court of London wrote, October 11th, 1763, to the duc de Choiseul, Minister of the King of France : ' It is not known what religious system the English will cause to be adopted in Canada ; but it is not doubted that in permitting the exercise of the Catholic religion, they will, in the meantime, suppress the convents of each sex, which they regard as useless in the colonies.' If this writer was well informed, and he must have been in a position to obtain correct information, the capitulation must have been considered as superseded by the treaty, and the free exercise of the Roman Catholic religion regarded as possible where convents are not allowed to exist. But perhaps he listened to the loose talk of persons who had not fully mastered the facts of the case.

The convents are in possession of large amounts of real estate, which is constantly increasing, and which does not contribute its share to the municipal burdens. Of these institutions there are in the Dominion two hundred and twenty-four, of which one hundred and sixty are situated in the Province of Quebec.* Some of the older convents in Quebec must be very wealthy, and in all parts

* The following figures come to hand while this work is passing through the press :- Rolland's Almanack for 1878 makes the Roman Catholic population of Canada 1,792,000 ; and states the number of Bishops at 22 ; Priests, 1,521 ; Churches or Mission Chapels, 1,591 ; Seminaries, 16 ; Ecclesiastics, 486 ; Colleges, 47 ; Convents, 224 Hospitals, 30 ; Asylums, 42 ; Academies, 99 ; Religious Communities, 76 ; Schools, 3,322.

71

of the country conventual wealth is rapidly increasing, from direct acquisitions and from the natural increase in the value of property.

These institutions have extraordinary facilities for increasing their wealth. Sometimes they are able to borrow from the faithful at about half the current rate of interest; and sometimes they give no other security than the receipt of the Superior. If the school fees they charge Protestant parents for educating their daughters be low, there is no reason to suppose they do not leave a profit. At the present rate of accumulation, it is difficult to set bounds to the future wealth of the convents; and their influence will be in proportion to their riches, if, as houses of education, they continue to have opportunities thrown in their way of moulding the minds of girls born of Protestant parents.

If education be secularized anywhere, the education of the daughters of Protestant parents in convents ought, by the very nature of the contract, to be secular. Of two things one: either no religious instruction can be given to these pupils, or it must be in accordance with the doctrines of the Church of Rome; if none is given the contract is so far observed. In that case what becomes of the cry of godless education? In the Province of Quebec the Archbishop decides that a particular catechism 'shall be the only one the use of which shall be permitted in the public instructions of the diocese.'* But no attempt will be made to teach a Roman Catholic catechism to Protestant pupils. Such a measure would defeat its own ends, by immediately awakening alarm. By undertaking to educate Protestant children, as the convents do, the Church forfeits its right to denounce secular education as godless.

In session of the Quebec Legislature 1876-77 the Sisters of Providence obtained the passage of an Act by a

* Mandement de Monseigneur l'Evêque de Québec, March 2, 1829.

large majority—the vote was forty against thirteen—
giving them authority to carry on every kind of manufactures in the convent. An attempt was made by the
minority to abolish the exemption from taxation which
the property of the Sisters enjoys, as a corollary of the
new competitive powers granted them, but it failed of
success. A general proposition to subject to taxation the
property of all religious communities which engage in
manufactures shared the same fate. But it is something
that the question of taxing ecclesiastical the same as lay
property has been raised in what Pope Pius IX. styles
the ' city which has the right to be called the metropolis
of the Catholic religion in North America.'*

In the other Provinces of the Dominion the wealth of
the Church is relatively much less than in Quebec. But
it is everywhere increasing in a variety of shapes : in
lands, in churches and chapels, in seminaries and colleges, in convents and hospitals, in asylums, academies,
and communities. If Bishop Strachan's estimate of the
value of the property of the Roman Catholic Church in
Quebec in 1854 be even approximately correct, and if we
make a moderate allowance for the rest of the Provinces,
that Church must be in the enjoyment of what is equal to
the revenue derivable from sixty-five millions of dollars
worth of property. But the truth is that the Church, and
the Church alone, is in possession of the means of arriving
at the extent of its wealth, and without its aid perhaps
no close or reliable estimate can be made. It is not impossible, however, that it is even more wealthy than the
figures we have given indicate.

Nearly all the priests in the Province of Quebec who
leave property behind them make a practice of bequeath-
ing it to the Church for one purpose or another.†

* Bull canonically erecting the University of Laval.

† Mémoir de Mgr. J. N. Provencher, Evèque de Julipoolis, 20 Mars, 1836.

In Manitoba, and possibly some other portions of the
North-west, the Church of Rome bids fair to become as
wealthy as it is in Qu ebec.   Of the one million four hundred thousand acres set apart for the half-breeds of that
Province, a large part is certain to become sooner or later
the property of the Church. It is in this indirect way that
most of her large acquisitions are made. The half-breeds
are attached to the roaming life of the hunter, which they
will not readily change for the steady and painful labour
of the agriculturist.   The superstition of the Indian, of
which they retain strong traces, makes them particularly sensible to religious impressions of whatever kind ;
and the influence over them of a priesthood which holds
the keys of heaven and hell, and can shorten the stay of
their souls in purgatory, must be all but omnipotent. That
it will be used, in their case as it has in others, to add to
the Church's wealth it is not uncharitable to believe.

     There, as almost everywhere else on this continent, the
Roman Catholic missionaries were first in the field.   In
the year of the Peace of Utrecht they had a mission at
the Grand Portage on Lake Superior, and they afterwards
slowly penetrated the interior, inciting the French Government to make those discoveries in which the Varennes
de Verandrye were engaged, and which shortly before the
conquest led the French as far as the Rocky Mountains.*
At a much earlier period they had been on some parts of
Lake Superior.   The North-west country was erected into a Vicarship in 1847 ; until then it had been under the
jurisdiction of the Bishop of Quebec.   The diocese of
St. Boniface, Manitoba, over which Archbishop Taché
presides, was divided in 1862 by the erection of the Mackenzie River Vicarship ; in 1867 the Vicarship of the
Saskatchewan was added, and in 1870 there were Catholic missions at over a hundred different points.

* Pierre Margry, in the Moniteur, Sept. 14 and Nov. 1, 1852.

Though there are at present no indications of the realization of the predictions of the late Anglican Bishop of
Toronto, we must not forget that an agitation for the
abolition of tithes in Lower Canada sprung up some time
ago, and was maintained with persistency, if not with much
energy, for several years.

'No degree ·of the ecclesiastical hierarchy,' said
L'Avenir, 'is exempt from the vices which the love of
power and of riches entails. The Catholic clergy is far
too rich ; the tithe gives it an undue influence, which it
has so much abused to the misfortune of the country.,
But the assault was ill conducted, and *L'Avenir* greatly
over-shot the mark. When it argued that a democratic
republic had no need of priests, it naturally shocked the
religious sentiment of a people so devoted to their Church
as are the great body of French Canadians. That agitation has subsided into a dead calm, whether to be renewed again or not is a question that belongs to the
future.

The New School takes new ground on the subject of
tithes as on almost every other question ; ground which
the Church never thought of assuming during the French
dominion. The new doctrine is that 'the interference
by the civil power in the administration of ecclesiastical
property is a sacrilegious usurpation, a manifest and revolt--
ing absurdity ; ' besides being a folly as great as it would
be for the same authority to undertake to make the course
of the stars dependent on its will. ' The Church alone,'
the modern doctrine runs, ' has a right to legislate on the
subject of tithes ; the rules it makes are strictly obligatory,
and the civil power has nothing to do with this or any
similar matter. It is permitted to do one thing only,
and not only permitted but commanded, if it desires to
exercise its legislative power with regard to ecclesiastical property : and that is to promulgate, as laws of the

State, the laws of the Church in a like matter; to use every means at its disposal to put them into execution and cause them to be observed.'*

The amount of the tithes depended on the will of the civil government. Numerous edicts were passed on the subject of tithes, in which original and absolute legislative jurisdiction was exercised. There was then no pretence that the Church had the right to fix the amount. If the Church could levy what rate of tithe it thought proper, it would be in its power to impoverish the entire body of farmers who adhered to the Roman faith.

The Abbé Pelletier contends that the Church's right of possession is one which the civil power cannot limit. The right to possess must carry with it the right to acquire, and if both propositions are admitted in their full import, the laws of mortmain must be swept away. Writers like this may support their claims by reference to the Syllabus, but in all Christendom there are few governments which are so far prepared to abdicate their functions as to allow the Church all it claims under this head. If anything could endanger the endowments of the Roman Catholic Church in Quebec, it would be the putting forth of extreme pretensions such as these. Any attempt materially to increase the amount of tithes which the Church might make, would oblige both the Legislature and the judicial tribunals to interfere. Even if the Church could temporarily succeed in practically applying these doctrines, it would only pave the way for its own final ruin.

The more sagacious members of the clergy see clearly enough that a Church which can be reproached with the possession of enormous wealth is in a dangerous position. There used to be Sulpician priests who believed that the Seminary of Montreal could, by pursuing an

* Abbé Pelletier. Le Don Quichotte Montréalais sur sa Rossinante, ou M. Dessaulles et la Grande Guerre Ecclésiastique.

indiscreet line of conduct, cover itself with discredit and ruin. 'The Seminary' was told that it was 'not assured of its existence. Its rights and possessions are contested;. and we have reason to fear for the future.'†

Villeneuve has employed arguments which, pushed to their legitimate extent, would authorize the bishop to despoil the Sulpicians of their estates. 'Their property,' he says, 'has been given to God for the service of the Catholics, in the Island of Montreal.' And to the question whether the property does not belong to the Sulpicians, he replies: 'It belongs to God, to the Church, to the faithful in the Island of Montreal.'

The means by which the Bishopric of Montreal has become the second largest proprietor in the city consist chiefly of gifts. Many of the properties of which it thus became possessed are charged with life annuities, varying in amounts from five hundred to six thousand dollars a year. The bishop is also made administrator of many other funds, such as the hundred thousand dollars given for the support of worship, education, and missions in Joliette. By the fire of 1852 the Bishopric lost, after deducting the amount of insurance it received, a hundred and sixty thousand dollars. The episcopal palace and other buildings were not built without the aid of a large amount of borrowed capital. But when the life annuities. expire, and the real estate increases in value, the Bishopric will become very, not to say enormously, wealthy. It is pretended that the ten priests connected with the Bishopric suffer the privations of poverty; their income, over and above their food and clothing, being put at thirty cents per day each.‡ They envy the Sulpicians the

† Déclaration et observations présentées par J. B. Ch. Bédard, Ptre, du Séminaire de Montreal, à M. Rioux, Supérieur de cette Maison, et aux autres Prêtres, ses. Confrères, Membres du même Séminaire, au sujet du Gouvernement Ecclésiastique du. District de Montreal, Juin 1824.

‡ Villeneuve.

possession of their wealth, and will probably never be satisfied until they can get a share of it.

It seems to be not impossible that the diocesan might dispute the title of the Sulpicians to their property in some possible event, such, for instance, as the extinction of the special objects for which the title was confirmed; but even then the State would have a much better right to do it. A commission of theologians, to whom some question were put by the bishops of Montreal and Rimouski, and who held their sittings at Quebec, cited authorities to show that religious communities are not proprietors, that their rights are only those of persons in the enjoyment of the usufruct and of administrators. And the authority quoted (the Nouveau Denisart) adds: 'The property is the property of the Church, to which it has been given by the State into which the Church has been received for the benefit of the people of whom it is composed.' Doctrines which the New School reject with indignation and abhorence. 'The property,' the quotation continues, ' belongs to the Church to which it has been given. The reason which causes us to regard the Church and the State as the real proprietors of ecclesiastical property is founded on the distinction between different kinds of communities. The different persons, whether physical or moral, who form what we call the clergy are not really the proprietors of the property of which they are in possession.'

When the bishops referred this question to those eminent theologians, they did not desire that the answers should be of this complexion; and when they were received they were rejected with haughty disdain. 'Cæsarism and Gallicanism, the most accentuated,'* shouted in chorus the army of writers by which the Bishop of Montreal had undertaken to subdue all hostile opinions.

* *La Rédaction du Franc-Parleur.*

' The Church a chattel of the State!'   The Episcopate of Quebec in council has reversed the maxim, and presented, as a pleasing thing, a picture of the State as a chattel of the Church.

The doctrine that the property of the Sulpicians of Montreal is the property of the Roman Catholic Church is one that may be pushed to much greater extent, and be turned against the parties by whom it is now used against the Seminary.   A slight change of phraseology is all that is necessary.   If the broader ground be taken that the property was given for the support of religion, and if the great majority of the people changed their religion, the property would, according to this doctrine and to equity, follow the change.   The argument has not only been used before, but it has frequently been applied in practice.   It is a perilous weapon for the bishopric of Montreal to wield against the Sulpicians.

The views of these Quebec theologians would carry us much further ; for as they assume that the property belongs to the Church and the State, there are conceivable cases in which resumption by the State would become a duty.   Judge Baudry† draws a very important conclusion from the fact that the parishioners are obliged to contribute to the construction of churches and presbyteries. After admitting that the property of the Fabrique is the property of the Church, and that the control of it properly belongs to the religious authority, he adds, as a matter of fact, that ' this property is subject to the control of the civil authority, for the reason that the obligation is imposed on the parishioners to contribute to the purchase of materials and the construction of the edifices, and that they are in possession thereof.'   Pagnuello contests this conclusion, but only by quoting the decrees of the Council of Trent, which are not in force in Canada.   The pretence

† Code des Curés.

that the Council of Trent could impose involuntary taxes on Her Majesty's subjects in Canada, involves the further assumption that the State only interferes, as in obedience bound, to lend the strength of the secular arm to enforce the decrees of a General Council. If the State were under this obligation, it would be equally bound to enforce all the propositions (reversed) in the Syllabus, and every-thing which the Pope may take on himself to define dogmatically, since General Councils have become useless in presence of an infallible Pontiff. When the State compels the citizens to pay any tax, whether for secular or religious purposes, there lies at the bottom of its action the theory that some public or national end is to be served, and if that tax be expended on permanent objects, it is clear that if these objects cease to serve the end for which they were created, they may be devoted to some other purpose, in order to carry out the original intention of promoting the national weal. The argument that a person who hires a pew in a church cannot be a co-proprietor, since he is certainly a tenant, is easily answered. A stockholder in a theatre company occupies the double position : he is at once co-proprietor and tenant; and there is nothing to prevent a parishioner who holds a pew in a church being co-proprietor of the building to the construction of which he was obliged to contribute. Is that a moral theory which denies the right of ownership to the creators of a property? If it be sound it will take us a long way, much farther than some have had to travel to reach the penitentiary.

The perpetuity of spontaneous gifts has in these latter days been treated as contrary to public policy. A man cannot, in this country, entail, even on his own direct descendants, that wealth which he spent a life of toil and self-denial in acquiring. What reason is there that bequests to Churches should be on a different footing? If corporations do not die, so successive generations of human beings fill up the gaps which death creates, and in any case entail must cease in default of heirs.

If in the train of this rapidly accumulating corporate wealth a desolating corruption do not follow, the world will have a new experience, of which the past presents no example and affords no reasonable ground of hope.

XVIII.

A RECOIL AT ONE POINT OF THE LINE.

The decisions of the Courts in the contested elections of Charlevoix and Bonaventure, by which the undue influence of the curés was condemned, attested the gravity of the crisis which had been brought about by the conflict into which the ecclesiastics had entered against the civil authority. On one side were the bishops and the priests, proclaiming aloud that they were backed by the approval of the Pope; on the other, the unfaltering voice and sinewy arm of the civil power, as represented in the highest court in the country. The delicacy of the situation was at once seen at Rome; and the worldly wisdom of the Vatican was called into action. In the early part of 1877, Dr. Conroy, Bishop of Ardagh, Ireland, was in Rome, where he attended several meetings of the Congregation of the Propaganda, and was admitted to more than one audience with the Pope, at which the crisis in Canada was the subject of discussion. The metropolis of Roman Catholicism in America needed instant attention. Thither Dr. Conroy was accredited as Ablegate. His instructions were drawn up by the Propaganda. When France was master of the country, this functionary would have been required to lay his instructions before the Government ; we are now left to divine their tendency through the medium of the causes which gave rise to this Papal embassy and from what it may lead to.

The facts are eloquent, and from no one are they a

hidden secret. On the verge of the precipice to which she had marched, Rome halted, recoiled. There were the Joint Letter, and the brief of Pope Pius IX. approving of that episcopal mandate; there were pastorals from more than one bishop identifying the approval of the Pope with the action of the priests. Retreat seemed cut off. The Joint Letter, the brief, and the separate pastorals could not be withdrawn or repudiated. But they could be explained in a way that would leave a loop-hole of escape from the difficulty. So the bishops met in Consistory, and in a joint pastoral, dated October 11, 1877, let the world know that they had never intended to authorize the priests to descend to the battle-ground of political parties and get into direct antagonism with individuals. The Joint Letter had been misunderstood; and strange as it may seem, the bishops had misunderstood themselves. But we are still to find in the Joint Letter 'the true doctrine on the constitution and rights of the Church;' that is, we are there to learn that the State is in the Church, and that the Church is superior to the State. The Pope's brief addressed to the Bishop of Three Rivers is not to be regarded as condemning any political party whatever, but as having reference solely to Liberal Catholics and their principles, wherever they may be found. The bishops leave each one of the faithful to judge 'who are the men to whom these condemnations apply, whatever the political party to which they belong.'

This retreat is only made at one point of the line ; every where else the old attitude is preserved. Besides, liberal Catholics are under the same condemnation as before ; the new difficulty will be to affix that stigma to any candidate ; if once made to adhere, it will not be less fatal in the future than it has been in the past. If this halt at one point of the line, this recoil before the menaced penalties of a parliamentary enactment, were to be followed by a stoppage of the entire aggressive movement of the Ultramontanes in Canada, of which there is not the least probability, that movement would still form one of the most striking episodes which the recent action of the Church of Rome anywhere presents.

THE END.

www.ingramcontent.com/pod-product-compliance
Lightning Source LLC
Chambersburg PA
CBHW032338280326
41935CB00008B/377